KARL BARTH

CHURCH DOGMATICS

A SELECTION

KARL BARTH

CHURCH DOGMATICS

A SELECTION

With an Introduction by HELMUT GOLLWITZER

Translated and Edited by G. W. BROMILEY

HARPER TORCHBOOKS
THE CLOISTER LIBRARY
HARPER & BROTHERS,
NEW YORK

CONTENTS

EDITOR'S PREFACE

Although Karl Barth has an established name in the theological world, and even in wider spheres, the content and significance of his main work, the *Church Dogmatics*, are not so widely known or appreciated as they deserve. The vast nature of the work, and the extended process of composition, are partly responsible. In addition, the isolation of the war years, and the inevitable lag in translation, have proved contributory factors in English-speaking areas.

In the circumstances, it is natural that there should have been various attempts to introduce readers rather more gently to the *Dogmatics*. This is the purpose of Professor Gollwitzer in the present work, in which he has in view both a wider public, yet also students and pastors who feel the need of initial guidance. His method is not merely to select for purposes of information, but also to group under leading themes to serve the purposes of interpretation. He has also contributed a fine introductory essay which admirably helps to an understanding of the mature Barth of the *Dogmatics*.

It should be emphasised that, while the work may lead more general readers to a fruitful acquaintance with Barth, it cannot replace the *Dogmatics* for serious students. If the main themes and extracts are judiciously selected, they are necessarily inadequate to convey the full sweep or content of the work. Many important themes have to be excluded, and the extracts themselves are naturally torn from their more immediate setting. This does not mean that the total effect is misleading. No more competent or sympathetic guide could be desired than Professor Gollwitzer. It means that the work primarily serves its intended purpose of introduction and orientation, as also, it is to be hoped, of stimulation.

The Introduction has been independently translated,

together with the brief theses at the head of the various sections. The extracts from the *Dogmatics*, which have been numbered and indexed for the sake of easier reference, follow the authorised English translation of the relevant volumes (*C.D.*, I, 1—IV, 2), all of which are now available. In an Appendix three passages have been added from IV, 3, which was not yet available, even in German, when the original choice was made.

PASADENA, *Michaelmas*, 1960.

INTRODUCTION

" The theology of Karl Barth is beautiful. Not merely
in the external sense that he writes well. He writes well
because he unites two things, namely, passion and objectivity. And his passion is for the object of theology, and
his objectivity that which is proper to so stimulating an
object. Objectivity means immersion in the theme. And
the theme of Barth is God as He has revealed Himself to
the world in Jesus Christ according to the witness of
Scripture. It is because Barth turns his glance wholly
away from the state of faith and directs it to the content
of faith . . . that he writes well, and ·we do not have
to fear from him pastoral edification ; the matter builds
up itself. But it is so captivating and challenging that
true objectivity necessarily coincides with a penetrating
but in no sense meretricious intensity. This union of
passion and objectivity is the basis of the beauty of Barth's
theology. Who in the last decades can be compared with
him in the exposition of Scripture, not exegetically, nor
in a biblicist sense, nor tendentiously, nor with pastoral
rhetoric, but with such concentration on the Word that
this alone shines out in its fulness and radiance ? And
who has possessed such unwearying perseverance and
vision, and possessed it because the matter itself unfolds
and displays itself in all its greatness before him ? We
have to go right back to Thomas to find a similar freedom
from all tension or narrowness, or so complete a mastery of
understanding and good temper, a good temper which in
Barth often takes the form of humour, but more especially
that of a pronounced taste for *tempo giusto*, of a lively
rhythm. Barth can make it quite convincing that for
him Christianity is something absolutely triumphant. He
does not write thus because he has the gift of style but
because he bears testimony, wholly objective testimony, to
something which has to do with God and which therefore
commands the very best style or writing. For Kierkegaard Christianity is otherworldly, ascetic and polemical.
For Barth it is the awe-inspiring revelation of God, of the

eternal light shining over all nature and fulfilling every promise, God's eternal Yea and Amen to Himself and His creation." [1]

These words, which do honour not only to the one whom they extol but to a writer who did not allow confessional barriers to hinder him from such grateful acknowledgment, apply to a theological work of unusual force which for the last thirty years has deeply influenced the inner development of the Evangelical church in the German-speaking world, and which the many translations and reactions show to have aroused no less attention, agreement and disagreement in the Christian churches of other lands.

Since the time of the Reformation no Evangelical theologian has received so much notice from Roman Catholic theology as Barth ; his work has created a new situation for the Evangelical-Roman Catholic debate. The development of the Ecumenical Movement would have been just as inconceivable without his contribution as would the Christian resistance to German National Socialism, or the richly varied wrestling of Christians and churches with Communism in the Eastern European states. It takes effect in the decisions of the young missionary churches of Asia and Africa in face of nationalistic and syncretistic movements no less than in the countless weekly sermons at which both preachers and listeners are hardly conscious how different the preaching would be if it had not been preceded by this dogmatic work. Both as literature and scholarship it is a product of the desk, yet it has not been restricted to the literary or academic level, but has exerted an influence on the active life of the 20th-century Christian churches and the practical conduct of innumerable individual Christians. If it has not had such strong emotional accompaniments as the so-called awakenenings of the 18th and 19th centuries, its ultimate effectiveness will probably be no less powerful.

What are the prospects of Christianity to-day ? What has it to say to-day and to-morrow in face and in the midst of the cataclysmic changes in which humanity is engulfed ? How can there be renewal in our ossified or quickly ossifying Church organisations ? How is Christianity to hold its own in competition with and under the assault of newly arisen political religions and reinvigorated

2

older religions ? How is it to fulfil its mission in the technical world of the future ? What is this mission ? What is Christianity, the Gospel, Christian faith ? In Barth's writing there is no practicable prescription for answering these questions. He is not indeed the only one to face them and to say important things regarding them. But those who tackle them—and which of our contemporaries, Christian or non-Christian, can fail to do so ?—are well advised not to overlook Barth's contribution. Hence it is not surprising that from the very outset his way is surrounded and accompanied by the attention not only of theologians but of many who are not theologians or even Christians. Many of them as academic colleagues have immediately perceived the vital significance of this work for the situation of the physician at the sick-bed, the merchant in economic life, the judge and the politician. The particularity of the Christian message, its claim and promise, its difference from all that man can tell himself about life and death, this world and the next, along the ordinary paths of religion and philosophy, have seldom been expressed with such resoluteness, with such power of sustained thinking, or with such confidence in the centre of this message.

Theology is the exposition or expository presentation of the Christian message. This statement has many implications. Barth never wearies of working it out for himself and others. Its first implication is the humility of theology. Theology does not create or fashion its subject. Its subject is presented to it. It is there before it and apart from it. It must take it as it is, as it offers itself. It can only think after it, following its movements—for it is a living theme or subject and not a dead object. It can only obediently and pliantly adapt itself to its particularity, resolutely refusing to attempt to bring it into conformity with the categories, thought-forms, concepts and needs which all human thought always brings with it. This special, unique subject must rule, and everything else must serve and be glad to be able to do so. This is the basis of what seems at first sight to be the provocatively sharp rejection by Barth of what is called "natural theology," i.e., the acknowledgment of a general framework of thought, derived perhaps from a general concept of

3

science, an established anthropology, a presupposed philosophical system or some other given knowledge of God, reality and man, into the co-ordinated system of which the Christian revelation has to be fitted. Yet it was by this rejection at the end of the twenties, when he stood almost alone and broke with a two-thousand-year-tradition in Christian theology, that Barth established a bulwark against the specific adaptation of the Christian faith to the norms of a supposed Germanic race consciousness (cf. his own exposition of the so-called Barmen *Declaration* as given on pp. 54–65). Revelation is not one species in a genus. It is the *concretissimum* which cannot be fitted into anything else and must be the starting-point of thought. We are well on the way to understanding Barth when we learn with him to reverse the usual movement of thought from the general to the particular and to move instead from the particular—this particular—to the general.

To the humility of theology there also belongs the knowledge that it never controls its subject. The subject of theology for Barth is not just God but God in His revelation, and His revelation is present only in the message which the Church brings to men. This ongoing message is the real theme which theology presupposes as the basis of its own existence and on which it reflects. It is never able to do this fully. It never achieves more than provisional results. It never produces a system of pure doctrine in which the nature of Christianity is conclusively fixed for all time. Theology is a historical work. With the message itself, which always turns anew to new men and ages, it is always on the way, *theologia viatorum*, a pilgrim theology. In Barth's own thinking this is shown in his readiness continually to strike his tents before settling down too comfortably. From the first edition of his *Epistle to the Romans* in 1917 to the latest volume of the *Church Dogmatics* he has been engaged in ceaseless revision with constant surprises no less for himself than for contemporaries working with him, and we have not yet seen the last of these surprises—for he is still young in his seventies. His thinking is of great systematic force and sustained power of concentrated thought. His doctrine of reconciliation in particular is a marvel of architectonic beauty. Yet he is not the creator of a system deducing from a single principle and therefore knowing everything in advance. It is because his thinking is a humble following that it is so alive, so vital.

If theology is exposition, this means concretely that it is bound to a text, to the text which the Church has recognised and acknowledged as the Canon, i.e., the standard, the normative, basic and exemplary form for the continuing delivery of its message, in other words to the Bible. Apart from Augustine, Luther and Calvin there has hardly been a great Christian thinker who has more clearly displayed the exegetical character of all theology, nor a dogmatic presentation of the Christian faith which has been worked out so clearly in terms of express exegesis of the whole content of the Bible. The small print exegetical passages in the *Church Dogmatics* are usually prepared by Barth before the composition of his own thematic expositions, though they are placed after them in the text. From this we infer that, if the temporal priority of exegesis shows the heteronomy, the dependence of theological thinking, its spatial priority in print shows its autonomy, freedom and individual responsibility, not as slavish repetition, but as the free expression, after humble listening, of its own understanding—the " freedom of those who are bound," according to the pregnant title selected by his friends, and forbidden by the German censor, for the volume prepared in 1936 in honour of his 50th birthday.[2]

Because theology is not free speculation but thinking which is referred to a specific place and set under concrete authority, the reader even of this selection must bear in mind that the theme rather than the author is responsible for many of the highly individual trains of thought which he finds. Barth's concern is not just with his own theology as a private view of things, or the programme of a theological school competing with other trends. His concern is always with the content of the Christian message. For Barth every sentence is as it were a proposal for the understanding of this message and it is accompanied by the question whether the message does not impose this understanding. Hence even when we come across very strange lines of thought it is as well not to reject them forthwith

5

but first to ask whether they have any basis in the message itself.

Barth never strives after originality for its own sake. In many of his theses he has contradicted hoary Christian traditions, but he has never done so lightly, nor in proud and arbitrary opposition to the fathers. In no Evangelical dogmatics since the great works of the older Protestant orthodoxy is there such a mass of historico-theological material, not merely in the form of exposition but of discussion. In none is there more intensive wrestling not merely with the theology of the Reformation but with the fathers and the great thinkers of mediaeval Scholasticism. For this theology, listening to the Bible means also attentive listening to other men. Even in the case of the great opponent Schleiermacher there is a constant concern to know what positive lessons he may have to teach. The sharp blade which Barth uses in polemics is always in fact a very humane instrument, and leaves the final judgment to the One who alone is Judge. As he himself says (IV, 2, p. 570), the word conflict or " falling-out " " has to be used very cautiously and selectively in theology. We cannot wish to fall out with God, with Jesus Christ, with the Holy Spirit. We can only be glad and thankful that God is on our side. It is also better not to fall out with Holy Scripture or the Church as the communion of saints. And it is better that there should be no falling out in our relationship with our neighbours. But there is every cause . . . to fall out with oneself." This is practised by Barth even in relation to the period which he first opposed so vehemently, namely, the theology of the 19th century, to which he has devoted one of his finest books.[3] For him tradition is neither a burdensome yoke nor a divine dictate. It is the voice of the fathers and brethren to be heard both with gratitude and freedom. It does not prevent his venturing into the new and unknown. Yet he always finds satisfaction when he can say that for all the " critical freedom which I have had to exercise . . . I have always found myself content with the broad lines of Christian tradition " (IV, 2, p. xi).

This peace with tradition, so different from the hybris of the revolutionary, is the Catholic element in the *Church Dogmatics* as the critical freedom is the Protestant.

6

Ecumenical breadth is one of the most important characteristics of this work. In passages where the motifs of Roman
Catholic, Eastern Orthodox and Pietist theology are
explicitly or implicitly taken up and heard, the expert is
continually forced to ask himself whether what they try
to say is not better brought out here and better and more
biblically expressed. There can be no mistaking Barth's
Reformed origin. He never conceals his particular gratitude
to the much slandered and misunderstood Calvin. But
it would be foolish for this reason to describe him as a
Reformed or Calvinistic theologian in the narrower sense.
Confessional definiteness does not mean confessional con-
striction. The division of the Church into confessions is
abruptly described by him as a scandal for which there is
no justification (IV, 1, p. 675). Theology as a serious
matter must always be prepared firmly and uncompromisingly to say Yes and No. It must always be prepared to
take its place in the conflict of confessions. But it must
also recognise that confessional traditions " exist in order
that we may go through them (not once but continually),
but not in order that we may return to them and take up
our abode in them " (III, 4, Preface). Thus Barth as an
acknowledged heir of the Reformation has contributed
essentially to the rediscovery of the theology of Luther
and Calvin which is such a feature of the modern epoch
of Protestant theology, and yet, although often chidden for
his orthodoxy, he has powerfully opposed every orthodox
repristination. Hence it is not surprising that in debate
with Roman Catholics his theology is regarded on the one
side as the most consistent realisation of the intention of
the Reformation (E. Przywara) and on the other as the
opening up of " a new possibility of fruitful interconfessional
conversation " (R. Grosche), or indeed as both " the
strongest development of Protestantism and the closest
approximation to Catholicism " (H. U. von Balthasar,
J. Küng). Yet it is unmistakeably Protestant in its consciousness of the responsibility of the individual, whom
no tradition nor ecclesiastical court can relieve of the duty
of publicly stating what he has heard and perceived, and
who therefore, in the bold words of the Preface to the first
volume, must " in all modesty venture to be such a Church
in his own situation and to the best of his ability."

7

Theology is impossible without humility because the truth at issue is a person who says : " I am the Truth " (Jn. 14⁶). We cannot possess a person, or rather this person. If He gives Himself, He does not give Himself away. Because its subject is so intractable, theology is an enterprise which cannot guarantee its own success. Hence there are many passages in the *Church Dogmatics* in which the author reminds himself and his readers of the essential reserve laid upon this thinking. It cannot take place without prayer for the fulfilment of the promise by which it is initiated—a fulfilment which it cannot produce nor demand, but for which it can only pray as for free grace. If theology is not pointless chatter, if it is " different from Rabbinic learning or Greek speculation . . . then it is so at every point on the basis of election, and not otherwise " (I, 2, p. 349 ; cf. II, 1, p. 70 ff.). The appeal must be to no less than the supreme court, and confidence in the supreme help and assistance, if theology is to be a meaningful undertaking. This was the real meaning of the earlier designation " dialectical theology " by which Barth and his friends first came to be spoken of after the first world war. Barth himself has later said rather brusquely that the label was attached to them by spectators, and he himself has become increasingly reluctant to use the ambiguous term " dialectical." He certainly used it freely enough in his earlier period. But he never had in view a Hegelian dialectic, i.e., a method of successfully viewing things together, and therefore a triumph of thought over the contradictions of reality. What he meant was rather a confession of the brokenness of our thinking, to which only contradictory parts are given and which cannot hope to achieve the synthesis reserved for God alone. In his development reflection on this brokenness belongs to his earlier period, whereas later he has given greater emphasis to the promise given to human thinking as it may enter the service of the message. This has meant a yielding of the influence of the paradoxical thinking of Kierkegaard before the attempt to understand the unity of the divine action in the incomprehensibilities of the divine decisions.

For theology should seek in all humility to understand. If it is exposition, this implies that it has a subject. Hence

there can be no question of a " blind and formless and
inarticulate and irrational stirring " to which there
corresponds on our side only a " blind and formless incite-
ment or even pacification." Revelation is rather an event
by which man becomes " one who sees and understands
and knows," and can give " a logical answer corresponding
to the logical attitude of God " (IV, 2, p. 313). Christian
faith is as remote from irrationalistic mysticism as it is
from a rationalism which posits the axioms of human
reason as a measure of the possibility and actuality of God.
It is essentially *fides quaerens intellectum,* faith seeking
after understanding.[4] Revelation neither lulls the understanding nor eliminates it. It mobilises it, both humbling
and yet also encouraging it. In the volumes of the doctrine
of reconciliation especially Barth applies all the energy of
his thinking to banish any suggestion of caprice or whim-
sicality from the understanding of divine grace. Rejecting
modern irrationalism, against which we are warned by its
dreadful fruits in the Third Reich, he honours man as a
rational being (III, 2, pp. 419 ff.), and he particularly
values revelation as that which is not in any sense a-logical
but genuinely rational. In God there is no conflict between
mystery and rationality. For this reason theology does
not violate but recognises the mystery of God in its attempt
to trace the wisdom of God in His acts.

Barth once wrote in 1922 that he had got over the
childish ailment of being ashamed of theology,[5] and
already in the Preface to the second edition of his *Epistle
to the Romans* he points out that what awaits the reader is
full-blooded theology. " If in spite of this warning non-
theologians take up the book—and I know some who will
understand its contents better than many theologians—I
shall be very pleased ; for I firmly believe that its subject
concerns everyone because its question is the question of
everyone. Yet even with this audience in view I could
not make it any easier. If I am not mistaken . . . we
theologians best serve the interests of the laity if we do not
expressly or purposefully address ourselves to them but
keep to our calling like all honest workmen." His aim
is not to be a prophet or renovator or reformer or revolutionary, but simply an honest workman, one who is charged
by the Church to expound the Christian message in the

9

service of this message and with a view to its better transmission. Convinced of the incomparable importance of this message for every man and age, and not least for our own age and its problems, he is sure that a life is not wasted if all its time and energy are devoted to the service of theology, and that this service is not incidental, and should not be rendered in a dilettante, rhetorical or sentimental manner, but must be undertaken only as sober work, with pitiless self-criticism, in the full strictness of the concept, without fearing the reproach of intellectualism, with the most highly intellectual eloquence and objective self-absorption. " Politics is the most manly of occupations next to theology," he could once write in relation to some political memoirs, thus showing how highly he esteemed his own task.

The theological work of Barth, therefore, is for a Christianity supremely threatened by arbitrariness and *allotria* an unmistakeable summons back to its true theme and task. Even the non-theological and especially the non-Christian reader, or the reader who does not regard himself as a Christian, finds himself invited to participate in objective thinking, though he must admit that no particular concession is made to him. If he reads impartially and with sufficient seriousness, he will hopefully note how often his own questions are treated. But they are not treated with express reference to him, nor with any anxious concern for particularly original or modern language. Barth has never dealt specifically with the demand so often put to the Church that it should more fully speak the language of the age, nor with the question so often discussed in Church circles how the Gospel should be preached to the modern man. But he has always thought that the question of content should take precedence of that of manner, that the correct recognition of what the Church has to say will also produce the right way of saying it, that if only it is correctly perceived the matter will speak for itself and create for itself an appropriate language. The fact that Barth rejects the attempt of " natural theology " frees him from any fear that there might be an age when it could be proclaimed either with triumph or sorrow that God is dead—an age, therefore, which might discard all earlier religious traditions and thus be unreceptive to the Gospel. Expecting receptivity to the Gospel only by the miracle of the Holy Spirit, he has implicit trust in this miracle, and does not therefore think in terms of ages which are more religious or more profane, closer to God or more distant from Him. The non-Christian can put no question which is not necessarily that of the Christian dogmatician as well. In solidarity with the non-Christian, he has no prior knowledge. He must begin from the very beginning with no presupposed consciousness of God. He must learn to spell out the message which comes to him as to every man. He must apply himself to understand its content, context and consequences. The fact that hearing is the only way to faith continually brings the Christian and the non-Christian into the same situation. Hence there is no reason for us to be concerned first with our own faith or lack of faith, but only with the unique theme which here breaks into the sphere of our lives as we are told of it. All the cards are on the table. Nothing more is required of any of us than in other branches of intellectual life, namely, seriousness of objective thought and living interest in the theme. The rest does not lie in the hands of men, whether they are the speakers or hearers, and therefore it cannot be forced by a particular method or mode of speech. If Barth's *Epistle to the Romans* was already sharply distinguished from the usual type of biblical commentary by its lively expressionistic style, this style was only the natural result of the overwhelming of the author by his great discoveries. In the event, and especially in the development of the successive volumes of the *Dogmatics*, Barth's style has more and more lost its prophetic quality, but also its academic flavour, which is most pronounced in the first. The language of the scholar has given way to that of direct presentation or even narration, the nature of the subject being such that it can " only be told " and not considered and described as a system (II, 2, p. 188). It is because the theme of this narration is as inexhaustible as it is enthralling that Barth is so eloquent, that his eloquence is never empty or merely rhetorical, that new expressions and comparisons continually occur to him, that the flow of his eloquence is so living and powerful and that he need not strive after modernity. If modernity of jargon is not found in his work, the passion of objectivity and " sober exuberance " (II, 1, p. 219) make his language genuinely modern.

His work did not begin at a professor's desk or with the aspirations of a young man of the new generation. The origins are to be found in the embarassment of an honest man in a Swiss parsonage who could have no more illusions as to the contrast between the claim of his work and its actuality. According to its claim as expressed in the tolling of the bell, preaching from the pulpit, the opening of the Bible and the administration of the sacraments, this work stands in the service of the intervention of another and eternal reality, being the place at which account has to be taken of this reality. But in actuality men were taking it up as a conventional task without the corresponding movement, so that it was valued like all other ecclesiastical activities and trends as the preaching of a culture which thought it meritorious to be Christian but saw to it in every possible way that there should be no genuine intervention to shake and question it. In actuality, therefore, the attack and claim which are so unmistakeable in the New Testament were muted and neutralised by the official recognition, the cultural integration and the social control of Christianity as a middle-class institution. In actuality the factory owners in the small industrial town of Safenwil in Aargau naturally expected the minister to be on their side in the bitter class war between them and their workers, and to use his preaching to summon the latter to good conduct, contentment and restraint from strike action. In actuality even the spiritual equipment which the young pastor had received from his theological teachers contradicted the task with which he found himself charged when he mounted the pulpit and opened the Bible.

In its resistance to the great attack on traditional dogma launched by the Enlightenment, the Protestant theology of the 19th century, on the basis of the Pietist movement and the Roman Catholic theology of the Counter-reformation, had very largely agreed in taking up a defensive position in which the truth of Christian faith was to be proved by demonstrating the indispensability of religious feeling to all higher humanity, it being also shown that all previous historical religions constitute an evolutionary ladder at the head of which stands Christianity, which embraces all their positive qualities and surpasses them in its spiritual and ethical development of the consciousness of God. In this way it seemed to be made clear that the most progressive civilisation and the highest religion, that Christianity, the West and progress all belong together, and that Christianity is an irreplaceable instrument for the humanisation of humanity which the century had adopted as its programme. The justification of Christianity had its roots, therefore, in that of religion generally, and this was accomplished by understanding it as an expression of the noblest need and the noblest assurance which man could discover in himself, as the revelation of his highest feature, his transcendentally related spirituality. If this defence did not find the hoped for response in the educated circles for which it was intended, it did at least give the representatives of Christianity the satisfaction of finding themselves in step with the march of civilisation and not of belonging to a past epoch as maintained by anti-Christian *Aufklärer* of every type. Yet on this basis it was not possible to refute the contention of Ludwig Feuerbach that the secret of theology is anthropology.[6] For on this view the revelation which could establish and validate all others was found in the breast of man himself, in the structure of human consciousness. His self-certainty was the basis of the certainty of God and the legitimation of the specifically Christian certainty of God. The secret of God was in truth that of self-glorifying man speaking of God and extolling his own divinity. But in these circumstances the need of man, his adaptation for the goal of culture, could not fail to become the standard by which the traditional form of the Christian message was judged and what was temporally conditioned in the Bible and ecclesiastical dogma was separated from what is still valid, i.e., serviceable, to-day. But once this standard was adopted, it is hard to see where a line could be drawn, and it seems fairly obvious that what we have here are only last-ditch attempts to resist those who with greater resolution were prepared to consign the whole of Christianity to the historical past. As knowledge of other cultures increased, and particularly of the great religions of Asia, the argument that Christianity stands at the top of a ladder of religious development had necessarily to give ground to a relativism which could recognise it as the supreme expression of religion only for our European civilisation. When one of our clearest theological thinkers, Ernst Troeltsch, came to see this, he was only being more consistent when in 1914 he moved to a philosophical chair. But the self-understanding of the Christian message as contained in the biblical writings stood in irreconcilable conflict with this integration into the religious history of humanity, with this understanding of a consciousness of God innate from the very first in man. The revelation of which Christian proclamation had to speak was a happening from above downwards in which man was measured by God's standard and which was directed against a thinking from below upwards, a grounding of the assertions of Christianity in human immanence.

The theological or religio-philosophical training of the young minister in Safenwil was thus quite unsuitable for the task with which he saw himself to be charged, especially when he had to preach. Unlike many others, however, he could have no further illusions as to his position. The son of a New Testament professor at Berne, Fritz Barth, who stood on the positive side, and the pupil of leading liberal theologians in Berlin and Marburg, he realised that the differences between the positive and liberal trends were of little account in face of their common features. The year 1914 saw the outbreak of a world war which educated circles in Europe had regarded as impossible and the enlistment of the vast majority of the adherents of these circles into the various propaganda fronts of this war. This new turn in events made it unmistakeably clear that the only alternatives were either to continue to build God on man and thus to move further and further away from the true starting-point of Christianity until finally humanity was lost as well as Christianity, as the war now revealed, or to make a new and resolute attempt to think in biblical terms and thus seriously to accept as such the revelation of God attested in the Bible, making it the measure of all things. "For me personally a day at the beginning of August in that year (1914) was the *dies ater* (the black day), when ninety-three German intellectuals published an endorsement of the military policy of Kaiser Wilhelm II and his councillors, on which to my horror I found the names of almost all the theological teachers whom hitherto I had confidently respected. If they could be so mistaken in ethos, I noted that it was quite impossible for me to adhere any longer to their ethics or dogmatics, to their exposition of the Bible or presentation of history. So far as I was concerned, there was no more future for the theology of the 19th century." [7]

In those first weeks of the first world war some of the ministers in Aargau met for one of their usual conferences, and, shaken by the fury of war which they saw unleashed beyond the Swiss frontiers, the majority thought that they should postpone their discussion of theological questions until more peaceful times. The young Barth, however, took the opposite view that theological work was the most urgent imperative of the hour, and he set himself to examine the foundations hitherto accepted and to look for better. He has remained true to the conviction that the way must always lead from within outwards, from the centre to the periphery, and that reflection on this centre is thus the most relevant and promising of all undertakings in unsettled times. Hence he did not follow the example of many others like F. Naumann, Albert Schweitzer and the Christian Socialists, who, equally dissatisfied with contemporary theology and philosophy, turned to supposedly more practical tasks. Instead he remained faithful to his pastoral office and sought a new way out of the dilemma in which it involved him.

There now fell on fruitful soil a number of voices from the outer edges of the main ranks of Christianity which might have been heard before but thus far had spoken in vain—the voice of Kierkegaard, of the unique Dutch-Rhenish preacher H. F. Kohlbrügge, of the two Swabian preachers of the kingdom of God, the elder and the younger Blumhardt (whose influence is shown by the sequel, and particularly by the volumes on reconciliation, to be the most enduring), of the spiritually powerful Zurich pastor and philosopher Hermann Kutter, of the Basle Church historian Franz Overbeck and his merciless criticism of the contemporary Christianity of culture, of Dostoievski and above all of the newly articulate Reformers.[8] All these combined, however, to point to the particularity of

15

the biblical Word. It was not that recourse was had to the Bible because a traditional dogma demanded it, but that alongside other voices the Bible had also to be tested, as it were, in the search for a way out. In fact, however, the Bible came right into the forefront, and it is perhaps consonant with this experience that Barth has always refused to find a principial basis of the particular authority of the Bible in the Christian Church and has always regarded it as a sufficient basis that it does in fact impose and continually assert itself in a way which is unique and irreplaceable.

It soon became apparent how the Bible began to speak when consulted in this predicament. In 1918 there was published a small Swiss edition of an exposition of the Romans which in the months before and after the German collapse many who were seeking new guidance took up and then passed on to others. What they found here was Paul speaking in up-to-date terms, not of human cultural ideals but of the judgments of God, not in an attempt to find parallels but in demonstration of the antithesis between the Gospel and human striving, not on the basis of human need but of his commission vertically from above, not as a genius but as an apostle, triumphant only in brokenness. The prophetic force of this exposition fell on receptive ears, and it was quickly reissued by C. Kaiser of München. A volume of sermons followed in which Barth co-operated with his friend E. Thurneysen, who has always been his most loyal partner and whose contribution to the early work particularly cannot be ignored. These sermons show what a new and strange and stimulating sound preaching can still achieve. Fresh adherents were gained as the new or dialectical theology attracted younger men and found a focus in the journal *Zwischen den Zeiten*. With Barth and Thurneysen, Friedrich Gogarten, Emil Brunner, Georg Merz and then Rudolf Bultmann became the leaders of the new movement.

The sermons published by Barth and Thurneysen in 1924 under the title *Komm Schöpfer Geist* bear as a motto the saying of Calvin : *Deus in sua inscrutabili altitudine non est investigandus* (God is not to be sought out in His inscrutable loftiness). The pathos of distance was directed against the comfortable mysticism of Neo-Protestantism,

16

against the notion of man bearing God within his own breast and knowing well the right way. All the things which had seemed to be self-evident were now shown not to be so at all : that man knows about God ; that human questioning finds a divine answer ; that God can be known ; that God hears and speaks ; that God is love ; that God is concerned about man ; that the address of God means life for man and not death. Barth's correspondence in 1923 with his former teacher A. von Harnack[9] should be read to understand how revolutionary, menacing and inhuman the contesting of these supposedly self-evident truths must have seemed to the older generation.

In the Preface of his second edition of the *Epistle to the Romans* Barth writes : " If I have a system it consists in the fact that I keep as consistently as possible before me the negative and positive significance·of what Kierkegaard has called the ' infinite qualitative distinction ' between time and eternity. ' God is in heaven, and thou on earth.' The relation of this God to this man, and this man to this God, is for me the theme of the Bible and the sum of philosophy." If we ask concerning the relationship between the earlier Barth and the later, we may say that the second of the two statements quoted is the one which has remained, whereas the first shows us the difference. The pathos of distance, the contesting of supposedly self-evident truths, the recognition of God as the Wholly Other whom to encounter is mortal judgment, the preaching of the *diastasis* of Christianity and culture, the exclusion of mysticism and ethicism, the questioning of all hyphens, the championing of exclusivism against inclusivism—all these were necessary if revelation was to be recognised and taken seriously as miracle, grace as a far from self-evident gift, the Gospel as something really new which man cannot tell himself, and the Christian message as a message which has its own self-grounded and unique quality. But this was not all that was required. There had to be a positive as well as a negative movement.[10] If Barth saw this more quickly than his fellow-workers, this is because he cannot rest content with a single insight and spend the rest of his days in its systematic development. His self-criticism is too great and his urge for total knowledge too strong to allow him to remain blind for

17

long to the inadequate, truncated and one-sided aspects of a given position. It is for him a practical and not just a theoretical truth that all theology is *theologia viatorum* or " broken thought and utterance to the extent that it can progress only in isolated thoughts and statements directed from different angles to the one subject. It can never form a system, comprehending and as it were ' seizing ' the object " (III, 3, p. 293). In his own practice this does not mean, however, that he can accept the most disparate elements or the most paradoxical propositions as though paradox were an indication of truth. It means that he is committed to an unceasing movement from what is known to what is not yet known, to an active pilgrimage. On the other hand, his thinking cannot consist in the development of axioms into a system. It is always stimulated from without. It has a partner outside itself. It has a theme which is continually given it by something else. For Christian theological thinking this other is in the first instance—and whatever else may have to be said on the subject—the Bible as the basic and canonical witness to revelation. For Barth this has meant in practice that there is for him no distinction between exegetical and systematic theology. He is constantly occupied in exegetical work. He has embarked on his fresh developments in and by means of exegesis. In contrast to the builder of systems, whose steps can always be foreseen, he sees himself and his readers constantly faced by surprises in virtue of it. Exegetical labours of acknowledged rank have thus led him on and forced upon him changes which have alienated many who previously made common cause with him.

The main change is that the pathos of distance has now been replaced by the pathos of the Gospel, of the glad tidings that the distance has been overcome, though the earlier insight is retained that this is not self-evident, so that there can be no return to the old equations, to thinking from below. " God is God." In 1921 this was a warning against the identification of God with what man thinks he can find in himself by way of the consciousness of God. Thirty years later it is a grateful confession of the condescension of God, of His grace and self-offering on the cross. The titles " dialectical theology " and " theology

18

of crisis " vanished even before the group thus designated was rent by the material differences which emerged between Barth and some of the others, but the title " Theology of the Word " is still apposite, and the concept Word has been increasingly filled out by the concrete name of Jesus Christ.

This main change has taken some twenty years, and three points may be noted : the publication of the *Christian Dogmatics in Outline* in 1927, which offended many because the prophet had now turned dogmatician ; the publication of the first volume of the *Church Dogmatics* in 1932, with its almost complete obliteration of the earlier outline ; and the publication of the essay *Justification and Law* in 1938. The way from the *Epistle to the Romans* to the *Dogmatics* was necessary and unavoidable if the antithesis formulated against Neo-Protestantism was not to remain in the framework of basic Neo-Protestant concepts but to be a real antithesis. How else could the new preaching of God as the Wholly Other, of the crisis of everything temporal in relation to eternity etc., be more than the articulation of a new facet of the consciousness of the age or the expression of a distinctive religious mentality no less justified than others but with no claim to exclusive justification ? How far was it not merely a religious possibility but a Christian necessity ? How far was it to be taken seriously that the " essence of Christianity " does not consist in ideas and ideals but in a concrete person Jesus of Nazareth, as is undoubtedly the view of the whole of the New Testament ? What was the result of taking this seriously ? In relation to this question everything that is merely an expression of the mood of the age, or that rests on a generally philosophical foundation, or that has recourse to a general dialectic of the infinite and the finite, is consistently rejected in favour of a persistent concern to bring all the essential statements of the Christian faith back to their christological basis, and thus to clarify their content and show them to be specifically Christian, i.e., to show how they are made possible but also necessary by the manifestation of Jesus Christ, and how it is only in relation to Him that they take on their own significance but also their impregnable certainty. There is thus achieved a christological concentration unparalleled in the history of Christian thought, a focusing upon this one central human fact, which is not, however, a measurable fact but a Word which comprehends and reveals the whole history between God and man. This being the case, there can be no weighing of its significance without participation. When it speaks of this Word, language necessarily loses the character of academic neutrality and constantly reveals that it speaks in the presence of this subject, taking the form of worship and confession as is so often the case— though without sentimentality or vehemence—in the *Church Dogmatics*.

The essay *Justification and Law* (1938) brought to light, although naturally not without preparation,[11] an implication of the christological concentration which still occupies us to-day, namely, the political relevance of the Christian message. What we have thus far expounded can never be regarded merely as the movement of an individual thinker. The attention claimed by Barth since the *Epistle to the Romans* and the inner necessity of his understanding of the Gospel produced an inward correspondence of the history of his thinking to that of German Protestantism between the two world wars. When German Evangelical Christianity was confronted in 1933 by the demand that it should view National Socialism as a divine revelation, purge the Christian tradition according to the norm of a supposed German consciousness of God, and place preaching in the service of national renewal as Hitler understood it, and when it seemed for the most part inclined willingly to comply with this demand, it was of providential significance that the theological work associated with the name of Barth, though not, of course, prosecuted by him in isolation, disclosed and brought into even sharper focus the difference between Christian revelation and everything else that might claim to be revelation, the critical freedom of the Gospel in relation to all human claims and aspirations, and the exclusive authority of the Word of God over the action of the Church. Hence Barth's polemical work *Theologische Existenz heute* in the summer of 1933 was a basic document of the Confessing Church then in process of formation, and the Declaration of the Confessional Synod of Barmen of May, 1934, which still serves to direct the Evangelical Church, derived in all its main essentials from him.[12]

Although as a Swiss he was hampered in his participation and often hindered, he, too, was initially of the opinion that there should be a careful separation between the ecclesiastical opposition to National Socialism and the political. In view of the weighty reasons for this view only ill-wishers or fools can reproach him for it, as sometimes happens. But as the true nature of National Socialism emerged, he realised that the separation could not be maintained, and the theological work which he still prosecuted for all his participation in current events also served to force him into a more radical position. For the idea of separation presupposed an ultimate distinction between the religious and political spheres which reflection on the universal significance of the manifestation of Jesus Christ necessarily called in question. That there is an essential relevance of Christianity in politics, and that the Christian as such is charged with political responsibility, had always been recognised by Barth. For him the Gospel had always struck a revolutionary rather than a conservative note. It had always seemed to call for the alteration and amelioration of the *status quo* rather than its legitimation. For this reason he had supported Social Democracy in Switzerland from as early as 1915. But now he attained to theological clarity and understanding in the matter through his recognition that grace is commitment. To be graciously blessed is not merely to be spared punishment or loaded with benefits ; it is to be commissioned for active service. Already in the second edition of the *Epistle to the Romans* (p. 414) we read : " Admonition is the assertion of grace as demand." Grace demands, and for those who are graciously blessed by God there is no other demand than that which derives from grace. Hence the commands of God are not divorced from His grace ; they are its orders and applications to life. In political life this means that the Christian as a citizen stands under no other command than that of his Lord, and that in his political action he cannot be obedient to an autonomous decree of the state as a final authority, but must understand and test it as an answer to the grace of his Lord addressed not only to himself and his nation but to all men. The positions adopted by Barth, which have been much contested and misunderstood and cannot be more precisely indicated in the present context, are his own attempts to put this into practice. Those who do not merely attack them on the basis of passing hearsay, but attentively study them, can hardly fail to see both his loving concern for the ways and destiny of the German people to whom he is so closely related and his consistency in spite of every difference in detail, especially in relation to National Socialism and Communism. There is no question of any interest in the domination or self-preservation of the Church, nor in the execution of a programme deduced from the articles of the Christian faith. This would be to change the Gospel into an ideology. The concern is always for a daily answer to the lordship of grace of Jesus Christ. This is worked out in an answering of political questions which cannot be laid down in advance after the manner of casuistry, but which is guided by the recognition that politics must serve the life of the man saved by Christ, and that no man is excluded from His saving act.

Many difficult decisions have to be made in attempting a small selection from the *Church Dogmatics*. The work is a cosmos with no dead or isolated sections. Art consists in omission according to Liebermann, but what can we omit from the *Dogmatics* without hurt ? If we choose only passages which are accessible without prior knowledge or which appeal to those whose interest is only superficial, the real content of the work is left undisclosed and many statements even in the selected passages are rendered incomprehensible. On the other hand, if we introduce the leading trains of thought by assembling decisive portions, there is the danger that such a mosaic will demand no less and perhaps more of the receptivity of the ordinary reader than the original itself. Yet I have decided for the latter method on the assumption that such a collection will better serve the reader than a few choice morsels, since it will not only bring out the originality of Barth but also provide an outstanding example of the work of theology generally. Limitation of space naturally means that many indispensable expositions have had to be omitted. Thus the doctrine the Trinity and' the important new conception of the doctrine of predestination appear only on the margin, and there are no sections on the doctrine of the Church, on the doctrine of angels, on the eschatology already visible in outline in the present volumes, or on the significance of the people of Israel, whose election and destiny have been more highly evaluated in Barth than in any previous Christian theology, so that a new basis is here provided for discussion between the Church and the Synagogue. But if a reading of this selection gives rise to questions which are not answered, the reader will perhaps blame the fact that it is a selection and be stimulated to investigate the works of Barth himself.

THE " CHURCH DOGMATICS "

In its totality the *Church Dogmatics* is planned in five volumes, and thus far (1961) a single part of Volume IV has still to appear and the whole of Volume V on the doctrine of redemption (eschatology). The interrelationship of the existing parts, all of which are now available in English, is as follows.

Volumes I, 1 and I, 2 contain the prolegomena to the dogmatics, i.e., an attempt to understand the task, theme, presuppositions, methods and modes of knowledge both of theology in general and dogmatics in particular. Included are expositions of the doctrine of the Trinity, Christology and the doctrine of Holy Scripture.

Volumes II, 1 and II, 2 deal with the so-called doctrine of God in the narrower sense, i.e., in II, 1 the question of the possibility of the knowledge of God and the doctrine of the attributes of God (love, freedom, omnipotence, wisdom, presence etc.), and in II, 2 the doctrine of the election of grace (predestination) and basic definitions in relation to the commanding of God and therefore the foundation of Christian ethics.

Volume III deals with the doctrine of creation under the following heads :

III, 1, the basis in a great meditation on the creation stories of Genesis 1 and 2 ;

III, 2, the Christian view of man (theological anthropology) ;

III, 3, the doctrines of providence, nothingness and angels ; and

III, 4, the ethical questions raised by the creatureliness

23

of man, namely, his relationship to animals, his sexuality (male and female, marriage), parents and children, nation and humanity, respect for life (e.g., suicide, sickness, capital punishment and war), work, calling, honour etc.

Volume IV contains the doctrine of the reconciliation of God and man in Jesus Christ, as told in three great movements in the parts thus far completed.

IV, 1, Jesus Christ is the condescension of the Son of God as Judge to solidarity with the man who has fallen victim to judgment, the Lord becoming a servant (the high-priestly office of Christ), sin being unmasked as pride and opposed by the divine verdict which effects man's justification, and reconciliation being actualised on man's side by the work of the Holy Spirit in the gathering of the community and the awakening of individual faith ;

IV, 2, Jesus Christ is the restitution of man from the fall to life with and for God, the servant becoming Lord (the kingly office of Christ), sin being unmasked as sloth and opposed by the divine direction which effects man's sanctification, and reconciliation being actualised on man's side by the work of the Holy Spirit in the upbuilding of the community and the awakening of individual love ;

IV, 3, Jesus Christ the God-man is the victorious revelation of the accomplished reconciliation (the prophetic office of Christ), sin being unmasked as falsehood and opposed by the divine promise which effects man's vocation, and reconciliation being actualised on man's side by the work of the Holy Spirit in the calling of the community and the awakening of individual hope.

Help to an understanding of the whole work may be found in the so-called *Introductory Report* to the *Dogmatics* by Otto Weber (Verlag der Buchhandlung des Erziehungsvereins Neukirchen, Kreis Mörs, 1950 ff., E.T., Lutterworth Press, 1953).

OTHER MAIN WORKS OF BARTH

(Cf. the *Bibliographia Barthiana* of Charlotte von Kirschbaum in the "Festschrift" *Antwort* (1956), which lists 406 titles up to 1955.)

DOGMATIC WORKS

Credo (an exposition of the Apostles' Creed), München, 1935.
Gotteserkenntnis und Gottesdienst (an exposition of the *Scots Confession*), Zürich, 1938. E.T., *The Knowledge of God and the Service of God*, Hodder and Stoughton, 1938.
Dogmatik im Grundriss, München, 1947. E.T., *Dogmatics in Outline*, S.C.M. and Harpers, 1949.
Die Christliche Lehre nach dem Heidelberger Katechismus, München, 1949.

EXEGETICAL WRITINGS

Römerbrief, 2nd edit., München, 1921. E.T., *Epistle to the Romans* (6th ed.), O.U.P., 1950.
Die Auferstehung der Toten (I Kor), München, 1924. E.T., *The Resurrection of the Dead*, F. H. Revell, 1933.
Erklärung des Philipperbriefes, München, 1927.
Kurze Auslegung des Römerbriefes, München, 1956. E.T., *A Shorter Commentary on Romans*, S.C.M. and John Knox, 1959.

SERMONS

Suchet Gott, so werdet ihr leben (with E. Thurneysen), Bern, 1917, 2nd edit., München, 1928.
Komm Schöpfer Geist (with E. Thurneysen), München, 1924. E.T., *Come Holy Spirit*, Round Table Press and T. & T. Clark, 1933.
Die grosse Barmherzigkeit (with E. Thurneysen), München, 1935. Cf. E.T., *God's Search for Man*, Round Table Press and T. & T. Clark, 1935.
Fürchte dich nicht, München, 1949.
"*Fides quaerens intellectum.*" *Anselms Beweis der Existenz Gottes*, München, 1931. E.T., S.C.M. and John Knox, 1960.

Die protestantische Theologie im 19 *Jahrhundert. Ihre Vorgeschichte und Geschichte,* Zürich, 1947. E.T., *Protestant Thought from Rousseau to Ritschl,* S.C.M. and Harpers, 1959.

ESSAYS

Das Wort Gottes und die Theologie, München, 1924. E.T., *The Word of God and the Word of Man,* Hodder and Stoughton, 1928.
Die Theologie und die Kirche, München, 1928.
Eine Schweizer Stimme, 1938–1945, Zürich, 1945.
Karl Barth zum Kirchenkampf (Theologische Existenz heute, N.F., No. 49), München, 1956.
Theologische Fragen und Antworten, Zürich, 1957.
Many essays and articles by Barth have appeared in the two series *Theologische Existenz heute* (edited by Barth until 1936 and since then by K. G. Steck and G. Eichholz, München, Kaiser-Verlag), and *Theol. Studien* (edited by Karl Barth and Max Geiger, Evangelischer Verlag, Zürich-Zollikon). All the monographs of Barth have been published by the Verlag C. Kaiser, München, and the Evangelischer Verlag, Zürich-Zollikon (German edition, C. Kaiser).

LITERATURE ON KARL BARTH

This constitutes already a small library. One of the remarkable signs of the theological situation is that after a lively discussion of his earlier work German Protestantism has nothing to say about the *Church Dogmatics.* The fullest monographs concerning the *Dogmatics* in German are by two Swiss Roman Catholics and a Dutch Reformed, and all three are worth noting in virtue of their knowledge and discussion of the theme. They are :
Hans Urs von Balthasar, *Karl Barth, Darstellung und Deutung seiner Theologie* (Verlag J. Hegner, Köln, 1951) ;
Hans Küng, *Rechtfertigung, Die Lehre Karl Barths und eine katholische Besinnung. Mit einem Geleitbrief von Karl Barth* (Johannes-Verlag, Einsiedeln, 1957) ;

G. C. Berkouwer, *Der Triumph der Gnade in der Theologie Karl Barths* (Verlag der Buchhandlung des Erziehungsvereins, Neukirchen bei Mörs, 1957). E.T., *The Triumph of Grace in the Theology of Karl Barth*, Paternoster Press, 1956.

The great extent of Barthian work is made strikingly clear in the Festschrift prepared by his friends and pupils for his 70th birthday under the title *Antwort* (edited by E. Wolf, Evang. Verlag, Zürich-Zollikon, 1956). Among English works which call for notice are the two volumes prepared for Barth's 60th and 70th birthdays under the titles *Reformation Old and New* (edited by F. W. Camfield, Lutterworth Press, 1947) and *Essays in Christology for Karl Barth* (edited by T. H. L. Parker, Lutterworth Press, 1956).

NOTES

(1) Hans Urs von Balthasar, *Karl Barth. Darstellung und Deutung seiner Theologie*, Verlag J. Hegner, Köln, 1951, p. 35 f.
(2) *Theologische Aufsätze, Karl Barth zum 50. Geburtstag*, München, 1936.
(3) *Die protestantische Theologie im 19. Jahrhundert*, Zürich, 1947 ; cf. his article *Evangelische Theologie im 19. Jahrhundert*, Zürich, 1957.
(4) The title of his book on Anselm : " *Fides quaerens intellectum*," *Anselms Beweis der Existenz Gottes*, München, 1931.
(5) In the essay " Not und Verheissung der christlichen Verkündigung " (1922) in *Das Wort Gottes und die Theologie*, München, 1924, p. 99.
(6) Cf. Barth's essays on L. Feuerbach in *Die Theologie und die Kirche*, 1928, pp. 212–239, and *Die protestantische Theologie im 19. Jahrhundert*, pp. 484–489.
(7) K. Barth, *Evangelische Theologie im 19. Jahrhundert*, 1957, p. 6.
(8) On Blumhardt : E. Thurneysen : *Chr. Blumhardt*, München, 1926 ; on Overbeck : K. Barth : *Unerledigte Anfragen an die heutige Theologie* (1920), now in *Die Theologie und die Kirche*, pp. 1–25 ; on Dostoievski : E. Thurneysen : *Dostojewskij*, München, 1922 ; on the whole mood and development of the period 1914–1921 cf. E. Thurneysen's essay " Die Anfänge K. Barths Theologie der Frühzeit " in the Festschrift *Antwort*, 1956, pp. 831–864.
(9) Now in K. Barth : *Theologische Fragen und Antworten*, Zürich, 1957, pp. 7–31.
(10) This is Barth's own retrospective judgment on his own earlier period in the essay *Die Menschlichkeit Gottes*, Zürich, 1956.
(11) The most important preparatory work is to be found in the

27

article *Evangelium und Gesetz* (now in the series *Theologische Existenz heute*, N.F., No. 50, 1956).

(12) Barth's utterances during the Church conflict in Germany have now been collected in *K. Barth zum Kirchenkampf* (*Theologische Existenz heute*, N.F., No. 49, 1956), and, with his pronouncements during the second world war, in *Eine Schweizer Stimme* 1938–1945, Zürich, 1945.

I. REVELATION

1. GOD

The whole world speaks of God. Human history is a history of the relationship of men to their gods. Does Christian utterance concerning God mean the same as the rest of the world when it speaks of God, the gods and the divine ? Is it a particular result of the rich religious production of humanity and its unceasing reflection on the ultimate bases of human existence ? Barth perceives that what the biblical authors say about God is opposed to any such integration. His concern, then, is to work out the distinction. In Christian parlance the word God is used only to denote the One who has revealed Himself as the Lord of all being by His concrete intervention in His address to Israel and the manifestation of Jesus Christ.

[1] Who God is and what it is to be divine is something we have to learn where God has revealed Himself and His nature, the essence of the divine.   [IV, 1, p. 186]

[2] God is indeed the genuine Counterpart which alone can finally and primarily satisfy man and all creation as such. Far too often, however, this has been said in so general and therefore unconvincing a manner that we cannot be content to make the word " God " our final, or perhaps even our basic, term. Far too often this word is used simply as a pseudonym for the limitation of all human understanding, whether of self or the world. Far too often what is meant by it is something quite different, namely, the unsubstantial, unprofitable and fundamentally very tedious magnitude known as transcendence, not as a genuine counterpart, nor a true other, nor a real outside and beyond, but as an illusory reflection of human freedom, as its projection into the vacuum of utter abstraction. And it is characteristic of this transcendence that it neither has a specific will, nor accomplishes a specific act, nor speaks a specific word, nor exercises a specific power and authority. It can neither bind man effectively nor effectively liberate him. It can neither justify him nor satisfy him. It cannot be for his life either a clear meaning or a distinct purpose.

Its high-priests and prophets usually interrupt those who dare to say such things, telling them that it is only in the form of " mythologisation " that we can say anything definite, i.e., that we can ascribe to it a person and form, an ability to act and speak, or even specific words and acts, so that we are better advised not to make any attempts in this direction. Transcendence as they see it cannot mean anything more than that behind and above and before all human action there is this open sphere, this abyss as it were, into which every man is destined to plunge headlong, whether wise or foolish, whether blessed or judged, whether to salvation or perdition. And the only sure and certain result which accrues from contemplating this spectre seems to be the rather barren law of toleration, i.e., of refraining from absolutising, and therefore in fact of avoiding all positive statements concerning its binding content and direction. In the present context we need not join issue with this standpoint and its representatives on this aspect. We must certainly insist, however, that when we ourselves introduce the term " God " at this point, we necessarily have something very different in view.

The introduction of the term " God " is not an abuse of this name, but meaningful and helpful, if in respect of it we think of what is attested by Holy Scripture concerning God's speech and action. God is the One whose name and cause are borne by Jesus Christ. Hence there is no question of divinity in the abstract as suprahuman and supracosmic being. Holy Scripture knows nothing of this divinity. To be sure, the God of Holy Scripture is superior to man and the world as the Lord. But He has also bound Himself to man and the world in creating them. God is here introduced to us in the action in which He is engaged, not merely in His superiority over the creature, but also in His relationship to it. What is presented to us is the faithfulness of this God and His living approach to the creature. There is set before us His specific coming, acting and speaking in the creaturely world with the intention of asserting, protecting and restoring His right to the creature, and therefore the creature's own right and honour.   [III, 4, p. 479 f.]

[3] When Holy Scripture speaks of God, it does not

30

permit us to let our attention or thoughts wander at random until at this or that level they set up a being which is furnished with utter sovereignty and all other perfections, and which as such is the Lord, the Law-giver, the Judge and the Saviour of man and men. When Holy Scripture speaks of God it concentrates our attention and thoughts upon one single point and what is to be known at that point. And what is to be known there is quite simple. It is the God who in the first person singular addressed the patriarchs and Moses, the prophets and later the apostles. It is the God who in this " I " is and has and reveals sovereignty and all other perfections. It is the God who wills to be known and worshipped and reverenced as such. It is the God who created His people Israel by His Word, and separated them from all other peoples, and later separated the Church from Israel. It is the God who exercises His rule in what He wills and does with this people, the people first called Israel and later the Church. It is He, this God, who as the Lord and Shepherd of that people is also, of course, the World-ruler, the Creator of all things, the Controller of all events, both great and small. But in every way His government of the world is only the extension, the application and the development of His government in this one particular sphere. He does the general for the sake of the particular. Or to put it in another way, He does the general through the particular, and in and with it. That is God according to His self-revelation.

We may look closer and ask : Who and what is the God who is to be known at the point upon which Holy Scripture concentrates our attention and thoughts? Who and what is the God who rules and feeds His people, creating and maintaining the whole world for its benefit, and guiding it according to His own good-pleasure—according to the good-pleasure of His will as it is directed towards this people ? If in this way we ask further concerning the one point upon which, according to Scripture, our attention and thoughts should and must be concentrated, then from first to last the Bible directs us to the name of Jesus Christ. It is in this name that we discern the divine decision in favour of the movement towards this people, the self-determination of God as Lord and

Shepherd of this people, and the determination of this people as "his people, and the sheep of his pasture" (Ps. 100³). And in this name we may now discern the divine decision as an event in human history and therefore as the substance of all the preceding history of Israel and the hope of all the succeeding history of the Church. What happened was this, that under this name God Himself became man, that He became this particular man, and as such the Representative of the whole people that hastens towards this man and derives from Him. What happened was this, that under this name God Himself realised in time, and therefore as an object of human perception, the self-giving of Himself as the Covenant-partner of the people determined by Him from and to all eternity. What happened was this, that it became a true fact that under this name God Himself possesses this people : possesses it no less than He does Himself ; swears towards it the same fidelity as He exercises with Himself ; directs upon it a love no less than that with which in the person of the Son He loves Himself ; fulfilling His will upon earth as in the eternal decree which precedes everything temporal it is already fulfilled in heaven. What happened was this, that under this name God Himself established and equipped the people which bears the name to be "a light of the Gentiles," the hope, the promise, the invitation and the summoning of all peoples, and at the same time, of course, the question, the demand and the judgment set over the whole of humanity and every individual man. As all these things happened under this name, the will of God was done. And according to God's self-revelation attested in Scripture, it is wholly and utterly in these happenings that we are to know what really is the good-pleasure of His will, what is, therefore, His being, and the purpose and orientation of His work, as Creator of the world and Controller of history. There is no greater depth in God's being and work than that revealed in these happenings and under this name. For in these happenings and under this name He has revealed Himself. According to Scripture the One who bears this name is the One who in His own " I " introduces the concept of sovereignty and every perfection When the bearer of this name becomes the object of our attention and thoughts, when they are directed to Jesus

Christ, then we see God, and our thoughts are fixed on Him. [II, 2, p. 52 f.]

[4] The King of Israel is the God who rules all things.

At its simplest, this is the definition with which we have to fill out our hitherto formal consideration. And again, we can elucidate the definition most clearly and simply by saying that the God of Israel, and therefore the God who rules all things, is the Subject whose speaking and acting is the source and also the object and content of the witness of the Old and New Testaments. To put it in another way : The King of Israel is the One who according to the witness of the Old and New Testaments spoke the " I am," and in speaking it actualised it for seeing eyes and hearing ears by acts of power within the created cosmos and human history. The concrete name " the King of Israel" covers both the Old Testament and New Testament forms of the spoken and actualised " I am " in which we have to do with the Subject of the divine world-governance.

It may be noted that with this definition and its elucidation the idea of the divine world-governance, whatever may be our attitude towards it, does at least cease to be a mere idea and is related to a reality. The form of the idea acquires concrete substance. The colourless idea takes on colour. And this takes place when it is seen that in the idea of the divine world-governance the Subject God bears this concrete name. To apprehend and affirm the idea we have to think of definite periods in human history as this name leads us. And we have to think of definite places—the land of Canaan, Egypt, the wilderness of Sinai, Canaan again, the land on the two sides of Jordan, Jerusalem, Samaria, the towns and villages of Judaea and Galilee, the various places beyond in Syria, Asia Minor and Greece, and finally Rome. We have to think of definite events and series of events which according to the witness of the Old and New Testaments actually took place at these periods and in these places, relating them always to the spoken and actualised " I am." And then necessarily we have to think of the concrete Scripture which bears witness to these events, the text of the Old and New Testaments. And if we cannot apprehend and affirm the idea of the divine world-governance, then quite

33

concretely this means that we stand in a negative relationship to these events which took place at definite periods and in definite places, to this reality, and to this concrete Scripture. Belief or unbelief in the divine world-governance, whether we do or do not apprehend and confess it, is no longer a matter of the right or wrong development of the idea, but of the right or wrong relationship to this reality to which the idea has reference, and therefore to these definite events as according to the equally definite witness of the Old and New Testament Scriptures they took place at definite periods and in definite places. For the Subject who speaks and actualises the " I am " in these events, the King of Israel, is the God who rules the world.

Thomas Aquinas (*S. theol.*, I, *qu.* 103, *art.* 2) postulates and in his own fashion tries to prove that the Subject that rules the world and directs it to Himself as the one supreme end and goal is necessarily *aliquid extra mundum*, a *bonum* or *principium extrinsecum a toto universo*. We can and must accept this postulate. For if the Subject that rules the world is not recognisable and actually recognised as something distinct from the world, how can it really be a Subject that rules the world and posits itself as the goal of all world-occurrence, and how can it be recognisable or recognised as such ? But we may question whether this quite justifiable postulate ought to be filled out by the particular concept of God which Thomas presupposes and uses in his own demonstration. For this concept of God, the concept of a being in Himself, quite independent of all other being and to that extent absolutely superior to it, is indeed an attempt to point away beyond the world. But the reality of this supramundane being cannot be reached by an attempt of this kind. For the only reality that we can point to in this concept is that of the world as it attempts to transcend itself, so that even in such an attempt it is still the world and not this *principium extrinsecum* which might as such be the Ruler of the world and recognisable and recognised as such. We thus have a concept of God which demands proof of the existence of God. If it is to be recognisable and recognised as a being which is different from the world and therefore qualified to be its Ruler, something more is needed and something more must be perceived than the attempt of the world to transcend itself in this concept. What is needed is that the being itself should transcend the limit and self-knowledge of the world, and thereby demonstrate itself. For the idea of the world-governance of such a being can only have substance, the power postulated by Thomas, if by its own initiative and activity and revelation it actualises and makes perceptible the reality of its supramundane being over against the world, thereby demonstrating itself in the midst of the world. This supramundane being can make itself present in the world only by free grace. And it is the source and object and content of the biblical witness that this did actually occur. Of course, this witness does not refer us to the so-called natural proofs of God's existence in which Thomas found support at this critical point. It witnesses to the very intramundane and temporal and spatial " I am " as the work and revelation of grace in which the *principium extrinsecum*, which can as such be the World-ruler, has actually demonstrated itself to be such ; intramundane and temporal and spatial as opposed to the concept of God as an extramundane reality.

This is why in the biblical witness the divine world-governance is related to the King of Israel. From a philosophical standpoint the naivety with which it does this is highly objectionable. But it is in this naivety that its real strength lies. For it does not find any difficulty in the counter-question whether this supramundane being who as such can rule the world really exists. No second postulate is needed to fill out the first. No resort to natural proofs is needed to fill out the second postulate, and by means of the second the first. The outfilling is itself the starting-point. The basis is the intramundane self-demonstration of the extramundane God and World-ruler. And dogmatics has to take over this naivety and strength in its own thinking and utterance. There is no alternative if it is to be Christian thinking and utterance. If we are really to have a world-ruler, one who is capable of world-dominion as a *principium extrinsecum*, we have to relate the matter to the King of Israel. . . .

[III, 3, p. 177 f.]

[5] God Himself is the nearest to hand, as the absolutely simple must be, and at the same time the most distant, as the absolutely simple must also be. God Himself is the

irresolvable and at the same time that which fills and embraces everything else. God Himself in His being for Himself is the one being which stands in need of nothing else and at the same time the one being by which everything else came into being and exists. God Himself is the beginning in which everything begins, with which we must and can always begin with confidence and without need of excuse. And at the same time He is the end in which everything legitimately and necessarily ends, with which we must end with confidence and without need of excuse. God Himself is simple, so simple that in all His glory He can be near to the simplest perception and also laugh at the most profound or acute thinking—so simple that He reduces everyone to silence, and then allows and requires everyone boldly to make Him the object of their thought and speech. He is so simple that to think and speak correctly of Him and to live correctly before Him does not in fact require any special human complexities or for that matter any special human simplicities, so that occasionally and according to our need He may permit and require both human complexity and human simplicity, and occasionally they may both be forbidden us. . . .

Who and what is God Himself? We must not now go back and give an answer which declares what we think the conception of God ought to be, what God must be to be God according to all necessary postulates and ideas in respect of the concept of deity. God Himself is in fact simply the One of whom all prophets and apostles explained that they had heard His voice and had to obey Him, executing the messages and tasks He laid on them, and bearing witness of His will and work to others. In a remarkable way they also recognised His voice in the testimony of each other, at least to the extent that, in a long unbroken chain, admittedly in quite different ways, but in ways which at this point involved no contradiction, they all aimed to be servants and messengers of one and the same God. This One is God Himself, described by the unanimous testimony of prophets and apostles as the Subject of creation, reconciliation and redemption, the Lord. And as they describe and explain these works of His and His dignity, they characterise Him as the One who is gracious and holy, merciful and righteous, patient

36

and wise, but also omnipresent, constant, omnipotent, eternal and glorious. [II, 1, p. 458]

[6] Knowledge of this God brings those who partake of it under a claim that is total and unlimited as regards what is divine. It isolates them unescapably. It confronts them with an exclusive demand that nothing can soften. In respect of God it sets bounds for them which they can break only by giving up the knowledge of this God. In this they experience God's love as grace, mercy and patience. They experience it as God's election in virtue of His freedom, an election in which God not only chooses them for Himself, but in doing so chooses Himself for them, and marks Himself out as the one, true and therefore unique God. They experience His love as an election in which a final decision is reached at every point regarding what is and what is not divine. The decision is reached that this God, who chooses them, is God alone, and that all other so-called or would-be gods are not what they claim to be. He alone is God, because all that He is and does has its significance and power and stands or falls by the fact that He is it and does it in an incomparable and unique way. There is no other like Him. He does not have to face any competition, either hostile or friendly. His Word does not need to fear any contradiction or His work any opposition, nor of course do they stand in need or are they capable of any assistance, supplementation or authorisation from any other source. . . .

Knowledge of God in the sense of the New Testament message, the knowledge of the triune God as contrasted with the whole world of religions in the first centuries, signified, and still signifies, the most radical " twilight of the gods," the very thing which Schiller so movingly deplored as the de-divinisation of the " lovely world." It was no mere fabrication when the Early Church was accused by the world around it of atheism, and it would have been wiser for its apologists not to have defended themselves so keenly against this charge. There is a real basis for the feeling, current to this day, that every genuine proclamation of the Christian faith is a force disturbing to, even destructive of, the advance of religion, its life and richness and peace. It is bound to be so. Olympus and Valhalla decrease in population when the message of the

37

God who is the one and only God is really known and believed. The figures of every religious culture are necessarily secularised and recede. They can keep themselves alive only as ideas, symbols, and ghosts, and finally as comic figures. And in the end even in this form they sink into oblivion. No sentence is more dangerous or revolutionary than that God is One and there is no other like Him. All the permanencies of the world draw their life from ideologies and mythologies, from open or disguised religions, and to this extent from all possible forms of deity and divinity. It was on the truth of the sentence that God is One that the " Third Reich " of Adolf Hitler made shipwreck. Let this sentence be uttered in such a way that it is heard and grasped, and at once 450 prophets of Baal are always in fear of their lives. There is no more room now for what the recent past called toleration. Beside God there are only His creatures or false gods, and beside faith in Him there are religions only as religions of superstition, error and finally irreligion. [II, 1, p. 443 f.]

2. THE KNOWLEDGE OF GOD

The knowledge of God in the Christian sense is the result of an event which took place once and once for all. " The Word was made flesh " (Jn. 1[14]). God as Creator confronts the creature as an object (His primary objectivity), and He declares Himself as such by means of certain earthly realities, the reality of Jesus Christ and the witness to Him effected through Him and made efficacious by the power of His Spirit (His secondary objectivity). On the human side the corresponding factor is faith, i.e., an indirect knowledge of God which begins with the grateful recognition of this divine mode of revelation and keeps to the realities chosen by God.

[7] What God is as God, the divine individuality and characteristics, the *essentia* or " essence " of God, is something which we shall encounter either at the place where God deals with us as Lord and Saviour, or not at all. The act of revelation as such carries with it the fact that God has not withheld Himself from men as true being, but that He has given no less than Himself to men as the overcoming of their need, and light in their darkness—Himself as the Father in His own Son by the Holy Spirit. The act of God's revelation also carries with it the fact that man,

38

as a sinner who of himself can only take wrong roads, is called back from all his own attempts to answer the question of true being, and is bound to the answer to the question given by God Himself. And finally the act of God's revelation carries with it the fact that by the Word of God in the Holy Spirit, with no other confidence but this unconquerable confidence, man allows being to the One in whom true being itself seeks and finds, and who meets him here as the source of his life, as comfort and command, as the power over him and over all things.

[II, 1, p. 261 f.]

[8] The revelation of God, in which man's fulfilment of the true knowledge of God takes place, is the disposition of God in which He acts towards us as the same triune God that He is in Himself, and in such a way that, although we are men and not God, we receive a share in the truth of His knowledge of Himself. Certainly it is the share which He thinks proper and which is therefore suitable for us. But in this share we have the reality of the true knowledge of Himself. This share is given as God unveils Himself to us in that other, second objectivity, that is to say, in the objectivity of His works and signs in our creaturely sphere, before the eyes and ears and in the hearts which as such and of themselves alone are quite incapable of knowing Him. But the heart of it all is that it is He Himself, the one, supreme and true Lord, who thus unveils Himself to us ; that in revelation we have to do with His action as the triune God, and therefore with Himself in every creaturely work and sign that He uses. On this basis and only on this basis can there be real knowledge of God.

[II, 1, p. 51]

[9] In its subjective reality God's revelation consists of definite signs of its objective reality which are given by God. Among the signs of the objective reality of revelation we have to understand certain definite events and relations and orders within the world in which revelation is an objective reality, and therefore within the world which is also our world, the world of our nature and history. The special determination of these events and relations and orders is that along with what they are and mean within this world, in themselves, and from the standpoint of immanence, they also have another nature and meaning

39

from the side of the objective reality of revelation, i.e., from the side of the incarnation of the Word. Their nature and meaning from this transcendent standpoint is that by them the Word which entered the world objectively in revelation, which was spoken once for all into the world, now wills to speak further in the world, i.e., to be received and heard in further areas and ages of this world. By them it will have " free course " in this world. They are the instruments by which it aims at becoming a Word which is apprehended by men and therefore a Word which justifies and sanctifies men, by which it aims at executing upon men the grace of God which is its content. And their instrumental function is to veil the objective of revelation under a creaturely reality ; and yet to unveil it, i.e., in the actual form of such creaturely reality to bring it close to men, who are themselves also a creaturely reality. They point to revelation. They attest it. No, the Word of God made flesh attests by them that it was not made flesh in vain, that it was spoken once for all, that it is the valid and effective Word.   [I, 2, p. 223]

[10] He unveils Himself as the One He is by veiling Himself in a form which He Himself is not. He uses this form distinct from Himself, He uses its work and sign, in order to be objective in, with and under this form, and therefore to give Himself to us to be known. Revelation means the giving of signs. We can say quite simply that revelation means sacrament, i.e., the self-witness of God, the representation of His truth, and therefore of the truth in which He knows Himself, in the form of creaturely objectivity and therefore in a form which is adapted to our creaturely knowledge.   [II, 1, p. 52]

[11] At bottom, knowledge of God in faith is always this indirect knowledge of God, knowledge of God in His works, and in these particular works—in the determining and using of certain creaturely realities to bear witness to the divine objectivity. What distinguishes faith from unbelief, erroneous faith and superstition is that it is content with this indirect knowledge of God. It does not think that the knowledge of God in His works is insufficient. On the contrary, it is grateful really to know the real God in His works. It really lets itself be shown the objectivity of God by their objectivity. But it also holds fast to the

40

particularity of these works. It does not arbitrarily choose objects to set up as signs, in that way inventing a knowledge of God at its own good-pleasure. It knows God by means of the objects chosen by God Himself. It recognises and acknowledges God's choice and sanctification in the operation of this knowledge. And, for its part, it uses these special works of God as they ought to be used—as means of the knowledge of God. It lets their objectivity become a witness—yet only a witness—to the objectivity of God. Where the worship of God is made possible and necessary by God Himself, it does not establish an idol worship. Faith, and therefore the knowledge of God, stands or falls with all these determinations of the clothed objectivity of God. It is under these determinations that God is spoken about and heard in the Church of Jesus Christ. Not a single one of them can be set aside or altered without radically injuring the life of the Church.

[II, 1, p. 17 f.]

[12] In opposition to that we have to set first Ex. 33¹¹ ⁻²³. We can hardly understand this except as a confirmation of Luther's general rule, and it forms a background for the understanding of all the rest. It says there of Moses that the Lord spake with him face to face, as a man speaks with his friend (v. 11). What does that mean? We read in what follows that Moses called upon God in consequence of God saying to him : " I know thee by name, and thou hast also found grace in my sight." Thereupon Moses wished to know of God's " ways "—that is, to " know " Him (v. 13) as the One who would " go up with them " in the move from Sinai to Canaan which He had commanded. " If thy presence go not with me, carry us not up hence. For wherein shall it be known here that I and thy people have found grace in thy sight ? is it not in that thou goest with us ? so shall we be separated, I and thy people, from all the people that are upon the face of the earth " (v. 15 f.). God replies that this very thing shall take place. Moses insists that he would see the glory of the Lord (v. 18). And not even this request meets with a blank refusal. No ; God will make to pass before him " all his glory," and he shall hear the name of the Lord : " I will be gracious to whom I will be gracious, and will shew mercy on whom I will shew mercy " (v. 19). But it

41

is precisely in the passing before of God that Moses is to hear His name. " Thou canst not see my face : for there shall no man see me, and live " (v. 20). This "passing before " obviously means that His prayed and awaited going with them had begun, that God actually does go before him and the people. And in this " passing before " God will place him in the cleft of a rock and spread His hand over him so that he can only see Him from the back (and hence in the process of that passing before and going with and going before). It is in this way and not in any other that he can and shall see the glory of God. It is in this way that God speaks with Moses " face to face, as a man speaketh with his friend." God really speaks with him. Moses hears God's name. He is really encouraged and given directions by God Himself. He knows God, as he has prayed—God in His extremest objectivity. But all this comes to pass in God's passing before and going before, in God's work and action, in which he does not see God's face but in which he can only follow God with his eyes. In this case, more than that would not only be less, but even nothing at all—indeed, something negative. Man cannot see God's face, God's naked objectivity, without exposing himself to the annihilating wrath of God. It would indeed have to be a second God who could see God directly. How could man escape destruction by God ? Hence God shows Moses a twofold mercy : not only does He actually receive him according to His promise ; but also He does it in a way that is adapted to him as a creature, and speaks to him through the sign of His work. We can hardly presuppose that any of the other scriptural passages and references that should be considered in this context teach anything in opposition to this indirect knowledge of God. Rather we shall have to assume that, even in those passages where means and signs of God's appearance or speaking are not expressly mentioned, they are nevertheless taken for granted by the biblical writers. They always mean the God who is present and revealed to man in His secondary objectivity, in His work. . . .

Moreover, the message of the New Testament is nothing but the proclamation of the name of God on the ground of His gracious " passing before." And it is given in the form of a continual explanation of a definite historical event—of the same historical event that began with the Exodus, even with the call of Abraham, even with the covenant with Noah. But now its concrete aim and its totality become quite clear. The Messiah, the promised Son of Abraham and David, the Servant of Yahweh, the Prophet, Priest and King, has appeared ; and not only as sent by God, but Himself God's Son. Yet the Word does not appear in His eternal objectivity as the Son who alone dwells in the bosom of the Father. No ; the Word became flesh. God gives Himself to be known, and is known, in the substance of secondary objectivity, in the sign of all signs, in the work of God which all the other works of God serve to prepare, accompany and continue, in the manhood which He takes to Himself, to which He humbles Himself and which He raises through Himself. " We say his glory " now means : we say this One in His humanity, the humanity of the Son of God, on His way to death, which was the way to His resurrection. Hence, it is again an indirect encounter with God in which the apostles, as the witnesses of the New Testament, find themselves. They, too, stand before a veil, a sign, a work of God. In the crib of Bethlehem and at the cross of Golgotha the event takes place in which God gives Himself to them to be known and in which they know God. The fact that they see this in the light of the resurrection, and that in the forty days they see it as what it really is, God's own presence and action, does not alter the fact that in the forty days they do see this unambiguously secondary objectivity, and in it as such, and attested by it, they know the primary objectivity and hence God Himself. The fact that the God-manhood of the Mediator Jesus Christ is the fulfilment of the revelation and reconciliation proclaimed in the New Testament is equivalent to the fact that the knowledge of faith in the New Testament is indirect (and for that very reason real !) knowledge of God.

And it is precisely this knowledge of faith, attested in the Old and New Testaments as the knowledge of God from His works, which is now the content of knowledge in the Church of Jesus Christ. Since this message is the Gospel of its Lord and therefore of the God-man, the Mediator, it stands in explicit contrast to any message having the pure and naked objectivity of God Himself as its object. It is the Gospel of faith and the summons to faith in that it proclaims God—really God Himself—in His mediability, in the sign of His work, in His clothed objectivity. And it is this just because it does not leave the realm of indirect knowledge of God, but keeps to the fact that in this very realm God Himself—and therefore all things—is to be sought and found, and that this indirect knowledge is the right and true knowledge of God because it is chosen and ordained by God Himself. Letting this be enough for oneself is not resignation but the humility and boldness of the man who really stands before God in faith, and in faith alone. The Gospel of the Church of God is therefore of necessity a defined, circumscribed and limited message. It does not contain and say anything and everything. Its content is not the ἄπειρον, the boundless and groundless that human presumption would like to make God out to be. It does not destroy perception ; it integrates it. It does not oppose a definite and concrete view ; it establishes it. It does not teach thought to lose itself in an unthinkable one and all ; it forms it to very definite concepts, affirming this and denying that, including this and excluding that. It contains the veritable Gospel, the Gospel of Jesus Christ, the Messiah of Israel, the true God who became also true man in His own time and place. It explains, not an idea of God, but His name revealed in His deeds. And in correspondence with its content it is itself objective in form—visible Church, audible preaching, operative sacrament. These constitute an area of objectivity among and alongside so many other areas of objectivity ; but this is grounded on the witness of the apostles and prophets which must be shown and proved objectively. Nor is it ashamed of this witness ; on the contrary, it boasts of it as just one book among many others. Christian faith as knowledge of the true God lets itself be included in this area of objectivity, and allows itself to be kept in this area, which in itself and as such is certainly not identical with the objectivity of God. But in it God's work takes place, and hence God's own objectivity gives itself to be known and is to be known, and this on the strength of the choice and sanctification of His free grace. We shall have to destroy the very roots of the Church of Jesus Christ and annihilate faith itself if we want to deny and put an end to the area of secondary objectivity ; if, to reach a supposedly better knowledge of God, we want to disregard and pass over the veil, the sign, the work in which He gives Himself to be known by man without diminution but rather by manifestation of His glory as the One He is. Faith either lives in this sphere, or it is not faith at all. And just the same thing is also true of the knowlege of God through faith.

[II, 1, pp. 18 ff.]

[13] He exists, not only inconceivably as God, but also conceivably as a man ; not only above the world, but also in the world, and of the world ; not only in a heavenly and invisible, but in an earthly and visible form. He becomes and is, He exists—we cannot avoid this statement ; to do so would be the worst kind of Docetism—with objective actuality. Does this mean, then, that He exists as one thing amongst others, and that as such He can be perceived and may be known like other things ? Well, we cannot deny that He is a thing like this, and can be perceived and known as such, if He was and is a man in the world, with an earthly and visible form. But, of course, a man is not merely a thing or object. As a man among men he is a human Thou, and as such distinct from all mere things. Now as a Thou man is not merely an existential determination of the I, but the sum of all the objective reality of the world. And in Jesus Christ God becomes and is man, the fellow-man of all men. As God He is not merely one of many such fellow-men, nor is He merely the idea of fellow-humanity. We are speaking of " the Father's Son, by nature God." He became and is man, the fellow-man of all men ; and therefore Thou, not merely in a simple, but in a supremely objective reality, *the* human Thou, which as such is also directly the Thou of the one eternal God. It is not that a man has rightly or wrongly taken it upon himself to be the objective reality of this human Thou, and has been grasped and understood and interpreted by others as the objective reality of this Thou. The fact is rather that God Himself, in His deep mercy and its great power, has taken it upon Himself to exist also in human being and essence in His Son, and therefore to become and be a man, and therefore this incomparable Thou. God Himself is in the world,

45

earthly, conceivable and visible, as He is this man. We have to do with God Himself as we have to do with this man. God Himself speaks when this man speaks in human speech. God Himself speaks when this man speaks in human speech. God Himself acts and suffers when this man acts and suffers as a man. God Himself triumphs when this One triumphs as a man. The human speaking and acting and suffering and triumphing of this one man directly concerns us all, and His history is our history of salvation which changes the whole human situation, just because God Himself is its human subject in His Son, just because God Himself has assumed and made His own our human nature and kind in His Son, just because God Himself came into this world in His Son, and as one of us " a guest this world of ours He trod."   [IV, 2, p. 50 f.]

[14] If the fact that the Son of God became and is also the Son of Man may be known as such among all the other facts of world-occurrence, how else can it be but by His self-revelation ? Which of all the forms of contemplation and thought that we know and use for the perception of other subjects can be of any avail in this connexion ? What physics or metaphysics can even lead us to this subject, let alone enable us to know it—to know it, that is, in a way that permits us, as in theology, to see and handle it materially as a basis, and formally as an axiom, of all subsequent reflection ? What authority, even if it is that of an infallible Church or the apostles, can guarantee it if it does not guarantee itself in their witness ? If it is in fact guaranteed, it is by itself, because and as it is revealed in the sense described. Otherwise it is not guaranteed. Otherwise we will be forced to admit that we have only hazarded a hypothesis—a bold and profound hypothesis perhaps, but only a hypothesis. We have only *made* an assumption, and we will have to rely on the fact that we have made it consistently, and that it may be relevant and fruitful. But at bottom we will not really know. We will only suspect. And the whole Church will rest on this hypothesis. It will not really know, but only suspect, where and on what it really stands. If it does know, if we know, it is only on the ground that this fact is not merely a fact, but that as such it speaks for itself, that it makes that self-disclosure, that from its maintained

46

objectivity there springs the fact that it makes itself
known, that it therefore includes in itself a subject which
knows it as such. It is better not to conceal the truth
that there can be no sure knowledge of it at all except—
in this sense—from itself. [IV, 2, p. 123]

[15] The presupposition of this knowledge of the man
Jesus is the participation of the knowing subject in the
new thing which makes this One this man within the
cosmos. And the presupposition of this participation is
that the ground of being of this One penetrates and transcends of itself the limits of the sphere of what we can see
and interpret and know, that it discloses and declares and
attests and reveals itself in this sphere. But this means
that in the power and mercy of the same divine act of
majesty which is the ground of His being the man Jesus
speaks for Himself, expounds Himself and gives Himself
to be known, so that He is no longer just confessed in a
way, but known and recognised as the One He is. This
means that in and with His self-disclosure He induces and
initiates the human seeing and interpreting which attaches
itself to the divine act of majesty in and by which He has
His being, following and accompanying it, repeating the
being which He has on this basis, and therefore becoming
and being a relevant human seeing and interpreting (as
that which is mastered by Him). The essence of the
knowledge of this One is that the divine act of majesty in
and by and from which the man Jesus has His being
should be reflected and repeated in the human seeing and
interpreting which is awakened and controlled by Him and
therefore corresponds to Him. [IV, 2, p. 39]

[16] The Holy Spirit is the coming of the man Jesus,
who is the Son of God, to other men who are not this but
with whom He still associates. And the witness of the
Holy Spirit is the disclosure to these men, and therefore
their discovery, of the fact that because they are associated
with Him they can be called what they are certainly not
called of themselves, and be what they can certainly never
become or be of themselves—children of God, children of
light who in the midst of death are freed from the fear of
death because as sinners they are freed from the curse of
sin, and as such messengers to all those who, because they
do not see the light, are still in darkness, but are not to

47

remain in this darkness. And as and because the Holy
Spirit is the coming of Jesus Christ Himself, and His
witness this disclosure to men concerning themselves, He
and His witness are in fact the self-revelation of Jesus
Christ and as such the basis of the knowledge of Jesus
Christ.   [IV, 2, p. 128]

[17] We have to realise that God's revealedness for us
is God's own person and God's own work. All the comfort,
all the power, all the truth of this revealedness depends
upon the fact that it is with God that we are dealing. All
our understanding of this revealedness depends upon the
fact that we identify it with God Himself, ruling out all
other possibilities but God's possibility. We have therefore to realise that as the recipient of revelation man is
brought under God's judgment. It is only because of this
that he is brought under God's promise. It is only because
of this that God meets him as the One who intercedes for
him, who undertakes and directs his cause, who does not
therefore quench his own ability and will and accomplishment but subordinates it to His own, since man must
always be subordinated to God, if God's glory is to triumph
and man is to be helped. We are to understand, therefore, that for God to be revealed involves the dislodging
of man from the estimation of his own freedom, and his
enrichment with the freedom of the children of God. This
negation, the negation of man through God's eternal grace
and mercy, is only the obverse of his position as a child of
God, as a member of the covenant between God and man.
But this obviously means that the negation of man cannot
be put into effect any more than his position as a child of
God except through God's own action. Thus God's possibility triumphs over the very imprisonment in which we
are involved, where we only fulfil our own possibilities and
only believe in our own possibilities. The self-enclosed
uniqueness of man, who only has and knows his own
freedom, is overarched and enclosed and finally relativised
through the uniqueness of God and His freedom, the
freedom in which He is resolved to have fellowship with
this man and once and for all to be his Lord. How could
man ever foresee this triumph and the wonder of it ? How
could he ever anticipate this triumph or prepare himself for
it ? It is God's triumph. It is a state or position in which

man may very well find himself, but only with amazement, only with gratitude, only in humble recognition of
an accomplished fact, without any opportunity to think
how it might come to pass, without possessing any need or
capacity to derive it from his earlier state or to indicate
the way which led from the one to the other.

[I, 2, p. 259 f.]

[18] Knowledge of God is obedience to God. Observe
that we do not say that knowledge of God may also be
obedience, or that of necessity it has obedience attached
to it, or that it is followed by obedience. No ; knowledge
of God as knowledge of faith is in itself and of essential
necessity obedience. It is an act of human decision corresponding to the act of divine decision ; corresponding to
the act of the divine being as the living Lord ; corresponding to the act of grace in which faith is grounded and continually grounded again in God. In this act God posits
Himself as our object and ourselves as those who know
Him. But the fact that He does so means that our knowing
God can consist only in our following this act, in ourselves
becoming a correspondence of this act, in ourselves and
our whole existence and therefore our considering and
conceiving becoming the human act corresponding to the
divine act. This is obedience, the obedience of faith.
Precisely—and only—as this act of obedience, is the
knowledge of God knowledge of faith and therefore real
knowledge of God. Were it something else, did it not
spring from obedience and therefore from faith, it would
miss God and would certainly not be knowledge of God.
For God will be known as the One He is. But precisely
as the One He is, He acts. It is as this One who acts,
however, that He will be known. [II, 1, p. 26]

3. The Question of Natural Theology

By the natural knowledge of God (natural theology or general
revelation) there has always been understood in Christian theology
the knowledge of God which man has thought he could receive
apart from the concrete divine act of revelation and on the basis of
general human utterance concerning the gods and the divine. Barth
thinks that the linking of Christian thought about God with this

49

supposed general knowledge is a fateful error, because important characteristics are imparted by what man thinks he knows of himself. Revelation seeks to rescue man from his own imaginings concerning the divine. Hence there can be no concord but only conflict between religion (as the knowledge of God possible to man) and the Gospel. Historic Christianity itself is religion, and must constantly come under the criticism of the Gospel. This was for Barth the real issue in the German Church conflict after 1933, as recognised in the *Barmen Declaration* of 1934, which was essentially composed by him.

[19] When we spoke of the original and basic will of God, of His " first act " fulfilled in and with creation but transcending creation, we did not speak of an " original revelation " which we must differentiate from Jesus Christ because it is in fact different from Him. We did not speak in the light of the results of any self-knowledge or self-estimate of human reason or existence. We did not speak with reference to any observations and conclusions in respect of the laws and ordinances which rule in nature and human history. We certainly did not speak in relation to any religious disposition which is supposed to be or actually is proper to man. There is only one revelation. That revelation is the revelation of the covenant, of the original and basic will of God. How else could this be revealed to us ? The concept of an " original revelation " which must be differentiated from the revelation in Jesus Christ because it is actually different from it is a purely empty concept, or one that can be filled only by illusions.

In a word, the covenant of grace which is from the beginning, the presupposition of the atonement, is not a discovery and conclusion of " natural theology." Apart from and without Jesus Christ we can say nothing at all about God and man and their relationship one with another. Least of all can we say that their relationship can be presupposed as that of a covenant of grace. Just because it is a covenant of grace, it cannot be discovered by man, nor can it be demonstrated by man. As the covenant of grace it is not amenable to any kind of human reflection or to any questions asked by man concerning the meaning and basis of the cosmos or history. Grace is inaccessible to us : how else can it be grace ? Grace can only make itself accessible. Grace can never be recalled. To remember

50

grace is itself the work of grace. The perception of grace is itself grace. [IV, 1, p. 45]

[20] Natural theology is the doctrine of a union of man with God existing outside God's revelation in Jesus Christ. It works out the knowledge of God that is possible and real on the basis of this independent union with God, and its consequences for the whole relationship of God, world and man. It is a necessary undertaking in the sphere of man as such—presupposing that there is such a sphere and that it can therefore be the object of serious consideration. Whatever we may think of its character as reality or illusion, this sphere arises and exists in the fact that man depends on himself over against God. But this means that in actual fact God becomes unknowable to him and he makes himself equal to God. For the man who refuses his grace God becomes the substance of the highest that he himself can see, choose, create and be. It is of this that he gives an account in natural theology He must do it, because this is the self-exposition and self-justification of the being of man in this sphere.

[II, 1, p. 168]

[21] This "coming to us" of the truth is revelation. It does not reach us in a neutral condition, but in an action which stands to it, as the coming of truth, in a very definite, indeed a determinate relationship. That is to say, it reaches us as religious men; i.e., it reaches us in the attempt to know God from our standpoint. It does not reach us, therefore, in the activity which corresponds to it. The activity which corresponds to revelation would have to be faith; the recognition of the self-offering and self-manifestation of God. We need to see that in view of God all our activity is in vain even in the best life; i.e., that of ourselves we are not in a position to apprehend the truth, to let God be God and our Lord. We need to renounce all attempts even to try to apprehend this truth. We need to be ready and resolved simply to let the truth be told us and therefore to be apprehended by it. But that is the very thing for which we are not resolved and ready. The man to whom the truth has really come will concede that he was not at all ready and resolved to let it speak to him. The genuine believer will not say that he came to faith from faith, but—from unbelief, even though

51

the attitude and activity with which he met revelation, and still meets it, is religion. For in faith, man's religion as such is shown by revelation to be resistance to it. From the standpoint of revelation religion is clearly seen to be a human attempt to anticipate what God in His revelation wills to do and does do. It is the attempted replacement of the divine work by a human manufacture. The divine reality offered and manifested to us in revelation, is replaced by a concept of God arbitrarily and wilfully evolved by man. [I, 2, p. 301 f.]

[22] We begin by stating that religion is unbelief. It is a concern, indeed, we must say that it is the one great concern, of godless man. . . .

In the light of what we have already said, this proposition is not in any sense a negative value-judgment. It is not a judgment of religious science or philosophy based upon some prior negative judgment concerned with the nature of religion. It does not affect only other men with their religion. Above all it affects ourselves also as adherents of the Christian religion. It formulates the judgment of divine revelation upon all religion. It can be explained and expounded, but it cannot be derived from any higher principle than revelation, nor can it be proved by any phenomenology or history of religion. Since it aims only to repeat the judgment of God, it does not involve any human renunciation of human values, any contesting of the true and the good and the beautiful which a closer inspection will reveal in almost all religions, and which we naturally expect to find in abundant measure in our own religion, if we hold to it with any conviction. What happens is simply that man is taken by God and judged and condemned by God. That means, of course, that we are struck to the very roots, to the heart. Our whole existence is called in question. But where that is the case there can be no place for sad and pitiful laments at the non-recognition of relative human greatness.

That is why we must not omit to add by way of warning that we have not to become Philistines or Christian icono-clasts in face of human greatness as it meets us so strikingly in this very sphere of religion. Of course it is inevitable and not without meaning that in times of strong Christian feeling heathen temples should be levelled to the earth, idols and pictures of saints destroyed, stained glass smashed, organs removed : to the great distress of aesthetes everywhere. But irony usually had it that Christian churches were built on the very sites of these temples and with materials taken from their pillars and furnishings. And after a time the storm of iconoclasm was succeeded by a fresh form of artistic decoration. This goes to show that while the devaluation and negation of what is human may occasionally have a practical and symbolical significance in detail, it can never have any basic or general significance. And it must not, either. We cannot, as it were, translate the divine judgment that religion is unbelief into human terms, into the form of definite devaluations and negations. From time to time it has to be manifested in the form of definite devaluations and negations. But we must still accept it as God's judgment upon all that is human. It can be heard and understood, strictly and exactly as intended, only by those who do not despair of the human element as such, who regard it as something worth while, who have some inkling of what it means really to abandon the world of Greek or Indian gods, China's world of wisdom, or even the world of Roman Catholicism, or our own Protestant world of faith as such, in the thoroughgoing sense of the divine judgment. In this sense the divine judgment, which we have to hear and receive, can actually be described as a safeguard against all forms of ignorance and Philistinism. It does not challenge us to a venal and childish resignation in face of what is humanly great, but to an adult awareness of its real and ultimate limits, which do not have to be fixed by us but are already fixed. In the sphere of reverence before God, there must always be a place for reverence for human greatness. It does not lie under our judgment, but under the judgment of God.

[I, 2, p. 299 f.]

[23] It (religion) is a feeble but defiant, an arrogant but hopeless, attempt to create something which man could do, but now cannot do, or can do only because and if God Himself creates it for him : the knowledge of the truth, the knowledge of God. We cannot, therefore, interpret the attempt as a harmonious co-operating of man with the revelation of God, as though religion were a kind of outstretched hand which is filled by God in His revelation.

53

Again, we cannot say of the evident religious capacity of man that it is, so to speak, the general form of human knowledge, which acquires its true and proper content in the shape of revelation. On the contrary, we have here an exclusive contradiction. In religion man bolts and bars himself against revelation by providing a substitute, by taking away in advance the very thing which has to be given by God.

He has, of course, the power to do this. But what he achieves and acquires in virtue of this power is never the knowledge of God as Lord and God. It is never the truth. It is a complete fiction, which has not only little but no relation to God. It is an anti-God who has first to be known as such and discarded when the truth comes to him. But it can be known as such, as a fiction, only as the truth does come to him.   [I, 2, p. 303]

[24] We will conclude with a short historical commentary on the first article of the *Theological Declaration* of the Synod of Barmen on May 31st, 1934. The text is as follows :

" *I am the way, the truth, and the life :   no man cometh unto the Father, but by me* " (*Jn.* 14⁶).

" *Verily, verily, I say unto you, He that entereth not by the door into the sheepfold, but climbeth up some other way, the same is a thief and a robber. . . . I am the door : by me if any man enter in, he shall be saved* " (*Jn.* 10¹, ⁹).

Jesus Christ, as He is attested to us in Holy Scripture, is the one Word of God, whom we have to hear and whom we have to trust and obey in life and in death.

We condemn the false doctrine that the Church can and must recognise as God's revelation other events and powers, forms and truths, apart from and alongside this one Word of God.

This text is important and apposite because it represents the first confessional document in which the Evangelical Church has tacked the problem of natural theology. The theology as well as the confessional writings of the age of the Reformation left the question open, and it has actually become acute only in recent centuries because natural theology has threatened to turn from a latent into an increasingly manifest standard and content of Church proclamation and theology. The question became a burning one at the moment when the Evangelical Church in Germany was unambiguously and consistently confronted by a definite and new form of natural theology, namely, by the demand to recognise in the political events of the year 1933, and especially in the form of the God-sent Adolf Hitler, a source of specific new revelation of God, which, demanding obedience and trust, took its place beside the revelation attested in Holy Scripture, claiming that it should be acknowledged by Christian proclamation and theology as equally binding and obligatory. When this demand was made, and a certain audience was given to it, there began, as is well known, the so-called German Church conflict. It has since become clear that behind this first demand stood quite another. According to the dynamic of the political movement, what was already intended, although only obscurely outlined, in 1933 was the proclamation of this new revelation as the only revelation, and therefore the transformation of the Christian Church into the temple of the German nature- and history-myth.

The same had already been the case in the developments of the preceding centuries. There can be no doubt that not merely a part but the whole had been intended and claimed when it had been demanded that side by side with its attestation in Jesus Christ and therefore in Holy Scripture the Church should also recognise and proclaim God's revelation in reason, in conscience, in the emotions, in history, in nature, and in culture and its achievements and developments. The history of the proclamation and theology of these centuries is simply a history of the wearisome conflict of the Church with the fact that the " also " demanded and to some extent acknowledged by it really meant an " only." The conflict was bound to be wearisome and even hopeless because, on the inclined plane on which this " also " gravitated into " only," it could not supply any inner check apart from the apprehension, inconsistency and inertia of all interested parties. Actually in these centuries too the Church was —as always miraculously—saved because the Bible remained in face of the " also " of invading natural theology and it secret " only." For it threw its own " only " into the scales, and in this way—not without the co-operation of that

55

human apprehension, inconsistency and inertia—did at least maintain the point that for their part God's revelation in Jesus Christ and faith and obedience to Him are " also " not actually to be reduced to silence and oblivion. Thus things were not carried as far as the logic of the matter really demands. The logic of the matter demands that, even if we only lend our little finger to natural theology, there necessarily follows the denial of the revelation of God in Jesus Christ. A natural theology which does not strive to be the only master is not a natural theology. And to give it place at all is to put oneself, even if unwittingly, on the way which leads to this sole sovereignty. But during the developments of these centuries this whole state of affairs was almost entirely hidden, particularly from the eyes of those who wanted in good faith to defend the validity and value of the biblical revelation. It is noteworthy that it was conservative movements within the Church, like those inspired by Abraham Kuyper and Adolf Stöcker, which acted most naively. But the naivety reigned at every point. The concept of revelation and that of reason, history or humanity were usually linked by the copulative particle " and," and the most superficial provisos were regarded as sufficient protection against all the possible dangers of such combinations. Happy little hyphens were used between, say, the words " modern " and " positive," or " religious " and " social," or " German " and " Evangelical," as if the meaning then became self-evident.* The fact was overlooked that all this pointed to the presence of a trojan horse within which the superior enemy was already drawn into the city. For in the long run the fundamentally peaceful acknowledgment of the combination came to be accepted as the true orthodoxy, as the basis of theology (especially of Church governments). The resistance occasionally offered to it necessarily came under suspicion as fanatical one-sidedness and exaggeration.

This was how matters stood when the Church was confronted with the myth of the new totalitarian state of 1933—a myth at first lightly masked, but unmasked soon enough. It need not be said that at first the Church stood entirely defenceless before this matter and simply had to succumb to it for the time being. Once again, as so often for two hundred years—or so it seemed—the representative of a new trend and movement of the human spirit knocked at the door of the Church. Its petition was very understandable in the light of every precedent. It asked simply that its ideas and ideals should be allowed into the Church like those of all earlier times and phases. Its argument was that they constituted a more timely form, a new historical hinterland, a point of contact given by God Himself, *rebus sic stantibus*, for the proclamation of the Gospel, which in itself, of course, would remain unaltered. Exactly the same thing had happened at the beginning of the 18th century with the reviving humanism of the Stoa ; or a century later with idealism ; or, in its train, with Romanticism ; and then with the positivism of the bourgeois society and scholarship of the 19th century ; and the nationalism of the same period ; and a little later socialism : they had all wanted to have their say in the Church. And in face of these clear precedents there could be no basic reason for silencing this new nationalism of race. Whether it was as worthy as its predecessors to be heard and to have its say in the Church is a matter on which there might be different opinions outside Germany. A negative answer would normally be given where the phenomenon of race nationalism is unknown or known only from a distance, and a different political and philosophical position causes it to be regarded with repugnance. But we must not fail to realise that inside Germany an affirmative answer could be given with what is basically just the same right. If it was admissible and right and perhaps even orthodox to combine the knowability of God in Jesus Christ with His knowability in nature, reason and history, the proclamation of the Gospel with all kinds of other proclamations—and this had been the case, not only in Germany, but in the Church in all lands for a long time—it is hard to see why the German Church should not be allowed to make its own particular use of the procedure. And the fact that it did with its customary German thoroughness is not really a ground of reproach. What the " German Christians " wanted and did was obviously along a line which had for long enough been acknowledged and trodden by the Church of the whole world : the line of the Enlightenment and Pietism, of Schleiermacher,

Richard Rothe and Ritschl. And there were so many parallels to it in England and America, in Holland and Switzerland, in Denmark and the Scandinavian countries, that no one outside really had the right to cast a stone at Germany because the new combination of Christian and natural theology effected there involved a combination with the race nationalism which happened to be rather uncongenial to the rest of the world, and because this combination was now carried through with a thoroughness which was so astonishing to other nations. Now that so many other combinations had been allowed to pass uncontradicted, and had even been affectionately nurtured, it was about two hundred years too late to make any well-founded objection, and in Germany there were at first good reasons to make a particularly forceful stand for this new combination. It had the merit of recommending itself especially to German Lutheranism as, so to say, its distinctive and perhaps definitive solution of the question of the relationship of Christian and natural theology and proclamation. It could seem like the powerful river in which the different separate streams of the older and oldest history of the German Church and religion might possibly unite. It seemed to promise the exponents of culture and fellowship the unexpected fulfilment of their deepest wishes. It seemed to raise like a tidal wave the ship of the Church, which many people felt had run aground, and at last, at long last to be trying to bear it back again to the high seas of the real life of the nation and therefore into the sphere of reality. Humanly speaking, it was inevitable that in 1933 the German Evangelical Church should accede to the demand made of it, to the new " also," and the " only " which lay behind it, with exactly the same abandon as it had done to so many other demands, and as the Church in other lands—wittingly or unwittingly—had continually done to so many other demands. The only question was whether the Bible, which was not at first to be suppressed, and the usual apprehension, inconsistency and inertia of all concerned, would not this time too act as a counter-weight and prevent matters being carried to extremes.

It was, therefore, an astonishing fact—and this is the significance of the first article of the Barmen *Declaration*—

that within Germany there arose an opposition to the new combination which was aimed not only at this particular combination, but basically at the long-accustomed process of combination, at the " and " which had become orthodox in Germany and in the whole world, at the little hyphen as such and therefore at no more and no less than the condominion of natural theology in the Church. For when in Barmen Jesus Christ as He is attested to us in Holy Scripture was designated as the one Word of God whom we have to trust and to obey in life and in death ; when the doctrine of a source of Church proclamation different from this one Word of God was repudiated as false doctrine ; and when, in the concluding article of the whole *Declaration*, the acknowledgment of this truth and the repudiation of this error were declared to be the indispensable theological foundation of the German Evangelical Church—an assertion was made (far above the heads of the poor " German Christians " and far beyond the whole momentary position of the Church in Germany) which, if it was taken seriously, contained in itself a purifying of the Church not only from the concretely new point at issue, but from all natural theology. The German Christians were contradicted by the contradiction of the whole development at whose end they stood. The protest—this was expressed with blunt words at Barmen by Hans Asmussen, who had to explain the whole proposal—was " against the same phenomenon which for more than two hundred years had slowly prepared the devastation of the Church." The protest was without doubt directed against Schleiermacher and Ritschl. The protest was directed against the basic tendencies of the whole 18th and 19th centuries and therefore against the hallowed traditions of all other Churches as well. And it must be noticed that this protest was formulated in a contemporary application of the confession of the Reformation yet without the possibility of appealing to any express formula in that confession. In the unity of faith with the fathers something was expressed which they had not yet expressed in that way. The venture had to be made, even at the risk of the suspicion and later the actual charge of innovation in the Church. It was under the sign of this protest that the German Church conflict continued from this point.

59

All its individual and practical problems were and still are directly and indirectly connected with the first article of Barmen. The Church was the "confessional" Church precisely in the measure that it took this decision seriously in all its aspects. The conclusions of the Synod of Dahlem in November, 1934 clarified its position in relation to Church law. But this clarification was dependent upon the dogmatic clarification of Barmen and could be carried through only in conjunction with it. The accumulated errors and vacillations in the Confessional Church are connected with the fact that the insight expressed at Barmen—Jesus Christ is the one Word of God whom we have to trust and to obey—did not at first correspond to the flesh and blood reality of the Church but contradicted it, and had still to be repeated, attained and practised in a wearisome struggle. Where this did not happen, no other attitude could be reached in practice than that of continual partial retreats and compromises. Where it did happen, it carried with it automatically the will and the power to resist. The German Confessional Church has either the power of the ecumenical gift and task which it received and accepted at Barmen, or it has no power. It fights either for the purification of which the Evangelical Church has long been in need and is everywhere in need, or in reality it does not fight at all. Had it been concerned simply with the German error of 1933, or with certain fatal consequent manifestations of this error, its conflict would have had no less but also no more meaning than the different reactions within the great modern disorder which had never been entirely lacking earlier and are not entirely lacking elsewhere. It would then not have been a real and serious conflict. It is a real and serious conflict so far as it is concerned with the matter as a whole ; and not merely because what is at issue is obviously the opponent natural theology in its newest form, but because it is this time a question of the Church itself in its repudiation of natural theology as a whole, because it is a question of its own fundamental purification. But the very thing which (in what is best described as a cry of need and of joy) is expressed in the first article of the Barmen *Declaration* is that this is at issue. The fact that in 1934 the basic opposition could be made which is laid down in this article, and that, in spite of all uncertainty and reverses, this opposition could since prove and maintain itself as the nerve of the whole attitude of the Confessional Church in a position of the severest tribulation, is something which, however things may develop, we can already describe as one of the most notable events in modern Church history.

It was not the new political totalitarianism, nor was it the methods of beleaguerment which precipitated this event. And it is naive in the extreme to find in "Calvinism" or the activity of this or that professor of theology the effectual power of salvation (or corruption) in this affair. The fact is that, when nothing else was left for the Church, the one Word of God who is called Jesus Christ remained. The fact is that it could not let itself fall into the abyss, as was demanded, but that it could take and had to take a new stand. The fact is that this time the logic of the case worked irresistibly on the other side and therefore this time it was arrested in the Church. And all this has to be appraised spiritually or it cannot be appraised at all. What might have been expected was that, having so often blunted the temptation in its earlier, finer forms, the Church would now be tired and its eyes blurred and it would be inwardly exhausted, so that it would succumb all the more easily and this time for good to the assault of the blatant temptation. But the fact is that this did not happen. The Word of God still remained, in spite of everything, in the same Church in which it had been so often denied and betrayed. Men could still be so terrified by the spectre of the terrible form of the new god and his messiah as not to give way to it. They could still come to the position of knowing that there is another possibility than that of crashing into the abyss. In spite of every weakness they could still reach after this other possibility, reading the Bible again, confessing again its clear assertions, and therefore uttering the cry of need and of joy from Barmen. And they could at once stand and hold their position on this ground after all other grounds had crumbled under their feet. That this could be the case certainly has its spiritual-historical, theological and political presuppositions and determinations. But all the same it was impossible, and in the end a miracle, in the eyes of those who saw it at close quarters. And so the first article of Barmen was not merely a pretty little discovery of the theologians. The position in the spring of 1933 was not one in which a fortune could be made in Germany with little theological discoveries. Basically it was quite simply a public statement of the very miracle that against all expectation had once again happened to the Church. When it had lost all its counsellor and helpers, in the one Word of God, who is called Jesus Christ, it still had God for its comfort. Things being as they were, to whom else could it give its trust and obedience ; to what other source of its proclamation could it and should it cling ? *Rebus sic stantibus*, any other source could only be myth and therefore the end of all things and certainly the end of the Church. But from this very end the Church now saw itself pulled back and guarded by the Word of God in contemporaneous self-attestation. What option had it but to confess this Word of God alone ? If we want really to understand the genesis of Barmen, we shall be obliged to look finally neither to the Confessional Church as such nor to its opponents. For there is not much to be seen here. The Confessional Church was, so to speak, only the witness of a situation in which simultaneously there took place a remarkable revelation, as there had not been for a long time, of the beast out of the abyss, and a fresh confirmation of the one old revelation of God in Jesus Christ. It was only a witness of this event. Indeed, it was often a most inconspicuous and inconvenient witness. But it was a witness. It was obliged to notice what was going to be seen on this occasion—that Satan had fallen from heaven like lightning and that the Lord is mighty over all gods. What it noticed on this occasion was the fact of the unique validity of Jesus Christ as the Word of God spoken to us for life and death. The repudiation of natural theology was only the self-evident reverse side of this notice. It has no independent significance. It affirms only that there is no other help—that is, in temptation— when it is a question of the being or not being of the Church. What helps, when every other helper fails, is only the miracle, power and comfort of the one Word of God. The Confessional Church began to live at the hand of this notice and at its hand it lives to this day. And it is this notice which it has to exhibit to other Churches as the testimony which it has received and which is now laid upon it as a commission. It will be lost if it forgets this testimony, or no longer understands it, or no longer takes it seriously ; the power against which it stands is too great for it to meet it otherwise than with the weapon of this testimony. But it will also be lost if it does not understand and keep to the fact that this testimony is not entrusted to it simply for its own use, but at the same time as a message for the world-wide Church. And it may well be decisive for other Churches in the world, for their existence as the one, ecumenical Church of Jesus Christ, whether they on their side are able to hear and willing to accept the message of the Confessional Church in Germany.

For the understanding of what the first article of Barmen has to say in detail, it is perhaps advisable not to pass over the preceding verses from Jn. 14 and Jn. 10, but to understand everything from them as a starting-point. The emphasis of everything said previously lies in the fact that Jesus Christ has said something, and, what is more, has said it about Himself : I myself am the way, the truth, and the life. I myself am the door. The Church lives by the fact that it hears the voice of this " I " and lays hold of the promise which, according to this voice, is contained in this " I " alone ; and therefore it chooses the way, knows the truth, lives the life, goes through the door, which is Jesus Christ Himself alone. Moreover, it is not on its own authority, or in the execution of its own security programme, but on the basis of the necessity in which Jesus Christ Himself has said that no man comes to the Father but by Him, and that any by-passing of Him means theft and robbery, that the Church makes its exclusive claim, negating every other way or truth or life or door apart from Him. The negation has no independent significance. It depends entirely on the affirmation. It can make itself known only as the affirmation makes itself known. But in and with the affirmation it does and must make itself known. For this reason the positive assertion has precedence even in what follows, and for this reason the resulting critical assertion can be understood only as its converse and unambiguous elucidation. The Church lives by the fact that it hears the Word of God to which it can give entire trust and entire obedience, and that in life and in death—that is, in the certainty that it will be sustained in this trust and obedience for time and eternity. Precisely because it is allowed and invited to entire trust and obedience, it knows that the Word said to it is the one Word of God by which it is bound but in which it is also free, alongside whose Gospel there is no alien law and alongside whose Law there is no alien gospel, alongside or behind or above which we do not have to honour and fear any other power as way, truth, life or door. And this one Word is not first to be found, but has already given itself to be found : in Him who has the power and the right to call Himself the way, the truth, the life and the door because He is these things. This one Word means Jesus Christ from eternity to eternity. In this form it is attested in the Holy Scriptures of the Old and New Testaments. In this form it has founded the Church ; and upholds and renews and rules, and continually saves the Church. In this form it is comfort and direction in life and in death. In this form and not in any other ! It is of the " not in any other " that the concluding critical article speaks. We may notice that it does not deny the existence of other events and powers, forms and truths alongside the one Word of God, and that therefore throughout it does not deny the possibility of a natural theology as such. On the contrary, it presupposes that there are such things. But it does deny and designate as false doctrine the assertion that all these things can be the source of Church proclamation, a second source alongside and apart from the one Word of God. It excludes natural theology from Church proclamation. Its intention is not to destroy it in itself and as such, but to affirm that, when it comes to saying whom we have to trust and obey in life and in death, it can have no sense and existence alongside and apart from the Word of God. Whatever else they may be and mean, the entities to which natural theology is accustomed to relate itself cannot come into consideration as God's revelation, as the norm and content of the message delivered in the name of God. When the Church proclaims God's revelation, it does not speak on the basis of a view of the reality of the world and of man, however deep and believing ; it does not give an exegesis of these events and powers,

64

forms and truths, but bound to its commission, and made free by the promise received with it, it reads and explains the Word which is called Jesus Christ and therefore the book which bears witness to Him. It is, and remains, grateful for the knowledge of God in which He has given Himself to us by giving us His Son.   [II, 1, pp. 172 ff.]

The Gospel and the Bible

By the Gospel, i.e., the glad tidings of the enacted revelation of God, men are brought into the presence of this revelation. The messenger to whom this message is committed is the Church. The basic and therefore the normative form of the witness with which the Church is charged is the Bible. This is a human witness historically conditioned, yet by the concentration of its gaze on revelation it is also the standard or Canon for all further witness. The true understanding of the relationship between the Word of God and the word of man is a main theme in all Christian theology and therefore in the *Church Dogmatics*. The historico-critical investigation of the Bible as pursued for the last two centuries is affirmed by Barth as a legitimate consequence of its humanity and does not contradict its recognition as the Canon.

[25] (3) The third point to be mentioned is what we might call the *opus proprium* of the community, namely, its commission to preach the Gospel to the world. It is in this wider, deeper and more material sense that it is a missionary community. It is for this purpose that it must expand in the world, that it wills to renew itself by admission of men from the world. Through increasing and ever new witnesses the world must be given the intimation that God has espoused its cause, that God has aided it, that it is not a world left to itself but a world which He has loved and saved and which He preserves and rules and conducts to its salvation, and that everything that takes place in it, the whole of human life in all its confusion and affliction and sin and guilt and trouble, indeed, the whole of creaturely life in its subjection, hastens to meet the revelation of what God has accomplished in its favour. The community has to proclaim to the world the free grace of God and the hope which this carries with it. It has to declare to it that Jesus Christ, very God and very man, has come as its Saviour and will come again. This is the announcement of

the kingdom of God. This is the Gospel. The Christian community does not exist for itself ; it exists for the Gospel. It has accepted the primary fact that in Jesus Christ God has put matters right, securing once and for all His own glory as Creator but also the glory of His creature. It has seen that this first thing will also be the last. It has perceived that every happening has in it both its beginning and its end, deriving from it and hastening back to it. It has seen that time and all that is in it is lovingly, patiently, mercifully and helpfully included in it. Having perceived this, it lives among those who have not, at the heart of their great attempt to live without God, in the midst of their countless small attempts to help, justify, sanctify and glorify themselves, within the evils which they thereby inflict on themselves, in the misery which they bring upon themselves and in all the resultant excitement, anxiety and care in which they must exist. The Christian community knows that all this is unnecessary. It sees that No has already been said to it. This is what it has to say to men on the basis of what it has perceived. To be sure, it cannot conceal from them the fact that their great attempt is wrong and futile, that it is outmoded from the very outset, that it can be made only in new sin and with the prospect of new corruption, and therefore that all the small attempts in which the great is revealed and presented are radically overthrown. It cannot approve nor tolerate the way and ways of the world. It has to indicate a very different path. On the other hand, its decisive task is not to confront men with this objection, criticism and negation, nor with a programme, plan or law in the performance of which men must abandon that great attempt to live without God, counterbalancing it by the opposite attempt to return to God and with His help to make everything different and better. This is what the Synagogue does. This is what Freemasonry does. This is what Moral Rearmament does. But this is not what the Church of Jesus Christ does. It has no right to make proposals to men as though they could now help, justify, sanctify and glorify themselves more thoroughly and successfully than hitherto. It cannot set before them any better men, any sinless men, any innocent men, any men who escape the confusion and sorrow of the world. It has no such men to hold out as examples to

66

follow, as though others had only to imitate them to extricate themselves from the quagmire and hell in which they live. It realises indeed that men, belonging to God as His creatures, know deep down the perversity and futility of their attempt and attempts. It knows that at the true and final core of their being is a great weariness and sorrow which they can only conceal and suppress with all their running and clamouring and fighting. It knows that they are all in God's hand, that they cannot escape it, that they inflict so much sorrow on themselves only by continually trying to resist and oppose it. It knows, therefore, that it cannot help them by confirming their true state in the form of accusation. It knows that of themselves men certainly will not overcome and remove this opposition. It knows also that it cannot do it for them. It knows that it does not even say anything new, let alone give real aid, if it can do no more than propose the best and latest plans, programmes and laws, for the elimination of the suffering which results from this opposition, and of its underlying causes. It knows above all that it, too, stands under judgment with all others, that the same opposition is also to be found among Christians, that the community also, the Church in all its forms and enterprises, participates fully and very concretely in the perversity and futility of all human efforts, and that it is therefore useless from the very outset for it to offer or commend either itself or the Christians united within it as a salutary example. No, its great and simple but very different commission is that of declaring to them the kingdom of God, and not therefore a means to help them to do something, but the one truth that God has already begun to do something for them and that He will also complete it in spite of their opposition, outbidding all the attempts which spring from this opposition, overlooking and bypassing all their perversity and futility. What it has to attest to them is neither the divine No nor an improved and Christian Yes, but the divine Yes which does, of course, include a No, i.e., the divine judgment, and which also evokes and entails a new human Yes, but which over and above all is the wise and intrinsically powerful Yes which God has spoken to His creature and which He will finally execute and reveal. The presence of this divine Yes is the new and glorious message which is entrusted to the Christian community and which it is commissioned to deliver on earth. It need neither ask nor worry what the result will be, what success it will either enjoy or not enjoy, so long as it is obedient in this service. The power, fruitfulness, blessing and true help of the Word of God is God's own work, and He has His own varied and very secret ways to accomplish this work. All that the community can and should do is to attest this Word. It does not live by its own triumphs over the world, nor in order to be able to achieve and celebrate such triumphs. It does not live by its numerical growth, nor by asserting itself in the world. It lives by its commission. Its task is simply to see to it that the comfort and exhortation of the divine Yes are declared, and that they are declared as clearly and forcibly and impressively and universally as possible. It has simply to scatter the seed as it is, not on any account mixing with it its own ideas either in criticism of the world or for its amelioration. Nevertheless it must not be faint-hearted. It must be confident that just as it is this seed is the good seed which will bear fruit a hundredfold, sixtyfold or thirtyfold, possibly in very different ways from what it imagines, but all the same real fruit. It must be only the community of the Gospel, content to be no more. Whatever may be enterprised against it cannot prevent it from being the community of the Gospel, let alone destroy it as such. And whatever may have to be said against either it or its members cannot hinder it from being the community of the Gospel. The Word which it has to declare will always place it first under judgment in a far more serious manner than anything that may be said against it from without or that it may have to allege against itself. But the Word which it has to declare will always uphold it. As the community of the Word it may always and supremely live by the Gospel, accepting the divine Yes, taking to heart both its admonition and its consolation, and therefore, notwithstanding all its weakness and all the perversity and futility of human action in which it shares, being fundamentally sure of its cause and therefore undaunted.

[III, 4, pp. 506–508]

[26] In the Church which is charged with this ministry the commitment of the member is beyond computation. There is no possible place for idleness, indifference or luke-

warmness. No appeal can be made to human imperfection where the claim is directed to the very man whose incapacity and unworthiness for this ministry is known and admitted even when he is charged with it, without altering the fact that he really is charged with it. If there is no escape in arrogance, there is no escape in pusillanimity or indolence. He can entertain no illusions, but he has no excuse for diffidence or nonchalance. He can only address himself to the task without pretensions and without reservations. This is what the qualifications and elucidations imply. But they can never become arguments against the positive truth that the members of the Church in all their humanity are invited to share in God's own work of proclaiming His Word. They can never be obstacles to our believing in this positive truth and therefore to our accepting the vocation it implies and holding ourselves in readiness for the service it involves. If they do become obstacles for us, this only shows our failure to understand them, that they are not the great attack of God upon us, from which they derive when they have power. They are the accusations of a kind of scepticism in the guise of piety. We are making them ourselves, not as members of the Church, but in assertion of the arrogance and diffidence of those who wish to evade the power of the resurrection of Jesus Christ and the power of the Holy Spirit. The only power they can have is that of accusations which we ourselves can make. They cannot have real power unless they arise from the realisation that the Son of God has come in the flesh, that His Holy Ghost has been poured out upon the Church, and that the duty of speaking about God has been laid on the Church. They cannot have real power unless they arise, not from unbelief, but from faith. And the power which they then have will be not the power of destruction, paralysis and discouragement, but in a two-fold sense, directed against both our pride and our diffidence, the power of salutary criticism. And behind and above this criticism will stand the transformation which was wrought at the cross and on Easter Day. As members of the Church we share in this transformation (which we ourselves certainly cannot effect either in reality or in thought) in so far as we accept its reality in faith. But that means that we do not escape but accept the salutary criticism and the great assault. And to accept this transformation means to recognise and confess : " He is present with us, in the power of His Spirit and gifts." To accept it means, in all our reflection about the humanity of the Church and ourselves, to look beyond it, and beyond all its incapacity and unworthiness, to the foundation and beginning of the Church and to its existence in Jesus Christ. There, in Him, it is not unworthy and not incapable of speaking about God. There it is all that it has to be for this purpose. There it has everything that it needs for it. There it is justified and sanctified, blessed and authorised in its action. There the miracle has already happened which has to happen to a man if he is to speak about God— really speak about God. The Church looks to Jesus Christ. It allows Him to be its own life, and therefore its consolation. It does not cling to its own humanity—either in arrogance or diffidence—but to the task imposed upon it in its humanity. And as it does so, it can confess, but with a final certainty, that as it speaks about God in human words, it proclaims God's own Word.   [I, 2, p. 756 f.]

[27] We have stated that we are told such and such in the New Testament. We are, in fact, told these things. That is where we must begin. And, as we have put it, we for our part must let ourselves be told these things, whether or not they seem either illuminating or acceptable. It is quite indispensable that we should let ourselves be told these things, whatever may be the outcome. But these stiff and cold and non-committal expressions are not the end of the matter. For what the New Testament tells us, at the very heart and centre which is our present concern, it tells us in a specific and distinctive way which addresses and summons us, applying what it says to ourselves and claiming us for it. It tells it to us as witness : witness to a person, to Jesus Christ, to the whole nexus and history of reality and truth bound up in this name, as it is given by those who have the necessary information ; but also witness addressed to persons, to us, who can also acquire this information by receiving the witness, and who are already claimed in anticipation as those whom it concerns. What we have said about the objective content of truth of the reality of Jesus Christ, which includes our own reality, presses in upon us, from its objectivity to our subjectivity,

in order that there should be in us a correspondence. We have already seen this from what we find in its human attestation as it concerns us in the New Testament. It has its historical form in the existence of the New Testament. It becomes a historical event in the encounter between this witness and us. In the name and commission of the reality and truth of Jesus Christ we are concretely seized, whether we like it or not, in the course of this address and summons and application and claim. It is not with aloof detachment, but seizing us in this way, that the New Testament tells us what it has to tell us and what we have to let ourselves be told : who and what is real and true, Jesus Christ as the Lord and we as His ; who and what is also active and effective and reaches and affects us. This is not told us merely as an imparting of information, but as that which lays claim on us for what is imparted. In relation to all generations, and therefore to us, the New Testament has always come with this demand. It has always dared to claim man in this way. It has always dared to lay hold of him, for the impartation of its content, in order that he should receive it and at once become a new witness of its message. Thus to allow ourselves to be told what it tells us means rather more than is at first suggested by this formula. It is to be exposed to this attack which takes place in the New Testament. It is to be involved in the wrestling with this demand. When the New Testament encounters us, we are not at all the " we " that we think (but only think) we know so well, and that so boldly try to control themselves, in all their neutrality and with all their reservations and question-marks and pretexts and caprices and individual activities. But when its witness reaches us, when we are confronted by its witnesses, we are already in the circle of the validity of what they say to us, and are no longer the same in the sense that we are now marked, like trees for cutting, for the fulfilment of our own actual acknowledgment of its validity. This is how the prophets saw and treated their contemporaries, as did also the apostles, both Jews and Gentiles. They confronted them, and the world, with the very sober and not at all enthusiastic presupposition that they belonged to Jesus Christ, and were therefore ordained to hear the news concerning Him. By

71

their very existence these witnesses are never present in vain for the rest, for the world around, for us. To hear them is to hear Him, and to hear Him is to be placed directly before and in the altered world situation, before one's Lord who is the Lord over all. The only thing is that we must not imagine that we are still somewhere alongside or outside the Word that God has spoken through these witnesses. We stand already under the Word.

[IV, 2, p. 303 f.]

[28] The attitude of the biblical witnesses is decided by the fact that, whatever else may rightly or wrongly be said about their other attitudes, they are in the position and are called to give information upon a question put to them from without. They are called by God in the face of all other men to be witnesses of His own action. They can and must attest, before all the world and so that every one may hear, that God has spoken and acted and how He has spoken and acted in Jesus Christ and to His people. Their starting-point is this speaking and acting of God in its determinate reality, and they think and speak before the face of the same God, who now as Judge asks of them nothing but the truth concerning this reality, concerning His own speaking and acting which has taken place once for all. They speak under this twofold presupposition, with the weight of it, and therefore with the unchecked flow of a headlong mountain stream. Of course, they also describe, narrate, reflect and argue. How can any witness speak without to some extent doing these things too ? But these things do not make him a witness. Nor did they make the prophets and apostles witnesses of God's revelation. What makes them its witnesses is the fact that they speak under this twofold presupposition : they believe and therefore speak.   [I, 2, p. 817]

[29] The Church is apostolic and therefore catholic when it exists on the basis of Scripture and in conformity with it, i.e., in the orientation which it accepts when it looks only in the direction indicated by the witness which speaks to it in Scripture, with no glances aside in any other direction. The Bible itself cannot do this merely as a sacred but closed book. As such it belongs to the very constitution of all supposed or actual, more or less Christian Churches. But this does not of itself make them true

Churches. What counts is that the Bible speaks and is heard. Again, the Bible cannot do it merely as the book of the law of the Church's faith and order. To the degree that it is treated as such, it is, in fact, controlled. Like the apostles, it does not will to rule but to serve. And it is where it is allowed to serve that it really rules ; that it is not betrayed to any human control. It is not a prescript either for doctrine or for life. It is a witness, and as such it demands attention, respect and obedience—the obedience of the heart, the free and only genuine obedience. What it wants from the Church, what it impels the Church towards—and it is the Holy Spirit moving in it who does this—is agreement with the direction in which it looks itself. And the·direction in which it looks is to the living Jesus Christ. As Scripture stirs up and invites and summons and impels the Church to look in this same direction there takes place the work of the Spirit of Scripture who is the Holy Spirit. Scripture then works in the service of its Lord, and the Church becomes and is apostolic and therefore the true Church. [IV, I, p. 722 f.]

[30] By recognising the existence of a Canon, the Church declares that particularly in its proclamation it realises that it is not left to its own devices, but that the commission which underlies its proclamation, the object of its proclamation, the judgment to which it is subject and its actual eventuation must all come from another source, and that they must do so concretely in the utter externality of the concrete Canon as an imperative which is categorical yet also historical, being issued in time. And by acknowledging that this Canon is actually identical with the Bible of the Old and New Testaments, with the word of the prophets and apostles, it declares that this connexion of its proclamation with something external and concrete is not a general principle, nor a mere determination of form the content of which might be totally different, but that this connexion is completely determined in content, that it is an order received, an obligation imposed, that this piece of past occurrence composed of definite texts constitutes its working instructions, its marching orders, by which itself as well as its preaching stands or falls, so that in no circumstances, not even hypothetically, can they be thought away, or thought to be replaced by

73

others, if proclamation and the Church itself are not to be thought away. [I, 1, p. 113 f.]

[31] In every age, therefore, the Evangelical decision will have to be a decision for Holy Scripture as such. As such, of course, it is only a sign. Indeed, it is the sign of a sign, i.e., of the prophetic-apostolic witness of revelation as the primary sign of Jesus Christ. Of course, the Church can only read Scripture to hear the prophets and apostles, just as it can only hear the latter to see Jesus Christ with them, and to find in Him, and properly, ultimately and decisively only in Him, the prior direct and material and absolute authority from which its authority depends, on which it is founded and by which it is everywhere and always measured. But again, it can distinguish between seeing Jesus Christ, hearing His prophets and apostles and reading their Scriptures, and yet it cannot separate these things, it cannot try to have the one without the other. It cannot see without hearing and it cannot hear without reading. Therefore if it would see Jesus Christ, it is directed and bound to His primary sign and therefore to the sign of this sign—if it would see Jesus Christ, it is directed and bound to Holy Scripture. In it His authority acquires and has that concreteness as an authority higher than the Church which arrests the apparently irresistible revulsion of obedience to self-government. We can appropriate God and Jesus and the Holy Ghost and even the prophetic-apostolic witness in general, and then exalt the authority of the Church under the name and in the guise of their divine authority. But in the form of Holy Scripture God and Jesus Christ and the Holy Ghost and the prophets and apostles resist this change. In this form their divine authority resists the attack which the Church and its authority is always making upon it. Whenever this attack is made and seems to have succeeded, it again escapes it. Rightly or wrongly, in loyalty or disloyalty, the Church may say a thousand things expounding and applying Scripture. But Scripture is always autonomous and independent of all that is said. It can always find new and from its own standpoint better readers, and obedience in these readers, even in a Church which has perhaps to a large extent become self-governing, and by these readers a point of entry to reform and renew the whole Church and to bring it back from self-government

to obedience. If the Reformation of the 16th century means the decision for Holy Scripture, conversely we must also say that for every age of the Church the decision for Holy Scripture means the decision for the reformation of the Church : for its reformation by its Lord Himself through the prophetic-apostolic witness which He established and the force of which is revealed and effective because it is written. Let the Church go away from Scripture as such. Let it replace it by its traditions, its own indefinite consciousness of its origins and nature, its own pretended direct faith in Jesus Christ and the Holy Ghost, its own exposition and application of the word of the prophets and apostles. In the proportion in which it does this, it will prevent that entry upon which its whole life and salvation rests, and therefore at bottom refuse to be reformed. All kinds of " life," evolutions and revolutions will be possible in the Church. It can include conservative and progressive thinking in their constant action and reaction. There can be undeniable tensions and party conflicts like those between Catholicism and Neo-Protestantism, or like the internal Catholic battles between Realists and Nominalists, Episcopalians and Curialists, Benedictines and Jesuits, or the internal Neo-Protestant between Orthodox and Pietists, " Positives " and " Liberals." And these may give the deceptive appearance that the Church is really alive. But it does not live in the inner movement of these tensions. In them we see rather the process of decay to which the Church is at once subject when it ceases to live by the Word of God, which means by Holy Scripture. What is ultimately at issue in these tensions is the very secular antithesis of various human principles which can all be reduced easily to the denominator of this or that philosophical dialectic, and which ultimately reflect only the deep disunity of man with himself. And in these tensions the Church is obviously only disputing with itself. And in this debate properly both partners are right and both wrong. According to the circumstance of the age the debate may end with a victory for this side or that, but neither party, not even the victor, can say Amen with an ultimate certainty and responsibility, because neither way is it or can it be a matter of confession, i.e., of responsibility to a higher tribunal confronting both partners with concrete authority. These debates in the Church are conducted in the absence of the Lord of the Church. But are they then really conducted in the Church ? Has the Church not ceased to be the Church the moment it wants to be alone with itself ? And does it not want to be alone with itself, if it will not stand with its authority under the Word in the concrete sense of the concept, and therefore under Holy Scripture ?

It is here that we come to the final positive meaning of the Evangelical decision : it is taken in the thankful recognition that the Church is not alone, that it is not left to its own discussions and especially that it is not left to itself. It would be the moment its authority ceased to be confronted by that divine authority. For then clothed with divine dignity the Church would have to stand and live by itself like God. And however grand it might seem to be in its godlikeness, for the creature which is distinct from God that means only misery, the misery of sin and death. From this misery of the solitariness of the creature fallen in sin and death the Church is snatched away by the fact that God in Jesus Christ is present and gracious to it in concrete authority, which means in an authority which is different from and superior to its own. It is the Word of God as Holy Scripture which puts an end to this misery. Because Holy Scripture is the authority of Jesus Christ in His Church, the Church does not need to smooth out its own anxieties and needs and questions, it does not need to burden itself with the impossible task of wanting to govern itself, it can obey without having to bear the responsibility for the goal and the result. [I, 2, p. 583 ff.]

[32] 1. The history of Holy Scripture. We are thinking now of its origin and transmission, and its exegesis and influence in the course of history generally. Certainly we cannot say that from this standpoint it sheds any compelling, universal, direct or necessary light upon its content, i.e., the occurrence of that particular and sacred history, and therefore the King of Israel as the Lord of world-occurrence. For there is no doubt that these aspects can be considered and explained as simply the result of a particular epoch in the religious development of mankind, or even as the result of certain peculiar superstitions and delusions, or it may be of the most serious and profound

experiences and insights of the human race, according to the standpoint of the individual observer. And this certainly does not mean that they can be regarded as the result of a demonstration of the world-governance of the One concerning whom this Scripture speaks. We cannot say more than that the history of Holy Scripture can also be considered quite differently from this standpoint. But this we can say. We can take up the position which man necessarily occupies according to the content of this Scripture. And then we can receive and accept its witness, and the Old and New Testament message of the Word and work of God to which it bears testimony. It can then be the case that as we encounter this witness we encounter God Himself and His gracious and compelling existence, and that we are claimed and liberated and captivated by it. It can then be the case that in consequence we are men in whose lives the governance of this God—far from being the governance of a particular god in his own sphere, or the power of a particular idea—has actually shown itself to be the governance of the world. Clearly, the history of Holy Scripture can be considered from quite a different angle on this presupposition, and we may think that on this presupposition it has to be considered from this quite different angle.

We can see this already in relation to its origin. If we accept the witness of Holy Scripture, then implicitly we accept the fact that, quite irrespective of the way in which they were humanly and historically conditioned, its authors were objectively true, reliable and trustworthy witnesses. It is not merely that we recognise their opinions to be good and pious, or appreciate their part and significance in religious history. We perceive rather that it pleased God the King of Israel, to whom the power of their witness is pledged as to the Lord, to raise up these true witnesses by His Word and work. In this fact, at the very beginning of the history of Scripture, and at the heart of world-occurrence, even while the fact itself is a moment in occurrence generally, what we see is not merely a moment in occurrence generally, and in religious occurrence in particular, but a trace of the governance of God as the one and only true God, a trace of this God as the Lord of all world-occurrence.

77

And this is what we also see in the continuation of this history, the rise, completion and transmission of the Canon of the Old and New Testaments. Certainly it is not a history which is apart from the developments and complications which affect all human history. Certainly it is not a history which is preserved inwardly from the follies and errors and oddities of all human history. It is a history which is not accidental but necessary in its whole course and sequence. It is a true history, not a perverted history. It is a history whose necessity and truth have constantly to be recognised, understood, tested, and actualised. And as such it is a history which can be interpreted in many different ways at different times. But however it is considered and interpreted, it is a history whose meaning persists and maintains itself. It is a history which gives rise to constant questioning, but which constantly puts more important questions on its own account. From this angle again, what we see is not a trace of creaturely occurrence but of the plan and will which rule this occurrence—the plan and will of the One whose Word and work are the subject of the Scripture whose peculiarity is so much emphasised.

And this is also what we can and must see in the history of exegesis which begins already with the history of the text and Canon and necessarily returns again and again to this history. Here, too, we are not outside the sphere of world-occurrence generally, but inside it. Here, too, we see the powerful and far-reaching effect of the various languages and racial characteristics, the politics, economics, philosophy, scholarship, artistic sense, faith, heresy and superstition of the different ages, the individual talents of the various individual readers and exegetes. And here, too, we must give sober consideration to all these factors : how it was all a help or a hindrance ; how it was that such singular honour came to be paid to the Old and New Testaments, and what they had to put up with ; to what extent men faithfully reproduced the teaching of Scripture, and to what extent they wilfully read their own teaching into it ; how again and again Scripture was continually discovered and forgotten, esteemed and despised ; how at all times it was continually understood and misunderstood. Should our estimate of this history be an optimistic or a pessimistic one ? If our attitude to the content of the texts which we are considering is the attitude of that original freedom and constraint, there can be no doubt at least that we shall always see in that history a history of their own self-exegesis. And this means that we shall never look upon the prophets and apostles as merely objects for the study and assessment of later readers ; they will always be living, acting, speaking subjects on their own account. The fact that they have spoken once does not mean that they have now ceased to speak. On the contrary, they take up and deliver the Word afresh in every age and to every people, at every cultural level and to every individual. And they do it in such a way that what they have to say is far more acute and relevant than what may be said or thought about them. What are all the commentaries and other expositions of the Bible but a strong or feeble echo of their voice ? If we are in that direct relationship to the Bible, then in the last and decisive analysis we shall not consider the history of biblical exegesis in the light of what took place outwardly. On the contrary, we shall consider the history of its outward experiences in the light of its own continually renewed and for that reason always surprising action, as a history of its self-declaration and self-explanation in the midst of that general occurrence to which it belongs and within which it constitutes its own life-centre and origin in virtue of its affinity with the divine Word and work to which it testifies. It was not merely a rhetorical flourish when at the time of the Reformation Scripture was gladly described and magnified as *dux* and *magistra*, or even as *regina*. The fact is—and it does not make the slightest difference whether it is recognised or not—that in all ages Scripture has been the subject of its own history, the guiding, teaching, ruling subject, not under men but over men, over all the men who in so many ways, and with such continual oddities and contradictions, have applied themselves to its exposition. And for this reason its history is in this respect too—those who have eyes to see, let them see—a trace of the ruling God whom it declares. It has a concealed but not a completely hidden part in His kingly rule.

And finally, we have to consider the history of its influence or effects. What happened to that witness ? What is happening to it now ? What does it actually accomplish in the world in which it is spoken and transmitted and continually expounded ? In this respect, too, we have to consider it in the sequence of all the other factors of world-occurrence and their effects. Let us take as an illustration the well-known theory that what we call Western Christendom is a hybrid product deriving from biblical Christianity on the one hand and Graeco-Roman antiquity on the other. But how many other causes do we have to mention side by side with the Bible, some of them oriental and some occidental, some of them spiritual and some very strongly material ? If we have not already done so, we shall have to accustom ourselves to thinking of the historical effect of the biblical witness as one effect among many others. And when we do this, we cannot be too serious in reckoning with the fact that what we have to do with here—we need only think of what we call Western Christendom—is a historical effect which is very much diluted and distorted, and which in addition is always restricted in power, and constantly threatened with extinction. In a genuinely historical investigation it can even be asked whether one day this force will not be exhausted and lost like so many others. But what is this force, the influence of the Bible in world history ? If we consider it in the light of the influence which we know as an event in our own lives, then we know it as a wonderful election and calling which we cannot explain merely as a possibility of our own. To our own astonishment we find that we are added to the people, the Church, the community of the King of Israel. We find this particular influence of the biblical witness in the quite extraordinary existence of this community and its commission in the world. And in face of this influence we can only be amazed, first that we are not excluded from it, that we can be aware of it in our own lives, and then that we are not alone in this experience, but can publicly share it with so many others both past and present, both far and near. It claims our whole attention to take this influence seriously, and gratefully to do justice to it. And this means that we have neither the time nor the energy for general historical considerations. We have a prior claim and commission within and in face of all other occurrence. And

80

we shall not experience any surprise at the way in which the influence of the biblical witness is necessarily diluted and distorted and threatened as seen against world-occurrence generally. This fact will not cause us any anxiety or despair. We shall be well enough aware of it from the way in which this influence is diluted and distorted and threatened in our own lives as members of the people of God both individually and corporately. Far from despairing, we shall be ashamed, and do penance, and pray, and work, not only for ourselves, but for the whole people of God. And we shall remember that it would be something far more strange if this high and solemn thing were something triumphant in the midst of world-occurrence, if it were an enormous and undiluted and unequivocal success, if it were something popular. We know that all the influence of the biblical witness can itself have only the form of a witness, the witness of most inadequate creatures. By our commission and its execution we shall not cease to aim at what the Church either is accomplishing or could accomplish by means of it. And there can be no mistake as to the influence which—with all the ambiguity and weakness of that which results from it—the biblical witness does actually have, and always has had, and always will have, in the fact that new witnesses are called out and new confessing communities are assembled by this witness. In the vast ocean of other influences we shall be aware of the fact that at all times and in all places this calling out and assembling has taken place and still does take place. And we shall not look at this influence merely as one among many. We shall not weigh and evaluate it optimistically or pessimistically in relation to the others. In this influence, in the power of the prophetic and apostolic witness at all times and in all places to call out and assemble, we shall again find traces of the One with whom that witness has to do, of the One who is manifestly present as King not only in this influence, but everywhere and always.

[III, 3, pp. 200–204]

5. THEOLOGY

Like all knowledge of God, theology is an impossible enterprise from the human standpoint and can never escape the limitations of humanity. Yet it is both possible and necessary. It is possible because God's revelation is such that it does not exclude the action of man but enlists it into service, the human understanding thus being given a proper role. It is necessary because it can never be taken for granted that the men called to service, i.e., the Church, will give true service and therefore critical testing is constantly demanded. The work of theology is thus wholly related to the task of the Church which is that of every Christian. Whether we can call theology a science depends on what we mean by science. If we do not mean a systematic world-view, but strict objectivity and method, then theology must also, though not exclusively, be pursued in scientific terms.

[33] All theology is *theologia viatorum*. It can never satisfy the natural aspiration of human thought and utterance for completeness and compactness. It does not exhibit its object but can only indicate it, and in so doing it owes the truth to the self-witness of the theme and not to its own resources. It is broken thought and utterance to the extent that it can progress only in isolated thoughts and statements directed from different angles to the one object. It can never form a system, comprehending and as it were " seizing " the object. [III, 3, p. 293]

[34] But the claim is issued—and in this it shews itself to be a true claim—in spite of our powerlessness. It is disclosed to us that we do not view and think of God, that we cannot speak of Him ; and because this is disclosed to us, it is brought home to us that this is the very thing which has to happen no matter what the circumstances, that we must not fail to do it. It is the one characteristic of the revelation of God attested in the Bible that when it is issued it is impossible for man not to proceed to think of God, or to be silent about God. When it is issued, man is convicted of his inability to think of God and to speak of God. And when it is issued, it is required of man that in spite of his inability, and even in his inability, he should still do both. On the ground of this requirement, thanks to the truth of God in it, there is a true knowledge of God on the part of man. The human knowledge of God is true in so far as it does not evade this requirement, but fulfils it in obedience. [II, 1, p. 212]

[35] But the authorisation given us by God's revelation demands our trust and its command our obedience. In its consequences it is nothing more nor less than a denial of Jesus Christ and blasphemy against the Holy Spirit,

82

resembling the act of the servant who took and hid the one talent entrusted to him, if we try to value our incapacity more highly than the capacity which God Himself in His revelation confers upon our incapacity ; using the appeal to it, and the resigned complaint that God is a hard Master, to justify our failure to attempt to view and conceive Him, and our resort to the way of mystical theology. As God encounters us visibly and conceivably in the witness of His revelation, in the creaturely form of a historical occurrence or a succession of such occurrences, and in the relationships of our own life to these occurrences, we are invited and summoned to know Him as the One who acts and rules in these occurrences and relationships. But this means that our human viewing and conceiving are claimed within their natural limits. They are, of course, claimed by God's revelation of Himself in these visible occurrences and relationships—of God Himself, who as such neither is nor becomes visible. [II, 1, p. 201]

[36] In this sober exuberance there takes place the true human knowledge of God and the undertaking to view and conceive God humanly and to speak of Him in human words. It is not the undertaking of a slave but of a child. It is childlike even in the restrictive sense of the term, but in such a way that the very limitation of that which is childlike is also the earmark of the peculiar freedom here bestowed upon man. In this exuberance, which has nothing to do with conceit and presumption, in the exuberance of the worship of God in the heart and mouth of the sinful creature, human knowledge of God is an act of gratitude and therefore partakes of the veracity of the revelation of God. [II, 1, p. 219]

[37] We say awe, having previously said thanksgiving, and having referred finally to the necessary joyfulness of the knowledge that participates in the veracity of the revelation of God. But as in the case of thanksgiving, and therefore joyfulness, we have to say awe of necessity. Awe refers to the distance between our work and its object. This distance is certainly overcome. But it is still a distance which is overcome only by God's grace, the distance between here and there, below and above. In awe we gratefully let grace be grace, and always receive it as such. We never let reception become a taking. Our knowledge of God is always compelled to be a prayer of thanksgiving,

83

penitence and intercession. It is only in this way that there is knowledge of God in participation in the veracity of the revelation of God.   [II, 1, p. 223]

[38] Theology can, of course, be sheer vanity. It is this when it is not pertinent, and that simply means—not humble. The pertinence of theology consists in making the exposition of revelation its exclusive task. How can it fail to be humble in the execution of this programme, when it has no control over revelation, but has constantly to find it, or rather be found by it ? If we presuppose this happening—and we can, of course, presuppose it only as we pray and work—theology is as little vanity as the " old wife's " stammering. If she may stammer, surely theology may also try to speak. The attempt may and must be made, within the limits of human cognition, to ask about the truth, to distinguish the true from the false, and continually to carry the " approximation " further—although always knowing that the goal as such is attainable only to faith and not to our viewing and conceiving as such. This means, to seek after better human views and concepts in closer correspondence with their object, and therefore, so far as we are able, to make the witness to the reality of God more complete and clear. If this presupposition is valid—as it can and will be valid—theology can be pursued in the confidence which is not forbidden but commanded us against the background of the hiddenness of God, without any pretensions, but also without any false shame, so much the more so because it is not an arbitrary undertaking, but one which is necessary to the task of the Church's proclamation. If this presupposition is valid, theology is on firm ground for its undertaking—indeed, on disproportionately firmer ground than all other sciences.   [II, 1, p. 203 f.]

[39] As a theological discipline dogmatics is the scientific self-examination of the Christian Church with respect to the content of its distinctive utterance concerning God.
                                    [I, 1, p. 1 ; thesis of § 1]

[40] The Church produces theology in this special and peculiar sense by subjecting itself to self-examination. It puts to itself the question of truth, i.e., it measures its action, its utterance concerning God, by its being as the Church. Thus theology exists in this special and peculiar sense because before it and apart from it there is in the

84

Church utterance concerning God. Theology follows the utterance of the Church to the extent that in its question as to the correctness of this utterance it does not measure it by an alien standard but by its own source and object. Theology guides the utterance of the Church to the extent that it concretely reminds it that in all circumstances it is fallible human work which in the matter of relevance or irrelevance lies in the balance and must be obedience to grace if it is to be well done. Theology accompanies the utterance of the Church to the extent that it is itself no more than human " utterance concerning God," so that with this utterance it stands under the judgment that begins at the house of God and lives by the promise given to the Church.   [I, 1, p. 2 f.]

[41] To participate in this, and therefore to accompany even the work of erudite theology in the stricter sense, is the task of the community and therefore of each individual member. The Christian is not free to adopt any current religious idea, to espouse his own private philosophy, and then to urge this upon the community. On the other hand, he is both free and yet also summoned and obliged to reflect on the Word which underlies the community and is to be declared by it, and to give responsible expression to his reflections. No one will do this obediently unless he is prepared to let himself be stimulated, advised and guided by others, including professional theologians. No one will do it obediently if he is not in dialogue not only with God but also with his fellow-men and fellow-Christians. The freedom at issue is freedom in the community and not a foolish freedom on one's own responsibility and on the basis of hopeful or defiant private inspirations. No one, however, can be content at this point to be a mere " layman," to be indolent, to be no more than a passive spectator or reader. No one is excused the task of asking questions or the more difficult task of providing and assessing answers. Preaching in the congregation, and the theology which serves its preparation, can be faithful to its theme and therefore relevant and adapted to the circumstances and edifying to the community, only if it is surrounded, sustained and constantly stimulated and fructified by the questions and answers of the community. With his own questions and answers in matters of right understanding

and doctrine, each individual Christian thus participates in what the community is commanded to do. If he holds aloof, or slackens, or allows himself to sleep, or wanders into speculation and error, he must not be surprised if sooner or later the same will have to be said about the community as such and particularly about its more responsible members. How many complaints about the "Church" would never be made if only those who make them were to realise that we ourselves are the Church, so that what it has or has not to say stands or falls with us. There can be no doubt that all the great errors which have overtaken the preaching and theology of the community in the course of its history have had their true origin, not so much in the studies of the well-known errorists and heretics who have merely blabbed them out, but rather in the secret inattention and neglect, the private drowsing and wandering and erring, of innumerable nameless Christians who were not prepared to regard the listening of the community to the Word as their own concern, who wanted privacy in their thinking, and who thus created the atmosphere in which heresy and error became possible and even inevitable in the community. Conversely, there can be no doubt that the revivals and quickenings continually granted to the preaching and theology of the community have had their basis, not so much in the bearers of the great names which have come down to us in Church history as representatives of these movements, but effectively, if secretly, in the community from which they sprang, by which they were surrounded and as the mouthpiece of which they spoke, and therefore again in the innumerable nameless Christians for whom the question of correct doctrine was a burning one which they tried to address to the right quarter, and who then quietly if inarticulately found and espoused the relevant new and better answers until someone was found to bring them to expression. In this matter of co-operation in the service of the community, each must consider whether and in what sense he has thus far participated in the service of the Word which is so central for its inner life. Each must remember that as a Christian he is fully responsible, either directly or indirectly. Each must see to it that he begins to take this responsibility seriously, or more seriously than previously.   [III, 4, p. 498 f.]

86

II. JESUS CHRIST

1. THE CHRISTOLOGICAL BASIS

The statements of Christian proclamation must be statements of
certainty, not of conjecture or private opinion. They are such
when they derive from the basis which Christian faith recognises
and acknowledges as the sum of certainty, as the truth itself. A
Christian faith which did not say this of Jesus Christ would not be
Christian faith. Hence Barth seeks to anchor to this place of certainty all the declarations of theology, whether concerning God or
—and here he is an innovator—concerning man and his nature and
action. Man does not know himself of himself, but has to be told
about himself through the manifestation of Jesus Christ.

[42] But the voice which reigns, the voice by which we
were taught by God Himself concerning God, was the voice
of Jesus Christ. Along all the path now behind us we could
not take a single step without stumbling again and again
across that name. And " across that name " does not mean
across an empty title. It does not mean across a form or
figure in which God could declare Himself to us or exist for
us and yet be quite different in and by Himself. It does
not mean across a name which is only a means or medium,
and which God could ultimately discard, because ultimately
it is not the real name of God, but only of a divine arrangement which in the last analysis is quite different from God
Himself. The truth is that we continuously stumbled
across that name in matter and substance. We stumbled
across it necessarily. For as we proceeded along that path,
we found that that name was the very subject, the very
matter, with which we had to deal. In avoiding the
different sources of error, we saw that they had one feature
in common : the negligence or arbitrariness with which
even in the Church the attempt was made to go past or
to go beyond Jesus Christ in the consideration and conception and definition of God, and in speech about God.
But when theology allows itself on any pretext to be jostled
away from that name, God is inevitably crowded out by a
hypostatised image of man. Theology must begin with
Jesus Christ, and not with general principles, however

better, or, at any rate, more relevant and illuminating, they may appear to be : as though He were a continuation of the knowledge and Word of God, and not its root and origin, not indeed the very Word of God itself. Theology must also end with Him, and not with supposedly self-evident general conclusions from what is particularly enclosed and disclosed in Him : as though the fruits could be shaken from this tree ; as though in the things of God there were anything general which we could know and designate in addition to and even independently of this particular. The obscurities and ambiguities of our way were illuminated in the measure that we held fast to that name and in the measure that we let Him be the first and the last, according to the testimony of Holy Scripture. Against all the imaginations and errors in which we seem to be so hopelessly entangled when we try to speak of God, God will indeed maintain Himself if we will only allow the name of Jesus Christ to be maintained in our thinking as the beginning and the end of all our thoughts.

[II, 2, p. 4 f.]

[43] This name is the answer to our earlier question. In the Christian " God with us " there is no question of any other source and object than that indicated by this name. Other than in this name—as on the basis of the necessity and power of its conceptual context—it cannot be truth, either on the lips of those who speak it or in the ears and hearts of those who receive it. Without this name it is left insecure and unprotected. It is exposed to the suspicion that it might be only a postulate, a pure speculation, a myth. It is truth as it derives from this name and as it points to it, and only so. Where is it that the men stand who declare this message ? The answer is that they stand in the sphere of the lordship of the One who bears this name, in the light and under the impelling power of His Spirit, in the community assembled and maintained and overruled by Him. They have not placed themselves there but He has placed them there, and it is as they stand there by Him that their report is a report of actuality. Again, where will those others stand to whom they address their report and witness, who both receive it and then, on their own responsibility, spread it further ? The answer is that they too stand in the sphere of the

lordship, which has now claimed them, of the One who bears this name, of His Spirit, of the call to His community which has now come to them. They too have not placed themselves there. And those who said to them " God with us " have not brought it about. But, again, it is He Himself who bears this name that has called and led and drawn them, and it is as that happens that it is given to them, too, to pass on to others their report of actuality as such. Therefore the One who shows and persuades and convinces and reveals and communicates from man to man that it is so, " God with us," is the One who bears this name, Jesus Christ, no other, and nothing else. That is what the message of the Christian community intends when at its heart it declares this name. If it were a principle and not a name indicating a person, we should have to describe it as the epistemological principle of the message. Where between man and man there is real communication of the report of what took place in Him and through Him, He Himself is there and at work, He Himself makes Himself to be recognised and acknowledged. The Christian message about Him—and without this it is not the Christian message—is established on the certainty that He is responsible for it, that He as the truth speaks through it and is received in it, that as it serves Him He Himself is present as actuality, as His own witness. He Himself by His Spirit is its guarantor. He Himself is the One who establishes and maintains and directs the community which has received it and upon which it is laid. He Himself is the strength of its defence and its offensive. He Himself is the hope of freedom and enlightenment for the many who have not yet received and accepted it. He Himself above all is the comfort, and the restlessness, and yet also the uplifting power in the weakness of its service. In a word : the Christian message lives as such by and to the One who at its heart bears the name of Jesus Christ. It becomes weak and obscure to the extent that it thinks it ought to live on other resources. And it becomes strong and clear when it is established solely in confidence in His controlling work exercised by His Spirit ; to the extent that it abandons every other conceivable support or impulse, and is content to rest on His command and commission as its strength and pledge. He, Jesus Christ, is Emmanuel, " God with

89

us." How else can He be proclaimed except as the One who proclaims Himself ? And how else can human activity and speech and hearing be effective in His service except in the prayer and expectation that He will constantly do it ?   [IV, 1, p. 17 f.]

[44] But the Christian message does say something individual, new and substantial because it speaks concretely, not mythically, because it does not know and proclaim anything side by side with or apart from Jesus Christ, because it knows and proclaims all things only as His things. It does not know and proclaim Him, therefore, merely as the representative and exponent of something other. For it, there is no something other side by side with or apart from Him. For it, there is nothing worthy of mention that is not as such His. Everything that it knows and proclaims as worthy of mention, it does so as His.

It is not, therefore, doing Him a mere courtesy when it names the name of Jesus Christ. It does not use this name as a symbol or sign which has a certain necessity on historical grounds, and a certain purpose on psychological and pedagogic grounds, to which that which it really means and has to say may be attached, which it is desirable to expound for the sake of clarity. For it, this name is not merely a cipher, under which that which it really means and has to say leads its own life and has its own truth and actuality and would be worth proclaiming for its own sake, a cipher which can at any time be omitted without affecting that which is really meant and said, or which in other ages or climes or circumstances can be replaced by some other cipher. When it speaks concretely, when it names the name of Jesus Christ, the Christian message is not referring simply to the specific form of something general, a form which as such is interchangeable : in the phrase of Lessing, a " contingent fact of history " which is the " vehicle " of an " eternal truth of reason." The peace between God and man and the salvation which comes to us men is not something general, but the specific thing itself : that concrete thing which is indicated by the name of Jesus Christ and not by any other name. For He who bears this name is Himself the peace and salvation. The peace and salvation can be

90

known, therefore, only in Him, and proclaimed only in His
name.   [IV, 1, p. 21]

[45] If the freedom of divine immanence is sought and
supposedly found apart from Jesus Christ, it can signify
in practice only our enslavement to a false god. For this
reason Jesus Christ alone must be preached to the heathen
as the immanent God, and the Church must be severely
vigilant to see that it expects everything from *Jesus
Christ*, and from Jesus Christ *everything* ; that He is
unceasingly recognised as the way, the truth, and the life
(Jn. 14⁶). This attitude does not imply Christian absolu-
tism or ecclesiastical narrowmindedness because it is
precisely in Jesus Christ, but also exclusively in Him, that
the abundance and plenitude of divine immanence is
included and revealed. If we do not have Christ, we do
not have at all, but utterly lack, the fulness of God's presence. If we separate ourselves from Him, we are not
even on the way to this richness, but are slipping back
into an impoverishment in which the omnipresent God is
not known. . . .

The legitimacy of every theory concerning the relationship of God and man or God and the world can be tested
by considering whether it can be understood also as an
interpretation of the relationship and fellowship created
and sustained in Jesus Christ. Is it capable of adaptation
to the fundamental insights of the Church concerning the
person and work of Jesus Christ—the *analogia fidei* ? Or
does it stand in isolation from Christ's person and work,
so that it can be brought into connexion with these insights
only as an introduction or an appendix, neither deriving
from them nor leading back to them. There are strictly
speaking no Christian themes independent of Christology,
and the Church must insist on this in its message to the
world. It is at all events impossible to assert the contrary with reference to God and His freedom. If we
appeal to God and His freedom, in the last resort, directly
or indirectly, we can expound and elucidate only this one
theme.   [II, 1, p. 319 f.]

[46] Eliminate this name and the religion is blunted
and weakened. As a " Christianity without Christ " it
can only vegetate. It has lost its only *raison d'être*. Like
other religions, for other reasons, it can look only for a

91

speedy dissolution. It we try to look away from the name of Jesus Christ even momentarily, the Christian Church loses the substance in virtue of which it can assert itself in and against the state and society as an entity of a special order. Christian piety (no matter whether it vaunts itself as a piety of head or heart or action) loses the substance in virtue of which it can be something distinctive alongside morals, art and science. Christian theology loses the substance in virtue of which it is not philosophy, or philology, or historical science, but sacred learning. Christian worship loses the sacrificial and sacramental substance in virtue of which it is more than a solemn, half insolent and half superfluous pastime—its substance, and therefore its right to live, and at the same time its capacity to live. The Christian religion is the predicate to the subject of the name of Jesus Christ. Without Him it is not merely something different. It is nothing at all, a fact which cannot be hidden for long. It was and is and shall be only in virtue of the act of creation indicated by this name. And it is because of this act of creation that along with its existence it also receives its truth. Because it was and is and shall be through the name of Jesus Christ, it was and is and shall be the true religion : the knowledge of God, and the worship of God, and the service of God, in which man is not alone in defiance of God, but walks before God in peace with God.   [I, 2, p. 347]

2. " THE WORD WAS MADE FLESH "

The dogmatic definitions of the Early Church concerning the relationship of deity and humanity in the person of Jesus Christ, or the divine and human natures of Christ, are not regarded by Barth as the result of a distortion of primitive Christianity by Greek metaphysics, but as an irreplaceable introduction to the proper understanding of the New Testament statements about Christ. To guard against the misconception that these definitions refer to a strange and marvellous God-man, Barth interprets them as the description, not of a static essence, but of an action of God which takes place in Jesus Christ and is the determinative centre of cosmic and human destiny. The person and work of Jesus Christ are one, and cannot be separated even for the purpose of study. All that He is, is also His work for men ; He is man for other men. It is of a piece with the relating of all Barth's thinking to the manifestation of Jesus Christ that his ability to light up the biblical narrative is at its peak in respect of the New Testament tradition of the life and work of Jesus, as illustrated by a long extract from the sub-section " The Royal Man " (IV, 2, pp. 171–180). In Barth's exposition of the cross and resurrection of Jesus it is to be noted (1) how the understanding of the reconciliation of God and man is freed from the widespread notion of the placation of an angry God by innocent sacrifice, atonement being an undertaking of the love of God exposing Himself for us to the flames of His own wrath, the burning wrath of His love ; (2) how the same is true in relation to human sin as to the knowledge of God and the true reality of man, its nature and gravity being known only from its conquest and therefore from the history of Jesus Christ ; and (3) how the resurrection of Jesus is understood as God's confession of the self-sacrificing obedience of Jesus.

[47] A. Harnack opened his lectures on " What is Christianity ? " (1900) by recalling the dictum of John Stuart Mill that humanity cannot be reminded too often of the fact that there was once a man named Socrates ; and he added a sentence which is worth pondering, that although Mill was right it is even more important continually to remind humanity that there once stood in its midst a man named Jesus Christ. We may differ from Harnack as to the way in which we should remember this man. But we can agree that we cannot be reminded too often that this man once dwelt in the midst of humanity. In Him we have the central human factor.

[III, 2, p. 160]

[48] This same is God : " Christ Jesus is his name, The Lord Sabaoth's Son ; He, and no other one, Shall conquer in the battle." There we have the clearest expression of the Christian faith in the divine world-governance. And the Christian idea of the matter is not an empty idea, or an idea which can be filled out in a variety of ways. When we think of the divine governance we are not thinking of an empty form, of a general and overriding order and teleology in all occurrence. We are not looking either up above or down below. We are simply looking at the Old and New Testaments ; at the One whom Scripture calls God ; at the events which Scripture attests in their relationships the one to the other ; at the incursion of the supremacy of free grace which Scripture records ; at the Subject who is active in this incursion ; at His inconceivable but manifest act of election ; at the faithfulness

which He demonstrates and maintains ; and, at the very heart of these events, at Jesus Christ on the cross ; at the One who was not crucified alone, but two thieves with Him, the one on the right hand and the other on the left (Mt. 27³⁸) ; at the One who accepted solidarity with all thieves both Jew and Gentile ; at the One who is King over them all and on behalf of them all. It is from this point, and in this sense, and according to this purpose as it is active and revealed in these events, that the world is ruled, heaven and earth and all that therein is. This is the Christian belief in the divine world-governance. The history of salvation attested in the Bible cannot be considered or understood simply in and for itself. It is related to world history as a whole. It is the centre and key to all events. But again, world history cannot be considered or understood simply in and for itself. It is related to the history of salvation. It is the circumference around that centre, the lock to which that key belongs and is necessary.

[III, 3, p. 186]

[49] There is no discernible stratum of the New Testament in which—always presupposing His genuine humanity —Jesus is in practice seen in any other way or—whatever terms may be used—judged in any other way than as the One who is qualitatively different and stands in an indissoluble antithesis to His disciples and all other men, indeed, to the whole cosmos. There is no discernible stratum which does not in some way witness that it was felt that there should be given to this man, not merely a human confidence, but that trust, that respect, that obedience, that faith which can properly be offered only to God. Allowing for every difference in viewpoint and concept, the heavenly Father, His kingdom which has come on earth, and the person of Jesus of Nazareth are not quantities which can be placed side by side, or which cut across each other, or which can be opposed to each other, but they are practically and in effect identical. This would still be true even if it could be proved and not merely suspected that Jesus Himself did not expressly speak of His majesty, His Messiahship, His divine Sonship. In the context of what we know of the disciples and the community in the New Testament there is no ground for even suspecting the existence of disciples or a community

94

which could be practically related to Him except on the presupposition of His majesty.

So, then, we can speak of this and that title being " conferred " on Jesus only with the reservation that this conferring is not represented as something arbitrary which we might omit or handle otherwise. This conferring, and the valuation and estimation and judgment which underlies it, has nothing whatever to do with the free apotheosis of a man. In spite of all the mitigations of later Judaism this would have been an unprecedented thing in the original Palestinian community, in the direct sphere of the Old Testament concept of God. And since there has never been a Christian community without the Old Testament, it could not possibly have been carried through in Hellenistic Christianity (or only *per nefas*). The exaltation of a man as a cult-god, or his investiture with the dignity of a gnostic hypostasis, was not at all easy on this presupposition. We do not understand either the practical attitude to Jesus discernible on all levels of the New Testament tradition, or the titles of majesty conferred upon Him, if we do not at least hazard the hypothesis that the peculiar place and function of the man Jesus for New Testament Christians was not a hypothesis, that the practice and theory of their relationship to Him was not a religious experiment—however earnest and sincere—against the background of an " as though " which secretly left the question open. Their estimation and judgment of Jesus is as such something secondary, a necessary consequence. It is not itself their theme, the subject-matter of their preaching. They are occupied with Jesus Himself. They aim to be His witnesses. They answer His question. They give an account of His existence. He has placed them in this attitude. He has put these titles of majesty on their lips. They do not try to crown Him in this way, but they recognise Him as the One who is already crowned, to whom these titles belong. . . .

It is clear that we can reject this New Testament witness concerning the man Jesus. It has been rejected again and again—even within the community. But there can be no disputing the fact that, in the sense of those who gave it, this witness is to the simple effect that, prior to any attitudes of others to Him or statements of others about

Him, the man Jesus did in fact occupy this place and function, that, prior to any knowledge of His being or temporally conditioned confession of it, He actually was and is and will be what He is represented in the reflection of this witness, the Son of the Heavenly Father, the King of His kingdom, and therefore " by nature God." We have to let go the whole New Testament witness step by step and turn it into its opposite if we read it as a documentation of " religious valuations," if we do not see and admit that step by step it relates to the being and revelation of this man in the unprecedented and quite unique determination of His existence. It is not a Christian conception of Him, and to that extent not the Christian *kerygma*, but He Himself in His revelation and being, who according to the New Testament builds His community and calls the world to decision : He Himself in the power of His resurrection, the Lord who is the Spirit. Only when this is seen and admitted do we know what we are doing when we either accept or reject the New Testament witness.

[IV, 1, pp. 161–3]

[50] Jesus was not in any sense a reformer championing new orders against the old ones, contesting the latter in order to replace them by the former. He did not range Himself and His disciples with any of the existing parties. One of these, and not the worst, was that of the Pharisees. But Jesus did not identify Himself with them. Nor did He set up against them an opposing party. He did not represent or defend or champion any programme—whether political, economic, moral or religious, whether conservative or progressive. He was equally suspected and disliked by the representatives of all such programmes, although He did not particularly attack any of them. Why His existence was so unsettling on every side was that He set all programmes and principles in question. And He did this simply because He enjoyed and displayed, in relation to all the orders positively or negatively contested around Him, a remarkable freedom which again we can only describe as royal. He had need of none of them in the sense of an absolute authority which was vitally necessary for Him, and which He could prescribe and defend as vitally necessary for others because it was an absolute authority. On the other hand, He had no need consistently to break any

96

of them, to try to overthrow them altogether, to work for their replacement or amendment. He could live in these orders. He could seriously acknowledge in practice that the temple of God was in Jerusalem, and that the doctors of the Law were to be found in this temple, and that their disciples the scribes were scattered throughout the land, with the Pharisees as their most zealous rivals. He could also acknowledge that the Romans were in the land with their native satellites, and that the emperor in Rome bore supreme rule even over the land and people of the divine covenant. He could grant that there were families, and rich and poor. He never said that these things ought not to be. He did not oppose other " systems " to these. He did not make common cause with the Essene reforming movement. He simply revealed the limit and frontier of all these things—the freedom of the kingdom of God. He simply existed in this freedom and summoned to it. He simply made use of this freedom to cut right across all these systems both in His own case and in that of His disciples, interpreting and accepting them in His own way and in His own sense, in the light shed upon them all from that frontier. It was just that He Himself was the light which was shed upon all these orders from that frontier. Inevitably, then, He clashed with these orders in the interpretation commonly placed on them in the world in which He lived. Inevitably their provisional and relative character, the ways in which they were humanly conditioned, their secret fallibility, were all occasionally disclosed —not in principle, only occasionally, but on these occasions quite unmistakeably—in His attitude toward them and His assessment of their significance. But it was not these incidental disclosures of the freedom of God which made Him a revolutionary far more radical than any that came either before or after Him. It was the freedom itself, which could not even be classified from the standpoint of these orders. For where are these orders when He expresses both in word and deed that abasement of all that is high and exaltation of all that is low ? Do they not all presuppose that the high is high and the low low ? Was not the axe really laid at the root of all these trees in and by His existence ? In the last resort, it was again conformity with God Himself which constituted the secret of the

97

character of Jesus on this side too. This is the relationship of God Himself to all the orders of life and value which, as long as there is history at all, enjoy a transitory validity in the history of every human place. This is how God gives them their times and spheres, but without being bound to any of them, without giving any of them His own divine authority, without allotting to any of them a binding validity for all men even beyond their own time and sphere, without granting that they are vitally necessary and absolutely authoritative even for their own time and sphere. In this way God Himself is their limit and frontier. An alien light is thus shed on them by God Himself as on that which He has limited. This is how He Himself deals with them, not in principle, not in the execution of a programme, but for this reason in a way which is all the more revolutionary, as the One who breaks all bonds asunder, in new historical developments and situations each of which is for those who can see and hear—only a sign, but an unmistakeable sign, of His freedom and kingdom and overruling of history.

Attention should first be paid to what we might call the passive conservatism of Jesus. Rather curiously, Jesus accepts and allows many things which we imagine He ought to have attacked and set aside both in principle and practice and which the community in which the Gospels arose had to a very large extent outgrown. It did not—and obviously could not—find it a source of vexation to have to maintain this aspect of the traditional picture.

He accepted the temple as quite self-evidently the house of His Father (Lk. 2⁴⁹). Even the astonishing act of cleansing it of the traders and moneychangers presupposes (Mk. 11¹⁷) that it is for Him the house of God. As we see from Mt. 23¹⁶ᶠ·, He does not take it (or take the altar in it) less seriously but more seriously than the scribes and Pharisees. He assumes that the pious Israelite will still go up to it to bring his sacrifices (Mt. 5²³ᶠ·). When He Himself comes to Jerusalem, He does not teach in the streets and market-places, but daily in its forecourt (Mk. 12³⁵, 14⁴⁹). It is there that the Pharisee and publican make their prayers in the parable which brings out so strongly the difference between Himself and those around Him (Lk. 18⁹ᶠ·). We may also note the description of the conduct of His disciples in the closing verse of St. Luke's Gospel : " And they were continually in the temple, praising and blessing God." We may also recall that after His crucifixion, resurrection and ascension they still continued " daily with one accord in the temple."

But respect may also be seen for the order of the family, for according to Lk. 2⁵¹ Jesus was at first subject to His parents in Nazareth. And in Mk. 7¹¹ᶠ· He insisted that the duty of caring for father and mother must take precedence of all cultic obligations. We may also remember, with reservations, the provision which He made for His mother even on the cross, according to the saying handed down in Jn. 19²⁶.

Again, at least at the beginning of His teaching activity, He did not separate Himself from the Galilean synagogues (Mk. 1²¹, 3¹). Indeed, in Lk. 4¹⁷ᶠ· we have an obvious description of the way in which He adapted Himself to current synagogue practice. As concerns the Law, He not only protests (Mt. 5¹⁷ᶠ·) that He has not come to destroy it and the prophets, but He maintains that He has come to fulfil it, that not one jot or tittle shall pass from it until heaven and earth pass away, and that only those can be great in the kingdom of heaven who practise and teach even its most minute regulations. In Mt. 23¹ᶠ· He concedes (even if ironically) that the scribes and Pharisees who expound the Law sit in Moses' seat, so that if the people and His disciples have to be warned against their example, they are also enjoined : " All therefore whatsoever they bid you observe, that observe and do." And if in Mt. 23²³ᶠ· He accused them of hypocritically tithing mint and anise and cummin and omitting the weightier matters of the Law, judgment, mercy and faith, He added as something self-evident : " These ought ye to have done, and not to leave the other undone." In Mt. 13⁵² again, He recognised the possibility of the scribe " instructed unto the kingdom of heaven " who " is like unto a householder, which bringeth forth out of his treasure things new and old "—the old as well as the new. The antithesis in Mt. 5²¹ᶠ· (" Ye have heard that it was said by them of old time. . . . But I say unto you . . .") certainly implies a more radical understanding of the Ten Commandments, but this in turn involves a recognition. And the same is true of the more precise exposition of the three traditional exercises of almsgiving, prayer and fasting in Mt. 6¹ᶠ·. Even to the sayings on the cross, the tradition likes to see Jesus speaking in direct or indirect quotations from the Old Testament, and it sets Him generally in the confines, not merely of the world of religion, but of the special religious promise given to His own people. In Jn. 4²² we even have the express saying that " salvation is of the Jews." The point is made so emphatically that it can be reported without any inhibitions that some of His more kindly-disposed contemporaries regarded Him merely as " a prophet, or as one of the prophets " (Mk. 6¹⁵), or perhaps a particularly " great " prophet (Lk. 7¹⁵). Similarly, in the later search for the so-called " historical Jesus " the suggestion could be made that He might be reduced to the figure of a (very outstanding) representative of a reformed and deepened Judaism.

It is also to be noted that we never see Him in direct conflict with the economic relationships and obligations of His time and background. We have only to think of the uncritical equanimity with which He accepted in the parables of the kingdom the existence of free employers of labour and employees dependent on their good will, of masters and servants and capital and interest, as though all these things were part of the legitimate *status quo*. In Lk. 16¹ᶠ· unqualified praise was given to the οἰκονόμος, not as a deceiver, but at least as one who knew how to act wisely within the current arrangement in relation to rents. To the man who asks Him to see that his brother divides the inheritance fairly He replies in Lk. 12¹³ᶠ· that it is not His office to judge and divide in such matters. In this request, at any rate in the context in which Luke reports it, He sees only the cry of covetousness and not at all a cry for justice. " Ye have the poor with you always " (Mk. 17⁴), is His answer to the disciples who would have preferred a corresponding almsgiving to the woman's lavish devotion. He thus takes it as almost axiomatic that there must always be poor people—a thought which has given an illusory comfort to many in subsequent periods. And then in Lk. 16⁹, ¹¹ we are told to make friends with mammon (even the unrighteous mammon), and that the true riches (ἀληθινόν) will not be entrusted to those who are not " faithful " in relation to it. This was certainly not an invitation to maintain and augment our financial possessions as cleverly as possible—a process which later came to be regarded almost as a specific Christian virtue in certain parts of the Calvinistic world—but it is obviously not a summons to socialism.

Traces of the same attitude may finally be discerned in respect of political relationships and orders and disorders. It is freely presupposed in Mt. 5[25f.] and elsewhere that there are judges and officers and prisons. That there are those who " think to rule over the nations " (the qualifying δοκοῦντες is to be noted), and do in fact exercise dominion and authority over them, is certainly described in Mk. 10[42f.] as a procedure which is not to have any place in the community, but there is no direct criticism of it as such. The God who does not allow His elect to cry to Him in vain (Lk. 18[1f.]) can appear in the guise of a notoriously unjust judge who neither fears God nor has any respect for man. It is expressly recognised by Jesus in Jn. 19[11] that Pilate has an authority even in relation to Himself, and that this is given him from above. In Mt. 26[52] He did not allow Peter to put up any resistance to the Sanhedrin guard, but ordered him to put up his sword into its sheath. We do not find in the Gospels the slightest trace either of a radical repudiation of the dominion of Rome or Herod, or, for that matter, of any basic anti-imperialism or anti-militarism.

It is quite evident, however, and we must not ignore this aspect, that there is also no trace of any consistent recognition in principle. We can describe the attitude of Jesus as that of a passive conservatism in the further sense that it never amounted to more than a provisional and qualified respect (we might almost say toleration) in face of existing and accepted orders. Jesus acknowledged them and reckoned with them and subjected Himself to them and advised His disciples to do the same ; but He was always superior to them. And it was inevitable—we will now turn to this aspect—that this superiority, the freedom of the kingdom of God, should occasionally find concrete expression in His words and actions, that an occasional creaking should be unmistakeably heard in the timbers.

As regards the temple, He made it plain to the Pharisees

in Mt. 12⁶ that there is something greater than the temple. When He paid the temple tax for Peter and Himself in Mt. 17²⁴ᶠ·, He did not do so on the basis of an unqualified recognition which the disciple was to regard as binding, but "lest we should offend them." For : "What thinkest thou, Simon ? of whom do the kings of the earth take custom or tribute ? of their own children, or of strangers ? " And when Peter answered : "Of strangers. Jesus saith unto him, Then are the children free."

Again, it was an unmistakeable assault on the order of the family, which is so firmly stabilised by nature and custom, when in Mk. 3³¹ He gave to His mother and brethren, who had "sent unto him, calling him," the following answer : "Who is my mother, or my brethren ? " and then, "looking round about on them that sat about him " : "Behold, my mother and my brethren." And we need hardly refer to the even harsher saying in the story of the wedding at Cana : τί ἐμοὶ καὶ σοί, "What have we in common ? " (Jn. 2⁴). It also has a most destructive sound in this respect when He replied to the man who wanted to be His disciple, but only after he had buried his father : "Let the dead bury their dead : but go thou and preach the kingdom of God " (Lk. 9⁵⁹ᶠ·), and to the other who asked if he might first make his farewells to those at home : "No man, having put his hand to the plough, and looking back, is fit for the kingdom of God " (Lk. 9⁶¹ᶠ·).

Again, there are breaches of the prevailing religious or cultic order. The accusation was made in Mk. 2¹⁸ᶠ· that His disciples did not fast like those of the Pharisees or even the Baptist. To those who raised this point He gave the puzzling answer : "Can the children of the bride-chamber fast, while the bridegroom is with them ? " There was also the complaint in Mk. 7¹ᶠ· that His disciples neglected the purifications prescribed for meals : "Why walk not thy disciples according to the tradition of the elders ? " In reply, Jesus explains that it is not what is without but what is within that really defiles a man—the evil thoughts and acts which come from the heart (Mk. 7¹⁴ᶠ·). Above all, there is His attitude to the sabbath, which allowed His disciples to satisfy their hunger by plucking ears of corn (Mk. 2²³ᶠ·) and Himself to heal on the sabbath (Mk. 3¹ᶠ· ; Jn. 5¹ᶠ·, 9¹ᶠ·). The offence which He gave and the reproaches which He incurred at this point were particularly severe. His answers were as follows : " Is it lawful to do good on the sabbath days, or to do evil ? to save life, or to kill ? But they held their peace " (Mk. 3⁴). " If a man on the sabbath day receive circumcision, that the law of Moses should not be broken ; are ye angry at me, because I have made a man every whit whole on the sabbath day ? " (Jn. 7²³). And above all : " The sabbath was made for man, and not man for the sabbath : therefore the Son of man is Lord also of the sabbath " (Mk. 2²⁷ᶠ·). As appears in Mk. 3⁶ and elsewhere, this breach was one of the most concrete things which made His destruction necessary in the eyes of His opponents.

Again, there are some striking breaches of the contemporary (and not only the contemporary) industrial and commercial and economic order. We may mention certain features in the parables which are definitely not taken from real life but are quite foreign to customary practice in these spheres. As Goethe pointed out, no sensible husbandman would ever sow as did the man in Mt. 13³ᶠ·, scattering his seed irrespectively over the path and stony ground and among thorns as well as on good ground. And what servants will ever be prepared to say that they are unprofitable when they have done all that they are required to do (Lk. 17¹⁰) ? What king will ever be so magnanimous as to pronounce unconditional freedom from punishment or guilt on the steward who has so obviously misappropriated that which was entrusted to him (Mt. 18²³ᶠ·) ? What owner of a vineyard will ever pay his workmen as did the owner of Mt. 20¹ᶠ· ? And what sense does it make that the man whose land has been fruitful and who therefore plans (in good and sensible fashion) to pull down his barns and build greater, hoping to enjoy a future in which he can take his ease and eat and drink and be merry, is described by God as a fool—simply because he has the unavoidable misfortune to die before his enterprise can be completed, and he can no longer call all these goods his own (Lk. 12¹⁶ᶠ·) ? Nor does Jesus seem to have a proper understanding of trade and commerce when we consider the story, recorded in all four Gospels, of the expulsion from the temple of those who changed money and sold doves. " A den of thieves " (Mk. 11¹⁷) is rather a harsh description for the honest, small-scale financial and commercial activities which had established themselves there. These detailed signals only give warning of the real threat and revolution which the kingdom of God and the man Jesus signify and involve in relation to this sphere, but they are signals which we ought not to overlook.

There are similar signals in the political sphere as well. Can we adduce in this respect the not very respectful way in which Jesus describes His own particular ruler, Herod, as a " fox " (Lk. 13³²) ? However that may be, the question and answer in Mk. 12¹³ᶠ· are certainly relevant. Ought tribute to be paid to Cæsar or not ? Well, the coin bears the image of Cæsar, and there can be no doubt that authority rests in his hands, so : " Render to Cæsar the things that are Cæsar's—precisely those things, and no more, is the obvious meaning—and to God the things that are God's." There is not a second kingdom of God outside and alongside the first. There is a human kingdom which is authoritative and can demand obedience only as such. And this kingdom is sharply delimited by the one kingdom of God. According to Jn. 19¹⁰ Pilate's power over Jesus is only the power to release Him or to crucify Him. When He asked : " Art thou the king of the Jews ? " Jesus did not owe him a defence which He never made—for although Pilate, like the high-priests, made a case against Him, Jesus did not conduct any case—but only the confession : " Thou sayest it." Even the more explicit statement recorded in Jn. 18³³ᶠ· is only a paraphrase of this confession, this καλὴ ὁμολογία as it is called in 1 Tim. 6¹³. With this confession as the one thing that He had to set against it He both honoured the imperial kingdom and yet at the same time drew unmistakeable attention to its limitations, setting it under a cloud and calling it in question. " Behold, I cast out devils, and I do cures to day and to morrow, and the third day I shall be perfected," was His answer when Herod threatened Him (Lk. 13³²). To the extent that it is another form of the same confession this saying is also relevant in this context.

But the crisis which broke on all human order in the man Jesis is more radical and comprehensive than may be gathered from all these individual indications. Our best starting-point for this deeper consideration is the comparison recorded by all the Synoptics in connexion with the question of fasting : " No man also seweth a piece of new cloth on an old garment : else the new piece that filled it up taketh away from the old, and the rent is made worse. And no man putteth new wine into old bottles : else the new wine doth burst the bottles, and the wine is spilled, and the bottles will be marred : but new wine must be put into new bottles " (Mk. $2^{21f.}$). For Jesus, and as seen in the light of Jesus, there can be no doubt that all human orders are this old garment or old bottles, which are in the last resort quite incompatible with the new cloth and the new wine of the kingdom of God. The new cloth can only destroy the old garment, and the old bottles can only burst when the new wine of the kingdom of God is poured into them. All true and serious conservatism, and all true and serious belief in progress, presupposes that there is a certain compatibility between the new and the old, and that they can stand in a certain neutrality the one to the other. But the new thing of Jesus is the invading kingdom of God revealed in its alienating antithesis to the world and all its orders. And in this respect, too, the dictum is true : *neutralitas non valet in regno Dei.* There is thus concealed and revealed, both in what we called the passive conservatism of Jesus and the individual signs and penetrations which question the world of human orders as such, the radical and indissoluble antithesis of the kingdom of God to all human kingdoms, the unanswerable question, the irremediable unsettlement introduced by the kingdom of God into all human kingdoms.

In Mk. $13^{1f.}$, when His disciples were admiring the temple, Jesus answered them : " Seest thou these great buildings ? there shall not be left one stone upon another " —a saying that was brought against Him in Mk.14^{58} (and again on the cross in Mk. 15^{29}) as implying that He Himself would destroy the temple made with hands and replace it in three days by another not made with hands. Mark and Matthew ascribed this version of the saying to false witnesses. But according to the version preserved in Jn. 2^{19}, although He did not speak of Himself destroying the temple, He certainly spoke of its rebuilding in three days. The comment of John is that He spoke of the temple of

His body (Jn. 2²¹). Either way, while He honoured the temple as the house of God and was even jealous for its sanctity, He could not ascribe to it any permanent place or significance in the light of what He Himself brought and was. Unlike the Law in Mt. 5¹⁷ᶠ·, it was not to continue until heaven and earth passed away. The saying to the Samaritan woman is relevant in this connexion : " Woman, believe me, the hour cometh, when ye shall neither in this mountain, nor yet at Jerusalem, worship the Father " (Jn. 4²¹). And what is said about the heavenly Jerusalem in Rev. 21²² is like an echo of all these sayings : " And I saw no temple therein : for the Lord God Almighty and the Lamb are the temple thereof."

Everything else that we have to say concerning the radical antithesis of the new thing which was actualised and appeared in Jesus to the totality of the old order can be said only in relation to its complete ignoring and transcending of this order. We can merely attempt to see with what profundity He attacked it by this ignoring and transcending. He attacked it—in a way from which it can never recover—merely by the alien presence with which He confronted it in its own sphere. What was, in fact, this way in which He confronted it ?

In the first place, He himself remained unmarried—no one has ever yet explained with what self-evident necessity. And in Mt. 19¹² He reckoned with the fact that there might be others who would remain unmarried for the sake of the kingdom of heaven. In this way He set against the whole sphere of the family (in addition to the sayings already adduced) the basic question of its right and permanence to which there could be given only a provisional and relative answer. " For when they shall rise from the dead, they neither marry, nor are given in marriage " (Mk. 12²⁵).

But above all we must take up again the question of His relationship to the economic order. It, too, was simply but radically called in question by the fact that neither He Himself nor His disciples accepted its basic presupposition by taking any part in the acquisition or holding of any possessions. It is as if the declaration and irruption of the kingdom of God had swept away the ground from under us in this respect. We have already mentioned the passage in the commissioning of the disciples in Mt. 10⁹ which refers to the total insecurity to which He abandons His disciples. Those who followed Him had left everything (Mt. 19²⁷), their nets and boats (Mk. 1¹⁸ᶠ·), their families and houses and lands (Mt. 19²⁹). " Lacked ye anything ? " He asks them, and their answer is : " Nothing " (Lk. 22³⁵). But this is not due to acquisition or possession. Those who came to Him, those who went through the narrow gate, were told : " Sell whatsoever thou hast, and give to the poor, and thou shalt have treasure in heaven " (Mk. 10²¹). Those who were sad and went away grieved when they came to this narrow gate (v. 22) did not come to Him. A dangerous alternative for all the economic attitudes and practices conceivable or serviceable to man ! As is well-known, in Ac. 2⁴⁴ we read of a bold attempt by the most primitive post-Pentecostal community to take up this basic challenge. " And all that believed were together, and had all things common ; and sold their possessions and goods, and parted them to all men, as every man had need." There is only one other direct mention of this attempt, in Ac. 5¹ᶠ· It has often been taken up since in different forms. But in whatever form can it ever have more than the significance of an attempt ? It is worth pondering that the venture was at least made. And it will always be inevitable that there should be impulses in this direction wherever the Gospel of Jesus is proclaimed and heard. But it has never happened—least of all in the modern system called " Communism "—that even in smaller circles the way which leads in this direction has been trodden to the end. And the proclamation in Mt. 6¹⁹ is even more dangerous : " Lay not up for yourselves treasures upon earth, where moth and rust doth corrupt, and where thieves break through and steal," and especially in Mt. 6²⁵ᶠ· : " Take no thought for your life, what ye shall eat, or what ye shall drink ; nor yet for your body, what ye shall put on. . . . Take therefore no thought for the morrow : for the morrow shall take thought for the things of itself." Surely there could be no sound or solid economy, either private or public, without this laying up and taking thought ? But this is what Jesus says in words which are strangely illuminating and pregnant and penetrating—who can escape their truth and comfort and inspiration ?—even though they obviously do not give to the community in which the Gospels arose any directions as to their practical realisation, and have a final validity even though they are exposed from the very outset to the accusation that they are incapable of practical realisation. And how dangerous it is when this laying up and taking thought are scorned as " Gentile " and there is opposed to them the freedom of the fowls of the air and the lilies of the field which neither worry nor work ! How dangerous it is that the concept of mammon, which seems to denote only the idea of material possession, is used as a comprehensive term for the whole of that dominion which is opposed to the kingdom of God, the antithesis of the rich and the poor being adopted as a basic *schema* for all the blessedness or otherwise of man ! Obviously this is to shake the basic pillars of all normal human activity in relation to the clearest necessities of life—and in the irritating form, not of the proclamation of a better social order, but of the free and simple call to freedom. This is indeed a new piece which cannot be sewn on the old garment, new wine which cannot be put into old bottles. Its relation to the old is that of something which is unmistakeably different and opposed, the strident proclamation of its end and of a new beginning beyond this end, a question and challenge and invitation and demand which cannot as such be silenced. It was the new thing—we must be content, for the moment, with the simple affirmation—of the royal man Jesus penetrating to the very foundations of economic life in defiance of every reasonable and to that extent honourable objection.

It is exactly the same in relation to the juridical and political sphere. Here, too, we have a questioning of the very presuppositions which is all the more powerful in its lack of any direct aggressiveness. What are all the attempts at reform or revelation in which Jesus might have taken part or which He might have instigated or directed compared with the revolution which He did actually accomplish in this sphere ? He did not oppose the evil which He came to root out. He was the Judge and He did not judge : except, perhaps, those who thought that they could be the judges ; except by causing Himself to be judged for these usurpers of judgment. His injunction to

His followers, not as a law, but as a free call to freedom, is of a piece with this. They are not to resist evil (Mt. 5[38f.]). They are to let themselves be smitten on the left cheek as well as the right. They are to give away their cloak if their coat is taken from them. They are to go two miles with those who compel them to go one. More than that, if they do not want to be judged, they are not to judge (Mt. 7[1f.]). More still, they are to love their enemies (Mt. 5[43f.]) and pray for their persecutors, as children of their Father in heaven who causes His sun to shine on the good and the bad and His rain to fall on the just and the unjust, and obviously as brothers of Jesus, who, when His enemies (really the enemies of God) did their worst against Him, prayed for them (Lk. 23[34]) : " Father, forgive them ; for they know not what they do." It is again clear—for what political thinking can do justice or satisfaction to this injunction and to the One who gives it ?—that this involves a shaking of every human foundation ; that the right of God is in irreconcilable conflict with every human right ; that the divine state is quite incompatible not merely with the wicked totalitarian state but with every conceivable human regime ; that the new thing cannot be used to patch or fill the old. It is evident that human order is here betrayed into the proximity of a final and supreme menace. The community has again and again stifled and denied and even forgotten this, so that it could also be forgotten by the world around. But in this dimension too it has never been able to free itself completely from the unsettlement which it has within itself—whether it accepts the fact or not—as the community of this royal man. Nor has it been able completely to hide it from the world around. For in so far as it has been present as the community of this man, it has been present as such for the world, and the confrontation of the old order with the incommensurable factor of the new has been inescapable in this respect too. From the very outset and continually— cost what it may—the presence of this man has meant always that the world must wrestle with this incommensurable factor.

In all these dimensions the world is concretely violated by God Himself in the fact that the man Jesus came into it and is now within it.

But we have not yet mentioned the decisive point at which the man Jesus is the image and reflection of God Himself. In all the matters that we have emphasised so far we have been protecting this point against any attempt to render it innocuous or trivial. We have been forestalling the opinion that what we have to call the decisive point is something that can be attained and conceived and controlled by men, and incorporated into the scale of known relationships of magnitude and value. That is why we have first had to set Jesus against man and his cosmos as the poor man who if He blessed and befriended any blessed and befriended the poor and not the rich, the incomparable revolutionary who laid the axe at the root of the trees, who pitilessly exposed the darkness of human order in the cosmos, questioning it in a way which is quite beyond our capacity to answer. We do not know God at all if we do not know Him as the One who is absolutely opposed to our whole world which has fallen away from Him and is therefore self-estranged ; as the Judge of our world ; as the One whose will is that it should be totally changed and renewed. If we think we know Him in any other way, what we really know (in a mild or wild transcendence) is only the world itself, ourselves, the old Adam. In the man Jesus, God has separated Himself from this misinterpretation. And we have had to copy this divine separation in all that we have said so far. But again, we do not really know Jesus (the Jesus of the New Testament) if we do not know Him as this poor man, as this (if we may risk the dangerous word) partisan of the poor, and finally as this revolutionary.

[IV, 2, pp. 171–180]

[51] The subject-matter, origin and content of the message received and proclaimed by the Christian community is at its heart the free act of the faithfulness of God in which He takes the lost cause of man, who has denied Him as Creator and in so doing ruined himself as creature, and makes it His own in Jesus Christ, carrying it through to its goal and in that way maintaining and manifesting His own glory in the world.

[IV, 1, p. 3 ; thesis of § 57]

[52] Between God and man there stands the person of Jesus Christ, Himself God and Himself man, and so medi-

ating between the two. In Him God reveals Himself to man. In Him man sees and knows God. In Him God stands before man and man stands before God, as is the eternal will of God, and the eternal ordination of man in accordance with this will. In Him God's plan for man is disclosed, God's judgment on man fulfilled, God's redemption of man accomplished, God's gift to man present in fulness, God's claim and promise to man declared. In Him God has joined Himself to man. And so man exists for His sake. It is by Him, Jesus Christ, and for Him and to Him, that the universe is created as a theatre for God's dealings with man and man's dealings with God. The being of God is His being, and similarly the being of man is originally His being. And there is nothing that is not from Him and by Him and to Him. He is the Word of God in whose truth everything is disclosed and whose truth cannot be over-reached or conditioned by any other word. He is the decree of God behind and above which there can be no earlier or higher decree and beside which there can be no other, since all others serve only the fulfilment of this decree. He is the beginning of God before which there is no other beginning apart from that of God within Himself. Except, then, for God Himself, nothing can derive from any other source or look back to any other starting-point. He is the election of God before which and without which and beside which God cannot make any other choices. Before Him and without Him and beside Him God does not, then, elect or will anything. And He is the election (and on that account the beginning and the decree and the Word) of the free grace of God. For it is God's free grace that in Him He elects to be man and to have dealings with man and to join Himself to man. [II, 2, p. 94 f.]

[53] " God with us " means more than God over or side by side with us, before or behind us. It means more than His divine being in even the most intimate active connexion with our human being otherwise peculiar to Him. At this point, at the heart of the Christian message and in relation to the event of which it speaks, it means that God has made Himself the One who fulfils His redemptive will. It means that He Himself in His own person— at His own cost but also on His own initiative—has become

III

the inconceivable Yet and Nevertheless of this event, and so its clear and well-founded and legitimate, its true and holy and righteous Therefore. It means that God has become man in order as such, but in divine sovereignty, to take up our case. What takes place in this work of inconceivable mercy is, therefore, the free overruling of God, but it is not an arbitrary overlooking and ignoring, not an artificial bridging, covering-over or hiding, but a real closing of the breach, gulf and abyss between God and us for which we are responsible. At the very point where we refuse and fail, offending and provoking God, making ourselves impossible before Him and in that way missing our destiny, treading under foot our dignity, forfeiting our right, losing our salvation and hopelessly compromising our creaturely being—at that very point God Himself intervenes as man. Because He is God He is able not only to be God but also to be this man. Because He is God it is necessary that He should be man in quite a different way from all other men : that He should do what we do not do and not do what we do. Because He is God He puts forth His omnipotence to be this other man, to be man quite differently, in our place and for our sake. Because He is God He has and exercises the power as this man to suffer for us the consequence of our transgression, the wrath and penalty which necessarily fall on us, and in that way to satisfy Himself in our regard. And again because He is God, He has and exercises the power as this man to be His own partner in our place, the One who in free obedience accepts the ordination of man to salvation which we resist, and in that way satisfies us, i.e., achieves that which can positively satisfy us. That is the absolutely unique being, attitude and activity of God to which the " God with us " at the heart of the Christian message refers. It speaks of the peace which God Himself in this man has made between Himself and us. [IV, 1, p. 12 f.]

[54] But it is something very bold and profoundly astonishing to presume to say without reservation or subtraction that God was truly and altogether in Christ, to speak of His identity with this true man, which means this man who was born like all of us in time, who lived and thought and spoke, who could be tempted and suffer and die and who was, in fact, tempted and suffered and

died. The statement of this identity cannot be merely a postulate. . . . It aims very high. In calling this man the Son or the eternal Word of God, in ascribing to this man in His unity with God a divine being and nature, it is not speaking only or even primarily of Him but of God. It tells us that God for His part is God in His unity with this creature, this man, in His human and creaturely nature —and this without ceasing to be God, without any alteration or diminution of His divine nature. But this statement concerning God is so bold that we dare not make it unless we consider seriously in what sense we can do so. It must not contain any blasphemy, however involuntary or well-meant, or however pious. That it does do this is to this very day the complaint of Judaism and Islam against the Christian confession of the deity of Christ. It cannot be taken lightly. It cannot be secured by a mere repetition of this confession. We must be able to answer for this confession and its statement about God with a good conscience and with good reason. We must be able to show that God is honoured and not dishonoured by this confession. [IV, I, p. 183 f.]

[55] We may believe that God can and must only be absolute in contrast to all that is relative, exalted in contrast to all that is lowly, active in contrast to all suffering, inviolable in contrast to all temptation, transcendent in contrast to all immanence, and therefore divine in contrast to everything human, in short that He can and must be only the " Wholly Other." But such beliefs are shown to be quite untenable, and corrupt and pagan, by the fact that God does in fact be and do this in Jesus Christ. We cannot make them the standard by which to measure what God can or cannot do, or the basis of the judgment that in doing this He brings Himself into self-contradiction. By doing this God proves to us that He can do it, that to do it is within His nature. And He shows Himself to be more great and rich and sovereign than we had ever imagined. And our ideas of His nature must be guided by this, and not *vice versa*.

We have to think something after the following fashion. As God was in Christ, far from being against Himself, or at disunity with Himself, He has put into effect the freedom of His divine love, the love in which He is divinely free.

He has therefore done and revealed that which corresponds to His divine nature. His immutability does not stand in the way of this. It must not be denied, but this possibility is included in His unalterable being. He is absolute, infinite, exalted, active, impassable, transcendent, but in all this He is the One who loves in freedom, the One who is free in His love, and therefore not His own prisoner. He is all this as the Lord, and in such a way that He embraces the opposites of these concepts even while He is superior to them. He is all this as the Creator, who has created the world as the reality distinct from Himself but willed and affirmed by Him and therefore as His world, as the world which belongs to Him, in relation to which He can be God and act as God in an absolute way and also a relative, in an infinite and also a finite, in an exalted and also a lowly, in an active and also ·a passive, in a transcendent and also an immanent, and finally, in a divine and also a human—indeed, in relation to which He Himself can become worldly, making His own both its form, the *forma servi*, and also its cause ; and all without giving up His own form, the *forma Dei*, and His own glory, but adopting the form and cause of man into the most perfect communion with His own, accepting solidarity with the world. God can do this. And no limit is set to His ability to do it by the contradiction of the creature against Him. It does not escape Him by turning to that which is not and losing itself in it, for, although He is not the Creator of that which is not, He is its sovereign Lord. It corresponds to and is grounded in His divine nature that in free grace He should be faithful to the unfaithful creature who has not deserved it and who would inevitably perish without it, that in relation to it He should establish that communion between His own form and cause and that of the creature, that He should make His own its being in contradiction and under the consequences of that contradiction, that He should maintain His covenant in relation to sinful man (not surrendering His deity, for how could that help ? but giving up and sacrificing Himself), and in that way supremely asserting Himself and His deity. His particular, and highly particularised, presence in grace, in which the eternal Word descended to the lowest parts of the earth (Eph. 4⁹) and tabernacled in the man

114

Jesus (Jn. 1¹⁴), dwelling in this one man in the fulness of His Godhead (Col. 2⁹), is itself the demonstration and exercise of His omnipresence, i.e., of the perfection in which He has His own place which is superior to all the places created by Him, not excluding but including all other places. His omnipotence is that of a divine plenitude of power in the fact that (as opposed to any abstract omnipotence) it can assume the form of weakness and impotence and do so as omnipotence, triumphing in this form. The eternity in which He Himself is true time and the Creator of all time is revealed in the fact that, although our time is that of sin and death, He can enter it and Himself be temporal in it, yet without ceasing to be eternal, able rather to be the Eternal in time. His wisdom does not deny itself, but proclaims itself in what necessarily appears folly to the world ; His righteousness in ranging Himself with the unrighteous as one who is accused with them, as the first, and properly the only one to come under accusation ; His holiness in having mercy on man, in taking his misery to heart, in willing to share it with him in order to take it away from him. God does not have to dishonour Himself when He goes into the far country, and conceals His glory. For He is truly honoured in this concealment. This concealment, and therefore His condescension as such, is the image and reflection in which we see Him as He is. His glory is the freedom of the love which He exercises and reveals in all this. In this respect it differs from the unfree and loveless glory of all the gods imagined by man. Everything depends on our seeing it, and in it the true and majestic nature of God : not trying to construct it arbitrarily ; but deducing it from its revelation in the divine nature of Jesus Christ. From this we learn that the *forma Dei* consists in the grace in which God Himself assumes and makes His own the *forma servi*. We have to hold fast to this without being disturbed or confused by any pictures of false gods. It is this that we have to see and honour and worship as the mystery of the deity of Christ. [IV, 1, pp. 186–188]

[56] As applied to Jesus Christ we can legitimately call th term " Son of God " a true but inadequate and an inadequate but true insight and statement. This means that on the one side we can be sure that the term as applied in

115

this way does correspond to its object, that it does express it, that it is therefore true, that it tells us what Jesus Christ in fact is. We have no better term, and this one forces itself necessarily upon us. From the standpoint from which we have tried to understand Jesus Christ it is very suitable and indeed indispensable if we are to say what has to be said concerning His deity. It is quite right that it should have acquired its very particular importance and role in the New Testament and in the language of the later Church. It confesses the final thing that we have to confess of Him, and therefore necessarily it takes the first place. But it confesses it in the way that we men can confess the mystery to which it points. As a true description of Jesus Christ it goes far beyond anything that it can say in any other application. As applied to this " Son " it is in a certain sense burst wide open, it can be thought through to the end only as we bring into it meanings which it cannot have in any other use which we can make of it. As applied in this way it deserves our every confidence because it is true, but it must be used with great reserve because of its inadequacy. And is it not fitting that the true deity of the One who is obedient in humility, of the Son who is in this way the only begotten Son of the Father, wills to be known and can be known only in this way—with every confidence but also with great modesty ? For in this matter, as others, what can all our Christian statements be but a serious pointing away to the One who will Himself tell those who have ears to hear who He is ? [IV, 1, p. 210]

[57] What does the man Jesus say in the midst of the cosmos and all other men ? If we are to put the matter in the simplest terms we must undoubtedly say—Himself. He speaks by the mere fact of his existence. By the very fact that He is, He is the Word of God. And the Word of God at its simplest is to the effect that He, this man Jesus, is. Thus His own existence is the content of the speech of this man. He speaks of the creaturely presence, action and revelation of God actualised in Himself ; of the saving action of God, and therefore of His kingdom, of the doing of His will, of His own creaturely being as wholly dedicated to this purpose, of God's lordship over Him, and therefore of His own freedom for this service. The

116

man Jesus Himself is in fact this act of salvation, His doing of the will of God, this service, this sovereignty of the Creator and freedom of the creature. And He also speaks of it. He declares and shows that the created cosmos, men and each individual man are not without Him. He thus declares that what is needed to deliver the creature from the evil of nothingness is about to be done. He declares that the creature is not abandoned by its Creator ; that it is not left to itself and its own defencelessness. He declares that the yawning abyss of nonbeing will not be allowed to engulf its being. The Creator of all being is beside it in person—He who knew, negated, and rejected non-being as such, and by His wisdom, goodness and power imparted being to His creation, thus judging between light and darkness and separating the one from the other. He makes Himself responsible for the preservation of being, and in so doing He vindicates His own honour as the Creator. If the creature as such is endangered by its own impotence, the kingdom of the Creator comes to it, and the will of the Creator is done in regard to it. The very existence of Jesus tells us this. He is thus the light of the divine election and mercy to the creature. He is the utterance of the promise which the creature is given and under which it can stand from the very outset. He is the expression of the friendliness with which God adopted it in creation. He also declares the righteousness with which God resolved to maintain and order it in creation. Creation is not to be undone or to perish. It belongs to its Creator and to no one else. This is what is declared by the man Jesus within it ; by the man Jesus as the Word of God, and therefore as a Word which is unassailable and irrevocable. And so the world, and in particular the sphere of man, is not without this Word. When we say " man " we have to remember above all that there is one man among many who is this Word, and in respect of the many that it is in their sphere that this Word is to be found—the Word which is for them, which is the Word of their hope, and which in defiance of every threat promises them freedom, security and life.   [III, 2, p. 148 f.]

[58] The Cross.

It cannot be ignored that many men have suffered

117

grievously, most grievously, in the course of world history. It might even be suggested that many men have perhaps suffered more grievously and longer and more bitterly than did this man in the limited events of a single day. Many who have suffered at the hands of men have been treated no less and perhaps more unjustly than this man. Many have been willing as He was to suffer in this way. Many in so doing have done something which, according to their intention and it may be in fact, was significant for others, perhaps many others, making a redemptive change in their life. And in face of any human suffering do we not have to think ultimately of the obscure but gracious control of divine providence and therefore of the goodwill of God which becomes act and event in it ? The suffering of man may be deserved or undeserved, voluntary or involuntary, heroic or not heroic, important for others or not important for others. But even if it is only the whimper of a sick child it has in it as such something which in its own way is infinitely outstanding and moving and in its human form and its more or less recognisable or even its hidden divine basis something which we can even describe as shattering. This is true of the passion of Jesus of Nazareth, but in so far as it is a human passion it is not true in a way which is basically different from that of any other human passion. If this is the scope of the Gospel story and the starting-point of Gospel proclamation, it was not the intention of the New Testament, nor was it seriously the intention of the Church as it understood itself in the light of the New Testament, that the fundamentally unique occurrence should be found in the human passion as such. If we single out this human passion above others, we may be able to see and to say something which is noteworthy as such, but we shall not be helped forward a single step towards an understanding of what this occurrence is all about. For this reason we have already had to look beyond the human story at every point.

The mystery of this passion, of the torture, crucifixion and death of this one Jew which took place at that place and time at the hands of the Romans, is to be found in the person and mission of the One who suffered there and was crucified and died. His person : it is the eternal God

Himself who has given Himself in His Son to be man, and as man to take upon Himself this human passion. His mission : it is the Judge who in this passion takes the place of those who ought to be judged, who in this passion allows Himself to be judged in their place. It is not, therefore, merely that God rules in and over this human occurrence simply as Creator and Lord. He does this, but He does more. He gives Himself to be the humanly acting and suffering person in this occurrence. He Himself is the Subject who in His own freedom becomes in this event the object acting or acted upon in it. It is not simply the humiliation and dishonouring of a creature, of a noble and relatively innocent man that we find here. The problem posed is not that of a theodicy : How can God will this or permit this in the world which He has created good ? It is a matter of the humiliation and dishonouring of God Himself, of the question which makes any question of a theodicy a complete anticlimax ; the question whether in willing to let this happen to Him He has not renounced and lost Himself as God, whether in capitulating to the folly and wickedness of His creature He has not abdicated from His deity (as did the Japanese Emperor in 1945), whether He can really die and be dead. And it is a matter of the answer to this question : that in this humiliation God is supremely God, that in this death He is supremely alive, that He has maintained and revealed His deity in the passion of this man as His eternal Son. Moreover, this human passion does not have just a significance and effect in its historical situation within humanity and the world. On the contrary, there is fulfilled in it the mission, the task, and the work of the Son of God : the reconciliation of the world with God. There takes place here the redemptive judgment of God on all men. To fulfil this judgment He took the place of all men, He took their place as sinners. In this passion there is legally re-established the covenant between God and man, broken by man but kept by God. On that one day of the suffering of that One there took place the comprehensive turning in the history of all creation—with all that this involves.

Because it is a matter of this person and His mission, the suffering, crucifixoin and death of this one man is a unique occurrence. His passion has a real dimension of depth which it alone can have in the whole series of human passions. In it—from God's standpoint as well as man's—we have to do not merely with something but with everything : not merely with one of the many hidden but gracious overrulings of God, but in the fulness of its hiddenness with an action in which it is a matter of His own being or not being, and therefore of His own honour or dishonour in relation to His creation. We are not dealing merely with any suffering, but with the suffering of God and this man in face of the destruction which threatens all creation and every individual, thus compromising God as the Creator. We are dealing with the painful confrontation of God and this man not merely with any evil, not merely with death, but with eternal death, with the power of that which is not. Therefore we are not dealing merely with any sin, or with many sins, which might wound God again and again and only especially perhaps at this point, and the consequences of which this man had only to suffer in part and freely willed to do so. We are dealing with sin itself and as such : the preoccupation, the orientation, the determination of man as he has left his place as a creature and broken his covenant with God ; the corruption which God has made His own, for which He willed to take responsibility in this one man. Here in the passion in which as Judge He lets Himself be judged God has fulfilled this responsibility. In the place of all men He has Himself wrestled with that which separates them from° Him. He has Himself borne the consequence of this separation to bear it away.

The New Testament has this in mind when in the Gospels it looks forward to the passion story of Jesus Christ and in the Epistles it looks forward from it to the future of the community and therefore to the future of the world and of every man. It is a matter of history. Everything depends upon the fact that this turning as it comes from God for us men is not simply imagined and presented as a true teaching of pious and thoughtful people, but that it happened in this way, in the space and time which are those of all men. But it is a matter of this history. That it took place once at this time and place as this history is what distinguishes the passion, crucifixion and death of this one Jew from all the other occurrences in time and space with which the passion of Jesus Christ is otherwise similar in every respect. Distinguished in this way, it is the subject of Christian faith and proclamation.

[IV, 1, pp. 246–248]

[59] It is one thing for God to elect and predestinate Himself to fellowship with man, and quite another for God to predestinate man to fellowship with Himself. Both are God's self-giving to man. But if the latter means unequivocally that a gift is made to man, the former certainly does not mean that God gives or procures Himself anything—for what could God give or procure Himself in giving to man a share in His own being ? What we have to consider under this aspect is simply God's hazarding of His Godhead and power and status. For man it means an infinite gain, an unheard of advancement, that God should give Himself to him as his own possession, that God should be his God. But for God it means inevitably a certain compromising of Himself that He should determine to enter into this covenant. Where man stands only to gain, God stands only to lose. And because the eternal divine predestination is identical with the election of Jesus Christ, its twofold content is that God wills to lose in order that man may gain. There is a sure and certain salvation for man, and a sure and certain risk for God. [II, 2, p. 162]

[60] What is quite certain is that for God it means severe self-commitment. God does not merely give Himself up to the risk and menace, but He exposes Himself to the actual onslaught and grasp of evil. For if God Himself became man, this man, what else can this mean but that He declared Himself guilty of the contradiction against Himself in which man was involved ; that He submitted Himself to the law of creation by which such a contradiction could be accompanied only by loss and destruction ; that He made Himself the object of the wrath and judgment to which man had brought himself ; that He took upon Himself the rejection which man had deserved ; that He tasted Himself the damnation, death and hell which ought to have been the portion of fallen man ? What did God choose of glory or of joy or of triumph when in Jesus Christ He elected man ? What could this election bring except something of which God

121

is free in Himself and for which He cannot truly have any desire : darkness, and the impossibility of our existence before Him as sinners, as those who have fallen victim to His penalties ? If we would know what it was that God elected for Himself when He elected fellowship with man, then we can answer only that He elected our rejection. He made it His own. He bore it and suffered it with all its most bitter consequences. For the sake of this choice and for the sake of man He hazarded Himself wholly and utterly. He elected our suffering (what we as sinners must suffer towards Him and before Him and from Him). He elected it as His own suffering. This is the extent to which His election is an election of grace, an election of love, an election to give Himself, an election to empty and abase Himself for the sake of the elect. Judas who betrays Him He elects as an apostle. The sentence of Pilate He elects as a revelation of His judgment on the world. He elects the cross of Golgotha as His kingly throne. He elects the tomb in the garden as the scene of His being as the living God. That is how God loved the world. That is how from all eternity His love was so selfless and genuine. And, conversely, if we would know what rejection is as determined in God's eternal counsel, the rejection of which we cannot but speak even in our doctrine of predestination, then we must look in the same direction. We must look to what God elected for Himself in His Son when in that Son He elected for Himself fellowship with man.

[II, 2, p. 164 f.]

[61] For how can we explain the rise of a tradition whose content is so singular and contradictory—not the acts and achievements and works of a historical figure, but his shameful end, his destruction which so totally compromises everything that precedes it ? and this as an event of such dimensions, of a relevance which is so positive in every respect ? How does it help us to refer to the possibilities of myth, its invention, formation and elaboration ? How could a myth originate at this point or develop in these surroundings ? How could it come about that only 30–70 years after the death of a historical man, and in these different ways, all this could be narrated and said with such remarkable concentration about His death ? However that may be, there is no doubt that in

the 1st century there were people—and they were the first members of the Christian community and Church—who did know and tell and say of His death, His death on the cross, that it had positive meaning as a decisive redemptive turning-point for them and for all men, His life being the way which led to this turning-point, and therefore to His death on the cross as the confirmation of His existence, His relationship to God, and all that He said and did. And if they were asked how they knew this, and could tell and say it, their answer (and they usually volunteered the information of themselves) was simply that He had encountered them as the One who had risen again from the dead, thus revealing the secret of His death, and therefore of His life, as the work of the saving and enlightening power of God, or, decisively and comprehensively, revealing Himself as the incomparable royal man. We cannot develop the theme in this context. But at some point and in some way the Christian Church did in fact begin to have this massive certainty. And we must beware of facile explanations of this beginning. [IV, 2, p. 257 f.]

[62] We must pause for a moment to consider a statement which plays no little part in the New Testament, that the coming into the world of the Son of God includes within itself the appearance and work of the Judge of the world and of every man. If He were not the Judge, He would not be the Saviour. He is the Saviour of the world in so far as in a very definite (and most astonishing) way He is also its Judge. . . .

All sin has its being and origin in the fact that man wants to be his own judge. And in wanting to be that, and thinking and acting accordingly, he and his whole world is in conflict with God. It is an unreconciled world, and therefore a suffering world, a world given up to destruction.

It is for this reason—the fault and evil are evidently great and deep enough to make it necessary—it is for this reason that God Himself encounters man in the flesh and therefore face to face in the person of His Son, in order that He may pass on the one who feels and accepts himself as his own judge the real judgment which he has merited. This judgment sets him in the wrong as the one who maintains his own right against God instead of bowing

123

to God's right. We will have to explain this when we come to speak of sin as such. For the moment it is enough to maintain that because it is a matter of the appearance and work of the true Judge amongst those who think they can and should judge and therefore exalt themselves, therefore the abasement of the Son to our status, the obedience which He rendered in humility as our Brother, is the divine accusation against every man and the divine condemnation of every man. The whole world finds its supreme unity and determination against God in looking for justification from itself and not from God. And as a world hostile to God it is distinguished by the fact that in this way it repeats the very sin of which it acquits itself. In this way that which is flesh is flesh. And for this reason the incarnation of the Word means the judgment, the judgment of rejection and condemnation, which is passed on all flesh. Not all men commit all sins, but all men commit this sin which is the essence and root of all other sins. There is not one who can boast that he does not commit it. And this is what is revealed and rejected and condemned as an act of wrong-doing by the coming of the Son of God. This is what makes His coming a coming to judgment, and His office as Saviour His office as our Judge.

But those who are judged and rejected and condemned by God as wrong-doers are lost and condemned to perish, indeed, they are already perishing. They stand on the left hand of God, under the divine No, in the sphere of that which God does not will but rejects, and therefore in the sphere of that which is not, in the darkness in which there is no light, in the affliction in which there is no help, in the need from which there is no redemption. The power of God still rules over them, but as the power which holds and imprisons them, the power of His condemnation. The loves of God burns where they are, but as the fire of His wrath which consumes and destroys them. God lives for them, but the life of God can only mean death for those who are His enemies. That is how the men exist who will be their own judges, who will acquit themselves, who in so doing commit all sins *in nuce*, and who are therefore judged and rejected and condemned by God as wrong-doers. And because all men are determinedly against God in this, this is how every man necessarily exists—in a lost state as one who is lost. God would not be God if there could be any altering the universality and logic and completeness of what is necessarily done here, if there could be any escaping this sequence of sin and destruction. It means eternal perdition to have God against us. But if we will what God does not will, we do have God against us, and therefore we hurry and run and stumble and fall into eternal perdition.

But again God would not be God if His reaction to wrong-doers could be compared to a mechanism which functions, as it were, independently of His free ruling and disposing. That is not how it is on His right hand, where He says Yes to the creature, where He frees his powers and blesses his love and gives him life which is life indeed. God is the Lord in all His rule, even in that of His wrath and the destruction and perdition which it brings. He Himself determines the course and direction and meaning of it : not some necessity immanent to its occurrence ; not a force to which man when he sins against God becomes subject absolutely, i.e., otherwise than in conformity to the sovereign will and disposing of God which obtains even in His rule on the left hand. How God will fulfil the sentence to which man has fallen inescapably victim is a matter for Him to decide. He can fulfil it—in all its strictness—in such a way that in fulfilling it there is attained that which man in his perversity tried and never could secure for himself—his pardon. Without relaxing or mitigating the sentence, let alone as a judge who is unjust by reason of his laxity, He can exercise grace even with His judgment and in execution of it. He can be so much in earnest against sinful man that He is for him. He can bring on him all that must come on him as a wrong-doer at the left hand of God and under His No, in order to set him at His right hand, in order finally to say Yes to him, in order to address and treat him as one who does right and not wrong. God is free to judge in this way. He is not obliged to do so. There is no inner compulsion forcing Him to exercise this strange judgment. Even less is there any right or claim on the part of man on the ground of which he can expect this strange judgment. Everything is against any such judgment being even conceivable : a serious judgment of God's enemies the result of which is grace, liberation, redemption proceeding out of captivity, love out of wrath, life out of death ; a judgment which in the event makes the enemies of God His friends ; a judgment in which this does not happen arbitrarily but in a fixed order, not in a wild divine inconsequence but with a clear purpose and according to a firm plan ; and therefore a judgment beside and after and beyond which there need be no further fear of judgment ; a judgment which concludes once and for all with the redemption and salvation of the man who had been rightly accused and condemned and had fallen a helpless victim to destruction. Everything is against the possibility of a judgment like that. But we cannot encroach on the freedom of God. We cannot, therefore, say that it could not please God in His grace, out of sheer faithfulness and mercy to us men, to be our Judge in this strange fashion.

But in the last resort there is only one thing which tells us that this is in fact possible—that in Jesus Christ His Son our Lord He has acted in this and no other way as our Judge and the Judge of all men. We now return to our question : Why did the Son of God become man, one of us, our Brother, our Fellow in the human situation ? The answer is : In order to judge the world. But in the light of what God has actually done we must add at once : In order to judge it in the exercise of His kingly freedom to show His grace in the execution of His judgment, to pronounce us free in passing sentence, to free us by imprisoning us, to ground our life on our death, to redeem and save us by our destruction. That is how God has actually judged in Jesus Christ. And that is why He humbled Himself. That is why He went into the far country as the obedient Son of the Father. That is why He did not abandon us, but came amongst us as our Brother. That is why the Father sent Him. That was the eternal will of God and its fulfilment in time—the execution of this strange judgment. If this strange judgment had not taken place, there would be only a lost world and lost men. Since it has taken place, we can only recognise and believe and proclaim to the whole world and all men : Not lost. And since it did take place, what does it matter what may be said against the possibility of it ?

But what did take place ? At this point we can and must make the decisive statement : What took place is that the Son of God fulfilled the righteous judgment on us men by Himself taking our place as man and in our place undergoing the judgment under which we had passed. That is why He came and was amongst us. In this way, in this " for us," He was our Judge against us. That is what happened when the divine accusation was, as it were, embodied in His presence in the flesh. That is what happened when the divine condemnation had, as it were, visibly to fall on this our Fellow-man. And that is what happened when by reason of our accusation and condemnation it had to come to the point of our perishing, our destruction, our fall into nothingness, our death. Everything happened to us exactly as it had to happen, but because God willed to execute His judgment on us in His Son it all happened in His person, as His accusation and condemnation and destruction. He judged, and it was the Judge who was judged, who let Himself be judged. Because He was a man like us, He was able to be judged like us. Because He was the Son of God and Himself God, He had the competence and power to allow this to happen to Him. Because He was the divine Judge come amongst us, He had the authority in this way—by this giving up of Himself to judgment in our place—to exercise the divine justice of grace, to pronounce us righteous on the ground of what happened to Him, to free us therefore from the accusation and condemnation and punishment, to save us from the impending loss and destruction. And because in divine freedom He was on the way of obedience, He did not refuse to accept the will of the Father as His will in this self-giving. In His doing this for us, in His taking to Himself—to fulfil all righteousness—our accusation and condemnation and punishment, in His suffering in our place and for us, there came to pass our reconciliation with God. *Cur Deus homo ?* In order that God as man might do and accomplish and achieve and complete all this for us wrong-doers, in order that in this way there might be brought about by Him our reconciliation with Him and conversion to Him. [IV, 1, pp. 216 f., 220–223]

[63] But how is man to see this, to take sin as seriously as this—his own sin and that of others, however plain ?

Are we not continually surprised by the insignificance of that act in which the first man—and with him every other man—became a sinner according to the story in Genesis ? And do we not take a restricted view of the guilt and sinfulness of evil in all the measures that we believe we can and should take against its origins and effects (our pedagogic and political and moral enterprises) ? How small the harm appears when we think we can botch it up in this way ! The truth is that Anselm's question : *quanti ponderis sit peccatum ?* is given an answer either from the cross of Christ or not at all. It is given an answer from the cross of Christ. The serious and terrible nature of human corruption, the depth of the abyss into which man is about to fall as the author of it, can be measured by the fact that the love of God could react and reply to this event only by His giving, His giving up, of Jesus Christ Himself to overcome and remove it and in that way to redeem man, fulfilling the judgment upon it in such a way that the Judge allowed Himself to be judged and caused the man of sin to be put to death in His own person. It is only when it is seen that this was the cost to God— in the person of His Son—of our reconciliation with Him, that the frivolously complacent assumption is destroyed that our evil is always limited by our good (our good nature and our good actions), and that it is excused and mitigated by this compensation. Our evil is indeed limited and compensated and more than counterbalanced, but not by our good, only by the goodness of God. And because this is the only possible limitation and compensation we cannot think too stringently or soberly about the seriousness of the human situation.   [IV, 1, p. 411 f.]

[64] There, on the cross of Golgotha, hangs the man who in His own name and person represented me, my name and person, with God ; and who again in His own name and person represented God to me in my name and person. Everything, therefore, that God has to say in His relationship to me is originally and properly said to Him ; everything that I have to say to God in this relationship is originally and properly said by Him. All that I have to do, therefore, is to repeat what is already said in this conversation between God and the Son. But what takes place in this conversation is that in the person of Jesus

Christ I am addressed as a sinner, a lost son, and that again in the person of Jesus Christ I confess myself to be a sinner, a lost son. In this conversation the voice of denial is absolutely silenced. For in the death of Jesus Christ, this conversation between Father and Son is conducted with me and about me—with me and about me in His person as my Advocate before God. Even in the soliloquy and self-judgment which I cannot escape in face of the divine colloquy and judgment the voice of denial cannot be raised. I am not one who, as a hearer of this divine conversation, and a participator in this divine judgment, can either hear or make any kind of excuse. At the point where God deals with me, where He has sought and found me, at the cross of Golgotha, I am exposed and addressed as a sinner. Indeed, I have found and confessed myself to be this. I have nothing to add to what is said and confessed there, nor to subtract from it. The transgression in all transgressions, the sin in all sins, namely, that I should refuse the name of a sinner, is made quite impossible. It is literally nailed to the cross with Jesus Christ. It can only die. The only thing that I can do is recognise that my sin is really dead—the sin from which I cannot cleanse myself, the sin which I cannot even recognise and confess, the sin which I could only see awakening, and myself awaken, to constantly new forms of life if it were not already dead in the fact that God has pronounced and executed His sentence on His beloved Son in my place, and that the latter has accepted it in my place. [II, 2, p. 750 f.]

[65] How, then, did He traverse this earth of ours? How was He and is He among us? As a man like ourselves, with all our frailty and limitation! In solidarity with us—indeed bearing our guilt and shame and misery in our place! Finally betrayed and rejected and condemned, dying a criminal's death! Yet all this pales before the way in which He was man and lived and acted and suffered as such. For in all this, not least but supremely in His death and passion, He lived the superior life of a new man completely different from us. What a Lord among a race of servants was this one perfect servant in His very being as a servant! What a cause He espoused for us all against us all—for us who are so occupied with

wretched causes ! What words He spoke—in human language and with human limitations—but what words ! And what acts He performed—human acts and with human limitations—but what acts ! This man came, and in and with Him there came the kingdom. In and with Him there took place the divine seizure of power on earth. Nor was this arrested or reversed by His death, when He trod the way of His humiliation to the bitter end. On the contrary, it was completed, definitively completed, by His death. What is it that we beheld ? Flesh of our flesh ? And therefore the judgment of God fulfilled on all flesh in Him ? And therefore His own and our misery ? No, we beheld His glory—" the glory as of the only begotten of the Father, full of grace and truth " (Jn. 1^{14}). What is it that we heard ? That no man has seen God at any time ? That we are so far from God, so godless and god-forsaken ? No, for although we did hear this, we heard also the declaration of God brought us by the One who is in the bosom of the Father, and " of his fulness have all we received, and grace for grace " (Jn. 1^{16}). This is paradoxical, not merely because it is said of the man Jesus, of the eternal Word which became flesh, of the humiliated Son of God as the Son of Man, of the One who entered into the great concealment of His Godhead, but also because this man was so superior and exalted, so genuine and glorious a man. The riddle of the existence of Jesus Christ has also this quite other side. There is in it not only night but also day, not only confusing darkness but also—no less and perhaps even more strangely—blinding light ; the sharp light of contrast, but genuine light. Thus we have not only to ask where and how we are to see and have access to the reconciliation of the world with God as it has taken place in Him, its and our salvation, the kingdom of God drawn near and its peace. With the answer to this question we have also to ask how that which is really present and visible can be seen by human eyes ; how we can stand before this man ; where and how there is a place in our heart and reason for the glory of man as it is present in Him ; whether and how we are endowed and adapted to receive grace of His fulness, or even to realise the presence of the fulness of divine, and therefore of human, glory. Is it really the case that the riddle of the existence of Jesus Christ has only the aspect on which it appears to signify that on account of the lowliness in which God meets us in it we can make too little, or nothing at all, of this God ? Is it not perhaps the case that it has, especially, this other aspect on which it signifies that we are quite impotent in face of it because in this man too much, indeed everything, is made of us, because there has taken place in Him an exaltation, a new beginning of our human being, which is quite beyond us, because there encounters us in Him a life that we cannot even conceive, let alone think or live, either as the life of this man or as the life which we are also given in Him ?

It is again the case that the Christian community and the individual Christian, coming from the resurrection of Jesus Christ, find themselves on the far side of this question, actually saying Yes to this royal man, to the glory of the Son of God revealed in His human majesty, to His human life and therefore to the exaltation of our life as it has taken place in Him. If we assume that we are Christians, and that we come from Easter, we do not close our eyes to this light, or gape and stare at it as at an alien marvel. There is a place in our heart and reason for the reconciliation of the world with God as it has taken place in this true Son of God and Son of Man, for the covenant as it has been fulfilled even on man's side for the kingdom, the peace, the salvation of God, concluded in the existence of this man. We hear the Word incarnate, this man, and we obey Him. We can and must be His witnesses. We believe in the Lord Jesus Christ, the Crucified, but the One who conquers as the Crucified, and the One who is raised again and manifested as the Conqueror. We confess His human name as the name which is above every name. Whether we fully understand this and give ourselves to it, or draw back half-way, the fact itself is indisputable. The Christian community is the Easter community. Our preaching is Easter preaching, our hymns are Easter hymns, our faith is an Easter faith. We not only have a *theologia crucis*, but a *theologia resurrectionis* and therefore a *theologia gloriae*, i.e., a theology of the glory of the new man actualised and introduced in the crucified Jesus Christ who triumphs as the Crucified ; a theology of the promise of our eternal life which has its

131

basis and origin in the death of this man. It would be a false seriousness to try to disguise the fact that the Christian answer to the one puzzle of the existence of Jesus Christ has also this other aspect. To affirm it is not to deny or forget or conceal the first side. It is only in the light of the first that it can have this second aspect. It is great and wonderful and necessary enough that in face of the deep humiliation and concealment of the Son of God there should be a violently resisting and attacking Christian Notwithstanding and Nevertheless ; that in face of the cross there should be an acceptance and repetition, piercing the threatened despair, of the Yes that is spoken in and under this powerful No ; that there should be therefore a Good Friday faith, a *theologia crucis*. At all periods in its history the Christian community has ventured fearfully but boldly to proclaim this Notwithstanding and Nevertheless. And it will never cease fearfully but boldly to proclaim it. The Holy Spirit encourages and instructs and impels it to make this defiant penetration, and will never cease to kindle and therefore to characterise Christian faith and confession on this first side. But is it not more great and wonderful and necessary that the one riddle of the existence of Jesus Christ is disclosed to the same Christian community—at all periods in its history—by a very different aspect ? that the same faith in Him is set in its heart, and the same confession on its lips, in a very different form, in the form in which the Nevertheless has become a Hence and the Notwithstanding a Therefore ? This is in fact the case. The acceptance and repetition of that Yes are more than a desperate resistance and attack. They are more than the piercing of a threatened despair. They are this, but they are also more. They are a simple acceptance free from all the strain and stress of conflict. It is not merely that the Yes is spoken in and under the powerful No of the cross, and has to be received and repeated in defiance of it. The fact is that in and under the No of the cross a powerful Yes is also spoken : " Christ is risen," and that this powerful Yes may also be received and repeated. This being the case, faith and confession are characterised more by joy and thankfulness than by fearfulness and boldness. The liberation has given rise to liberty. The riddle of the existence of Jesus Christ, which is the point of reference for the Christian answer and Christian faith and confession, is thus the fact that in the humiliation of the Son of God there is actualised and revealed the exaltation of the Son of Man, and our own exaltation in Him as our Brother and Head.

[IV, 2, pp. 353–355]

III. NOTHINGNESS

The question of the origin and purpose of evil has always been a basic question of human thought. In Christian thinking certain tenets are sure even though they are hard to bring into logical connexion : (1) that God, the Author of all that is, is not the Author of evil, and yet the latter is a powerful reality and not a mere appearance ; (2) that evil is really evil, i.e., that it is that which is not willed by God, and cannot therefore be somehow regarded as purposeful, and yet God is a match for it, mastering it and turning it to good ; and (3) that the creaturely nature of man makes it possible for him to choose evil and sin, and yet this is not the will or plan of God, so that man alone is responsible and not God. Barth takes up the questions raised by these basic propositions. In his attempt the following points are to be noted : (1) the title " nothingness," which he gives to evil, does not mean that it does not exist but that it is rejected and overcome, so that man can only turn away from it and cannot respect it ; (2) he differentiates evil strictly from the shadow-side of creation—night, sorrow, finitude and need—which are meaningful and belong to the good creation of God, in no way detracting from it ; (3) he thinks that justice is done to the resurrection of Christ, the triumph of grace, only when the triumph of God is believed and evil is not therefore taken with final seriousness.

[66] It is a mark of the divine nature as distinct from that of the creature that in it a conflict with Himself is not merely ruled out, but is inherently impossible. If this were not so, if there did not exist perfect, original and ultimate peace between the Father and the Son by the Holy Spirit, God would not be God. Any God in conflict with Himself is bound to be a false God. On the other hand, it is a mark of created being as distinct from divine that in it conflict with God and therefore mortal conflict with itself is not ruled out, but is a definite possibility even if it is only the impossible possibility, the possibility of self-annulment and therefore its own destruction. Without this possibility of defection or of evil, creation would not be distinct from God and therefore not really His creation. The fact that the creature can fall away from God and perish does not imply any imperfection on the part of creation or the Creator. What it does mean positively is that it is something created and is therefore

dependent on preserving grace, just as it owes its very existence simply to the grace of its Creator. A creature freed from the possibility of falling away would not really be living as a creature. It could only be a second God— and as no second God exists, it could only be God Himself. Sin is when the creature avails itself of this impossible possibility in opposition to God and to the meaning of its own existence. But the fault is that of the creature and not of God. In no sense does it follow necessarily from what God is in Himself. Nor does it result from the nature of creation. It follows inevitably only from the incomprehensible fact that the creature rejects the preserving grace of God. What belongs to the nature of the creature is that it is not physically hindered from doing this. If it was hindered in this way, it could not exist at all as a creature. In that case, grace would not be grace and the creature would inevitably be God Himself. The fact of evil in the world does not cast any shadow on God, as if evil, i.e., opposition to Him, had any place either in Himself or in His being and activity as the Creator.

[II, 1, p. 503 f.]

[67] We cannot complain because God put a creaturely being on this frontier, a being unlike Himself in that it was subject to temptation. We cannot blame God for confronting man with evil, an evil which in His own case was excluded by the divine nature, but which in man's case could be excluded only by the divine Word and commandment. We cannot hold it against God that He did not prevent but permitted the fall of man, i.e., his succumbing to the temptation of the devil and his incurring of actual guilt. In God's eternal decree these things did not involve any injustice to the creature, for by this same decree God decided that the risk which He allowed to threaten the creature and the plight into which He allowed it to plunge itself should be His own risk and His own plight. God created man. In that sense He exposed him to the risk. Yet from all eternity God did not let him fall, but He upheld him even when Satan's temptation and his own culpability resulted in a fall into sin. Thus even when we think of man in this negative determination, we still think of him as the one whom God loved from all eternity in His Son, as the one to whom He gave Himself

135

from all eternity in His Son, gave Himself that He might represent him, gave Himself that He might bear and suffer on His behalf what man himself had to suffer. We must insist upon man's responsibility for his failure to do on that frontier what he ought to have done as a creature of God and hearer of the Word of God. But much more, we must insist upon the responsibility which God Himself shouldered when He created man and permitted the fall of man. Man cannot evade his own responsibility by complaining that God required too much of him, for what God required of Himself on man's behalf is infinitely greater than what He required of man. In the last analysis what God required of man consists only in the demand that he should live as the one on whose behalf God required the uttermost of Himself. " Thou wilt say then unto me, Why doth he yet find fault ? For who hath resisted his will ? Nay but, O man, who art thou that repliest against God ? " (Rom. 9$^{12f.}$). And the answer is : The man to whom God Himself turned from all eternity in His Son, even in the subordination to His will which is so strange to you ; the man at whose strange need and danger God estranged Himself from all eternity, making it His own ; the man who has no cause to reproach God, but if he will reproach anyone can only reproach himself ; the man who is justly reproached by God if he attempts to reply against Him, if he does not live as the one on whose behalf God has taken to Himself every reproach, if he does not live in a state of thankfulness towards God.

[II, 2, p. 165 f.]

[68] What is real nothingness ?

1. In this question objection may well be taken to the word " is." Only God and His creature really and properly are. But nothingness is neither God nor His creature. Thus it can have nothing in common with God and His creature. But it would be foolhardy to rush to the conclusion that it is therefore nothing, i.e., that it does not exist. God takes it into account. He is concerned with it. He strives against it, resists and overcomes it. If God's reality and revelation are known in His presence and action in Jesus Christ, He is also known as the God who is confronted by nothingness, for whom it constitutes a problem, who takes it seriously, who does not deal with it

136

incidentally but in the fulness of the glory of His deity, who is not engaged indirectly or mediately but with His whole being, involving Himself to the utmost. If we accept this, we cannot argue that because it has nothing in common with God and His creature nothingness is nothing, i.e., it does not exist. That which confronts God in this way, and is seriously treated by Him, is surely not nothing or non-existent. In the light of God's relationship to it we must accept the fact that in a third way of its own nothingness " is." All conceptions or doctrines which would deny or diminish or minimise this " is " are untenable from the Christian standpoint. Nothingness is not nothing. Quite apart from the inadmissibility of its content, this proposition would be self-contradictory. But it " is " nothingness. Its nature and being are those which can be assigned to it within this definition. But because it stands before God as such they must be assigned to it. They cannot be controverted without misapprehending God Himself.

2. Again, nothingness is not simply to be equated with what is *not*, i.e., not God and not the creature. God is God and not the creature, but this does not mean that there is nothingness in God. On the contrary, this " not " belongs to His perfection. Again, the creature is creature and not God, yet this does not mean that as such it is null or nothingness. If in the relationship between God and creature a " not " is involved, the " not " belongs to the perfection of the relationship, and even the second " not " which characterises the creature belongs to its perfection. Hence it would be blasphemy against God and His work if nothingness were to be sought in this " not," in the non-divinity of the creature. The diversities and frontiers of the creaturely world contain many " nots." No single creature is all-inclusive. None is or resembles another. To each belongs its own place and time, and in these its own manner, nature and existence. What we have called the " shadow side " of creation is constituted by the " not " which in this twofold respect, as its distinction from God and its individual distinctiveness, pertains to creaturely nature. On this shadow side the creature is contiguous to nothingness, for this " not " is at once the expression and frontier of the positive will, election and

activity of God. When the creature crosses the frontier from the one side, and it is invaded from the other, nothingness achieves actuality in the creaturely world. But in itself and as such this frontier is not nothingness, nor has the shadow side of creation any connexion with it. Therefore all conceptions and doctrines which view nothingness as an essential and necessary determination of being and existence and therefore of the creature, or as an essential determination of the original and creative being of God Himself, are untenable from the Christian standpoint. They are untenable on two grounds, first, because they misrepresent the creature and even the Creator Himself, and second, because they confound the legitimate " not " with nothingness, and are thus guilty of a drastic minimisation of the latter.

3. Since real nothingness is real in this third fashion peculiar to itself, not resembling either God or the creature but taken seriously by God Himself, and since it is not identical either with the distinction and frontier between God and creation or with those within the creaturely world, its revelation and knowledge cannot be a matter of the insight which is accessible to the creature itself and is therefore set under its own choice and control. Standing before God in its own characteristic way which is very different from that of the creature, the object of His concern and action, His problem and adversary and the negative goal of His victory, nothingness does not possess a nature which can be assessed nor an existence which can be discovered by the creature. There is no accessible relationship between the creature and nothingness. Hence nothingness cannot be an object of the creature's natural knowledge. It is certainly an objective reality for the creature. The latter exists objectively in encounter with it. But it is disclosed to the creature only as God is revealed to the latter in His critical relationship. The creature knows it only as it knows God in His being and attitude against it. It is an element in the history of the relationship between God and the creature in which God precedes the creature in His acts, thus revealing His will to the creature and informing it about Himself. As this occurs and the creature attains to the truth—the truth about God's purpose and attitude and therefore about

itself—through the Word of God, the encounter of the creature with true nothingness is also realised and recognised. Of itself, the creature cannot recognise this encounter and what it encounters. It experiences and endures it. But it also misinterprets it, as has always happened. Calumniating God and His work, it misrepresents it as a necessity of being or nature, as a given factor, as a peculiarity of existence which is perhaps deplorable, perhaps also justifiable, perhaps to be explained in terms of perfection or simply to be dismissed as non-existent, as something which can be regarded as supremely positive in relation to God, or even as a determination of God Himself. All these conceptions and doctrines, whatever their content, are untenable from a Christian standpoint if only because they are contingent upon an arbitrary and impotent appraisal of what can only make itself known in the judgment of God, and is thus knowable only as God pronounces His sentence, while its malignity and corruption find supreme expression in the assumption of the creature that of itself and at its own discretion it is able to discover its nature and existence.

4. The ontic context in which nothingness is real is that of God's activity as grounded in His election, of His activity as the Creator, as the Lord of His creatures, as the King of the covenant between Himself and man which is the goal and purpose of His creation. Grounded always in election, the activity of God is invariably one of jealousy, wrath and judgment. God is also holy, and this means that His being and activity take place in a definite opposition, in a real negation, both defensive and aggressive. Nothingness is that from which God separates Himself and in face of which He asserts Himself and exerts His positive will. If the biblical conception of the God whose activity is grounded in election and is therefore holy fades or disappears, there will also fade and disappear the knowledge of nothingness, for it will necessarily become pointless. Nothingness has no existence and cannot be known except as the object of God's activity as always a holy activity. The biblical conception, as we now recall it, is as follows. God elects, and therefore rejects what He does not elect. God wills, and therefore opposes what He does not will. He says Yes, and therefore says No to that to

which He has not said Yes. He works according to His purpose, and in so doing rejects and dismisses all that gainsays it. Both of these activities, grounded in His election and decision, are necessary elements in His sovereign action. He is Lord both on the right hand and on the left. It is only on this basis that nothingness " is," but on this basis it really " is." As God is Lord on the left hand as well, He is the basis and Lord of nothingness too. Consequently it is not adventitious. It is not a second God, nor self-created. It has no power save that which it is allowed by God. It, too, belongs to God. It " is " problematically because it is only on the left hand of God, under His No, the object of His jealousy, wrath and judgment. It " is," not as God and His creation are, but only in its own improper way, as inherent contradiction, as impossible possibility. Yet because it is on the left hand of God, it really " is " in this paradoxical manner. Even on His left hand the activity of God is not in vain. He does not act for nothing. His rejection, opposition, negation and dismissal are powerful and effective like all His works because they, too, are grounded in Himself, in the freedom and wisdom of His election. That which God renounces and abandons in virtue of His decision is not merely nothing. It is nothingness, and has as such its own being, albeit malignant and perverse. A real dimension is disclosed, and existence and form are given to a reality *sui generis*, in the fact that God is wholly and utterly not the Creator in this respect. Nothingness is that which God does not will. It lives only by the fact that it is that which God does not will. But it does live by this fact. For not only what God wills, but what He does not will, is potent, and must have a real correspondence. What really corresponds to that which God does not will is nothingness.   [III, 3, pp. 349–352]

[69] The character of nothingness derives from its ontic peculiarity. It is evil. What God positively wills and performs in the *opus proprium* of His election, of His creation, of His preservation and overruling rule of the creature revealed in the history of His covenant with man, is His grace—the free goodness of His condescension in which He wills, identifying Himself with the creature, to accept solidarity and to be present with it, to be Him-

140

self its Guarantor, Helper and King, and therefore to do the best possible for it. What God does not will and therefore negates and rejects, what can thus be only the object of His *opus alienum*, of His jealousy, wrath and judgment, is a being that refuses and resists and therefore lacks His grace. This being which is alien and adverse to grace and therefore without it, is that of nothingness. This negation of His grace is chaos, the world which He did not choose or will, which He could not and did not create, but which, as He created the actual world, He passed over and set aside, marking and excluding it as the eternal past, the eternal yesterday. And this is evil in the Christian sense, namely, what is alien and adverse to grace, and therefore without it. In this sense nothingness is really privation, the attempt to defraud God of His honour and right and at the same time to rob the creature of its salvation and right. For it is God's honour and right to be gracious, and this is what nothingness contests. It is also the salvation and right of the creature to receive and live by the grace of God, and this is what it disturbs and obstructs. Where this privation occurs, nothingness is present ; and where nothingness is present this privation occurs, i.e., evil, that which is utterly inimical first to God and then to His creature. The grace of God is the basis and norm of all being, the source and criterion of all good. Measured by this standard, as the negation of God's grace, nothingness is intrinsically evil. It is both perverting and perverted. In this capacity it does not confront either God or the creature neutrally. It is not merely a third factor. It opposes both as an enemy, offending God and threatening His creature. From above as well as from below, it is the impossible and intolerable. By reason of this character, whether in the form of sin, evil or death, it is inexplicable as a natural process or condition. It is altogether inexplicable. The explicable is subject to a norm and occurs within a standard. But nothingness is absolutely without norm or standard. The explicable conforms to a law, nothingness to none. It is simply aberration, transgression, evil. For this reason it is inexplicable, and can be affirmed only as that which is inherently inimical. For this reason it can be apprehended in its aspect of sin only as guilt, and in its aspect of evil and death only as retribution and misery, but never as a natural process or condition, never as a subject of systematic formulation, even though the system be dialectical. Being hostile before and against God, and also before and against His creature, it is outside the sphere of systematisation. It cannot even be viewed dialectically, let alone resolved. Its defeat can be envisaged only as the purpose and end of the history of God's dealings with His creature, and in no other way. As it is real only by reason of the *opus Dei alienum*, the divine negation and rejection, so it can be seen and understood only in the light of the *opus Dei proprium*, only in relation to the sovereign counter-offensive of God's free grace. It " is " only as the disorder at which this counter-offensive is aimed, only as the non-essence which it judges, only as the enemy of God and His creation. We thus affirm that it is necessary to dismiss as non-Christian all those conceptions in which its character as evil is openly or secretly, directly or indirectly, conjured away, and its reality is in some way regarded or grouped with that of God and His creature. Where God and His creature are known, and His free grace as the basic order of their relationship, nothingness can only be understood as opposition and resistance to this basic order and cannot therefore be regarded or grouped with God and His creature.

[III, 3, p. 353 f.]

[70] Thus it follows that the controversy with nothingness, its conquest, removal and abolition, is primarily and properly the cause of God Himself. At first sight we might regard the converse as true. Nothingness is the danger, assault and menace under which the creature as such must exist. Therefore the creature as such is surely the hero who must suffer and fight and finally conquer this adversary, and the conflict with it is the problem of his destiny and decision, his tragedy and courage, his impotence and comparative successes. But there can be no greater delusion nor catastrophe than to take this view. For it would not be real nothingness, but only an ultimately innocuous counterfeit, if the attack were primarily and properly directed against the creature, and its repulse could and should be primarily and properly the creature's concern. And while the creature is preoccupied with the assault and repulse of these counterfeits, it is already

subject to the attack of real nothingness and its defence against it is already futile. In face of real nothingness the creature is already defeated and lost. For, as Gen. 3 shows, it regards the conflict with it as its own cause, and tries to champion it as such. It tries to be itself the hero who suffers and fights and conquers, and therefore like God. And because this decision is a decision against the grace of God, it is a choice of evil. For good—the one and only good of the creature—is the free grace of God, the action of His mercy, in which He who has no need to do so has made the controversy with nothingness His own, exposing Himself to its attack and undertaking to repel it. He knows nothingness. He knows that which He did not elect or will as the Creator. He knows chaos and its terror. He knows its advantage over His creature. He knows how inevitably it imperils His creature. Yet He is Lord over that which imperils His creature. Against Him, nothingness has no power of its own. And He has sworn fidelity to His threatened creature. In creating it He has covenanted and identified Himself with it. He Himself has assumed the burden and trouble of confrontation with nothingness. He would rather be unblest with His creature than be the blessed God of an unblest creature. He would rather let Himself be injured and humiliated in making the assault and repulse of nothingness His own concern than leave His creature alone in this affliction. He deploys all His majesty in the work of His deepest condescension. He intervenes in the struggle between nothingness and the creature as if He were not God but Himself a weak and threatened and vulnerable creature. " As if "—but is that all ? No, for in the decisive action in the history of His covenant with the creature, in Jesus Christ, He actually becomes a creature, and thus makes the cause of the creature His own in the most concrete reality and not just in appearance, really taking its place. This is how God Himself comes on the scene.

But it is really God who does so in His free grace. And therefore it is He as the first and true and indeed the only man, as the Helper who really takes the creature's place, lifting from it all its need and labour and problem and placing them upon Himself, as the Warrior who assumes the full responsibility of a substitute and suffers and does everything on its behalf. In the light of this merciful action of God, the arrogant delusion of the creature that it is called and qualified to help and save and maintain itself in its infinite peril is shown to be evil as well as foolish and unnecessary. So, too, is the arrogant illusion that it is the principal party affected, that its own strength or weakness, despair or elation, folly or wisdom, modicum of " existential " insight and freedom, is the problem in solution of which there takes place the decisive encounter with nothingness, the repelling of its assault, and perhaps its defeat. In the light of the merciful action of God, only God Himself, and trust in Him, and perseverance in His covenant, can be called good, even for the creature too. Hence the creature has only one good to choose, namely, that it has God for it, and that it is thus opposed by nothingness as God Himself is opposed, the God who can so easily master it.

In this way, in this trust and perseverance, in this choice of God's help as its only good, the creature can and will have a real part in the conflict with nothingness. It is certainly no mere spectator. But only in this way does it cease to be such. Only in this way is it rescued from illusory struggles and strivings with what are only counterfeits of nothingness, and from inaction in the event in which the onslaught of nothingness is real but its repulse is effective and its conquest in sight. In this way alone is the situation of the creature, its fall and rehabilitation, its suffering, action and inaction, full of meaning and promise. As the action of God is primary, the creature can and will also play its part. For it is the salvation of the creature which God makes a matter of His own honour. It is for the right of the creature that He establishes and defends His own right. The *opus alienum* of divine jealousy, wrath and judgment is no less for the creature than the *opus proprium* of divine grace. For it is the sin and guilt, the suffering and misery of the creature that God makes His own problem. The creature is not its own. It is the creature and possession of God. It is thus the object of His concern. And therefore conflict with nothingness is its own problem as it is the cause of God. The full intervention of God is needed, and this action of His mercy is the only compelling force, to make the creature willing and able to act on its own behalf in the conflict with nothingness. As God takes action on its behalf, the creature itself is summoned and empowered. It has no arrogant illusion as to its own authority or competence. It really trusts in God, perseveres in His covenant and chooses His help as the only effective good. But if it does this it can and will take action in the conflict with nothingness. It is not under the wings of divine mercy but in the vacuum of creaturely self-sufficiency that the laziness thrives which induces man to yield and succumb to nothingness. And it is not in the vacuum of creaturely self-sufficiency but under the wings of divine mercy that the fortitude thrives in which man is summoned and equipped to range himself with God, so that in his own place he opposes nothingness and thus has a part in the work and warfare of God.

[III, 3, pp. 357–359]

[71] What is nothingness? In the knowledge and confession of the Christian faith, i.e., looking retrospectively to the resurrection of Jesus Christ and prospectively to His coming again, there is only one possible answer. Nothingness is the past, the ancient menace, danger and destruction, the ancient non-being which obscured and defaced the divine creation of God but which is consigned to the past in Jesus Christ, in whose death it has received its deserts, being destroyed with this consummation of the positive will of God which is as such the end of His nonwilling. Because Jesus is Victor, nothingness is routed and extirpated. It is that which in this One who was both very God and very man has been absolutely set behind, not only by God, but in unity with Him by man and therefore the creature. It is that from whose influence, dominion and power the relationship between Creator and creature was absolutely set free in Jesus Christ, so that it is no longer involved in their relationship as a third factor. This is what has happened to nothingness once and for all in Jesus Christ. This is its status and appearance now that God has made His own and carried through the conflict with it in His Son. It is no longer to be feared. It can no longer " nihilate." But obviously we may make these undoubtedly audacious statements only on the ground of one single presupposition. The aspect of creaturely activity both as a whole and in detail, our consciousness both of

the world and of self, certainly do not bear them out. But what do we really know of it as taught by this consciousness? How can this teach us the truth that it is really past and done with? The only valid presupposition is a backward look to the resurrection of Jesus Christ and a forward look to His coming in glory, i.e., the look of Christian faith as rooted in and constantly nourished by the Word of God. The knowledge and confession of Christian faith, however, inevitably entails the affirmation that by the divine intervention nothingness has lost the perpetuity which it could and must and indeed did have apart from this intervention. It can no longer be validly regarded as possessing any claim or right or power in relation to the creature, as though it were still before and above us, as though the world created by God were still subject to and dominated by it, as though Christians must hold it in awe, as though it were particularly Christian to hold it in the utmost awe and to summon the world to share in this awe. It is no longer legitimate to think of it as if real deliverance and release from it were still an event of the future. It is obvious that in point of fact we do constantly think of it in this way, with anxious, legalistic, tragic, hesitant, doleful and basically pessimistic thoughts, and this inevitably where we are neither able nor prepared to think from the standpoint of Christian faith. But it is surely evident that when we think in this way it is not from a Christian standpoint, but in spite of it, in breach of the command imposed with our Christian faith. If our thought is conditioned by the obedience of Christian faith, we have only one freedom, namely, to regard nothingness as finally destroyed and to make a new beginning in remembrance of the One who has destroyed it. Only if our thought is thus conditioned by the obedience of Christian faith is it possible to proclaim the Gospel to the world as it really is, as the message of freedom for the One who has already come and acted as the Liberator, and therefore of the freedom which precludes the anxiety, legalism and pessimism so prevalent in the world. We need hardly describe how throughout the centuries the Christian Church has failed to shape its thought in the obedience of Christian faith, to proclaim it to the world in this obedience, to live in this freedom and to summon the world to it. For this reason and contrary to its true nature, so-called Christianity has become a sorry affair both within and without. It is shameful enough to have to admit that many of the interpretations of nothingness which we are forced to reject as non-Christian derive their power and cogency from the fact that for all their weakness and erroneousness they attest a Christian insight to the extent that they do at least offer a cheerful view and describe and treat nothingness as having no perpetuity. It ought to be the main characteristic of the Christian view that it can demonstrate this more surely because on surer ground, more boldly because in the exercise and proclamation of the freedom granted to do so, and more logically because not in a venture but in simple obedience. We must not imagine that we serve the seriousness of Christian knowledge, life and proclamation by retreating at this point and refusing to realise and admit that the apparently audacious is the norm, the only true possibility. The true seriousness of the matter, and we may emphasise this point in retrospect of the whole discussion, does not finally depend upon pessimistic but upon optimistic thought and speech. From a Christian standpoint " to be serious " can only mean to take seriously the fact that Jesus is Victor. If Jesus is Victor, the last word must always be secretly the first, namely, that nothingness has no perpetuity.

[III, 3, p. 363 f.]

IV. CREATION AS BENEFIT

Barth's exposition of the first article of the creed is characterised by the fact that he does not regard the creatureliness of the world and the providence of God as something which can be known from other indications and demonstrated as attempted by the older proofs of God, but as something which can be known only in faith, i.e., in acknowledgment of the Word of revelation. It is also characterised by the closely related fact that he does not see only a subsequent but an original relationship between creation and salvation. God does not first posit in being and then bring salvation to certain creatures under specific conditions. He creates out of grace. This is what is meant by the two main propositions that creation is the external basis of the covenant and the covenant the internal basis of creation. In relation to God this means that His creation is not a causation but the overflowing of His love, His being for the creature. And in relation to us it means the unheard-of fact that our very being is grace, for which all of us, whoever we are, can only be absolutely thankful and with which we can only come to terms.

[72] God is unknown to us as our Father or as the Creator to the extent that He is not known through Jesus. . . . If this exclusive statement is accepted and taken seriously . . . there can be no possibility of regarding the first article of the creed as an article of natural theology. The message of Jesus concerning God the Father cannot be taken to mean that Jesus uttered the well-known truth that the world must have and really has a Creator, that He ventured to give to this Creator the familiar human name of " Father," that He took what all serious philosophy has called the supreme good, the *esse a se*, the *ens perfectissimum*, the *universum*, the ground or abyss of meaning, the unconditional, the limit, the critical negation or the origin, and gave to it this name which was already current in the language of religion, thus baptising it and interpreting it in a Christian sense. Concerning such a view we can only say that, whether or not it is given the name of Father, this entity, the supposed philosophical equivalent of the Creator God, has nothing whatever to do with the message of Jesus concerning God the Father. It still has nothing whatever to do with it even

if it is related and perhaps identified with the principle of dying to become, with the superior origin and goal of the dialectic of losing one's life to gain it. An idea projected with the claim to be the idea of God is as such an idol in the light of the exclusiveness of the biblical witnesses, not because it is an idea but because of its claim. This applies even to the genuinely pure and for that reason misleading idea of God advanced by a Plato. If our exclusive statement is true, Jesus did not proclaim again the well-known Creator of the world and reinterpret Him by investing Him with the not unknown name of Father. On the contrary, He revealed the unknown Father, His Father, and in so doing, but only in so doing, He said who and what the Creator is, and that the Creator as such is our Father. [I, 1, p. 448 f.]

[73] The doctrine of the creation no less than the whole remaining content of Christian confession is an article of faith, i.e., the rendering of a knowledge which no man has procured for himself or ever will ; which is neither native to him nor accessible by way of observation and logical thinking ; for which he has no organ and no ability ; which he can in fact achieve only in faith ; but which is actually consummated in faith, i.e., in the reception of and response to the divine witness, so that he is made to be strong in his weakness, to see in his blindness and to hear in his deafness by the One who, according to the Easter story, goes through closed doors. It is a faith and doctrine of this kind which is expressed when in and with the whole of Christendom we confess that God is the Creator of heaven and earth. [III, 1, p. 3 f.]

[74] Creation is the freely willed and executed positing of a reality distinct from God. The question thus arises : What was and is the will of God in doing this ? We may reply that He does not will to be alone in His glory ; that He desires something else beside Him. But this answer cannot mean that God either willed and did it for no purpose, or that He did so to satisfy a need. Nor does it mean that He did not will to be and remain alone because He could not do so. And the idea of something beside Him which would be what it is independently of Him is quite inconsistent with His freedom. In constituting this reality He cannot have set a limit to His glory, will and

149

power. As the divine Creator He cannot have created a remote and alien sphere abandoned to itself or to its own teleology. If, then, this positing is not an accident, if it corresponds to no divine necessity and does not in any sense signify a limitation of His own glory, there remains only the recollection that God is the One who is free in His love. In this case we can understand the positing of this reality—which otherwise is incomprehensible—only as the work of His love. He wills and posits the creature neither out of caprice nor necessity, but because He has loved it from eternity, because He wills to demonstrate His love for it, and because He wills, not to limit His glory by its existence and being, but to reveal and manifest it in His own co-existence with it. As the Creator He wills really to exist for His creature. That is why He gives it its own existence and being. That is also why there cannot follow from the creature's own existence and being an immanent determination of its goal or purpose, or a claim to any right, meaning or dignity of its existence and nature accruing to it except as a gift. That is why even the very existence and nature of the creature are the work of the grace of God. It would be a strange love that was satisfied with the mere existence and nature of the other, then withdrawing, leaving it to its own devices. Love wills to love. Love wills something with and for that which it loves. Because God loves the creature, its creation and continuance and preservation point beyond themselves to an exercise and fulfilment of His love which do not take place merely with the fact that the creature is posited as such and receives its existence and being alongside and outside the being and existence of God, but to which creation in all its glory looks and moves, and of which creation is the presupposition. [III, 1, p. 95 f.]

[75] Creation is one long preparation, and therefore the being and existence of the creature one long readiness, for what God will intend and do with it in the history of the covenant. Its nature is simply its equipment for grace. Its creatureliness is pure promise, expectation and prophecy of that which in His grace, in the execution of the will of His eternal love, and finally and supremely in the consummation of the giving of His Son, God plans for man and will not delay to accomplish for his benefit. In this

way creation is the road to the covenant, its external power and external basis, because for its fulfilment the latter depends wholly on the fact that the creature is in no position to act alone as the partner of God, that it is thrown back wholly and utterly on the care and intercession of God Himself, but that it does actually enjoy this divine care and intercession. . . . The covenant is the internal basis of creation. . . . This consists in the fact that the wisdom and omnipotence of God the Creator was not just any wisdom and omnipotence but that of His free love. . . . The fact that the covenant is the goal of creation is not something which is added later to the reality of the creature. . . . It already characterises creation itself and as such, and therefore the being and existence of the creature. The covenant whose history had still to commence was the covenant which, as the goal appointed for creation and the creature, made creation necessary and possible, and determined and limited the creature. If creation was the external basis of the covenant, the latter was the internal basis of the former. If creation was the formal presupposition of the covenant, the latter was the material presupposition of the former. If creation takes precedence historically, the covenant does so in substance. [III, 1, p. 231 f.]

[76] The ordaining of salvation for man and of man for salvation is the original and basic will of God, the ground and purpose of His will as Creator. It is not that He first wills and works the being of the world and man, and then ordains it to salvation. But God creates, preserves and overrules man for this prior end and with this prior purpose, that there may be a being distinct from Himself ordained for salvation, for perfect being, for participation in His own being, because as the One who loves in freedom He has determined to exercise redemptive grace—and that there may be an object of this His redemptive grace, a partner to receive it. . . . The " God with us " has nothing to do with chance. As a redemptive happening it means the revelation and confirmation of the most primitive relationship between God and man, that which was freely determined in eternity by God Himself before there was any created being. In the very fact that man is, and that he is man, he is as such chosen by God for salvation . . .

151

not because God owes it to him; not in virtue of any quality or capacity of his own being; completely without claim. [IV, 1, p. 9 f.]

[77] Divine creation is divine benefit. What takes shape in it is the goodness of God. This is the character without which it would not be a work of God. . . .

This statement is not made in the void, nor need it to used with such reserve as is sometimes the case, but it is of essential importance if it is referred to the character proper to creation in virtue of its connexion with the covenant. The process whose fundamental purpose, as we have learnt from the biblical testimony to creation, is the history of salvation which culminates in Jesus Christ, cannot itself be hostile or indifferent, but can only be a benefit and can only be understood as such. . . .

Creation is blessing because it has unchangeably the character of an action in which the divine joy, honour and affirmation are turned towards another. What God has created is as such well done. . . .

This affirmation is not an irresponsible venture. It is not only permitted; it is commanded. We cannot understand the divine creation otherwise than as benefit. We are not free to think and speak in this matter otherwise or even uncertainly and equivocally. The Christian apprehension of creation requires and involves the principle that creation is benefit. It shows us God's good-pleasure as the root, the foundation and the end of divine creation. It suggests the peace with which God separated and protected what He truly willed from what He did not will, and therefore from the unreal. It implies that God Himself, in and with the beginning of all things, decided for His creation and made Himself the responsible Guarantor of it. Creation, as it is known by the Christian, is benefit. . . . We may add in explanation that this statement is demanded and supported by the Christian knowledge of the Lord who alone can be the Creator at the beginning of all things. Who is this Lord? He is the God of Israel who in Jesus Christ has loved man, and sought and found him in his lostness and drawn him to Himself, averting from him the suffering of His righteous judgment, and in grace giving him life with the promise of eternal life. If the God who has expressed and revealed His nature in this way is the Creator, He has already expressed and revealed the same nature as the Creator, not saying No, or Yes and No, but an unqualified Yes to what He has really willed and created. What this God has created is good as such. Only if we lose sight of this God and His nature can we say otherwise. [III, 1, pp. 330–332]

[78] We have referred to the subordination of all creaturely occurrence to the one goal posited by God, which is itself God, and also to the mutual co-ordination of its individual moments and actions as thereby conditioned. Now it is clear that both these concepts involve a thoroughgoing relativisation of all creaturely occurrence. If God gives it His own end and ends, then this means that the occurrence has a significance outside itself. It is not moving in circles, but moving towards a destiny which is posited and given from without, whose fulfilment it can only await as it makes this movement. In the most literal sense creaturely occurrence is only preparatory, i.e., it is engaged in a process. The creature itself cannot decide either why it moves or whither it moves. This decision belongs to God who rules the creature. It is His action which determines the world-process in its true and definitive form. This is in a sense the vertical relativisation of creaturely occurrence. God co-ordinates the various events and the various activities and effects of individual creaturely subjects. He allots to each one its own place and time and function in relation to all the rest. And this means that we can speak of the significance of any one thing only in the light of its connexion with all other things. The individual thing is as it were a word or sentence within a context. It is indispensable to this context. But only within this context does it say what is really intended. Only within this context can it be read and understood rightly. And this is in a sense the horizontal relativisation of creaturely occurrence.

But we must be more precise. The twofold relativisation of creaturely occurrence has reference to its relationship to the rule of God. It is God who arranges for each creature its end and ends. Thus He subordinates all creatures to Himself. And under Himself He co-ordinates all the ends, and therefore all the activities and effects of all creatures into a totality. To this extent all creaturely occurrence and all creatures are relegated to a position of lowliness and dependence and relativity. This means that in themselves they are nothing, and that of themselves they can neither mean anything nor do anything. God is the "yonderside" of all creaturely being and activity from which alone the light and life and power of creaturely occurrence can derive. In relation to God the creature is lowly and dependent and relative. But this position of lowliness and dependence and relativity in relation to God does not involve a degradation or depreciation or humiliation of the creature. To be lowly before God is its exaltation. If it is nothing without Him it is everything by Him : everything, that is, that He its Creator and Lord has determined and ascribed and allotted to it ; everything that He will continue to be for it, and to execute with and by it. And since this is the optimum of light and life and power, making possible its own value and dignity, it is really everything. If we are to understand the divine world-governance rightly, there is one idea that we can never resist too strongly, one notion that we can never reject too sharply. The fact that God causes His will and His will alone to be done in all things, does not mean that the ruling God is an oppressor who grudges it to the creature even to exist at all, let alone to have its own value and dignity over against him. It is the glory of the creature to be lowly in relation to God. For when it is relative to Him, it participates with all its activities and effects in His absoluteness. To be able to serve Him alone with all its activities and in all its joint-effects, to be in His hands and under His control only as a means, an instrument, the clay of the potter—this is its direct and original glory. It is exalted in this necessity ; it is rich in this poverty ; it can go forward on the basis of this humiliation. To exist in any other way but in this relativity towards God would mean misery and shame and ruin and death for the creature. Its full and perfect salvation consists in this subordination to Him, and in this subordination in the co-ordination with its fellow-creatures which is ordained by Him.   [III, 3, 170 f.]

[79] The theological concept of Creator and creating, of creation and creature, must be kept in view. God the Creator must not be equated with a mere manufacturer,

or His work with a manufactured article. The man who makes something, however noble, talented or powerful he may be, can easily leave what he makes to itself, and the more easily the more perfect it is. But the Creator cannot do this in relation to His creature. Between Creator and creature in the sense of biblical theology there is a connexion which makes it impossible for the Creator to leave His work to itself, and makes immediately necessary the reality and knowledge of a second action of the Creator following the first, i.e., His action in the sense of the concept of providence. In no sense is God a creature in Himself. He has in Himself absolutely nothing of the nature of a creature. He does not need a creature to be perfect in Himself. Alongside and apart from Him there can be nothing like Him with its origin, meaning and purpose in itself. Yet on these strict conditions of His own being this God posits Himself as Creator, and apart from and alongside Himself He posits the creature, a reality distinct from Himself. This God who confronts His creature with such transcendence obviously stands, in respect of its continuation and history, in a relationship which could only be contingent and possibly alien to a supreme being or demiurge. The majestic freedom in which the relationship of Creator and creature is grounded is the guarantee of its preservation. The eternity of God is the pledge that He will give it time so long as He wills.

[III, 3, p. 9 f.]

[80] Of all creatures the Christian is the one which not merely is a creature, but actually says Yes to being a creature. Innumerable creatures do not seem to be even asked to make this affirmation. Man is asked. But man as such is neither able nor willing to make it. From the very first man as such has continual illusions about himself. He wants always to be more than a creature. He does not want merely to be under the universal lordship of God. But the Christian makes the affirmation that is demanded of man. . . .

He sees what the others do not see. The world-process in which he participates in solidarity with all other creatures might just as easily be a vain thrusting and tumult without either master or purpose. This is how many see it. But the Christian sees in it a universal lordship.

The lordship might just as easily be that of natural law, or fate, or chance, or even the devil. This is how many see it. But the Christian sees in it the universal lordship of God, of the God who is the Father, who is the Father to him, his Father. He sees the constitutive and organising centre of the process. What makes him a Christian is that he sees Jesus Christ, the Son of God, in the humiliation but also in the exaltation of His humanity, and himself united with Him, belonging to Him, his life delivered by Him, but also placed at His disposal. And seeing Him, he sees the legislative, executive and judicial authority over and in all things. He sees it as the authority of God. He sees it as the authority of the Father. He sees himself subjected to this authority as the one who is united with and belongs to the Son. Only the Christian sees this centre of the world-process. Only the Christian sees at this centre, as the One who has all power in heaven and on earth, the Son of God, and through Him God the Father, and on the circumference himself as a child of the Father for the sake of the Son. The whole Christian community is simply a gathering together by the Word which tells us this and explains and reveals it to us ; a gathering together of those whose eyes are opened to the fact of it. Only the Christian is a member of this community, i.e., one who is gathered together with others by this Word, one whose eyes are opened to this fact. There are some creatures which do not need to have eyes for it because even without seeing it they are carried along by the power of this order and are secure in its peace. There are other creatures which have eyes for it but they will not and cannot open them. But the Christian has open eyes. That is why he has the reality freely and joyfully to confess his creatureliness and his consequent subjection to the universal rule of God without reserve and without claim. What he sees at that centre and on that circumference is not something which frightens him, something which he has to reject. God the Father as the ruling Creator is obviously not an oppressor, and Christ as a subject creature is obviously not oppressed. There is nothing here which need frighten him. There is nothing here which need cause him to flee or rebel. To be wholly and unreservedly under the universal lordship of God, to be wholly and unreservedly a creaturely

156

subject, is not in any sense a constraint, a misfortune, an outrage or a humiliation for the man who as a Christian can see actualised in Jesus Christ both the lordship of God and also the subordination of the creature. For him all attempts to evade this fact are purposeless, and the illusion by which it is obscured or avoided is superfluous. If the relation between the Creator and the creature is the relation which he can see in Jesus Christ, then existence in this relation is the existence which is to be truly desired, an existence in the highest possible freedom and felicity. To have to confess this is not an obscure law, but a friendly permission and invitation. It is not unwillingly but spontaneously, not grudgingly but gladly, that the Christian will affirm and lay hold of this relation and his own existence in it. Hence the reality does not cost him anything. He does not have to force it. He does not have to struggle to attain it. It comes to him in the same way as what he sees comes to him. And this means that he does not screw himself up to a height when he is a real creature. It also means that there does not arise any claim or merit on his part just because he confesses so unreservedly what other creatures and other men cannot and will not confess. The fact that he does so is not a kind of triumph for his individual honesty. Other people are just as honest, perhaps more so. He is simply made real by what he sees. And as such he is simply availing himself of a permission and invitation. He is going through an open door, but one which he himself has not opened, into a banqueting hall. And there he willingly takes his place under the table, in the company of publicans, in the company of beasts and plants and stones, accepting solidarity with them, being present simply as they are, as a creature of God. It is the fact that he sees, and that which he is able to see as the centre and the circumference, the Creator and the creature, which constitute the permission and invitation and open door to his peculiar reality. . . .

In practice, of course, he is faced every day afresh with the riddles of the world-process, with the precipices and plains, the blinding lights and obscurities, of the general creaturely occurrence to which his own life's history also belongs. Of course he can only keep on asking : Whence ? and Whither ? and Why ? and Wherefore ? Of course he has no master-key to all the mysteries of the great process of existence as they crowd in upon him every moment in a new form, to all the mysteries of his own existence as a constituent existence in the historical process of all created reality. On the contrary, he will be the one man who knows that there is no value in any of the master-keys which man has thought to discover and possess. He is the one man who will always be the most surprised, the most affected, the most apprehensive and the most joyful in the face of events. He will not be like an ant which has forseen everything in advance, but like a child in a forest, or on Christmas Eve ; one who is always rightly astonished by events, by the encounters and experiences which overtake him, and the cares and duties laid upon him. He is the one who is constantly forced to begin afresh, wrestling with the possibilities which open out to him and the impossibilities which oppose him. If we may put it in this way, life in the world, with all its joys and sorrows and contemplation and activity, will always be for him a really interesting matter, or, to use a bolder expression, it will be an adventure, for which he for his part has ultimately and basically no qualifications of his own.

And all this is not because he does not know what it is all about, but just because he does know. All this is because he has an " understanding " with the source from which everything derives, from which directly or indirectly everything happens to him ; the " understanding " of the creature with its Creator, which is, for him, that of the child with its father. One thing at least he does not need to puzzle about. About this one thing he has no need to enquire, to be always on the look-out for new answers, new solutions. For he has learned once and for all who is this source, and what basically he can expect from it, and what will always actually come from it. But how the decision is reached, and in what form everything will come as it proceeds from this source, he is as tense and curious as a child, always open and surprised in face of what comes. Yet whatever comes, and in whatever form it comes, he will see that it comes from this one source. However strange it may seem, however irksome in the form in which it comes, he will approve it as coming from this source. He will always be, not perhaps able, but at least willing and ready to perceive the positive—and in the light of its source the most definitely positive—meaning and content of what comes. He will always be willing and ready—again a daring expression—to co-operate with it instead of adopting an attitude of supercilious and dissatisfied criticism and opposition, or, if it were possible, retiring sulkily into a corner as a sceptical spectator. He will always allow everything to concern him directly, and, with all the dialectic of his experiences and attitudes, he will ultimately and basically allow everything to concern him positively. Ultimately and basically he will always be thankful, and in the light of this thankfulness he will look forward to what has still to come. He will always know both what was intended and what is intended. He will always be the child having dealings with its father. This is the knowledge of the Christian in matters of the divine lordship. There is nothing arrogant about it. It remains within the bounds of the reality in which the Christian can know himself—know himself as a creature under the lordship of God like all other creatures. [III, 3, pp. 240–243]

[81] I must again revert to Wolfgang Amadeus Mozart. Why is it that this man is so incomparable ? Why is it that for the receptive, he has produced in almost every bar he conceived and composed a type of music for which " beautiful " is not a fitting epithet : music which for the true Christian is not mere entertainment, enjoyment or edification but food and drink ; music full of comfort and counsel for his needs ; music which is never a slave to its technique nor sentimental but always " moving," free and liberating because wise, strong and sovereign ? Why is it possible to hold that Mozart has a place in theology, especially in the doctrine of creation and also in eschatology, although he was not a father of the Church, does not seem to have been a particularly active Christian, and was a Roman Catholic, apparently leading what might appear to us a rather frivolous existence when not occupied in his work ? It is possible to give him this position because he knew something about creation in its total goodness that neither the real fathers of the Church nor our Reformers, neither the orthodox nor Liberals, neither

the exponents of natural theology nor those heavily armed with the " Word of God," and certainly not the Existentialists, nor indeed any other great musicians before and after him, either know or can express and maintain as he did. In this respect he was pure in heart, far transcending both optimists and pessimists. 1756–1791 ! This was the time when God was under attack for the Lisbon earthquake, and theologians and other well-meaning folk were hard put to it to defend Him. In face of the problem of theodicy, Mozart had the peace of God which far transcends all the critical or speculative reason that praises and reproves. This problem lay behind him. Why then concern himself with it ? He had heard, and causes those who have ears to hear, even to-day, what we shall not see until the end of time—the whole context of providence. As though in the light of this end, he heard the harmony of creation to which the shadow also belongs but in which the shadow is not darkness, deficiency is not defeat, sadness cannot become despair, trouble cannot degenerate into tragedy and infinite melancholy is not ultimately forced to claim indisputed sway. Thus the cheerfulness in this harmony is not without its limits. But the light shines all the more brightly because it breaks forth from the shadow. The sweetness is also bitter and cannot therefore cloy. Life does not fear death but knows it well. *Et lux perpetua lucet* (sic !) *eis*—even the dead of Lisbon. Mozart saw this light no more than we do, but he heard the whole world of creation enveloped by this light. Hence it was fundamentally in order that he should not hear a middle or neutral note, but the positive far more strongly than the negative. He heard the negative only in and with the positive. Yet in their inequality he heard them both together, as, for example, in the Symphony in G-minor of 1788. He never heard only the one in abstraction. He heard concretely, and therefore his compositions were and are total music. Hearing creation unresentfully and impartially, he did not produce merely his own music but that of creation, its twofold and yet harmonious praise of God. He neither needed nor desired to express or represent himself, his vitality, sorrow, piety, or any programme. He was remarkably free from the mania for self-expression. He simply offered himself as the agent by which little bits of horn, metal and catgut could serve as the voices of creation, sometimes leading, sometimes accompanying and sometimes in harmony. He made use of instruments ranging from the piano and violin, through the horn and the clarinet, down to the venerable bassoon, with the human voice somewhere among them, having no special claim to distinction yet distinguished for this very reason. He drew music from them all, expressing even human emotions in the service of this music, and not *vice versa*. He himself was only an ear for this music, and its mediator to other ears. He died when according to the worldly wise his life-work was only ripening to its true fulfilment. But who shall say that after the "Magic Flute," the Clarinet Concerto of October 1791 and the Requiem, it was not already fulfilled? Was not the whole of his achievement ˙implicit in his works at the age of 16 or 18? Is it not heard in what has come down to us from the very young Mozart? He died in misery like an "unknown soldier," and in company with Calvin, and Moses in the Bible, he has no known grave. But what does this matter? What does a grave matter when a life is permitted simply and unpretentiously, and therefore serenely, authentically and impressively, to express the good creation of God, which also includes the limitation and end of man.

I make this interposition here, before turning to chaos, because in the music of Mozart—and I wonder whether the same can be said of any other works before or after— we have clear and convincing proof that it is a slander on creation to charge it with a share in chaos because it includes a Yes and a No, as though orientated to God on the one side and nothingness on the other. Mozart causes us to hear that even on the latter side, and therefore in its totality, creation praises its Master and is therefore perfect. Here on the threshhold of our problem—and it is no small achievement—Mozart has created order for those who have ears to hear, and he has done it better than any scientific deduction could. This is the point which I wish to make.   [III, 3, pp. 297–299]

V. THE DETERMINATION OF MAN

If Jesus Christ is not just one light among others, but the " light of the world," Christian thinking which takes this seriously can find only in this source definitive information concerning man and his nature and goal. Barth thus projects in III, 2 an anthropology which certainly allows that other anthropological sciences and theories can establish and work out phenomena of the human but which derives its decisive definitions of real man from the human being of Jesus Christ. The central definitions of his nature are (1) his fellow-humanity, (2) his being as body and soul in inseparable unity and indissoluble differentiation, and (3) his temporality as a unique opportunity in the span bounded by his beginning and end.

[82] God's glory is the answer evoked by Him of the worship offered Him by His creatures. This is not of their own ability and inclination, their creaturely capacity and good-will, least of all the wisdom and desire of man who is flesh. It derives from the presence of the Creator which is granted to the creature. This is not an idle or unfruitful presence. It is not the presence of a cold confrontation. It is not a presence which leaves blind eyes blind or deaf ears deaf. It is a presence which opens them. It is a presence which also looses at once tongues that were bound. God's glory is the indwelling joy of His divine being which as such shines out from Him, which overflows in its richness, which in its super-abundance is not satisfied with itself but communicates itself. All God's works must be understood also and decisively from this point of view. All together and without exception they take part in the movement of God's self-glorification and the communication of His joy. They are the coming into being of light outside Him on the basis of the light inside Him, which is Himself. They are expressions of the infinite exultation in the depth of His divine being. It is from this point of view that all His creatures are to be viewed both first and last. God wills them and loves them because, far from having their existence of themselves and their meaning in themselves, they have their being and existence in the movement of the divine

self-glorification, in the transition to them of His immanent joyfulness. It is their destiny to offer a true if inadequate response in the temporal sphere to the jubilation with which the Godhead is filled from eternity to eternity. This is the destiny which man received and lost, only to receive it again, inconceivably and infinitely increased by the personal participation of God in man's being accomplished in Jesus Christ. The reaction of God even against sin, the meaning even of His holiness, even of His judgment, the meaning which is not extinguished but fulfilled even in damnation and hell, is that God is glorious, and that His glory does not allow itself to be diminished, to be disturbed in its gladness and the expression of that gladness, to be checked in the overflowing of its fulness. And this is what is expected from all creation because this is the source from which they come. It is in this light that they are to be seen and heard. This is their secret that will one day come out and be revealed. And it is to this that we are always required and will always find it worth our while to attend and look. It is for this revelation that we should always wait. The creature has no voice of its own. It does not point to its own picture. It echoes and reflects the glory of the Lord. It does this in its heights and its depths, its happiness and its misery. The angels do it (and unfortunately we have almost completely forgotten that we are surrounded by the angels as crown witnesses to the divine glory). But even the smallest creatures do it too. They do it along with us or without us. They do it also against us to shame us and instruct us. They do it because they cannot help doing it. They would not and could not exist unless first and last and properly they did this and only this. And when man accepts again his destiny in Jesus Christ in the promise and faith of the future revelation of his participation in God's glory as it is already given Him here and now, he is only like a late-comer slipping shamefacedly into creation's choir in heaven and earth, which has never ceased its praise, but merely suffered and sighed, as it still does, that in inconceivable folly and ingratitude its living centre man does not hear its voice, its response, its echoing of the divine glory, or rather hears it in a completely perverted way, and refuses to co-operate in the jubilation which surrounds him. This is the sin of man which is judged and forgiven in Jesus Christ, which God Himself has made good and cast behind man's back. It is this which in Jesus Christ has once for all become his past. In the eternal glory before us it will not exist at all even as the past. In the eternity before us the groaning of creation will cease, and man too will live in his determination to be the reflection and echo of God and therefore the witness to the divine glory that reaches over to him, rejoicing with the God who Himself has eternal joy and Himself is eternal joy.   [II, 1, pp. 647–649]

[83] And inevitably this distinction of man sheds light at least on earth and heaven and the whole cosmos as well. Man is not the world ; not even a reflection of the world ; not even its epitome or compendium. He is less than this, we said, but we also say that he is more than this. He is the point in the cosmos where, in spite of its very different nature, its relationship to God is illuminated. That the purpose of God towards it is revealed here, cannot be without significance for an understanding of its different nature. Heaven and earth, man's beyond and present, were created by the counsel and the act of God who created man. To the same end ? We have no direct knowledge of heaven and earth to justify us in affirming as much. And yet we affirm it by the indirect knowledge which we owe to our knowledge of man as grounded in the Word of God. He who is the Creator of man is also the Creator of the cosmos, and His purpose towards the latter, although hidden as such, is none other than His revealed purpose for us. Hence in the disclosed relationship of God with man there is disclosed also His relationship with the universe. It is not without significance that in Old and New Testament alike heaven and earth and their elements and inhabitants are always described not only as witnesses but as co-workers in the work of God and that of human praise. This does not rest on a world-view, but on a view of man which sees in him the point in the cosmos where the thoughts of its Creator are disclosed, illuminating man in his totality and also shedding light on the deepest and ultimate force which moves the cosmos—the cosmos which has for us no intrinsic light and cannot reveal the divine plan which governs it.

It is man in covenant with God who reveals this plan. He does so representatively for the whole cosmos. He is not actually alone. He is in the cosmos. He alone sheds light on the cosmos. As he is light, the cosmos is also light. As God's covenant with him is disclosed, the cosmos is shown to be embraced by the same covenant.

[III, 2, p. 18 f.]

[84] The grace of God in Jesus Christ is the noetic basis as and because it is also the ontic basis of man's creaturely being. But here it is both in almost indissoluble unity, and to avoid repetition we may consider it at once in this double quality.

What we really know of man, we know by means of this grace. For how things really stand with man, who and what he is, is grounded in it. What we claim to know about man apart from it, we only claim to know. On a closer examination, it consists only of the working hypotheses of man's self-understanding : perhaps in relation to his being as a natural being beside others and in the context of the being of nature as discernible to us ; perhaps in relation to his being as an ethical rational being with his ability to distinguish himself from nature and to become to a certain extent its master ; perhaps in relation to his being in the act of his existence with the capacity therein demonstrated to limit himself and to that extent to transcend himself in his totality ; or perhaps in relation to his being in the community of the history of his race with his ability to experience history and at the same time to make it. These are all permissible and necessary hypotheses with regard to definite aspects of human being, but they do not solve the question of the common denominator, i.e., of man himself. This question is solved, however, if we set out from the fact that man is the being to whom God is gracious in Jesus Christ. From this there result definitions which certainly do not extinguish as such or even obscure these phenomena of human existence, which do not contradict or render superfluous these working hypotheses of human self-consciousness, which give them a firm basis as hypotheses, but which, as opposed to them, refer to the real man, to man himself. In the fact, revealed to us in God's Word, that God is gracious to man in Jesus Christ, we do not see any of these views of man, either confirmed or questioned, nor do we see any new view of man, but we see man himself, what and how he really is.

This fact includes not only the " Behold your God," but also the *Ecce homo !* It is not only the mirror of the fatherly heart of God, but also of the particularity of man. In what way, and to what extent ? Simply to the extent that in distinction from all mere religion—even that of grace—it is the fact in which the true God is present and revealed in the true man. When we see the glory of God residing in Jesus Christ, then in and with the most high God Himself, we also see man : humbled, accused and judged as a guilty and lost creature, and only as such, only in the fire of judgment, upheld and saved ; but also exalted and glorified as the creature elected and affirmed by God from all eternity. This is real man, man himself in the mirror of God's grace addressed to him in Jesus Christ. [III, 4, p. 41 f.]

[85] This grace of God decides and has already decided concerning our human existence. What does it mean to be a man now that this decision has been reached by the grace of God ? It obviously means to be one who stands and walks and lives and dies within the fact that God is gracious to him, that He has made him His own. It obviously means to be one for whom God has intervened in this way, with whom He has dealt in this way. It obviously means to be one for whose human existence Jesus Christ Himself stands before God according to the will, in the name, and by the commission of God, in all the wisdom and the fulness of the might of God—so stands before God that he is completely covered by Him, completely destroyed both in his weakness and in his self-will, completely offered as a living sacrifice, but in this way made completely holy and completely glorious.

[II, 2, p. 558 f.]

[86] The ontological determination of humanity is grounded in the fact that one man among all others is the man Jesus. So long as we select any other starting-point for our study, we shall reach only the phenomena of the human. We are condemned to abstractions so long as our attention is riveted as it were on other men, or rather on man in general, as if we could learn about real man from a study of man in general, and in abstraction from the

fact that one man among all others is the man Jesus. In this case we miss the one Archimedean point given us beyond humanity, and therefore the one possibility of discovering the ontological determination of man. Theological anthropology has no choice in this matter. It is not yet or no longer theological anthropology if it tries to pose and answer the question of the true being of man from any other angle.

We remember who and what the man Jesus is. As we have seen, He is the one creaturely being in whose existence we have to do immediately and directly with the being of God also. Again, He is the creaturely being in whose existence God's act of deliverance has taken place for all other men. He is the creaturely being in whom God as the Saviour of all men also reveals and affirms His own glory as the Creator. He is the creaturely being who as such embodies the sovereignty of God, or conversely the sovereignty of God which as such actualises this creaturely being. He is the creaturely being whose existence consists in His fulfilment of the will of God. And finally He is the creaturely being who as such not only exists from God and in God but absolutely for God instead of for Himself.

From this knowledge of the man Jesus we have derived the criteria which indicate the limits within which the attempt to attain knowledge of human existence must always move. We have thus been warned against confusing the reality of man with mere phenomena of man. We have been unable to accept those determinations of man in which his relationship to God, his participation in the history inaugurated between him and God, and the glory, lordship, purpose and service of God, are not brought out as the meaning of human life. We have also had to be critical even where the concept of God seemed to play a certainly not unimportant role, but where it remained empty to the extent that there did not emerge anything of His saving action and the related actuality of the being of man. We have now to show the fact and extent that the ontological determination of man results from the fact that one man among all others is this creaturely being, the man Jesus.

Our first point is that the message of the Bible about

this one man has amongst other things this ontological significance. Speaking of this one man, it says of all other men—those who were before Him and those who were after Him, those who knew Him and those who did not know Him or did so only indirectly, those who accepted Him and those who rejected Him—at least that they were and are creaturely beings whom this man is like for all His unlikeness, and in whose sphere and fellowship and history this one man also existed in likeness with them. This means that a decision has been made concerning the being and nature of every man by the mere fact that with him and among all other men He too has been a man. No matter who or what or where he may be, he cannot alter the fact that this One is also man. And because this One is also man, every man in his place and time is changed, i.e., he is something other than what he would have been if this One had not been man too. It belongs to his human essence that Jesus too is man, and that in Him he has a human Neighbour, Companion and Brother. Hence he has no choice in the matter. The question whether and to what extent he knows this Neighbour, and what attitude he adopts to Him, is no doubt important but it is secondary to that which has already been decided, namely, whether he can be a man at all without this Neighbour. Once for all this question has been decided in the negative for every man. We cannot break free from this Neighbour. He is definitely our Neighbour. And we as men are those among whom Jesus is also a man, like us for all His unlikeness.

Theological anthropology must not be so timid that it does not firmly insist on this simplest factor in the situation. Nor must it be so distracted that it suggests every possible and impossible foundation for its thesis except the first and simplest of all, namely, that every man as such is the fellow-man of Jesus. The biblical message to which we must keep is neither timid nor distracted in this respect. It dares to be the message of this one man, and with all that it tells us concerning Him, and obviously in the light of it, it makes the massively self-evident ontological presupposition that the existence of this one man concerns every other man as such, and that the fact that He too is a man is the ground on which every other man is to be

168

addressed and to which every other man is to be kept. It is worth noting that the biblical message never addresses man on any other basis. It does not appeal to his rationality or responsibility or human dignity or intrinsic humanity. No other decisive presupposition is made except that every one who bears the name of man is to be addressed as such in the name of Jesus, and therefore that he stands in an indisputable continuity with Him which is quite adequate as a point of contact. The biblical message reckons with a humanity which as such stands in this continuity, and therefore with man as a being whom we immediately expect to respond to the call to order, to his own order, addressed in the name of Jesus. It reckons only with a creatureliness of man constituted by the fact that one man among all others is this man. This is the ontological undertone which we must not miss if we are to understand why as a message about what this One is and does, and as a message about faith in Him, it is so confident and unreserved, and yet not "enthusiastic" but sober. It speaks in fact about the One who not merely *a posteriori* but *a priori*, from the very outset, is the Neighbour, Companion and Brother of every man.

[III, 2, pp. 132–134]

[87] As the One who has done that, in whom God Himself has done that, who lives as the doer of that deed, He is our man, we are in Him, our present is His, the history of man is His history, He is the concrete event of the existence and reality of justified man in whom every man can recognise himself and every other man—recognise himself as truly justified. There is not one for whose sin and death He did not die, whose sin and death He did not remove and obliterate on the cross, for whom He did not positively do the right, whose right He has not established. There is not one to whom this was not addressed as his justification in His resurrection from the dead. There is not one whose man He is not, who is not justified in Him. There is not one who is justified in any other way than in Him—because it is in Him and only in Him that an end, a bonfire, is made of man's sin and death, because it is in Him and only in Him that man's sin and death are the old thing which has passed away, because it is in Him and only in Him that the right has been done which is

169

demanded of man, that the right has been established to which man can move forward. Again, there is not one who is not adequately and perfectly and finally justified in Him. There is not one whose sin is not forgiven sin in Him, whose death is not a death which has been put to death in Him. There is not one whose right has not been established and confirmed validly and once and for all in Him. There is not one, therefore, who has first to win and appropriate this right for himself. There is not one who has first to go or still to go in his own virtue and strength this way from there to here, from yesterday to to-morrow, from darkness to light, who has first to accomplish or still to accomplish his own justification, repeating it when it has already taken place in Him. There is not one whose past and future and therefore whose present He does not undertake and guarantee, having long since accepted full responsibility and liability for it, bearing it every hour and into eternity. There is not one whose peace with God has not been made and does not continue in Him. There is not one of whom it is demanded that he should make and maintain this peace for himself, or who is permitted to act as though he himself were the author of it, having to make it himself and to maintain it in his own strength. There is not one for whom He has not done everything in His death and received everything in His resurrection from the dead.   [IV, 1, p. 630]

[88] If it is not indifferent, incidental or subordinate but ontologically decisive, that one man among all others is the man Jesus ; if to be a man is to dwell with this man who is our true and absolute Counterpart ; if to be a man is to be concretely confronted with this man who is like us for all that He is so unlike in the full majesty of God, then the fact that we are with God is not merely one of many determinations of our being, derivative and mutable, but the basic determination, original and immutable.

Godlessness is not, therefore, a possibility, but an ontological impossibility for man. Man is not without, but with God. This is not to say, of course, that godless men do not exist. Sin is undoubtedly committed and exists. Yet sin itself is not a possibility but an ontological impossibility for man. We are actually with Jesus, i.e., with God. This means that our being does not include but

170

excludes sin. To be in sin, in godlessness, is a mode of being contrary to our humanity. For the man who is with Jesus—and this is man's ontological determination—is with God. If he denies God, he denies himself. He is then something which he cannot be in the Counterpart in which he is. He chooses his own impossibility. And every offence in which godlessness can express itself, e.g., unbelief and idolatry, doubt and indifference to God, is as such, both in its theoretical and practical forms, an offence with which man burdens, obscures and corrupts himself. It is an attack on the continuance of his own creatureliness : not a superficial, temporary or endurable attack, but a radical, central and fatal attack on its very foundation, and therefore its continuance. His very being as man is endangered by every surrender to sin. And conversely, every vindication and restoration of his relation to God is a vindication and restoration of his being as man. For he himself as a man is with Jesus and therefore with God. He himself stands from the very first and inescapably in the order which this fact implies. He himself is thus upheld if he keeps to this order, and he plunges into the void if he falls away from it.   [III, 2, p. 135 f.]

[89] I could not believe in the Church if in it and by it I did not find hope even for man as such.

We could call this awareness of the destiny of man the Christian conception of humanity. It is distinguished from the Stoic in three ways. First, it is not based on the perception and assessment of a so-called " nature " of man. Second, in ascribing to man as such a *character indelebilis* it does not mean statically a quality of his own. Third, it does not ascribe to him only—which is not enough—a so-called disposition or capacity which may perhaps be developed by instruction and education. It means actually and concretely his destiny, a historical differentiation of man and humanity, which consists in a mission and authorisation, and is fulfilled in an actual confrontation with the Church of Jesus Christ. It was in the light of this historical differentiation that in a particularly impressive way Paul (and, of course, all the mission of the primitive Church) considered the Gentiles. . . . The Church would not take itself seriously if confronting the world it did not regard it as a world already changed by this fact, if it did not find hope for man, not as such and before it has claimed him, but simply because it exists and will claim him. How can it ever cease to see him in advance in the light of " thou wilt," by which it lives itself ? How can it rest towards him in a barren " thou shalt " and therefore " thou art not " ? The Christian conception of humanity is, therefore, a very different one from the Stoic. But it is to be distinguished from it not by a lesser, but by a disproportionately much greater intensity and definition. What kind of power can and will that conception have which deals only with the " nature " of man and the still to be realised possibilities of education which must be weighed against it ? Again and again it will be corroded by a very justifiable scepticism, not only in respect of human nature, but also in respect of all human education. It is only in the Church or from the Church that there has ever been a free, strong, truly open and confident expectation in regard to the natural man, a quiet and joyful hope that he will be my neighbour, a conception of humanity which is based on ultimate certainty.   [I, 2, p. 423]

VI. AGAPE AND EROS

In the self-giving of Jesus Christ fulfilled in His crucifixion, God Himself intervenes for man who cannot help himself, as God the Son obedient to the will of God the Father, as the Judge bearing the judgment for the judged. To this action of God there corresponds on man's side the obedience of faith which accepts what is done (IV, 1). In the assumption of human nature by the incarnation of Jesus Christ God raises fallen man up again and exalts him to be a partner of His covenant and to new life in righteousness. To this action of God there corresponds on man's side the obedience of love in which man, freed for right action, imitates in relation to God and neighbour that which God has done towards him and for him. This is described in the second part of the volume on reconciliation (IV, 2) from which we take the great comparison of agape and eros.

[90] Christian love turns to the other purely for the sake of the other. It does not desire it for itself. It loves it simply because it is there as this other, with all its value or lack of value. It loves it freely. But it is more than this turning. In Christian love the loving subject gives to the other, the object of love, that which it has, which is its own, which belongs to it. It does so irrespective of the right or claim that it may have to it, or the further use that it might make of it. It does so in confirmation of the freedom in respect of itself which it has in its critical beginning. It does so with a radically unlimited liberality. Nor is this liberality confined to that which the loving subject " has." For in Christian love the loving subject reaches back, as it were, behind itself to that which at the first it denies and from which it turns away, namely, itself : to give itself (for everything would lack if this final thing were lacking) ; to give itself away ; to give up itself to the one to whom it turns for the sake of this object. To do this the loving man has given up control of himself to place himself under the control of the other, the object of his love. He is free to do this. It is in this freedom that the one who loves as a Christian loves. Where this movement is fulfilled in all its aspects, and reaches its goal in this self-giving of the loving subject,

173

there is Christian love. And this movement, together with faith (and hope, etc.) and inseparably and simultaneously fulfilled with them, is the life-act of the Christian both in detail and finally as a whole. Its fulfilment is the particular problem of Christian love.

As is apparent from this preliminary analysis, it is very different from any other movement which may have the name of " love " and in its own way is love, but which from first to last takes a very different form and direction. To sharpen the picture of the movement with which we are now concerned, we will attempt a brief analysis of this other kind of love. It does not have its origin in self-denial, but in a distinctively uncritical intensification and strengthening of natural self-assertion. It is in this that the loving subject finds itself summoned and stirred to turn to another. It is hungry, and demands the food that the other seems to hold out. This is the reason for its interest in the other. It needs it because of its intrinsic value and in pursuance of an end. As this other promises something—itself in one of its properties—there is the desire to possess and control and enjoy it. Man wants it for himself : for the upholding, magnifying, deepening, broadening, illuminating or enriching of his own existence ; or perhaps simply in a need to express himself ; or perhaps even more simply in the desire to find satisfaction in all his unrest. And so it takes place that, however much he may seem to give what is his, lavishing and dissipating it on the object of his love, he does not really give it up, but uses it as a means to win or keep or enjoy this object of his love (as the peacock displays its tail before its mate, or the woman exerts, as her own, all her inner and outer, natural and artificial advantages that the man may be hers also). And so it also takes place that the one who loves, however much he may apparently forget himself or however much he may transcend himself (in very high and noble and spiritual transports) in the direction of the object of his love, merely asserts himself the more strongly in face of it as he wins and keeps and enjoys it, since all the time it is himself that he has in view, and his own affirmation and development that he seeks. For all the self-emptying on the part of the one who loves, union with the beloved as the supreme goal of this love consists in the fact that this object of love is taken to himself, if not expressly swallowed up and consumed, so that in the event he alone remains, like the wolf when it has devoured, as it hopes, both Red Riding Hood and her grandmother. The movement of this love takes the form of a circle. It seeks the infinite in a transcendence of everything finite, but from the very first it is disposed in such a way that (even by way of the infinite) it must always return to its beginning. Its objects do not need to be sensual. It may be directed to the good, the true and the beautiful. Even in its sexual form, it may have reference (perhaps wholly and utterly) to the soul and not merely the body. Beyond all other goods and values, it may even reach out to the Godhead in its purest form and thus be a most wonderful love of God. But in all its forms it will always be a grasping, taking, possessive love—self-love—and in some way and at some point it will always betray itself as such.

But as such it is the direct opposite of Christian love—the love which seeks and attains its end as the self-giving of the one who loves to the object of his love. It is no light thing, of course, to dare to criticise and disqualify it from the standpoint of Christian love. For one thing, although Christian love is both permitted and commanded in the case of Christians, in a crude or subtle form (and perhaps both) they all love in this way too, according to the standards of this very different love. Thus they are all the first to be convicted by whatever may be said for the one love and against the other. And they have so much to do to wipe clean their own slate that it will be a long time before they can be too loud in their exaltation of Christian love and condemnation of the theoretical and practical forms of the other (whether Greek or otherwise). But above all reserve is enjoined by the fact that this other love can claim some of the greatest figures in the history of the human spirit, whom it would be a highly questionable enterprise to reject and repudiate in a curt and dogmatic Christianity, especially on the part of those who do not really know them and cannot therefore estimate them at their true worth. It has also to be taken into account that all of us (even we Christians) exist in a world which in its best and finest as well as its most basic phenomena is for the most part built upon this other rather than

175

Christian love, and that we live by the works and fruits and achievements of this love, so that when the Christian calls it in question in the light of Christian love he always takes on a highly ambiguous appearance. What is clearly brought out by this distinction between Christian and every other love as it may be seen—we stress this point—even in the life of the Christian himself, is the wholly alien character of Christianity in relation to the world around.

Yet these considerations must not prevent a sober affirmation of this distinction. Christian love cannot in fact be equated with any other, or with any of the forms (even the highest and purest) of this other, just as this other love has obviously no desire to be confused with Christian. Nor can Christian love be fused with this other to form a higher synthesis. We cannot say of any other love that it is a kind of preparatory stage for Christian love. Nor can we commend Christian love by representing and portraying it as the purified form, the supreme climax, of this other love. There is an element common to both types of love—we shall have to speak of this later. But remarkably enough it is precisely in view of this common element that there must and will always be decision and decisions between them : not only in the history of the Christian community in its relations with the world ; but also in the history of the Christian community itself, which is also of the world, and consists of men who both as a whole and as individuals can be moved by both types, but cannot possibly be moved by both at the same time or in the same way ; and finally and above all in the individual histories of these men themselves.

Even a superficial glance at the two phenomena and concepts, or rather at the realities of the two types of love, necessarily discloses that we have to do here with two movements in opposite directions, so that there can be no harmony but only conflict between them. The first type cannot pass over and be transformed into the second, nor the second into the first. Man loves either in one way or the other, and he has to choose whether it is to be in the one way or the other. If in fact he loves in both ways at the same time, as is often the case even with the Christian, this can only be with the disruption, the " falling out," which we had occasion to discuss in relation to " conversion." Where Christian love enters, there always begins at once the unceasing controversy between itself and every other love. The Christian life is existence in the history of the distinction between these opposing types of love. It has not yet begun, or has been extinguished again, where there is the desire or ability to be superior, or neutral, or tolerant in relation to the two ; where Christian love (perishing as such) can be brought to terms with this other love. Not the moment of this other love as such, but the moment of tolerance, of the agreement of Christian love with this other, of truce in the controversy, constitutes a hiatus, a cessation, a vacuum in the Christian life—a definitely non-Christian moment. There can be only conflict and not compromise between Christian love and this other. And there can be only conflict and not compromise between this other love and Christian.

The biblical basis for this distinction and opposition will emerge, like the material, only as we take up the various themes of the section. Our present task is simply to show that there is always this distinction and opposition.

Nevertheless, we are given a prior indication of the biblical basis when we remember the linguistic usage of the Bible. It is immediately apparent that the New Testament consistently avoids the use of the verb ἐρᾶν and the substantive ἔρως—the terms which in classical Greek plainly describe this other grasping, taking, possessing and enjoying love. Even in the apostolic fathers we find only a single occurrence of ἔρως (Ignatius, ad Rom. 7, 2), and here it is used only to denote the love which the author declares that he has left behind him as crucified. In the New Testament, however, it is not used at all, even in a depreciatory sense. The reader who meets the concept of love in these pages is obviously not even to be reminded of this other love. Apart from an occasional use of φιλεῖν with its emphasis on feeling, the normal term for love in the New Testament is ἀγαπᾶν, with the substantive ἀγάπη, which is unknown in classical Greek and only sparingly used in hellenistic. It is only in New Testament usage that this word has acquired the well-known meaning and content of a love opposed to ἔρως. In itself it is rather colourless. It has something of the sense of the English "like." It speaks of the acceptance or approval of something or someone. Perhaps this lack of distinctive significance was the very reason why it was adopted in the New Testament. It lent itself readily to the receiving of a new impress. But the New Testament was only following the Septuagint, which had had to find a supportable rendering for the verb *aheb* (and substantive *ahabah*), and its synonyms. *Aheb* can describe, with a positive emphasis, all kinds of familiar and friendly relationships. Indeed, in the first instance it is also used for that between a man and his wife, there being a material but no linguistic distinction in Hebrew between the love which is theologically significant and that which was later called "erotic." To avoid the latter, the Septuagint seized on the colourless terms ἀγαπᾶν and ἀγάπη, using them, strangely enough, even in the picture of the marriage between Yahweh and Israel in the Book of Hosea, and even more strangely in the Song of Songs. We can give as a reason for the choice of ἀγάπη only the intention to avoid at all costs the use of ἔρως to describe the love found in these passages. This intention was shared by hellenistic Judaism in its interpretation of the Old Testament and early Christianity in its attestation of Jesus Christ. Whatever we may say concerning ἀγάπη must be determined by the meaning and content which it was desired to give, and which were actually given, to this term (the other being completely eliminated) in the light of the origin, action and manner of this love which has to be so very differently described.

We must not form too impoverished a conception of the love which was linguistically eliminated by the Septuagint and the New Testament because it was the opposite of the kind of love that they were seeking to attest. That is to say, we must not seek it only in sexual love, or in degenerate and excessive forms of this love. The image of life and power and thought which is summed up under the catchword *eros*, and which dominated to a large extent the world of Greek antiquity and even the environment of the New Testament, is a magnitude which does, of course, include sexual love even in its more curious forms, and which no doubt has in this a striking symbol, but which cannot in any sense be understood in its depth and rich-

178

ness, and its dangerous opposition to Christian love, if it is considered exclusively or even preferentially with reference to its actuality in this sphere. Nor is it a magnitude which was potent and effective only in that particular period. On the contrary, although it did, of course, find particularly forceful expression in the Mystery religions and in thinking influenced by outstanding philosophers like Plato and Aristotle and later Plotinus, it is a general and very real human phenomenon which reaches back to the very beginnings of history and forward into every subsequent age, including our own. We are forced to say, indeed, that the warning given already by the biblical usage was largely in vain, and that the positive proclamation of Christian love has been a largely if not wholly futile swimming against the overwhelming flood of *eros*-love. As a proof of its power, *eros* invaded even Christian thought and life from the end of the 2nd century, and has been able to effect very radical and definite penetrations (sometimes with the conscious help or connivance of Christians, but the more effectively where there has been no awareness of its influence). The *caritas* which the Middle Ages had learned decisively from Augustine was a synthesis of biblical *agape* and antique or hellenistic *eros* in which the antithesis between the two can still be perceived, but not in any sense unequivocally, the tension having been largely destroyed with all its beneficial results. This was inevitable. As long as men love, even though they are Christians they will always live within the framework of *eros*, and be disposed to effect a synthesis between *eros* and *agape*, exercising all their powers both great and small to bring this about. . . .

We will now attempt to give some indication, in a few light strokes, of the form in which *eros* confronted and was perceived by the New Testament and later Septuagint-Judaism with their view of love. Who and what was this *eros* ? What was the experience, and action, of the one who loved in this erotic fashion ? This is the form which our question must first assume. We are asking concerning a definite experience and practice. In its origin in Orphism and its myth and mysticism *eros* was something far more than the philosophical concept which was first and unforgettably introduced into Western thought by Plato. *Eros* was a doctrine of redemption and salvation claiming to be revealed, and believed and proclaimed as such. Indeed, it was an experienced actuality of redemption and salvation which found expression both in solemn rites and everyday practice. As such, and hence not unlike Christian *agape*, it could and inevitably did stand in direct opposition to the latter, rousing in its advocates the critical concern so strikingly illustrated by the consistent elimination of the term *eros*. As such it could also provoke the question, which was often to be given a positive answer, whether *eros* and *agape* were not intrinsically comparable and combinable realities, and even at bottom one and the same reality—a view which was first explicitly held by Origen. In the actuality of *eros*, and its varied literature, edifying, poetic or dialectical, mythological or rational, it is always a matter of man, his limitation and its meaning and removal, his existence and transcendence, his need and hope. More precisely, it is always a matter of man hovering but in some sense moving upwards between a lower world and a higher, a world of darkness and a world of light. It is a matter of the experience and practice of this twofold reality. As it is seen and portrayed, this reality consists in his inalienable want and the desire which it kindles, or in his inalienable desire and the want to which it gives rise, as the very essence of this central position. This position is necessarily that of want and desire because it is the centre between his below and above, between his proper and improper being, between his fulness and emptiness, between his being in disintegration and in reintegration with himself. *Eros* is the experienced and self-attained turning from his being down below in darkness and return to his being up above in light. *Eros* is the power and act in which he must lose himself on the one hand to find himself again on the other. And so *eros* is a hypostatised form of man himself in this central position and the movement—the turning from and to— which is commensurate with it. As this hypostasis of man himself, the dæmon of man, powerful and manifest in him and known and expressed by him, *eros* is understood as a, and finally *the*, metaphysical link ($\mu\epsilon\tau\alpha\xi\acute{v}$) between the world of appearance and the world of reality, as the sum of the movement from the one to the other.

It was explained along these lines by Aristotle, who in this respect was more consistent than Plato. As he saw it, it is not merely an anthropological but a cosmological principle. It is the impulse in the power of which—at this point the concept of *eros* verges on that of entelechy—not merely psychic individuals but all cosmic elements, even the lower and higher physical bodies, strive after form in their materiality, actuality in their potentiality and the unmoved One in their movement and plurality, thus seeking their normal state, and being engaged in a universal dissolution and ascent. Plato was more restrained in his depiction of this great turning away and return, confining his gaze to the seizure and exercise of power by *eros* in man. On his view, in the visible *eidola* of transitory things and their relative values, there encounters man, not in visible form but perceptible to the enlightened eye, the *eidos*, the absolute value of that which immutably is, the beautiful, by which he is both attracted and impelled and therefore set in movement. How can he tarry with the *eidola* without being forced to flee them at once in the direction of the *eidos*? It is only for the sake of the *eidos* that he can love the *eidola*. But again, how can he flee them for the sake of the *eidos* without being forced to tarry with the *eidola* which have a distinct part in the beauty of the *eidos*? For its sake he may and must love them too. Plotinus brought out very strongly the religious significance of the *eros*-actuality, although here again we see affinities with originally platonic notions. His main contribution was to expand the theory to the point of maintaining that there is a departure of the soul from the higher world prior to its ascent from the lower, or an emanation of the soul from the deity prior to its return from the world, so that the want and desire, the turning from and to, the being in vacillation between world-denial and world-affirmation, can be described as a homecoming, as a return of the soul to its origin and therefore to itself— an innovation which merely serves to reveal the circular movement to which the practice and theory of the *eros*-actuality were exposed from the very outset. It is the actuality of the man who in his relationship to being both visible and invisible, and finally in his relationship to the Godhead, is engaged in realising his own entelechy, i.e., in needing and therefore in seeking, desiring and successfully finding and enjoying himself in his particularity. As he knows and approves and takes himself seriously in this actuality, as he presupposes himself in this form, he orders and understands the process of his life, and therefore loves.

This was the ἐρᾶν and ἔρως with which the authors of the New Testament and the translators of the Old before them refused to equate their own understanding of " love." In the foregoing sketch we have not touched on the concrete difficulties, the intellectual, moral and religious dangers and the corruptive effects which seemed to be involved in practice when the two types of love came face to face. The contrast between *agape* and *eros* arises even when we have to do with the latter in its essential nature and not in its degenerate form, in the vulgarisations to which that which Plato, Aristotle and Plotinus saw and understood as love was submitted on the streets and in the temples and dwelling-places of the antique and hellenistic world. If we are not merely to conceive but to grasp what Christianity and its " love " so resolutely rejected, nothing less than the best of what is held out to us by the plastic works of the time will suffice. If we do not take this into account, but capriciously restrict ourselves to the particular and very obvious antithesis between *agape* and the sinful forms of sexual love or even its most degenerate manifestations, then we shall not understand the consistency (so incisive in its very silence) with which *eros* is completely ignored in the language of the Bible, nor the fact that this could become so important a matter in the Christian sphere, nor finally the necessity of thinking and speaking of Christian love in a restrained and sober manner, i.e., on the basis of its own presuppositions, and therefore not in the *schema* of the actuality and doctrine of *eros*, and therefore not along orphic, platonic, aristotelian or neo-platonic lines. We have to do here with an opponent whom we must estimate at his true stature, and whom we can fully appraise as an opponent only if we do so.

We cannot be content, however, merely to state that there is a difference and antithesis between Christian and every other love. As we bring this introduction to a close we will thus turn to the question at what point and in what sense the two loves diverge. Unless we do this we cannot understand their relationship and antithesis, nor can we understand either *eros* on the one side or *agape* on the other. But to ask concerning this critical point is to ask concerning a common place from which they both come. We cannot ask concerning a place where they can be seen together and understood as components, as partial forms and aspects, of one and the same reality, and therefore in the last resort as one. The question of an original point of identity necessarily involves that of a synthesis compelling to a new identification which *eros* as well as *agape* (being what they are both in actuality and conception) must very definitely resist. Yet we can and must ask concerning the point from which they both come in their true nature, and can therefore be seen in full antithesis. We can and must ask concerning the point from which they cannot possibly co-exist in compromise or mutual tolerance, but only in the history of their controversy. We cannot fathom this matter unless we put this question and make some attempt to answer it. . . .

An obvious answer, and one which is not without real content, is that on both sides—whether we are thinking of *eros* or *agape*—we have to do with man, and with one and the self-same man in the case of the Christian. It is man who loves either in the one way or the other, or in both ways in the Christian conflict between the two. However sharply we may see and define the difference, there is no question of the love of two different beings, or even of different individuals 'when we are dealing with Christians. In this very different and even antithetical determination, direction and form we have to do with the same human being. It is always man who encounters us in the two forms.

This does not mean, in the case of either determination, that the two are peculiar to or inherent and grounded in the nature of man. We can say this neither of *eros* nor *agape*. Neither the one nor the other rests on a possibility of human nature as such. Neither the one nor the other is a perfection of human nature achieved or to be achieved in the actualisation of such a possibility. We can only say and must say—and we now take a second step—that they are both historical determinations of human nature. It is the same human nature which, as man loves in one way or the other, shows itself to be capable of this or that form of love, not with a capacity which is proper to it, but with one which is (shall we say) generally contingent to it, i.e., which comes upon it, in the history and existence of man. It is merely the case that man does actually express himself in the form of *eros* or *agape* or (in the case of the Christian) the two in contradiction ; and that to this extent (in view of the fact that he actually does so) he can express himself in this way. It is merely the case that man does always encounter us in these two forms of love, and to this extent in the corresponding forms of his nature.

He does so in a definite expression of his nature—this is the third step that we have to take. What actually comes upon him as the one who loves in the one way or the other is a distinct and even antithetical determination and direction of the act in which he himself, existing as the man he is, gives expression to his nature in its totality. . . .

Neither in *eros* nor *agape* therefore—this is the fourth step—can there be any question of an alteration of human nature. Whether he loves in the one way or the other he is the same man engaged in the expression of the same human nature. What comes upon him in his history, in the fulfilment of his self-expression, is the fact that in the two cases he is the same man in very different ways. As in neither case God ceases to be the Creator, in neither case does man cease to be the creature that God willed and posited when He made him a man, with the structure of human nature. Whatever form the history of man may take, there is broken neither the continuity of the divine will for man nor that of the nature which man is given by God. And although this may be seen in very different ways in the two forms of his loving, it can be seen in both of them. The only thing is that the human act is very different in the two cases. The only thing is that, as man loves in one way or the other, it comes upon him that the one unchangeable, perennial human nature is put by him to a very different use and given a very different character. The basis of the difference is not to be found in itself (so that it cannot be explained in terms of itself or deduced from itself), but in its historical determination.

Concerning this difference in the use and character of
184

human nature in *eros*-love on the one hand and *agape*-love on the other, we have first to make—the fifth step—a formal statement. We can and must speak of the difference of the new thing (in relation to human nature) which, as a matter of historical fact, overtakes or comes on man as he loves in the one form or the other. Without being grounded in his nature, this act of love takes place in a distinctive relationship to it, to that which makes him a man. This is not by a long way the whole of what has to be said about this love. Our present enquiry concerns only the common point of departure where comparison is possible, and at once becomes impossible, between the two ways of loving. The common point of departure consists in the fact that they both take place in relationship to the human nature chosen and willed and posited and ordered by God. They are both new in relation to this human nature, but they both take place in connexion with it. They are together in this relationship, and therefore comparison is possible. But they diverge in it, and therefore comparison becomes utterly impossible. The decisive statement must be ventured—decisive for the distinction— that *agape*-love takes place in correspondence and *eros*-love in contradiction to this nature ; the one as its "analogue " and the other as its " catalogue " ; the one as man does that which is right in relation to it, and the other as he does that which is not right in relation to it. *Agape*-love takes place in affinity, *eros*-love in opposition, to human nature. As we see, they both take place in relationship to it (and in this they can be compared). But in the one case the relationship is positive, in the other negative (so that they cannot be compared). In this antithetical use and character, in which the one unchanging human takes on form but which differ as Yes and No, being related only in respect of their object, *eros* and *agape* go their divergent ways.

This formal statement requires material clarification and substantiation in two directions which demand attention in this question. Our starting-point for a sixth step is that it is essential, natural and original to man, that it belongs to his very structure as this particular creature of God, to be with God, who is His Creator and Lord, as with his eternal Counterpart : deriving wholly from this

God, participating from the very first and in all circumstances (as His elect) in His preservation and effective help, and being sheltered absolutely by Him and in Him; and moving wholly towards Him, thanking Him (as the one who is called by Him), in responsibility before Him and obedience to Him, calling upon His name. From this vertical standpoint, as it were, the very nature and essence of man is to be freed by and for this God; to be engaged in the act of this twofold freedom (cf. *C.D.*, III, 2, § 44, 3). Man cannot escape or destroy or lose or alter the fact that it is only in this that he is truly and naturally and essentially a man. But in the life-act of every man (both as a whole and in detail) it is decided whether and to what extent, in relationship to that which he really is in his togetherness with God, he is true or untrue, in correspondence or contradiction, to himself (from this standpoint his being from God and to God). It is in this decision that there arises the new thing either of his *agape*-love in which he corresponds to his being from and to God or of his *eros*-love in which he contradicts it. In this respect *agape*-love consists in the fact that he accepts God as his eternal Counterpart, and therefore his own being as that of one who is elected by this God, being absolutely sheltered by His preservation and help, but who is also called by Him to thanksgiving, responsibility, obedience and prayer. It consists in the fact that he is determined and ready to live from and to God to the best of his knowledge and capacity: not raising any claim; not trying to control God; not with the ulterior motive of winning God for himself or demanding anything from Him; but simply because He is God, and as such worthy to be loved. *Agape* consists in the orientation of human nature on God in a movement which does not merely express it but means that it is transcended, since in it man gives himself up to be genuinely freed by and for God, and therefore to be free from self-concern and free for the service of God. *Eros*-love consists in this respect in the new thing (which is absurd in relation to human nature) that man shuts off himself against this freedom. In it he prefers a being from and by and in and for himself to togetherness with God as his eternal Counterpart, and makes God the origin of this self-inflated and self-enclosed being. In it he thus fabricates his God out of the compulsion and impulsion to this being, and therefore his own caprice. In the name of this reflection he chooses himself as the basis from which he comes, and therefore accepts the whole burden and responsibility for his help and preservation, for the securing and sheltering of his being. He also makes himself his goal, and therefore finds no place for thanksgiving, responsibility, obedience and calling upon God, but transposes them into a desire and longing and striving and transcending in which he spreads himself with some degree of coarse or refined appetite and more or less skill and consistency in the sensual and spiritual world, using it and making it serviceable to himself, as his environment, as that which satisfies his needs, as a place to sow and reap, as his sphere of work, or it may be only as his gymnasium and playground. *Eros* is love which is wholly claim, wholly the desire to control, wholly the actual attempt to control, in relation to God. This is inevitable, seeing it is the love in which the one who loves and the object of love are one and the same, so that from first to last it is self-love. In both cases we are dealing with love, even with the love of God, although in very different senses. In both cases it is love in relation to that which is essential to man, to that which is peculiar to him in his nature as it is formed and fashioned by God. The difference is that *agape* (irrespective of its strength or weakness) corresponds to this nature, and *eros* (irrespective of its form or intensity) contradicts it. The one transcends it; the other falls short of it. It will always be the case in practice that human nature orientated on God, and therefore *agape* as its correspondence, will be recognisable even in the negative of the most radical form of the contradiction and therefore of *eros*; and on the other hand that the most perfect form of the correspondence, and therefore *agape*, will reflect to some extent the contradiction, and therefore *eros*, in and with human nature. Yet the distinction, and the necessity of deciding, between them is perfectly clear from that which they have conceptually in common, and in the way in which they accompany one another in practice.

The starting-point for a seventh and final step is that it is essential and natural to man not only to be with God but also, on the horizontal level and in analogy with this

187

togetherness with God, to be with his fellow-man : not in isolation ; not in opposition or neutrality to this other ; not united with him in a subsequent relationship ; but bound to him basically and from the very first ; directed, that is, to the I-Thou encounter, in which there can be no I without the Thou, no man without the fellow-man, any more than there can be any man without God. He is a man as he sees the other man and is seen by him ; as he hears him and speaks with him ; as he assists him and receives his assistance. He is a man as he is free to do this ; as he can be a comrade and companion and fellow to the other, not under constraint, but voluntarily (cf. *C.D.*, III, 2, § 45, 2). In this respect, too, the nature of man is immutable, quite independently of his history. But in this respect, too, in indissoluble relationship with his decision in the connexion with God, it is decided in the history and life-act of man whether and how far he is true or untrue, in correspondence or contradiction, to his nature, to his humanity in this special sense, and therefore to himself. And in this connexion, too, *agape* means correspondence and *eros* contradiction. In *agape*-love the essential fellow-humanity of man is respected. For the one who loves in this way there can be no opposition or neutrality in relation to the other. In his love there takes place the encounter of I and Thou, the open perception of the other and self-disclosure to him, conversation with him, the offering and receiving of assistance, and all this with joy. In this respect, too, the real man is at work in *agape*, not merely expressing but transcending his nature. In this respect, too, *agape* means self-giving : not the losing of oneself in the other, which would bring us back into the sphere of *eros* ; but identification with his interests in utter independence of the question of his attractiveness, of what he has to offer, of the reciprocity of the relationship, or repayment in the form of a similar self-giving. In *agape*-love a man gives himself to the other with no expectation of a return, in a pure venture, even at the risk of ingratitude, of his refusal to make a response of love, which would be a denial of his humanity. He loves the other because he is this other, his brother. But as the one who loves in this way sees a brother in his fellow, and treats him as such, he also honours him as a man. While *agape* transcends humanity, the man who loves in this way is genuinely human ; he gives a true expression to human nature ; he is a real man. The same cannot be said of *eros*-love. In most cases this does, of course, consist in an address to one's fellow, and perhaps with considerable warmth and intensity. But as in relation to God, so also to his fellow, the man who loves erotically is not really thinking of the other but of himself. His fellow is envisaged only as an expected increase and gain for his own existence, as an acquisition, a booty, a prey, to be used by him in the pursuance of some purpose. In these circumstances how can he really be a comrade, companion and fellow ? How can he see him openly, or disclose himself to him ? How can he enter into honest conversation with him ? How can he assist him and receive his assistance ? It is only in semblance and not in truth that the one who loves erotically is well-disposed to him. As he grasps at him, he has already let him fall and rejected him. And it is inevitable that sooner or later he will do this openly. In the duality apparently sought and found by the one who loves erotically there lurks the isolation which he has never really left and in which he will finally remain. Erotic love is a denial of humanity. To be sure, it is love ; love for man ; an action in relationship, in this relationship, to humanity. Hence humanity and to that extent *agape* may be negatively seen in it, and it may be confessed in this perverted form ; just as *agape*-love as the act of man in his human nature is never so pure as not to betray in some way the proximity of the *eros*-love which is its opposite. Yet the two loves are still different—basically different in their relationship to humanity. And since they have this common point of departure from which they both come, it will always be the case that man can only choose between *eros* and *agape*. . . .

Since *agape* is from God—as we shall see in the next sub-section—and *eros* from self-contradictory man, is it not one of the things which make comparison impossible that the former is absolutely superior to the latter, not only in dignity, but also in power ? *Eros* can only flee and perish and cease, and with it the whole world which is dominated and impelled and built up and characterised by

189

it. But love, *agape*, never fails (1 Cor. 13⁸). With that which issues from it (as it does from God), it is imperishable even in the midst of a world which perishes.

For this reason, our final word can and must be conciliatory as we look back on our development of the problem of Christian love and therefore of its antithesis to *eros*. There can be no question of mediation, or of a weakening of the antithesis. But we can speak a word of reconciliation, not in respect of *eros*, but in respect of erotic man contradicting himself and shunning and opposing God and his neighbour. *Agape* cannot change into *eros*, or *eros* into *agape*. The one love cannot, then, be interpreted as the other. But if this is impossible, it is even more impossible that God should change into, or be interpreted as, another God who is no longer the God of man, even of the man who loves erotically ; and that this man should cease to be man, and therefore the creature elected and willed and fashioned by God, and therefore in the hands of God even in his corruption. But if he is in the hands of God, even erotic man must and will be affirmed in and with the love which is from God—Christian love. His erotic love will not be affirmed. But he himself will be affirmed as the man which he does not cease to be even as he loves erotically—God's man. And this affirmation proclaims his reconciliation ; the fact that God has loved, and loves, and will love even him. How can we love as Christians if we forget this, if we do not hold out this affirmation, this proclamation, even to the one who loves erotically ? How we judge ourselves—for we, too, love erotically—if we withhold this affirmation from the heathen who in contrast know no other love ! But if we love as Christians, and therefore with the love which is from God, and therefore in self-giving to God and our fellows, then in respect of the man who loves erotically our love must consist wholly and utterly in this affirmation : in the declaration that he, too, is loved by God and therefore in His hands ; that overlooking his erotic love God in His genuine, non-self-seeking love is the One who in His self-giving wills to be God only as his God, God for him, and to be majestic, all-powerful and glorious as such. If Christian love does not make this declaration to the non-Christian, it is not Christian love. It stops where the love of God, from which it derives, does not stop. And in so doing it parts company with the love of God. If a Christian believes, as he can and should, that he himself is not separated from the love of God by the fact that he loves erotically, he cannot refuse this declaration to the fellow-man whom he thinks he sees wholly entangled in the bands of *eros*-love.

The concrete content of this declaration, and therefore of the conciliatory word with which we must close our consideration of the antithesis between *agape* and *eros*, is to the effect that God simply espouses the cause of man, and therefore even the man who loves erotically. But this means that he understands him—far better than he understands himself. He cares for him—far better than he cares, or can care, for himself. This is how it is when he calls him out of the kingdom of *eros* and into the kingdom of His love, which consists in the act of self-giving and not in a campaign of aggression. And this is how it must be between the Christian and the non-Christian, the man who loves erotically. It is not a question of subjecting man to an alien, cold and gloomy law, in the following of which he will be afraid of falling short, and can expect only to be invaded and disarmed and oppressed and destroyed, so that he has every reason to try to evade it. There is no reason for this. For it is a matter of his liberation when God loves him—even him—in spite of his corruption, and calls him to decision in favour of *agape* against *eros*. This call is a message of light and not dark-ness, of promise and not threat, of joy and not sorrow. What is it, then, that the man who loves erotically wills and desires and seeks and strives after ? What is it that he would achieve and maintain ? We have seen that in the circle in which he turns to the natural and spiritual world, to God and his fellow-man, it is first and last him-self. May he not, then, be himself ? Will God refuse him this ? Can the God who has created him as he is refuse it ? Most certainly not. The truth is that he can never in all eternity find himself, his being as this self in the world before God and among his fellows, but, chasing his own shadow, can and will only lose it in all eternity, so long as he tries to will and desire and seek and strive after and achieve and maintain himself as the erotic man thinks it necessary to do. The love which is from God, the Christian love in which man can respond to the love of God, is his liberation from this supposed necessity, his dispensation from this forward-seeking in need and desire, his release from the obligation of this chase in which he is both the hunter and the hunted and which for this reason can only be utterly futile. Man can cease from this self-willing, and therefore from all the frenzied activity in which he can seek, yet never find, but only lose himself. For if the only meaning of life is that man must seek himself to find himself, he can only lose himself in this seeking, and life is meaningless. Christian love is his deliverance because the one who loves as a Christian gives up trying to save himself, to be his own deliverer. In Christian love a man can finally leave that circle of destruction, which is in the true sense a vicious circle. And not become himself? Quite the contrary! It is only in this way that he can and will become himself. To renounce that seeking, to leave that circle, is indeed a *conditio sine qua non* of Christian love. But positively this love is man's self-giving to God (not for what He can give, nor for the sake of some purpose that can be achieved with His help, but for God Himself), and his self-giving to his fellow (again, not for what he can give, nor for the sake of some purpose, but for the man himself). As this self-giving, the Christian love which is from God is man's response to God's own love. It is in this way that God loves man. He does not seek Himself, let alone anything for Himself, but simply man, man as he is and as such, man himself. And God does not in any sense fall short of Himself when He loves in this way. In this self-giving to man He is God in all His freedom and glory. If the love of man, as his response to the fact that God loves him in this way, itself consists in his self-giving, this certainly means that there can be no more self-love, no more desiring and seeking the freedom and glory of the self. But why, and how far, is this really the case? Simply because he has already found himself in great freedom and glory. What he cannot win by desiring and seeking, he has already attained, not in the power of his renunciation, but in the power of the self-giving in which he may respond to the love of God. He *himself* is the one who is loved by God. He *himself* is the one to whom God has given Himself in His Son, and gives Himself as He gives him His Holy Spirit. He is cut off from *eros*-love, and taken out of that circle, by the fact that, loving as a Christian, he is already at the place which he was vainly trying to reach in the Icarus-flight and self-assertion of *eros*-love. There is no further point in erotic love. *Eros* is made superfluous by the *agape* in which man may find himself and therefore has no more need to seek himself. He himself discovers himself to be secure in his response to the love of God.

It is obvious that at this point a second and theoretically more dangerous aberration would be worse than the first. I cannot try to love as a Christian in order to attain the goal and end which escapes me as one who loves erotically. An *ut finale* necessarily means a relapse into *eros*-love. The only valid *ut* is the radiant *ut consecutivum*. But this is indeed valid, and it makes any such relapse quite impossible. For in Christian love I am already at the goal. I have found myself, and cannot therefore lose myself by trying to love as a Christian in order to come to myself.

I have only to love continually as a Christian, and therefore without regard or purpose for myself, in self-giving to God and my fellows, and I will come to myself and be myself. This is what we are told in the saying in Mk. 8[35], which speaks about the saving and losing and the losing and saving of life ; and also in the saying in Mt. 6[33], which tells us that if we seek first the kingdom of God and His righteousness all other things are added to us. These sayings are not Law but Gospel. They describe the *agape* which conquers *eros* by making it pointless and superfluous. They describe the man who loves as a Christian as already at the goal which the man who loves erotically— poor dupe—wants to reach but never can or will reach in erotic love. They make no demand. They take nothing away. They do not blame or judge. They merely show him that he is understood and accepted and received by God—not his erotic love, but he himself. He may save himself and find himself and be himself. But this is something which is given, which comes, as he loses his life, as he renounces his whole self-seeking—" for my sake and the gospel's "—so that he is saved and has found himself already.   [IV, 2, pp. 733–751]

193

VII. MAN AND WOMAN

Because man is not merely a creature, but the knowledge derived from the reality of Jesus Christ shows that he is designed by God to be a covenant-partner and exists and can exist as man only in this covenant-relationship, real man is never solitary but is always man in relation, confronted by another for whom he exists, namely, God and the fellow-man. To be a fellow-man is the decisive determination of the nature of man. In the creaturely sphere this is revealed in the indissoluble bi-sexuality of man. Hence Barth gives to this phenomenon extended consideration (in III, 1, III, 2 and III, 4). What he has to say about the anthropological significance of the relationship of man and woman is a good example of the way in which his dogmatic insights produce ethical directions, the knowledge of the act of God for us leading to knowledge of His command to us. The selected passages on man and woman are the basis of Barth's thinking on questions of marriage and sexual life.

[91] The first and typical sphere of fellow-humanity, the first and typical differentiation and relationship between man and man, is that between male and female. . . .

Reflection upon the creaturely being of man as a co-existence of man and fellow-man confirms this reference. There are also other types of differentiation and relationship between man and man. But this relationship alone rests on a structural and functional distinction. So much cannot be said of the relationship between father and son or mother and daughter, nor of the relationship between men of different ages or different gifts and dispositions, nor of that between various peoples and historical epochs. Only that between man and woman rests upon a structural and functional difference. Notice that the distinction is merely structural and functional. It does not call in question the fact that male and female are both human. But structurally and functionally it is too clear and serious to be a mere variation upon a theme common to both— a neutral and abstract humanity which exists and can be considered independently. Man never exists as such, but always as the human male or the human female. Hence in humanity, and therefore in fellow-humanity, the decisive, fundamental and typical question, normative for all other relationships, is that of the relationship in this

194

differentiation. This is just as clear and serious as the distinction. For the differentiation itself, for all its incomparable depth, is one long reference to the relationship. We have to say both that man is necessarily and totally man *or* woman, and that as such and in consequence he is equally necessarily and totally man *and* woman. He cannot wish to liberate himself from the differentiation and exist beyond his sexual determination as mere man ; for in everything that is commonly human he will always be in fact either the human male or the human female. Nor can he wish to liberate himself from the relationship and be man without woman or woman apart from man ; for in all that characterises him as man he will be thrown back upon woman, or as woman upon man, both man and woman being referred to this encounter and co-existence. No other distinction between man and man goes so deep as that in which the human male and the human female are so utterly different from each other. And no other relationship is so obvious, self-explanatory and universally valid as that whose force resides precisely in the presupposed underlying otherness. The female is to the male, and the male to the female the other man and as such the fellow-man. It is with reason, therefore, that we first enquire what the divine command has to say in this sphere of fellow-humanity. [III, 4, p.117f.]

[92] It will serve to clarify and temper our understanding of the question if we begin by stating what it means, generally and fundamentally, that in this sphere too man is confronted by the divine command.

Consider the myths and sagas, the rites and customs, of so many religions in relation to this particular point. Think of the speculation of so much philosophy, psychology and poetry. Think finally of the tumult and violence of emotions which cannot be quite strange to any one who is slightly acquainted with this field, even though he be not capable of expressing them in happy and systematic form. These all point to the fact that here, more than anywhere else, man seems at least to stand on the threshold of a kind of natural mysticism. What else can stir him so much, bringing him as he thinks—whether he be a crude or a highly cultivated person—into such ecstasy, such rapture, such enthusiasm, into what seem to be the depths and essence of all being, into the vision of the Godhead and participation in it, supposedly exalting him into the vicinity at least of another God and Creator—what else can do this like the primal experience of encounter between male and female? Perhaps it is this experience itself in any one of its possible forms and varying degrees, perhaps it is a sublimation, transposition or spiritualisation of it— but always it is the experience of this encounter! Why this experience precisely? If we understand what is at issue here, we shall not ask. It is obviously on account of the truly breath-taking dialectic which arises in this encounter—the dialectic of difference and affinity, of real dualism and equally real unity, of utter self-recollection and utter transport beyond the bounds of self into union with another, of creation and redemption, of this world and the next. If humanity spells fellow-humanity and fellow-humanity is primarily experienced in this dialectic, how tempting it is to understand and experience this fellow-humanity as the bold and blessed intoxication of the deepest abasement and the supreme exaltation of human essence, as its deification! Is man not God to the extent that his being is being in this encounter?

But the command of God has precise reference to the being of man in this encounter. It is rewarding to linger a moment over this fact. Whatever the command requires of a man, it is the command of *God*. It shows that the throne of the true God is already occupied. It brings the real beyond into the picture. It makes us realise that there can be no question of man's experiencing himself as God, that the divine with which man would like to equate himself in the experience of this encounter can only be a miserable idol, a Baal or an Astarte, an Osiris or an Isis. It puts man in his place and confines him within his limits. It marks him as a creature. Even in the depths and heights, the self-recollection and rapture, the immanence and transcendence of this primal experience he is still a creature. And whatever the command wills of him, it is the *command* of God. An alien and superior will confronts him at this climax of his self-affirmation and self-denial, in this immanence and transcendence. It shows him that in all the seriousness and rapture of this dialectic he is still not his own master. In face of the dialectic which transports him it reveals a higher and impregnable place, and it lets it be understood that from this place there is One who rules, commands, permits and also forbids. From this place there is heard in the voice of the Law, in the midst of the storms of passion or the whispers of sublimated ecstasy, a critical and judicial Yes and No by which man is tested and must test himself.

What is the implication of this ? First and supremely, it obviously means that in this sphere he is not without a Master nor abandoned by his Creator ; that he does not here find himself plunged into a demonic world, into an abyss or jungle, but is at home and under the rule of his heavenly Father. Were it otherwise, God would not show him the grace to be present with him as a Ruler at this point too and in this matter. Where God is concerned for him, man and his humanity are not lost. He is still at home. It is still at bottom a question of things that are natural and right. If the command of God is relevant to the relationship of male and female, this means that God is concerned for man in this respect too. Here too, therefore, man is not lost but in his native sphere, and it is essentially a question of things that are natural and right.

Secondly, it is clear that the command of God which is relevant in this sphere, no matter what it prescribes, implies the radical relativisation of this encounter, and of the being of man in this encounter ; not its negation or destruction, but its radical relativisation. As the command enters the picture there is implied on the one hand a demythologisation of this field. If such a process is anywhere necessary, it is so here, where so many gods or demigods or partial gods try to speak and rule. The command of God carries through this process of demythologisation, and it does so radically. It sets aside these gods with a wave of the hand. It unmasks them as elemental spirits. It explains them naturally. What remains is man as the creature standing as such under his determination to be in this encounter, as male or female and as male and female, in this natural dualism. And it remains for man to confirm this natural dualism. On the other hand, the entry of the command of God means the ordering of this sphere. Whatever it asks of man, it certainly requires him to affirm this natural dualism ; not to deny

197

it nor to pervert it, but simply to express and reveal it as it is in his existence. As he does so, this sphere, and man within it, comes under control, and the task of man—for it is his own affair—is to exercise this control. To do so is the act of obedience required of him.

And now, thirdly, the fact that man is faced by the divine command at this point, too, implies that here again he is directed to freedom. He may be in the encounter of man and woman. He need not be afraid or ashamed of it. He need not have a bad conscience about the fact that his life is lived on this plane. He may relate himself to it as to everything else which concerns his human existence. He may even accept the fact that this seems to be a particularly exalted, important and beautiful aspect of his being. He may simply affirm this aspect. He may be a man in this respect too. He does not need any ecstasy or enthusiasm, any mysticism, rapture or deification, to accept this determination. He can and may take the dialectic in all seriousness. But he can and may spare himself the convulsions, pains and complications which would be inevitable if it were a question of a metaphysical and absolute dialectic, if in this dialectic he felt the desire and obligation to be himself God and his own master. In this respect, too, he may be man—only man, but real man. As God gives him His command at this point, as He is concerned for him and submits him to that radical relativisation, He gives him here too this freedom.

[III, 4, pp. 119–121]

[93] But what is the man in his sex and the woman in hers ? When it is not a question of psychology, pedagogy, hygiene and the like, but of ethics, of theological ethics, and therefore of the command of God, we cannot and may not prejudge the issue with an abstract definition. Man and woman as the man willed and created by God and now summoned by Him and placed under His command are in themselves as much and as little capable of description as the human individual in his particularity over against another. Male and female being is the prototype of all I and Thou, of all the individuality in which man and man differ from and yet belong to each other. We can, of course, denote the human individual with the demonstrative " this " or " that " or " the same." We can call

198

man and woman " he " and " she." We can describe
individual men and women by their Christian names and
surnames, their date of birth, family, birthplace or titles.
But we have to realise that when we say all this we merely
point to something which cannot be expressed, to the
mystery in which man stands revealed to God and to Him
alone. It is at the point where he is indefinable that he is
sought and found by the divine command, that the decision
is made, that he is obedient or disobedient, good or bad.
It is here that man and woman affirm their sex or deny it.
We cannot really characterise man and woman in the
form of a definition, but only as we recall that in their
very differentiation God has willed and made them in
mutual relation and that His command has also the
dimension or component that in the interests of this
relationship they must be true to their specific differentiation. We have no right, especially if we ask concerning
the command of God, to define or describe this differentiation. Even though we may think we know this or that
about it, it can never be known to us in advance if this is
our question. Otherwise we presume to know in advance
the content of the will of God concerning which ethics can
only ask. The command of God will find man and woman
as what they are in themselves. It will disclose to them
the male or female being to which they have to remain
faithful. It will tell them what they have to acknowledge
and may never deny as man or woman. In all this it
may perhaps coincide at various points with what we may
think we know concerning the differentiation of male and
female. But it may not always do this. It may manifest
the distinction in new and surprising ways. The summons
to both man and woman to be true to themselves may
take completely unforeseen forms right outside the systems
in which we like to think. In no event is it bound to a
scheme which we may presuppose. It is thus a mistake
to attach oneself to any such scheme, however well considered and illuminating it might appear to be. Such
schemes can sometimes render us heuristic, exegetic and
illustrative services. But it is not for us to write the text
itself with the help of any such system. It is not for us
to write the text at all. For the texts which we write, the
definitions and descriptions of male and female being

which we might derive from others or attempt ourselves, do not attain what is meant by the command when it requires of man that here, too, he should accept his being as man, as male or female, as it is seen to God. For it is a well-known fact, admitted by all wise exponents of such views, that these systems can take the form only of suppositions and assertions which rest upon impressions and personal experiences and are necessarily problematic if only because they are the suppositions and assertions of a man or a woman and it is most unlikely that any man has genuinely and deeply understood woman as woman, or any woman man as man. What we have here are simply opinions which may be very interesting and stimulating in themselves, which have their value for the current dealings of man with man, and which, as they are exchanged and compared, may produce all kinds of clarifications and agreements, but which cannot be known without doubt to be valid and necessary. If there is to be a knowledge of man and woman which in the enquiry concerning the command of God we can treat as unquestioned and presupposed, it will most certainly have to be a form of knowledge which rests upon secure foundations. That man and woman—in the relationship conditioned by this irreversible order—are the human creature of God and as such the image of God and likeness of the covenant of grace—this is the secure theological knowledge with which we ourselves work and with which we must be content. What God's command wills for man and woman is that they should be faithful to this their human nature and to the special gift and duty indicated in and by it.

This means that although we recognise their achievements we definitely reject every phenomenology or typology of the sexes. . . .

Example of such a typology : " The man is the one who produces, he is the leader ; the woman is receptive, and she preserves life ; it is the man's duty to shape the new ; it is the woman's duty to write it and adapt it to that which already exists. The man has to go forth and make the earth subject to him, the woman looks within and guards the hidden unity. The man must be objective and universalise, woman must be subjective and individualise ; the man must build, the woman adorns ; the man must conquer, the woman must tend ; the man must comprehend all with his mind, the woman must impregnate all with the life of her soul. It is the duty of man to plan and to master, of the woman to understand and to unite." I quote this passage because over and above the characterisation it brings us into the sphere of an " ought " or " must," of definite tasks supposedly set the sexes in virtue of their inherent characteristics. But here the matter becomes more than doubtful. Why should we not be content with these characterisations ? Why should we not agree that there is a good deal of truth in them ? Why should we not even accept the view that in the antithesis between Apollo and the chthonic-telluric divinities, man represents the former and woman the latter ? Yet how is it that we can hardly resist a certain levity in face of such antitheses, as though seeing in them, however serious their authors, a rather malicious caricature on the one side or the other, or perhaps both ? These things obviously cannot be said or heard in all seriousness. For they cannot be stated with real security. They cannot be stated in such a way that probably every third man and certainly every second woman does not become agitated and protest sharply against the very idea of seeing themselves in these sketches. Nor can they be stated in such a way that they will wholeheartedly accept the idea that this is what they, true man and true woman ought to be, that here they see their true nature portrayed. And how are these rather contingent, schematic, conventional, literary and half-true indicatives to be transformed into imperatives ? Real man and real woman would then have to let themselves be told : Thou shalt be concerned with things (preferably machines) and thou with persons ! Thou shalt cherish the mind, thou the soul ! Thou shalt follow thy reason and thou thy instinct ! Thou shalt be objective and thou subjective ! Thou shalt build and thou merely adorn ; thou shalt conquer and thou cherish etc. ! Thou shalt ! This is commanded thee ! This is thy task ! By exercising the one or the other function, thou shalt be faithful to thyself as man or woman ! This is quite impossible. Obviously we cannot seriously address and bind any man or woman on these lines. They will justifiably refuse to be so addressed in this way. On what authority are we told that these traits are masculine and these feminine ? And how can we be even sure that the last thing which can be said of the sexes on this plane will not be fatally identical with the first, namely, the hostility of the sexes ? Who can say whether the imperatives thus acquired, even if they command notice, will not be simply challenges in that conflict whose unhappy beginnings we observed in the world of the hamster. But if these descriptions fail us the moment we take them seriously and change them into imperatives, it is evident that we have moved on to ground which may be interesting but is extremely insecure. What, then, is the point of these typologies ? They may have value in other directions, but they are certainly not adapted to be a valid law for male and female, and we can only cause the greatest confusion if we try to exalt them into such a law and use them as such. It is for this reason that we for our part refuse to do so.

The specific differentiation particularly of male and female which is at issue in the divine command and its requirement of fidelity lies somewhere above and beyond the sphere in which such typologies are relatively possible and practicable. The command of God comes to man and woman in the relationship and order in which God created them to be together as His image, as the likeness of His covenant of grace, in the male or female existence which they gain in His eyes within the framework of their character as likeness and image. Thus it is the command of God itself which tells them what here and now is their male or female nature, and what they have to guard faithfully as such. As the divine command is itself free from the systematisation by which man and woman seek to order and clarify their thoughts about their differentiation, so, in requiring fidelity, it frees man and woman from the self-imposed compulsion of such systematisation. To what male or female nature must they both be true ? Precisely to that to which they are summoned and engaged by the divine command—to that which it imposes upon them as it confronts them with its here-and-now requirement. As this encounters them, their particular sexual nature will not be hidden from them. And in this way the divine command permits man and woman continually and particularly to discover their specific sexual nature, and to be faithful to it in this form which is true before God, without being enslaved to any preconceived opinions.

The temptation which arises in face of this first and fundamental demand for fidelity has two forms. The first is that the sexes might wish to exchange their special vocations, what is required of the one or the other as such. This must not happen. It involves a movement of flight which may be particularly attractive to those who for any reason cannot find a suitable partner and in the isolation of their existence feel so much the more oppressively the peculiar weakness of their sex. Yet they are none the less called to be whole and genuine men and women, not seeking to evade their sexuality, but in their own way having to express it just as honourably and being enabled to live in it just as cheerfully as others. But the problem may present itself just as acutely within marriage. And here supremely, as in all the concrete relationships between man and woman, it is important to recognise that each man and woman owes it not only to himself but also to the other always to be faithful to his own sexual characteristics. Fellowship is always threatened when there is a failure at this point either on the one side or the other. Of course, it is not a question of keeping any special masculine or feminine standard. We have just seen that the systematisations to which we might be tempted in this connexion do not yield any practicable imperatives. Different ages, peoples and cultures have had very different ideas of what is concretely appropriate, salutary and necessary in man and woman as such. But this does not mean that the distinction between masculine and non-masculine or feminine and unfeminine being, attitude and action is illusory. Just because the command of God is not bound to any standard it makes this distinction all the more sharply and clearly. This distinction insists upon being observed. It must not be blurred on either side. The command of God will always point man to his position and woman to hers. In every situation, in face of every task and in every conversation, their functions and possibilities, when they are obedient to the command, will be distinctive and diverse, and will never be interchangeable. Not every apparent violation is, of course, a real one. Life is richer, and above all the command of God is more manifold, than might appear from preconceived opinions. Not every apparent offence is a real one. But there are real violations and offences. They arise where the one sex or the other forgets, or for any reason refuses to acknowledge, that it has its right and dignity only in relation to the opposite sex and therefore in distinction from it. Such a forgetting or refusal will immediately disclose itself even outwardly as a blunder, error or disturbance. The root of fellow-humanity and of humanity generally is thus affected. A desire which at this point might include jealousy, envy, imitation or usurpation can never in any circumstances be good, whereas a pure desire will constantly and surely lead man and woman back to their place. . . .

Quite apart from the feminist movement, there is hardly a possibility of everyday life which is ethically irrelevant in this respect or falls outside the scope of this distinction, even down to the problems of dress and outward bearing. Nothing is indifferent in this connexion. The decision with regard to this requirement of faithfulness to sex is made at every point by both man and woman. The famous veil which the women of Corinth (1 Cor. 11) refused to wear any longer was obviously a subject of this decision in the then circumstances. This question is connected with that of order to which we shall come later. But it has also these general implications. The women of Corinth, like so many after them, had heard something of the truth which Paul himself had proclaimed in Gal. 3[28], that in Christ Jesus all are one—Jew and Greek, bond and free, and male and female. What was more natural than to infer that in their gatherings they should wish to have a similar external appearance to that of the men? But we must not blame Paul if he did not interpret his saying of Gal. 3[28] in this way, in the sense of a cancellation of the sexual distinction between man and woman, of an evasion of the command of God relevant at this point, but threatened these women with the greatest displeasure on the part of the watching angels (v. 10), and devoted sixteen whole verses to this question of their wearing veils. It was not a matter of superfluous legalism, nor of any depreciation or humiliation of woman—Gal, 3[28] makes this

204

inconceivable—but of reminding woman of her peculiar dignity and rights. The recollection of this brought Paul to a final stand where he could not yield an inch. But why should women blame him for this? In resisting the women of Corinth he was contending for their own true cause. And appearances must be very deceptive if in the much more debated direction of 1 Cor. 14$^{33ff.}$, where they are told not to speak but to be silent in the assembly, he was really relegating them to an inferior position. " If any man think himself to be a prophet, or spiritual, let him acknowledge that the things that I write unto you are the commandments of the Lord " (v. 37). The command of the Lord does not put anyone, man or woman, in a humiliating, dishonourable or unworthy position. It puts both man and woman in their proper place. Interpretations may vary as to where this place is, for the Lord is a living Lord and His command is ever new. It is certainly foolish to try to make an inflexible rule of the particular interpretation of Paul in this instance. It is undoubtedly the case that women may also not wear veils and actually speak in the assembly. But this is not the most important point to be gathered from 1 Cor. 11 and 14 in the present context. The essential point is that woman must always, and in all circumstances, be woman ; that she must feel and conduct herself as such and not as a man ; that the command of the Lord, which is for all eternity, directs both man and woman to their own proper sacred place and forbids all attempts to violate this order. The command may be given a different interpretation from that of Paul, for it is the living command of the living Lord, but if it is to be respected at all, it cannot even for a moment or in any conceivable sense be disregarded in this its decisive expression and requirement.

But the temptation which we have to see and avoid in this connexion may take a very different form. The desire to violate fidelity to one's own sex does not now think in terms of an exchange with the nature and characteristics of the opposite sex. It aspires beyond its own and the opposite sex to a third and supposedly higher mode of being, possible to both sexes and indifferent to both. What is sought is a purely human being which is male or female only externally, incidentally and on a lower plane, in respect of psychological and biological conditioning, perhaps only *per nefas* on the basis of a historical or metaphysical disturbance and perversion, but in any case only temporarily and provisionally. What is sought is a purely human being which in itself and properly is semi-sexual and therefore, in relation to its apparent bi-sexuality, sexless, abstractly human, and to that extent, a third and distinctive being as compared with male and female. There can be no doubt that what we have here is a more sublime and lofty and spiritualised form of that movement of escape. It is no accident that this type of consciousness has been traditionally impregnated with the magic fragrance of so much mysticism, mythology and gnosis. It is a movement in which man and woman aspire to overcome their sexual and separated mode of existence and to transcend it by a humanity which is neither distinctively male nor female but both at once, or neither.

On the one hand this movement can be presented and defended as the attempt at an idealistic solution of the problem of the single man or woman, or as a reason for the decision to live a sexually lonely life. What need have I of a sexual partner, and what difference does it make that in certain circumstances I have to resign the idea of one, and therefore of love and marriage, if at some depth of existence I can be feminine even as a man or masculine as a woman and thus embody in myself alone the whole of human being ? On the other hand, it can make itself out to be the deepest and truest fulfilment of love and marriage. The first and last word in this matter is not the fact that man and woman meet as such and unite in their dualism, but rather the overcoming of this dualism, the realisation of the destiny and aspiration of both to transcend their particularity and distinction, and together to be or to aspire to the one and undivided human being, in which not humanity, not the fellowship of the sexes, but sexual indifference and therefore the totality of humanity, or at any rate orientation towards this indifference and totality, is the meaning of *eros* and marriage.

It is obvious that this rejected religio-metaphysical interpretation of the whole sphere of man and woman can take very profound and concrete forms. Nor is it easy to criticise this theory and the corresponding practice. It seems somewhere very near the indisputable truth that in the being of man and woman, distinctive and related, we have to do with the genuine humanity of both. And it seems to commend itself only too well from an ethical standpoint as a serious illumination and purification of this whole sphere, emanating from a higher angle of vision. But the fact remains that if the divine command is valid and relevant in this sphere we must object no less earnestly to this view and the resultant conduct than to everything which necessarily entails effeminacy in the male or mannishness in the female. We can certainly accept the humanisation of this sphere, but not in such a way as would neutralise the sexes, for this would finally mean dehumanisation. Outside their common relationship to God there is no point in the encounter and fellowship of man and woman at which even as man and woman they can also transcend their sexuality. And precisely in the relationship to God, they cannot do this in such a way that they cease to be male and female or that their sexuality becomes non-essential, in such a way that they become or even can aspire to be a third higher type of being. In his relationship to God man does not become a god. He becomes genuinely and definitely a man. He is put in his proper place, which is that of a man or woman. The fact that man and woman transcend themselves in their relationship to God does not therefore mean that their encounter and fellowship would cease to be real encounter and fellowship. But they transcend themselves, becoming more than man and woman in their particularity and distinction, in the fact that God Himself in His unity is their unity, that their encounter and fellowship are guaranteed by His unity, and that this may be recognised and confessed by them. God is the One for them, and this very fact saves them from having to become one amongst themselves and prevents them from trying to do so. That God created man as male and female, and therefore as His image and the likeness of the covenant of grace, of the relationship between Himself and His people, between Christ and His community, is something which can never lead to a neutral It, nor found a purely external, incidental and transient sexuality, but rather an inward, essential and lasting order of being as He and She, valid for all time and also for eternity. The fact that they are male and female does not destroy the fact that they are man, nor merge into it. They are man as they are male and female, not as they are neither or both at some basic depth of the human, and not as they can expect to be neither or both in some *eschaton* of the human. And if the command of God concerns and reaches them at all, then it finds them as male and female, and in this way as man. And the first thing which it requires of them is simply that, confessing and acknowledging their unity in the unity of God, they should not leave behind or beneath them these concrete forms of their humanity, and especially that they should not aspire to sexless or bi-sexual humanity on the ground that it would be so fine and noble and glorious, so emancipating and purifying for human existence in this sphere, if male and female could somewhere transcend their sex, surrendering their sexual particularity and distinction in favour of a higher and better form of humanity which embraces both male and female and overcomes the division between them. We should never want to know better than God the Creator whose will in this respect as in others is simple and clear. We should be content to investigate and embody this simple and clear will of His—it is sufficiently deep and rich and living as such—and not try to emulate it with our own arbitrary profundities.

Here, too, we must see and respect the limit drawn by the command of God. It is incontestable that for male and female both in themselves and in their relationship to each other (through love and marriage or outside this special connexion), it is a question of the actualisation of humanity, and this must take place in the realisation of the fact that they belong indissolubly together and are necessary the one to the other for their mutual completion. But we have to remember that on this line of thought there is a point where good inevitably becomes evil and sense nonsense if this actualisation is sought outside obedience to God's command. There is a point at which the incontestable truth that male and female as such are together man becomes a lie when it is not significantly counterbalanced by the recognition that man as such is male or female and not a third term. There is a point at which the good work of mutual completion ceases to be good if it becomes the representation of a myth which has its foundation neither in the will of the Creator nor in the reality of His creature and therefore has no foundation at all, except to warn us against the sin of *hubris*, of wanting to be the whole either individually or together. There is a point at which even orientation towards the one God in which man and woman individually and together are true man can degenerate into the orientation towards an idea or principle or idol or demon if we do not take due warning of the possibility of exchanging the unity of God for a neutral unity of our own arbitrary invention. There is a point on this line where right can become wrong, the sublime ridiculous, freedom captivity. Here again we cannot lay down as a general rule what the point is when the faithfulness required of man is still preserved or already denied, and therefore what is the limit defined by the command of God. But there is a criterion which can help us to identify the limit in any given case. All is well so long and so far as man and woman, as they seek to be man individually and together whether in or outside the union of love and marriage, are not merely fully aware of their sexuality, but honestly glad of it, thanking God that they are allowed to be members of their particular sex and therefore soberly and with a good conscience going the way marked out for them by this distinction. But things are far from well if man or woman or both seek to be man in such a way that in virtue of a fancied higher being their sex becomes indifferent or contemptible or vexatious or even hateful, a burden which they bear unwillingly and from which they would gladly emancipate themselves as they ask after God and seek to be human. This is the starting-point of the flight from God which inevitably becomes a flight into inhumanity. This, then, is the limit to be drawn in this matter. And this is the question which has to be put to establish it, and to decide whether one has transgressed it or not. . . .

We proceed to a second principle, which again extends to the whole sphere. Looking now in the opposite direction, we maintain that in obedience to the divine command there is no such thing as a self-contained and self-sufficient male life or female life. In obedience to the divine command, the life of man is ordered, related and directed to that of the woman, and that of the woman to that of the man. What we have to say in this connexion is summed up in a verse which we have already quoted from 1 Cor. 11[11]: "Nevertheless neither is the man without the woman, neither the woman without the man, in the Lord." This is true of man and woman in marriage, but not only of them. We remember that to say man *or* woman is also, rightly understood, to say man *and* woman. The dissociation and diversity which we have so far emphasised, the demand for fidelity to one's own sex which has hitherto been our concern in its twofold aspect, certainly cannot be taken to mean that there is such a thing as an abstract masculinity and corresponding femininity which it is our task and aim to exalt, cherish and preserve as such. The position to which we were directed as the true and distinctive position for each sex is for each man and woman, whether within marriage or without, a position which is open to its opposite. One cannot occupy it, nor fulfil the requirement of fidelity to one's sex, without being aware of woman if one is a man, or of man if a woman. And openness to the opposite is not an incidental and dispensable attribute of this position ; it constitutes its very essence. All the other conditions of masculine and feminine being may be disputable, but it is inviolable, and can be turned at once into an imperative and taken with the utmost seriousness, that man is directed to woman and woman to man, each being for the other a horizon and focus, and that man proceeds from woman and woman from man, each being for the other a centre and source. This mutual orientation constitutes the being of each. It is always in relationship to their opposite that man and woman are what they are in themselves. We must be clear that relationship does not mean transition and dissolution. It does not mean a denial of one's own sex or an open or secret exchange with its opposite. On the contrary, it means a firm adherence to this polarity and therefore to one's own sex, but only in so far as such adherence is not self-centred but expansive, not closed but open, not concentric but eccentric. Relationship to woman in this sense makes the man a man, and her relationship to man in this sense makes the woman a woman. To become sexually awake, ripe and active, to be true to one's own sex, means for both man and woman to be awake to this polar relationship, ripe for it and active in it, to remain true to it. To this extent our second principle corresponds with the first, and the first can be properly grasped only in the light of the second. It is the equivalence of the being of both sexes with this relationship which legitimately replaces the many typologies which have been attempted, and makes them completely superfluous.

It cannot be objected that this relationship differs on the two sides. This is, of course, true, for man's relationship to and from woman is different from the corresponding relationship of woman. He is ordered, related and directed to her very differently from what she is to him. We shall return to this point in a third principle in which it will be a question of the order within the relationship. The relationship, and therefore the being of man and of woman, does not subsist apart from this order. But it is not this order which creates the relationship and makes the man man and the woman woman. It is where there is this relationship, where the man is man and the woman woman, that the order is operative and revealed. We shall have to concern ourselves with it as a *conditio sine qua non*, but only when we have recognised the relationship itself and therefore the being and distinctive difference of the sexes as determined by it, i.e., as they are ordered, related and directed the one to the other. And in this recognition the reciprocity of the sexes, and therefore that which they have in common, must take absolute precedence of the difference in their modes of interrelation. In other words, the similarity in their interrelationship must be more important in the first instance than the illuminating and fundamental dissimilarity in which it is realised. Or, to put it in yet another way, we must first consider their mutual co-ordination, for it is only on this basis that we can properly understand the order which obtains within it.

We have here a nodal point in our whole investigation and representation of " freedom in community " generally, and particularly typical of the freedom in the community of man and woman. The truth which we have to enunciate is that in Christ Jesus there is neither male nor female (Gal. 3[28]), which means that like Jew and Gentile or slave and free they are one in Him, and stand upon an equal footing. But if they are one in Him, standing upon an equal footing, this means that they are what they are for themselves as they are ordered, related and directed to each other. The Jew is a Jew in the Lord only, but precisely, to the extent that he confronts and is confronted by the Greek. The free man is free in the Lord only, but precisely, to the extent that the slave is associated with him and he with the slave. Similarly the male is a male in the Lord only, but precisely, to the extent that he is with the female, and the female likewise. That they are one in the Lord holds them together. It allows and commands them to be together. And it is the basis of their distinction, which is rooted in the fact that they have their essence in the fact that they are directed to be in fellowship. Because their freedom is that which they have from and before and for God, therefore it can take shape only in their fellowship with each other, and their humanity can consist concretely only in the fact that they live in fellow-humanity, male with female, and female with male. Every right of man and woman stands or falls with the observance and maintenance of this rule, and every wrong consists in its contravention.

This rule is from this standpoint the command of God. If we are to be obedient to the divine command we cannot regard ourselves as dispensed from its observance. It is clear that in it we have to do with the fundamental law of love and marriage in so far as it must be in particular the law of the being and attitude of a particular man in relation to a particular woman and *vice versa*. But the woman is the partner of the single man too, not woman in general, not an idea of woman, certainly not the Virgin Mary, but the concrete and definite form of woman encountering him in a particular way. She does actually encounter him too, being unmistakeably present for him at varying distances and in many different ways, even though she does not come into question as a companion in love or marriage. She is woman for him too, whether as mother, sister, acquaintance, friend or fellow-worker, just as she is also present in all these and other forms—and always as woman —for the man who is bound by love and marriage. Similarly, the man is undoubted partner of the single woman, not (it is to be hoped not!) as an epitome or ideal

212

form of manhood, as the heavenly bridegroom and such like, but as the real man who encounters her in concrete and definite form, not as a companion in love and marriage, but no less truly as a man in kinship, acquaintance, friendship and vocation than he is in relation to the woman to whom he is specially and individually bound. That the man is and should be with the woman, and the woman with the man, applies to the whole sphere of relationships now under consideration, and in this regard the primary and fundamental formulation of the relevant command should be as follows—that whether in love and marriage or outside this bond, every woman and every man should realise that he is committed to live consciously and willingly in this interrelationship, not regarding his being abstractly as his own but as being in fellowship, and shaping it accordingly.

As against this, everything which points in the direction of male or female seclusion, or of religious or secular orders or communities, or of male or female segregation—if it is undertaken in principle and not consciously and temporarily as an emergency measure—is obviously disobedience. All due respect to the comradeship of a company of soldiers ! But neither men nor women can seriously wish to be alone, as in clubs and ladies' circles. Who commands or permits them to run away from each other ? That such an attitude is all wrong is shown symptomatically in the fact that every artificially induced and maintained isolation of the sexes tends as such— usually very quickly and certainly morosely and blindly— to become philistinish in the case of men and precious in that of women, and in both cases more or less inhuman. It is well to pay heed even to the first steps in this direction.

These first steps may well be symptoms of the malady called homosexuality. This is the physical, psychological and social sickness, the phenomenon of perversion, decadence and decay, which can emerge when man refuses to admit the validity of the divine command in the sense in which we are now considering it. In Rom. 1 Paul connected it with idolatry, with changing the truth of God into a lie, with the adoration of the creature instead of the Creator (v. 25). " For this cause God gave them up unto vile affections : for even their women did change the natural use into that which is against nature : and likewise also the men, leaving the natural use of the woman, burned in their lust one toward another ; men with men working that which is unseemly, and receiving in themselves the recompence of their error which was meet " (vv. 26–27). From the refusal to recognise God there follows the failure to appreciate man, and thus humanity without the fellow-man (*C.D.* III, 2, p. 229 ff.). And since humanity as fellow-humanity is to be understood in its root as the togetherness of man and woman, as the root of this inhumanity there follows the ideal of a masculinity free from woman and a femininity free from man. And because nature or the Creator of nature will not be trifled with, because the despised fellow-man is still there, because the natural orientation on him is still in force, there follows the corrupt, emotional and finally physical desire in which—in a sexual union which is not and cannot be genuine—man thinks that he must seek and can find in man, and woman in woman, a substitute for the despised partner. But there is no sense in reminding man of the command of God only when he is face to face with this ultimate consequence, or pointing to the fact of human disobedience only when this malady breaks out openly in these unnatural courses. Naturally the command of God is opposed to these courses. This is almost too obvious to need stating. It is to be hoped that, in awareness of God's command as also of His forgiving grace, the doctor, the pastor trained in psycho-therapy, and the legislator and judge—for the protection of threatened youth—will put forth their best efforts. But the decisive word of Christian ethics must consist in a warning against entering upon the whole way of life which can only end in the tragedy of concrete homosexuality. We know that in its early stages it may have an appearance of particular beauty and spirituality, and even be redolent of sanctity. Often it has not been the worst people who have discovered and to some extent practised it as a sort of wonderful esoteric of personal life. Nor does this malady always manifest itself openly, or, when it does so, in obvious or indictable forms. Fear of ultimate consequences can give as little protection in this case, and condemnation may be as feeble a deterrent, as the thought of painful consequences in the case of fornication. What is needed is that the recognition of the divine command should cut sharply across the attractive beginnings. The real perversion takes place, the original decadence and disintegration begins, where man will not see his partner of the opposite sex and therefore the primal form of fellow-man, refusing to hear his question and to make a responsible answer, but trying to be human in himself as sovereign man or woman, rejoicing in himself in self-satisfaction and self-sufficiency. The command of God is opposed to the wonderful esoteric of this *beata solitudo*. For in this supposed discovery of the genuinely human man and woman give themselves up to the worship of a false god. It is here, therefore, that for himself and then in relation to others each must be brought to fear, recollection and understanding. This is the place for protest, warning and conversion. The command of God shows him irrefutably—in clear contradiction to his own theories—that as a man he can only be genuinely human with woman, or as a woman with man. In proportion as he accepts this insight, homosexuality can have no place in his life, whether in its more refined or cruder forms.

The commanded orientation of the sexes on one another, which constitutes the essence of each, can be summed up under three heads. They are to consider one another, to hear the question which each puts to the other and to make responsible answer to one another.

To consider one another means to know, or more precisely to want to know, about one another : not, then, as if they already knew about one another ; not on the basis of a preconceived general or even personal judgment of men about women or of women about men ; but with unprejudiced eyes and generous hearts, always ready to learn something new, to turn the corner and see something better. Among the immediate data of existence there is certainly no greater riddle for man than the fact of the existence of woman and the question as to her nature. And on the other hand the same applies to women. We need not think that a man can exist without encountering this riddle and being occupied with it, nor need we think that he has already solved it. To live humanly means never to escape the astonishment of one's own sex at the other, and the desire of one's sex to understand the other.

But each sex has also to realise that it is questioned by the other. The puzzle which the opposite sex implies for it is not theoretical but practical, not optional but obligatory, not factual but human. It is the great human puzzle which as man and woman they put to one another in their mutual confrontation. As man and woman are human in their co-existence and mutual confrontation, neither the one nor the other can be content with his own sexuality or heedlessly work out his sexually conditioned capacities, needs, interests, tendencies, joys and sorrows. Man is unsettled by woman and woman by man. There is always this unsettlement by the opposite sex where there is the encounter of man and woman. Each is asked by the opposite sex : Why, *quo iure*, are you *de facto* so utterly different from myself ? Can and will you guarantee that your mode of life which disconcerts me is also human ? Can you show me this in such a way that I can understand it ? There is such a thing as a silent but severe criticism which tacitly but persistently and in all conceivable forms passes between man and woman in their mutual relationships. The woman stands always in a certain tension to the man, and the man to the woman. No one can escape this unsettlement, this criticism and tension. To live humanly means to hear and face this question at the expense on both sides of self-glorification or simply of self-satisfaction.

And the question challenges both man and woman to act in responsibility to each other. As they consider one another and necessarily realise that they question each other, they become mutually, not the law of each other's being (for each must be true to his particularity), but the measure or criterion of their inner right to live in their sexual distinctiveness. Man can be and speak and act as a true man only as he realises that in so doing he must answer the question of woman, i.e., give her an account of his humanity. Much that is typically masculine would have to be left unsaid and undone, or said and done quite differently, if man remembered that in it, if it is to be truly masculine, he must prove his humanity in the eyes of woman, to whom he constitutes so great a question mark. For example, might not the very dubious masculine enterprise of war become intrinsically impossible if the remembrance of the confrontation with woman were suddenly to be given the normative significance which is undoubtedly its due ? When man excuses himself from this recollection, he strengthens rather than dispels woman's natural doubt of his humanity. And the more he strengthens her doubt, and the bond of fellowship between them is therefore weakened, so much the more doubtful does his humanity become even objectively, and so much the more is humanity as such called in question for both sides. On the other hand, exactly the same can be said of feminine being and speaking and acting. Woman, too, is challenged by the natural criticism of man to prove herself human in his eyes. If she may and must live out her life as woman, she too must consider that she has to render an account to man as he must render an account to her, that she is measured by his norms as he by hers. For this reason all the movements of man and woman in which there is an open or secret attempt to escape this reciprocal responsibility are suspect at least from the very outset. On both sides, everything is at stake here. They are not to elude their mutual responsibility, but to fulfil it. And, of course, they must fulfil it even when no representative of the opposite sex is present. As a norm and criterion the opposite sex is always and everywhere invisibly present. The divine decision that it is not good for man to be alone has been taken irrevocably ; and it applies to woman as well as to man. For both, therefore, there is only an incidental, external, provisional and transient isolation and autonomy. They elude themselves if they try to escape their orientation on one another, i.e., the fact that they are ordered, related and directed to one another. Their being is always and in all circumstances a being with the other. In obedience to God's command they will know that they are always and in all circumstances bound to remember and to do justice to the character of their existence as an existence in relationship.

We shall now take a third step, again with reference to the whole sphere of the relationship of man and woman. It brings us to the most delicate of the general questions which call for consideration at this point. The disjunction and the conjunction of man and woman, of their sexual independence and sexual interrelationship, is controlled by a definite order. As the attitude and function of the man and those of the woman must not be confused and interchanged but faithfully maintained, and as on the other hand they must not be divorced and played off against each other but grasped and realised in their mutual relatedness, so they are not to be equated, nor their relationship reversed. They stand in a sequence. It is in this that man has his allotted place and woman hers. It is in this that they are orientated on each other. It is in this that they are individually and together the human creature as created by God. Man and woman are not an A and a second A whose being and relationship can be described like the two halves of an hour glass, which are obviously two, but absolutely equal and therefore interchangeable. Man and woman are an A and a B, and cannot, therefore, be equated. In inner dignity and right, and therefore in human dignity and right, A has not the slightest advantage over B, nor does it suffer the slightest disadvantage. What is more, when we say A we must with equal emphasis say B also, and when we say B we must with equal emphasis have said A. We have considered this equality of man and woman as carefully as possible in our first two propositions, and not one iota of it must be forgotten or abrogated as we now turn in the third to the order in which their being no less than their being in fellowship is real, and therefore to the requirement of the divine command in so far as it includes the observance of this order. Man and woman are fully equal before God and therefore as men and therefore in respect of the meaning and determination, the imperilling, but also the promise, of their human existence. They are also equal in regard to the necessity of their mutual relationship and orientation. They stand or fall together. They become and are free or unfree together. They are claimed and sanctified by the command of God together, at the same time, with equal seriousness, by the same free grace, to the same obedience and the reception of the same benefits. Yet the fact remains—and in this respect there is no simple equality—that they are claimed and sanctified as man and woman, each for himself, each in relation to the other in his own

218

particular place, and therefore in such a way that A is not B but A, and B is not another A but B. It is here that we see the order outside which man cannot be man nor woman be woman, either in themselves or in their mutual orientation and relationship.

Every word is dangerous and liable to be misunderstood when we try to characterise this order. But it exists. And everything else is null and void if its existence is ignored, if we refuse to recognise it as an element in the divine command, if it is left to chance. If order does not prevail in the being and fellowship of man and woman— we refer to man and woman as such and in general, to the rule which is valid both in and outside love and marriage— the only alternative is disorder. All the misuse and misunderstanding to which the conception of order is liable must not prevent us from considering and asserting the aspect of reality to which it points. A precedes B, and B follows A. Order means succession. It means preceding and following. It means super- and sub-ordination. But when we say this we utter the very dangerous words which are unavoidable if we are to describe what is at issue in the being and fellowship of man and woman. Let us proceed at once to the very necessary explanation. When it is a question of the true order which God the Creator has established, succession, and therefore precedence and following, super- and sub-ordination, does not mean any inner inequality between those who stand in this succession and are subject to this order. It does indeed reveal their inequality. But it does not do so without immediately confirming their equality. In so far as it demands subjection and obedience, it affects equally all whom it concerns. It does not confer any privilege or do any injustice. It lays a duty on all, but it also gives to all their right. It does not deny honour to any, but gives to each his own honour.

Thus man does not enjoy any privilege or advantage over woman, nor is he entitled to any kind of self-glorification, simply because in respect of order he is man, and therefore A, and thus precedes and is superior in relation to woman. This order simply points him to the position which, if he is obedient, he can occupy only in humility, or materially only as he is ordered, related and directed to woman in preceding her, taking the lead as the inspirer, leader and initiator in their common being and action. He cannot occupy it, then, for himself, let alone against her, or in self-exaltation, let alone in exaltation over her and therefore to her degradation, but as he humbles himself in obedience to the command which concerns them both, as he first frees himself from sexual self-sufficiency and takes seriously his orientation on woman, as he first enters into fellowship with her, as he first bows before the common law of humanity as fellow-humanity. Only as he accepts her as fellow-man, only together with her, can he be the first in his relationship to her—the first in a sequence which would have no meaning if she did not follow and occupy her own place in it. If it is understood in any other way, and not as a primacy of service, the pre-eminence of man is not the divine order but a particular form of human disorder. The exploitation of this order by man, in consequence of which he exalts himself over woman, making himself her lord and master and humiliating and offending her so that she inevitably finds herself oppressed and injured, has nothing whatever to do with divine order. It is understandable that woman should protest and rebel against this exploitation, although she ought to realise at once that here as elsewhere protesting and rebelling are one thing and the way from disorder to order quite another. It cannot be a question of woman attaining her rights as opposed to man and his, but of man's understanding the order and sequence and therefore the obligation in which he is the first, of his primarily submitting and rendering obedience to the common law instead of standing upon his own rights, of his not neglecting in his own favour—or his own disfavour—the required initiative of service in the common cause of humanity, but of assuming and discharging it. By simply protesting and rebelling, woman, even though she were a thousand times in the right, does not affirm and respect the order under which she also stands and by which alone she can vindicate her rights. Indeed, it may well be that her protesting and rebelling spring from the same source of contempt for order with which man offends her so deeply. The real service which she ought to render in this matter—indirectly in her own favour—is certainly not yet performed by the mere fact of her opposing man when he turns order into disorder.

For woman does not come short of man in any way nor renounce her right, dignity and honour, nor make any surrender, when theoretically and practically she recognises that in order she is woman and therefore B, and therefore behind and subordinate to man. This order gives her her proper place, and in pride that it is hers, she may and should assume it as freely as man assumes his. She, too, has to realise that she is ordered, related and directed to man and has thus to follow the initiative which he must take. Nor is this a trifling matter. Properly speaking, the business of woman, her task and function, is to actualise the fellowship, in which matter man can only precede her, stimulating, leading and inspiring. How could she do this alone, without the precedence of man ? How could she do it for herself and against him ? How could she reject or envy his precedence, his task and function, as the one who stimulates, leads and inspires ? To wish to replace him in this, or to do it with him, would be to wish not to be a woman. She does not admit any false superiority on his part when she not merely grants him this primacy of service, for it can be nothing more, but is glad that man has and exercises this function in the common service of the common cause of humanity, he himself being also subject to order in his own place. Why should not woman be the second in sequence, but only in sequence ? What other choice has she, seeing she can be nothing at all apart from this sequence and her place within it ? And why should she desire anything else, seeing this function and her share in the common service has its own special honour and greatness, an honour and greatness which man in his place and within the limits of his function cannot have ? Is it then settled—if such things can be settled—that the honour and greatness peculiar to her position, the honour and greatness possible to her in her subordinate role, cannot possibly exceed his ? At least there can be no doubt that the subordination about which woman is entitled to complain is certainly not that which is envisaged in the divine order in which she has second place as woman. On the other hand the establishment of an equality with man might well lead to a state of affairs in which her position is genuinely and irreparably deplorable because both it and that of man are as it were left hanging in the void. If she occupies and retains her proper place, she will not merely complain even when man for his part does not keep to his place and thus encroaches upon her rights. The goodness and justice of the divine order are not transformed into evil and injustice even for those who have to suffer from its misunderstanding and abuse by others. Even then it is better that she on her side should not infringe but observe it. If there is a way of bringing man to repentance, it is the way of the woman who refuses to let herself be corrupted and made disobedient by his disobedience, but who in spite of his disobedience maintains her place in the order all the more firmly. . . .

The divine command, which is our concern, will thus always require from man that he should observe and maintain this order, wherever and in whatever circumstances man and woman meet and live together. Since God is the same God at all times, in all places and situations and in regard to all men, but is also a living God, Ruler and therefore Commander, it is not to be expected that the conduct which He requires, the obedience consistent with His command, will always and everywhere and for all individuals have the same form and expression. The divinely willed order remains the same. Its application to what God requires yesterday and to-day, here and there, from this man and that, varies, and so does also the content of the conduct which is commanded or forbidden, obedient or disobedient. Here again ethics must not become casual. Nor may we wish to fetter the divine command and thus the divine order concerning the relationship of man and woman by any system, whether old or new, traditional or progressive. It may not be adapted to any arrangements, customs, manners or even advances in human conduct and action, in which this order might be supposed to be preserved as opposed to other arrangements and customs in which it might be supposed to be infringed. But ethics can and must call our attention to the crossroads at which man and woman, every man and every woman both in marriage and outside it, are always placed by the very fact that God's command uncompromisingly requires of them the observance of divine order in their relationships. Here, too, ethics can and must suggest the points of view from which we should ask concerning good and evil in the light of this order. It can and must indicate the very question which man and woman must answer in this respect, and in the answering of which it will be seen whether they stand in obedience or in disobedience. This is the task to which we must now briefly address ourselves. It will inevitably entail a certain systematisation, almost a kind of woodcut.

The man who confronts woman in accordance with this order and therefore in obedience is always the strong man, which means the man who is conscious of his special responsibility for the maintenance of this order, and is engaged in practising it. It should be noted that it is not a question of his manly dignity and honour, even less of his masculine wishes and interests, but rather of his masculine responsibility for this order. The obedient man will in his proper place as a man set himself in its service. He will not leave it to chance whether the order subsists and prevails. Nor will he wait for woman to do her part in serving it. On the contrary, he will forestall her in this. And because for him, too, it is only a question of service, he will do so without arrogance or pretentiousness, but naturally and without embarrassment. In so doing, he will not feel superior to woman. He will really be superior only in so far as he will primarily accept as his own a concern for the right communion of the sexes as secured by this order, and therefore for the order itself. He is strong to the extent that he accepts as his own affair service to the order and in this order. He is strong as he is vigilant for the interests of both sexes. This is what is intended and tenable in the otherwise rather doubtful idea of chivalry. To the man who is strong in this sense there corresponds, when woman is obedient, the woman who is mature, i.e., whose only thought is to take up the position which falls to her in accordance with this order, desiring nothing better than that this order should be in force, and realising that her own independence, honour and dignity, her own special wishes and interests, are best secured within it. Thus in regard to the precedence which she sees man assume in this matter, she will feel no sense of inferiority nor impulse of jealousy. She will not consider herself to be attacked by this, but promoted and protected. She will see guarded by it just what she herself desires to see guarded. She has no need to assert herself by throwing out a challenge to man. She will perceive the opportunity which man places within her grasp. She will not merely accept his concern for the order and for herself, but make it her joy and pride as woman to be worthy of this concern, i.e., to be a free human being alongside man and in fellowship with him. If things go well, the strong man will summon woman to this maturity, and the mature woman will summon man to be a strong man. But the obedience of man and woman do not depend on the successful evocation of a response by this summons, on the actualisation of this reciprocity. There is on both sides also a solitary unanswered and apparently ineffective obedience which perhaps as such has all the more weight and inner grandeur. Wherever the true path may lead or not lead, there can be no doubt that it is to be sought in this direction both by man and by woman.

We may now oppose to this the contrasting picture, and we shall begin, as is fitting, with man. The tyrant is always disobedient in relation to this order. He need not be cruel or bad-tempered. There are quiet, gentle, amiable, easy-going tyrants who suit women only too well, and it is an open question in which form the male tyrant is worse and more dangerous. The distinctive characteristic of the tyrannical as opposed to the strong man is that he does not serve the order but makes the order serve himself. It interests him only in so far as he falsely supposes that it confers distinction upon him and gives him an advantage over women. He changes it into an instrument for the seizing and exerting of power in favour of his supposed masculine dignity and honour, wishes and interests. It is not for him a duty, but a need and a pleasure, to take precedence of woman. It is for him an end in itself to take advantage of her. Just because there cannot intrinsically be such a thing as the man who in himself and as such is a superior being, he must be all the more intensively concerned to play the role of lord and master, or at any rate of the all-wise and almighty, in relation to woman. And because the order persists even though it is misunderstood and abused, he finds ready to hand the means to do so. So he bluffs, and he has the advantage of possessing at least the instrument with which to do it. He preens himself, as the peacock its feathers. In his own refined or crude, convincing or ridiculous manner, he plays as best he can the part of the male. And only too often, unfortunately, complacent woman plays up to him, allowing such behaviour to impress and please her, and in fact actually inviting it. She forgets that she, too, has her responsibility. She is only too pleased to be relieved of it. She adapts herself to the attitude and role of the flexible and compliant person who waits on the other's moods. She plays on her side the counterpart which the tyrant expects to see and which is necessary to the success of his own performance. She discovers in advance what is expected of her and fulfils it to the letter. She finds it convenient to make things as convenient as possible for him. She also finds it attractive—and the clever tyrant will certainly support this view—to be his pliable kitten, his flattering mirror. In pleasing him, she thus pleases herself. And she, too, will play her part all the more craftily because it is only a part, because the submissive woman in this sense has no real existence, having no place in the order of the relationship of man and woman. She, too, abuses the order. She, too, lives on an appearance of it. She, too, is strong by the truth which she makes into a lie. In this case man and woman are thus corresponding forms of disobedience. The tyrannical man and the compliant woman mutually encourage each other. But this does not always happen. The submissive woman does not always encounter the tyrant, nor will the tyrant always encounter the submissive woman. The resultant conflict is at least more promising than the peace which ensues when these counterparts meet and find each other. But whether in isolation or co-operation, this is the contrasting picture of a disobedience which can take place on either side or both in violation of the order, but ought not to do so.

Let us now follow this development rather further, and first on the side of the woman. Since the tyranny of the man and compliance of the woman both imply what is disobedient and wrong, it is *ipso facto* decided that they cannot maintain the positions taken up. This impossibility is especially clear in the case of woman, for even when she co-operates she is in fact the one who is injured and suffers. The disorder will be avenged on her first, although it puts man, too, in an impossible position. But she will be the first to seek to extricate herself. By a return to order and therefore by becoming mature? Perhaps! But perhaps also by a deeper involvement in disorder. For somewhere in the submissive woman there lies concealed—not merely crouching in readiness, but already active—the rebellious woman. In her own way even the submissive woman illegitimately exercises power over man. By her very compliance—she knows well enough what she is about—she grasps at control over man. She avenges herself for his tyranny by performing so exactly the part which he desires her to play. In her voluntary weakness and readiness to yield, she acquires authority over him and is secretly the stronger. But this secret state of affairs can and must break out and come into the open. The order which is only apparently respected, but in reality abused and perverted, can clearly be challenged and infringed openly. Where it is not really obeyed, it may one day occur to woman to question not only the claimed prerogatives and postured lordship but also the real primacy of man, openly abandoning her position and snatching power from his hands. This dramatic turn obviously demands a change of scenery. Claim is now met by counter-claim, power by power, tyrant by tyrant. What objection can man bring when he himself and primarily is a transgressor of the order? The conflict thus starts in real earnest. It is now to be seen which will prove the stronger party. But whatever the result, on neither side is there right in the true and Christian sense. Let us suppose that woman's open or concealed revolt is successful. In fact it must often be more successful than would appear. The prospects of man in this encounter are none too good. In this case, man will obviously emerge as the weak man. That he was not really superior as he ought to have been according to the demands of the order, he has betrayed already by the fact that he felt compelled to proclaim his lordship so loudly and could thus become a tyrant. It is now clear that he could only assume the

226

role of lord, as also the submissive woman was only playing a part. The magnificent garb of the tyrant now becomes torn and thin. He may continue to play his role *pro forma*. But woman sees through him. She no longer believes, nor does he, that in their relationship he is the first and she the second. As he misused his position as the first and she refuses any longer to be the second, as neither is controlled nor assigned to his place by an order, there is no ambivalence, but the woman has now become the first in the bad sense, and the man has secretly or openly surrendered his position. What man will not desperately and indignantly strive against having to admit the truth of this ? To be sure, it cannot be the real truth. But where the tyranny of man and the submissiveness of woman can take place, there one day her revolt and his weakness and dependence will in some way be a fact. As the offended and humiliated party, woman does not have right on her side, but she has the appearance of right. And in this appearance of right, conjoined with the demonic power of her very weakness, she can in fact become the stronger and man the weaker. How can he now dare to assert his primacy over her ? Seeing he has failed to grasp this primacy, refusing the service in which alone he might have done so, it is his weakness that he must now try to assert it. The primacy of man is either there or not. The man who must defend or struggle for it shows by this very fact that he has lost it or never possessed it, that he is a poor weakling who can be twisted around one's finger—probably very gently, usually without anything sensational, but as effectively as only rebellious woman can do—and from whom there is no longer to be expected the leadership which he should exercise in virtue of the order and which he owes to woman, so that she, too, is now really poor. The weak man will become continually weaker through the rebellion of his wife, and the rebellious wife continually more rebellious through the weakness of her husband. In short, the order will be continually loosened and disrupted. And if the worst befalls, and man succeeds in reviving the tyranny with which it all began, the *circulus vitiosus* will be completed, and the game will start all over again.

But let us now return to our discussion of obedience to

the divine command and therefore observance of the order. We referred to the mature woman. This woman will never let herself be pushed into the role of the compliant wife, whether she has to do with the strong or the tyrannical man. She will endorse the strength of the strong man which is the strength of his sense of responsibility and service, and successfully or otherwise she will negate the tyranny of the tyrant. She will do both because she is an independent element in the order which binds both man and woman. The mature woman is as such the woman who knows and takes her proper place, not in relation to man but in relation to the order. She realises that as between man and woman there can be no question of claim and counter-claim or the brutal struggle for power, but of rivalry only in regard to the right following of the path common to both but specifically allotted to each. Therefore, while she compares herself to the man, she will not compare her place and right to his. If she is challenged by him, it is not whether his attitude and function might not equally well be hers, but whether she is truly fulfilling the position and function assigned her. If she is orientated on him, it is not with the intention of imitating him, but with that of doing her part in fellowship with him. In this self-knowledge there is no resignation on the part of woman. By it she asserts rather her independence, showing her mastery, her true equality with man. There can be in it no shadow of sadness and resignation and therefore no spark of rebellion even in relation to the tyrannical and weak man. In face of an erring man the mature woman will not only be sure of herself in her quiet self-restriction, but she will also know her duty and witness towards him. Successfully or otherwise—and we now turn over another leaf—she is in her whole existence an appeal to the kindness of man. In human relationships kindness is not the same thing as condescension. It means the free impulse in which a man interests himself in his neighbour because he understands him and is aware of his obligation towards him. The self-restricting woman appeals to the kindness of man. She puts him under an obligation to be kind. The opposite is also true, but in this respect the advantage is perhaps with woman. She may win the respect of man. If he is capable of this at all, it is in face of the mature and therefore self-restricting woman. He understands such a woman, not condescendingly, or superciliously, or complacently in respect of her pliability, but with a sincere and non-patronising respect for the independence, mastery and equality which she thus evinces. Such a woman puts man under an obligation. He can and must take such a one seriously. If anything can disturb his male tyranny and therefore his male weakness, if anything can challenge him to goodness and therefore to the acceptance of woman, it is encounter with the self-restricting woman. Why? Because her maturity is displayed in her self-restriction. She need not wait for the kind man to know and limit herself, as he need not wait for the modest woman to be kind. For kindness belongs originally to his particular responsibility as a man. But we come to the point where woman may in fact be the educator of man, so long, be it noted, as she does not evade her proper subordination. And now the circle may be closed. For the kind man, who is instructed in kindness by the self-knowledge and self-restriction of the woman, is identical with the strong man with whom we commenced this discussion. What is manly strength if not the power with which man in his relationships with woman may in obedience to the order of things seize responsibility and take the initiative? As a strong man he confirms the order, the order in which woman in her place is not simply subordinate to him, but stands at his side.

It is somewhere on the border-line between this *circulus veritatis* and the *circulus vitiosus* that the decision is made on those questions of good and evil which face man and woman in their relationship to the order under which they stand and which in their being, attitude and action they must answer both individually and in their manifold inter-relations. [III, 4, pp. 150–181]

APPENDIX

1. The Light of Life

[94] In sum, our statement distinguishes the Word spoken in the existence of Jesus Christ from all others as the Word of God. When we think of these others, we do well to include even the human words spoken in the existence and witness of the men of the Bible and the Church. In distinction from all these, Jesus Christ is the one Word of God. There are other words which are good in their own way and measure. There are other prophets in this sense. We shall return to this point. But there is only one Prophet who speaks the Word of God as He is Himself this Word, and this One is called and is Jesus. This is the substance of our statement, no more but also no less.

We shall now try to fix its more precise meaning by describing what it actually says. That Jesus is the one Word of God means first that He is the total and complete declaration of God concerning Himself and the men whom He addresses in His Word. God does satisfaction both to Himself and us in what He says in and with the existence of Jesus Christ. What He is for us and wills of us, but also what we are for Him and are ordained to be and will and do in this relationship, is exhaustively, unreservedly and totally revealed to us in Jesus Christ as the one Word of God. As this one Word He does not need to be completed by others. If we are to speak of completion, we must say that, as and because He is the living Lord Jesus Christ, He is engaged as the one Word of God in a continual completion of Himself, not in the sense that the Word spoken by Him is incomplete or inadequate, but in the sense that our hearing of it is profoundly incomplete. For He Himself is in Himself rich and strong enough to display and offer Himself to our poverty with perennial fulness. It is not His fault if we see and know so little of God and ourselves. There is thus no need to try to catch other words of God. Indeed, we must not do so, for any such word can only be the word of another god which is *per se* false in relation to the one God, and therefore it can only lead us astray from the truth of the one God and the consequent truth of man as His elect and beloved creature. Who and what the true God is, and through Him true man ; what the freedom of God is, and the freedom given by Him to man, is said to us in and with the existence of Jesus Christ as true Son of God and Son of Man in such a way that any addition can only mean a diminution and perversion of our knowledge of the truth.

That He is the one Word of God means further that He is not exposed on any third side to any serious competition, any challenge to His truth, any threat to His authority. Such a third side could only be a word of God different from that spoken in Him and superior or at least equivalent in value and force ; the word, perhaps, of a *Deus absconditus* not identical with the *Deus revelatus*, or identical only in irreconcilable contradiction. Now we have no cause to reckon with such an alien word, such a self-contradiction, on the part of God. But we have every cause to keep to the fact that He is faithful, and that in Jesus Christ we have His total and unique and therefore authentic revelation, the Word in which He does full justice both to Himself and us. To be sure, this Word meets opposition in the world, and also and supremely, as we must not forget, in the Church. To be sure, its light is resisted by darkness in the many forms of many sinister powers, all of which are connected with the sin of man, all empowered and unleashed by his falsehood, all to be taken seriously as opponents of the one Word of God. Jesus Christ can certainly be unrecognised, despised and rejected in the world and among His own people. He can be partially or even totally unheard as the one Word of God. That did happen, and happens still. But since God does not contradict but is always faithful to Himself, there is one thing that can never take place, namely, that such a sinister power and its lying words, revelations and prophecies should seriously threaten the validity and force of the one Word of God, invading and even destroying it. The living Lord Jesus Christ, risen again from the dead, has no serious rival as the one Prophet of God who does not merely attest but is the Word of God. There is none whose inferiority and final displacement is not already decided by His existence, presence and action. Who or what can rise up against God, or against Him as the one Word of God? This means in practice that no risk is involved if among the bids made by many supposed and pretended lords and prophets we trust and obey Him as *the* Lord and Prophet. He and He alone is worthy of complete trust and total obedience. None will ever repent of responding to His self-giving, and to the Word spoken in it, with a corresponding self-giving which is resolute and exclusive. " Whosoever believeth on him shall not be ashamed " (Rom. 10[11]). For, although He has enemies, He has none who can put Him to shame, or who will not be put to shame by Him.

That He is the one Word of God means further that His truth and prophecy cannot be combined with any other, nor can He be enclosed with other words in a system superior to both Him and them. As the one Word of God, He can bring Himself into the closest conjunction with such words. He can make use of certain men, making them His witnesses and confessing their witness in such a way that to hear them is to hear Him (Lk. 10[16]). He has actually entered into a union of this kind with the biblical prophets and apostles, and it is the prayer and promise in and by which His community exists that He will not refuse but be willing to enter into a similar union with it. Nor can any prevent Him entering into such a union with men outside the sphere of the Bible and the Church, and with the words of these men. Whether in the Church or the world, however, this type of union can be legitimate and fruitful only through His act, as His work, as a form of His free revelation of grace. Conversely, all syntheses which Christians or non-Christians may arbitrarily devise and create between Jesus Christ as the one Word of God and any other words, however illuminating, necessary or successful they may be; all well-meant but capricious conjunction of Jesus Christ with something else, whether it be Mary, the Church, the fate worked out in general and individual history, a presupposed human self-understanding, etc., all these imply a control over Him to which none of us has any right, which can be only the work of religious arrogance, in which we try to invest Him with His dignity as the Lord and Prophet, in the exercise of which He ceases to be who He is, not objectively, but for those who are guilty of this rash assault, and in and with which faith in Him, love for Him and hope in Him are abandoned, however loudly or with whatever degree of subjective sincerity they may be professed. There is no legitimate place for projects in the planning and devising of which Jesus Christ can be given a particular niche in co-ordination with those of other events, powers, forms and truths. Such projects are irrelevant and unfruitful enterprises because as the one Word of God He wholly escapes every conceivable synthesis envisaged in them. They are irrelevant and unfruitful because the men who attempt them will always be content with the revelations of the other elements.

We have here the irresistible and relentless outworking of the " Thou shalt have none other gods but me " of Ex. 20². The sin of Israel against the God of the covenant made and continually renewed with the patriarchs did not consist so much in direct apostasy from Yahweh as in the combination and admixture of His service, invocation and acknowledgment in practical obedience, with the adoration of the numina of Canaan and other surrounding peoples. It consisted in the fact that Israel made constant experiments to do the one and not leave the other undone, not losing Yahweh yet not missing the Baalim, and therefore halting between two opinions (1 K. 18²¹). It consisted in the fact that in its refusal to elect in accordance with its own election, it already elected, not electing Yahweh but deciding against Him and for the Baalim, and thus becoming a people alien like all others to the command of God. The remarkable but very relevant and accurate reference to the " jealousy " of Yahweh, which according to Ex. 20⁵ is directed against the attempt to worship Him in fashioned images as well as in His invisible majesty, shows us clearly that He radically and automatically refuses to allow His Godhead to be equated with other divinities, or His Word to be heard with other words. Israel can look to Him alone, or not at all. It can hear Him alone, or not at all. The whole prophecy of the history of Israel as attested by the Old Testament, and therefore explicitly and implicitly all its prophets, speak along these lines.

This combining of the Word of Jesus Christ with the authority and contents of other supposed revelations and

233

truths of God has been and is the weak point, revealed already in the *gnosis* attacked in the New Testament, at almost every point in the history of the Christian Church. The prophecy of Jesus Christ has never been flatly denied, but fresh attempts have continually been made to list it with other principles, ideas and forces (and their prophecy) which are also regarded and lauded as divine, restricting its authority to what it can signify in co-ordination with them, and therefore to what remains when their authority is also granted. Nor is this trend characteristic only of early and mediaeval Catholicism. It is seen in Protestantism too, from the very outset in certain circles, even in the Reformers themselves, and then with increasing vigour and weight, until the fatal little word " and " threatened to become the predominant word of theology even in this sphere where we might have hoped for better things in view of what seemed to be the strong enough doctrine of justification. It needed the rise of the strange but temporarily powerful sect of the German Christians of 1933 to call us back to reflection, and at least the beginning of a return, when the more zealous among them, in addition to their other abominations, awarded cultic honour to the portrait of the Führer. The overthrow of this whole attitude, and its provisional reversal, was accomplished in the first thesis of Barmen which is the theme of the present exposition. But there are other Christian nations in which it is customary to find a prominent place in the church for national flags as well as the pulpit and the Lord's table, just as there are evangelical churches which substitute for the Lord's table a meaningfully furnished apparatus for the accomplishment of baptism by immersion. These externals, of course, are trivial in themselves. But as such they may well be symptoms of the attempt which is possible in so many forms to incorporate that which is alien in other prophecies into what is proper to that of Jesus Christ. If these prophecies are prepared for this—and sooner or later they will make an open bid for sole dominion—the prophecy of Jesus Christ asks to be excused and avoids any such incorporation. If it is subjected to such combinations, the living Lord Jesus and His Word depart, and all that usually remains is the suspiciously loud but empty utterance of the familiar

name of this Prophet. " No man can serve two masters "
(Mt. 6²⁴). No man can serve both the one Word of God
called Jesus Christ and other divine words.

That He is the one Word of God means finally that His
prophecy cannot be transcended by any other. It cannot
be transcended in the content of its declarations, for it
tells us all that it is necessary and good for us to know
concerning God, man and the world, embracing, establishing and crowning all that is really worth knowing. It
cannot be transcended in the depth with which it speaks
the truth, for it is itself the source and norm of all truth.
It cannot be transcended in the urgency with which it
presents itself to man and demands to be acknowledged,
recognised and confessed by him, for everyone who gives
it a hearing sees that this is the one thing necessary compared with which all other hearing, however important,
must be given a secondary and subordinate place. Above
all, it cannot be transcended in the goodness, seriousness,
comfort and wisdom of what it imparts, for all other
things imparted to us, though these qualities may be
ascribed to them, are inferior to it, and in respect of goodness can only be abased and exalted, disqualified and
qualified, by it. In one respect alone can there be transcendence. This is not in relation to the content, depth,
urgency or goodness of the one Word of God spoken in
Jesus Christ. It is not its transcendence by any other
word. It is the self-transcendence of Jesus Christ as the
one Word of God in respect of the universality and direct
and definitive clarity of the knowledge which Christianity
and the world do not yet have in the time between His
resurrection and ascension, but to which they look and
move at His return, i.e., His total presence, action and
revelation which will conclude and fulfil time and history,
all times and all histories. In this *eschaton* of creation and
reconciliation there will not be another Word of God.
Jesus Christ will be the one Word and we shall then see
the final and unequivocal form of His own glory which
even now shines forth from His resurrection into time and
history, all times and all histories. The theme of Christian
hope, to the extent that it is not yet fulfilled nor cannot
be so long as time endures, is the revelation of the fact
that neither formally nor materially, theoretically nor

practically, can the one Word of God be transcended, as this is now confirmed in and through his self-transcendence, in virtue of which all ears hear and all eyes see all the things which already it is actually given to us to see and hear in Him. The inclusion of the eschatological element, then, does not imply any restriction, but the final expansion and deepening, of our statement that Jesus Christ is the one Word of God.   [IV, 3, pp. 99–103]

2. THE THREEFOLD COMING AGAIN OF JESUS CHRIST

[95] Let us try to be clear what it means if it is true that in the Easter event there has taken place the self-declaration of Jesus Christ, of His being and action in the relationship between God and man, and therefore the revelation of the reconciliation of the world with God, the immediate and perfect prophecy, by a new and specific divine act, of the divine-human High-priest and King. Let us have no reservations on the ground that what has taken place is perhaps too great for the measure of our being and understanding, nor prudent fears of the questions raised. These will come later. But they can properly come only when we first realise on what basis and with what reference they can be put and answered. Our first and unconditional objective must be to see and know what the Easter message no less unconditionally says.

In a first and very general formulation of its declaration, we venture the statement that the Easter event, as the revelation of the being and action of Jesus Christ in His preceding life and death, is His new coming as the One who had come before. As is made quite clear by the accounts in the Gospels, the One who now comes afresh and appears to His disciples is none other than the One who had come before. He is " Jesus Christ yesterday " (Heb. 13[8]), the One who yesterday acted and suffered and was finally crucified in His existence as temporally limited by His birth and death, with all the power and range and significance of this event for the whole world, but still enclosed yesterday within the limits of His existence, concealed and unknown in the world reconciled to God in

236

Him, not yet exercising the latent power and range and significance of His presence and therefore putting into effect what was done in Him for all men and for the whole created order. This One who came before now comes afresh in the Easter event. He is " Jesus Christ to-day," in all His being and action of yesterday, and its whole power for the world, new in the fact that to-day, His death and the empty tomb behind Him, He moves out from the latency of His being and action of yesterday and from the inoperativeness of His power, appearing to His disciples and in them potentially to all men and the whole cosmos, declaring Himself, making known His presence and what has been accomplished in Him for all men and for the whole created order, putting it into effect. With its manifestation and self-declaration, the fact of there and yesterday now becomes the factor of here and to-day. And in virtue of this event, newly come in His self-revelation as the One who came, Jesus Christ will not cease to be this factor and to work as such. Hence " Jesus Christ for ever " (Heb. 13⁸). As this factor, as the Prophet, Witness and Preacher entered into the world, as the light of His mediatorship, of the atonement made in Him, shining from this place, He is the living Jesus Christ, who has death behind Him, the light which shines in the world and can never be extinguished. And the world for its part is what it is enabled to be in the presence of this factor, in encounter with Him, in the shining of His light, in the determination given it by Him.

The citation in 1 Tim. 3¹⁶ from what is probably a liturgical text old even at the time of the composition of the Epistle should be allowed to speak for itself in this connexion : " He was manifest in the flesh, justified in the Spirit, seen of angels, preached unto the Gentiles, believed on in the world, received up into glory." The passage is introduced into the Epistle as a comprehensive definition of what is " by agreed confession " (ὁμολογουμένως) the one great " mystery of (Christian) godliness " (μέγα τὸ τῆς εὐσεβείας μυστήριον). Its six clauses can hardly be understood as a list of successive saving events such as we have in the oldest versions of the Christian creed. They are rather six references from different standpoints to a single event which can only be that of the resurrection or self-declaration of the living Jesus Christ as the divine act. All the references apply to this. If the passage is really a hymn, it must surely be an Easter hymn, or part of such a hymn.

It is not merely possible but imperative that what took place in the Easter event, the fresh coming of Jesus Christ as the One who came before, should be summed up under the New Testament concept of the *parousia* of Jesus Christ. However the New Testament writers may apply the term in other respects, or refer to it without application, the concrete perception with which they do so is that of the resurrection of Jesus Christ, just as conversely their notion of the resurrection is strictly identical with the full range of content of the concept of *parousia*.

The word παρουσία (cf. for what follows the article by A. Oepke in Kittel) derives from Hellenistic sources and originally means quite simply " effective presence." A *parousia* might be a military invasion, or the visitation of a city or district by a high dignitary who, as in the case of the emperor, might sometimes be treated so seriously that the local calendar would be dated afresh from the occasion. The term was also applied sometimes to the helpful intervention of such divine figures as Dionysius or Aesculapius Soter. What is signified by the term, if not the term itself, is familiar and important in the thinking of the Old Testament. From His place, whether Sinai, Sion or heaven, Yahweh comes in the storm, or enthroned over the ark of the covenant, or in His Word or Spirit, or in dreams or visions, or simply and especially in the events of the history of Israel. To the men of His people He comes finally as universal King in the unfolding of His power and glory. The coming of " one like the Son of man with the clouds of heaven " (Dan. 7[13]) ; the coming of the righteous and victorious Messiah-King abolishing war and establishing peace (cf. Zech. 9[9f.]) ; above all the recurrent Old Testament picture of the coming God of the covenant Himself manifesting Himself in movement from there to here—all these constitute materially the preparatory form of what in the New Testament is called παρουσία in the pregnant technical sense, namely, the effective presence of Jesus Christ.

What is formally meant by the word is best seen from

238

the fact that in the later New Testament (especially the Pastorals, yet also as early as 2 Thess. 2⁸) it is found in close proximity to, and sometimes replaced by, the term ἐπιφάνεια. In its Hellenistic origin at least ἐπιφάνεια denotes the making visible of concealed divinity. In 2 Thess. 2⁸ both terms appear in a way which is not just plerophoric (so W. Bauer) but materially instructive. With the breath of His mouth the Lord Jesus will slay a hidden but one day manifested ἄνομος, destroying him τῇ ἐπιφανείᾳ τῆς παρουσίας αὐτοῦ. What else can this genitive conjunction mean but that the epiphany of Jesus Christ is the manifestation of His *parousia* or effective presence, or conversely that His *parousia* takes place in His epiphany and therefore His manifestation?

As far as I can see, there are no passages (not even 2 Tim. 1¹⁰) where either term refers abstractly to the first coming of Jesus Christ as such, i.e., to His history and existence within the limits of His birth and death, of Bethlehem and Golgotha. In relation to these there would be no point in speaking either of ἐπιφάνεια (manifestation) or of παρουσία (effective presence). In them He is not even " manifest in the flesh " (1 Tim. 3¹⁶), and none of the other references in this passage can really apply to His pre-Easter existence as such. To be sure, the Word then became flesh, and His whole work was done in all its dimensions. But the incarnate Word was not yet revealed and seen in His glory (Jn. 1¹⁴). This took place in the event of Easter. In this event we certainly have the coming of the One who came before in that sphere. But it is now His coming in effective presence, because in visible manifestation in the world. It is now His coming in glory as the active and dominant factor within it. It is thus His new coming as the One who came before. It is now His " coming again," and in spite of Oepke I do not see how we can avoid this expression as we have provisionally and generally explained it.

We must now continue that, as concerns the scope and content of this event, the New Testament knows of only one coming again of Jesus Christ, of only one new coming of the One who came before, of only one manifestation of His effective presence in the world corresponding to His own unity as the One who came before. This does not

239

exclude the fact that His new coming and therefore His manifestation in effective presence in the world takes place in different forms at the different times chosen and appointed by Himself and in the different relationships which He Himself has ordained. Everything depends, of course, upon our seeing and understanding the one continuous event in all its forms. But in the time of the community and its mission after the Easter revelation it also takes place in the form of the impartation of the Holy Spirit, and it is with this that we are particularly concerned in this sub-section. It will also take place in a different and definitive form (of which we shall have to speak in eschatology), as the return of Jesus Christ as the goal of the history of the Church, the world and each individual, as His coming as the Author of the general resurrection of the dead and the Fulfiller of universal judgment. In all these forms it is one event. Nothing different takes place in any of them. It is not more in one case or less in another. It is the one thing taking place in different ways, in a difference of form corresponding to the willing and fulfilment of the action of its one Subject, the living Jesus Christ. Always and in all three forms it is a matter of the fresh coming of the One who came before. Always and in different ways it is a matter of the coming again of Jesus Christ.

The Easter event is only the first form of this happening. From the standpoint of its substance, scope and content, it is identical with its occurrence in the forms which follow. It is no less significant than these, nor is it to be depreciated in relation to them. On the contrary, the one and total coming in its other forms has its primal and basic pattern in the Easter event, so that we might well be tempted to describe the whole event simply as one long fulfilment of the resurrection of Jesus Christ. There are, of course, similar temptations in relation to the second and third forms of the event. We shall not attempt to reduce it in this way, since in so doing we should wander too far not only from the speech and terminology but also the material outlook of the New Testament. Thus, there can be no question that in all its forms the one totality of coming again does really have the character, colours and accents of the Easter event. There can also be no question that this is only the first if also the original form of this one totality.

If we allow the New Testament to say what it has to say, we shall be led in this matter to a thinking which is differentiated even in its incontestable unity, formally corresponding to that which is required for an understanding of the three modes of being of God in relation to His one essence in triunity : *una substantia in tribus personis, tres personae in una substantia.*

When the matter is usually spoken of in the New Testament under the terms *parousia* or epiphany, the reference is usually or chiefly to the third and final form, to the eschatological form in the narrower traditional sense, of the return of Jesus Christ, i.e., to His manifestation and effective presence beyond history, the community, the world and the individual human life, and as their absolute future. But reference to this climax of His coming dominates New Testament thought and utterance even where it is materially concerned with the subject without using these particular terms. We can hardly deny or explain this away in such typical passages as the *parousia* passages in the Synoptists, or the Thessalonian Epistles of Paul, or 1 Cor. 15, or the Apocalypse with its final $\check{\epsilon}\rho\chi\sigma\nu$ $\kappa\acute{\nu}\rho\iota\epsilon$ $'I\eta\sigma\sigma\hat{\nu}$ (22^{20}). Even the Gospel of John, which seems particularly to invite us to do this with its placing of both the gift of eternal life and the judgment in the present, resists it inasmuch as it is rather strangely the only book in the whole of the New Testament to speak of the last day ($\dot{\epsilon}\sigma\chi\acute{a}\tau\eta$ $\dot{\eta}\mu\acute{\epsilon}\rho\alpha$) when Jesus will awaken the dead ($6^{39, \ 40, \ 44, \ 54}$) and His Word spoken to men will judge them (12^{48}) ; and it is advisable not to solve the implied difficulty of interpretation by critical amputation. According to the New Testament, the return of Jesus Christ in the Easter event is not yet as such His return in the Holy Ghost and certainly not His return at the end of the days. Similarly, His return in the Easter event and at the end of the days cannot be dissolved into His return in the Holy Ghost, nor the Easter event and the outpouring of the Holy Spirit into His last coming. In all these we have to do with the one new coming of Him who came before. But if we are to be true to the New Testament, none of these three forms of His new coming, including

241

the Easter event, may be regarded as its only form. The most that we can say is that a particular glory attaches to the Easter event because here it begins, the Easter event being the primal and basic form in which it comes to be seen and grasped in its totality.

Yet, as we must plainly distinguish the resurrection, the outpouring of the Spirit and the final return of Jesus Christ, so we must understand and see them together as forms of one and the same event. A no less sharp warning must be issued against an abstract separation of the three forms of the new coming of Jesus Christ for which there is no basis in the New Testament. How else could we distinguish them except within the unity of the whole and therefore on the assumption of one event in these three forms?

Oepke is surely right when he says of the so-called last discourses in John that in them the "coming of the Resurrected, the coming in the Spirit and the coming at the end of the days merge into one another," and when he also says of the Synoptic Jesus that it is impossible to decide to what extent He made a clear distinction between His resurrection and His *parousia* in its final form. Yet may it not be that we can very definitely decide that He, or the Synoptic and also the Johannine tradition concerning Him, did not in fact make any absolute distinction between them at all in respect of either matter or form? What do we learn from the well-known passages (considered in detail in *C.D.*, III, 2, pp. 499 ff.) in which Jesus unmistakeably prophesies the manifestation of the kingdom of God $\dot{\epsilon}\nu$ $\delta\nu\nu\dot{a}\mu\epsilon\iota$ (Mk. $^{1f.}$), the coming of the Son of Man (Mt. 10^{23}, 26^{64}), or at least the sign which directly precedes (Mk. 13^{30} and *par.*) within the lifetime of those around Him? If we may eliminate in advance what is in its way the greatest triviality of any age, what are we to make of the assumption which underlay a particular school of Neo-Liberal theology, and which is unfortunately encountered only too often outside the narrow circle of this school, namely, that Jesus was deluded? If we find in the coming of the Resurrected, His coming in the Holy Spirit and His coming at the end of the age three forms of His one new coming for all their significant differences, there need be no artificiality in explaining that these passages refer to the first and immediate form in which His coming did really begin in that generation as the Easter event and in which the two remaining forms are plainly delineated and intimated. We are then forced to accept the statement of W. Michaelis which Oepke contests : " The resurrection . . . is the *parousia*," or again the statement of R. Bultmann (with particular reference to John's Gospel) : " The *parousia* has already taken place," although we must be careful to make the proviso that these statements are not to be taken exclusively but need to be amplified by the recollection that this is not the whole story. The outpouring of the Holy Spirit is also the *parousia*. In this it has not only taken place but is still taking place to-day. And as it has taken place in the resurrection and is taking place to-day in the outpouring of the Holy Spirit, it is also true that it will take place at the end of the days in the conclusion of the self-revelation of Jesus Christ.

It is thus impossible to relate a concept of the eschatological which is meaningful in the New Testament sense merely to the final stage of the *parousia*. Eschatological denotes the last time. The last time is the time of the world and human history and all men to which a term is already set in the death of Jesus and which can only run towards this appointed end. In the Easter event as the commencement of the new coming of Jesus Christ in revelation of what took place in His life and death, it is also revealed that the time which is still left to the world and human history and all men can only be the last time, i.e., time running towards its appointed end. In this sense the Easter event is the original because the first eschatological event. The impartation of the Holy Spirit is the coming of Jesus Christ in the last time which still remains. As we shall see, it is the promise, given with and through the Holy Spirit, by which the community, and with it the world in which it exists and has its mission, may live in this time which moves towards its end. Hence the new coming of Jesus Christ has an eschatological character in this second form too. If the *parousia* is an eschatological event in its third and final stage as well, this means specifically that in it we have to do with the manifestation and effective presence of Jesus Christ in their definitive form, with His revelation at the goal of the last time. It will consist again in a coming of Jesus Christ, and at this coming this last time, too, will reach the end which is already set for it in His death and revealed in His resurrection. The happening of the *parousia* is thus eschatological throughout its course. And it is this, as already indicated from the very first by the Easter event, because already and particularly in this event the term set to time in the death of Jesus Christ is revealed and the character and stamp of the last time is given to all the time which remains.

When we treat of the unity of the three forms or stages of the one event of the return of Jesus Christ, it is perhaps worth considering and exegetically helpful, again in analogy to the doctrine of the Trinity, to think of their mutual relationship as a kind of perichoresis (cf. *C.D.*, I, 1, p. 425). It is not merely that these three forms are interconnected in the totality of the action presented in them all, or in each of them in its unity and totality, but that they are mutually related as the forms of this one action by the fact that each of them also contains the other two by way of anticipation or recapitulation, so that, without losing their individuality or destroying that of the others, they participate and are active and revealed in them. As the Resurrected from the dead Jesus Christ is virtually engaged already in the outpouring of the Holy Spirit, and in the outpouring of the Holy Spirit He is engaged in the resurrection of all the dead and the execution of the last judgment. The outpouring of the Holy Spirit obviously takes place in the power of His resurrection from the dead, yet it is already His knocking as the One who comes finally and definitively, and it is active and perceptible as such. Similarly His final coming to resurrection and judgment is only the completion of what He has begun in His own resurrection and continued in the outpouring of the Holy Spirit.

To be sure, this is a view which is never systematised in the New Testament or presented in the form of instruction. But this does not mean that we are false to the Bible, or obscure its statements concerning the *parousia*, by adopting this view. Are we not more likely to throw light on them if we advance it with the necessary prudence yet also boldness ? Are there not many passages in the New

Testament which with their apparent contradictions cannot be satisfactorily explained except on the assumption of such a view ? This is not a key to open every lock. But it is one which we do well not to despise.

[IV, 3, pp. 290–296]

3. UNION WITH CHRIST

[96] Not by way of addition, but to give the most precise expression possible to what we have already stated in various ways, we must now take a further step. This is not merely because certain passages of the New Testament clearly direct us beyond the point already reached, but because the matter itself imperiously calls for further reflection. What is the nature of this fellowship of Christians with Jesus Christ if we have correctly understood it as the relationship of discipleship and possession, and finally as the powerful work of the Holy Spirit ? Are we not justified in asking whether the word " fellowship " is not too weak to embrace everything that is involved between Jesus Christ and the man called by Him, whether the word is not transcended and thus rendered unusable by the content which it acquires at this point ? Yet this is not the case. From all these different angles the relationship is always one of fellowship because, for all the intimacy and intensity of the connexion between them, there can be no question of an identification of the follower with his preceding leader, the possession with its owner, or the life of the one awakened by the Holy Spirit with the One who gives him this Spirit. There can thus be no question of an identification of the Christian with Christ. We have still to show, however, to what extent the fellowship of the Christian with Christ is one which is uniquely close and direct in the perfection of the mutual address of the two partners, so that it cannot be interchanged with any other.

We may begin by stating that it belongs to the perfection of this fellowship, and must not be overlooked or denied, that in it Christ does not merge into the Christian nor the Christian into Christ. There is no disappearance nor destruction of the one in favour of the other. Christ remains the One who speaks, commands and gives as the

Lord. And the Christian remains the one who hears and answers and receives as the slave of the Lord. In their fellowship both become and are genuinely what they are, not confounding or exchanging their functions and roles nor losing their totally dissimilar persons.

A delimitation is required at this point. In particular relation to its perfection, the fellowship here described, which is the goal of vocation, has often been linked with the concept of mysticism both in exposition of the relevant New Testament texts and elsewhere. As is well known, even Calvin referred once to a *unio mystica* (*Instit.*, III, 11, 10). But we should never do this unless we state precisely what we have in view when we speak of " mysticism "—and it would have to be a mysticism *sui generis* in this context. There can certainly be no question of what is usually denoted by the term in this relationship. That is to say, there can be no question of an experience of union induced by a psychical and intellectual concentration, deepening and elevating of the human self-consciousness. For while it is true that in his fellowship with Christ, now to be appreciated in all its perfection, the Christian acts as well as receives, neither his receiving nor his acting in this fellowship is the product or work of his own skill, but both can be understood only as the creation of the call of Christ which comes to him. Again, there can be no question of a disappearance of the true confrontation of God and man, of the One who addresses and the one who is addressed and answers. There can be no question either on the one side or the other of any depersonalising or reduction to silence. There can be no question of any neutralising of the distinction between Creator and creature or of the antithesis between the Holy One and sinners, nor of any establishment of the kind of equilibrium which may exist between things but can never obtain between persons, and especially between the divine Jesus Christ and the human person. Even as a child of God, and therefore in the analogy of his existence to that of the eternal Son in the flesh, the Christian is not what the latter is, and alone can be. His fellowship with the latter thus has and maintains the character of an encounter in which the grace of Jesus Christ in all its fulness, but His grace and therefore a grace which is always free, is addressed to him. Nor

246

does this grace fail to include a judgment passed on man. It does not cease to demand that he keep his distance. In face of it even his supreme and most joyous gratitude must always have, and continually acquire, the character of adoration. It is also important to notice that precisely in this fellowship of encounter there is not merely safeguarded the sovereignty of God, of Jesus Christ and of the Holy Spirit, but also the freedom of the human partner is preserved from dissolution. Indeed, it is genuinely established and validated. Unless we consider, safeguard and expressly state these things, we do better not to speak of " Christ-mysticism " when there is obviously no compelling reason to do so.

Having made this point, we may now proceed to state that the fellowship of Christians with Christ, which is the goal of vocation, is a perfect fellowship inasmuch as what takes place in it is no less than their union with Christ. The terms " attachment " and " co-ordination " are inadequate if they are not expressly understood in the sense of " union," i.e., the Christian's *unio cum Christo*. As we have shown, union does not mean the dissolution or disappearance of the one in the other, nor does it mean identification. It does not mean a conjunction of the two in which one or the other, and perhaps both, lose their specific character, role and function in relation to the other, the reciprocal relation being thus reversible. The union of the Christian with Christ which makes a man a Christian is their conjunction in which each has his own independence, uniqueness and activity. In this way it is, of course, their true, total and indissoluble union : true and not ideal ; total and not merely psychical and intellectual ; indissoluble and not just transitory. For it takes place and consists in a self-giving which for all the disparity is total on both sides. In this self-giving Christ and the Christian become and are a single totality, a fluid and differentiated but genuine and solid unity, in which He is with His people, the Lamb on the throne with the one who recognises in Him his Lord and King, the Head with the members of His body, the Prophet, Teacher and Master with His disciples, the eternal Son of God with the child of man who by Him and in Him, but only thus, only as His adopted brother, may be called and be the

247

child of God. Like His own unity of true deity and humanity, this unity is *hic et nunc* concealed. It may be known in faith but not in sight, not by direct vision. The revelation of its glory has still to come. But even *hic et nunc* there can be and is no question of creating it or giving it force, but only of making definitively and universally visible its possibility, nature and reality as something incomparably great and totally new. This, and this alone, is what the whole of creation, with all men and Christians too, is waiting and groaning for. The purpose for which Christians are already called here and now in their life-histories within universal history is that in the self-giving of Jesus Christ to them, and theirs to Him, they should enter into their union with Him, their *unio cum Christo*.

For the sake of practical perspicuity in our definition of the Christian we first spoke of his humanity in common with all men, then of his divine sonship, then, in description of his fellowship with Jesus Christ, of the relationship of discipleship, his existence as the possession of this Owner, and the powerful work of the Holy Spirit within him. It is only now that we have reached the heart of the matter in his union with Christ. In view of what we said about the problem of the *ordo salutis* in the preceding sub-section, there is obviously no question here of a description of the genetic sequence of the states of the Christian, nor is it to be assumed that in the *unio cum Christo* we reach the culminating point of such a sequence. Our present concern is not with the event of vocation at all, but with its meaning and goal. And our supreme and final definition of this as the union of the Christian with Christ describes the most essential element in it which underlies and comprehends all the others, so that from the purely material view we really ought to have put it first. This is what Calvin actually ventured to do (*Instit.*, III, 1) when he opened his whole doctrine *De modo percipiendae gratiae* with a depiction of this *unio*. If we have not followed him in this, and for the sake of clarity have thus departed in some sense from the matter, it is to be noted expressly that only now have we reached the central point which supports all that precedes and is tacitly presupposed in it. If we are to understand the nature of this union, then,

248

in relation to the emphasised independence, uniqueness and activity of Jesus Christ on the one side and the Christian on the other, we do well to begin, not below with the Christian, but above with Jesus Christ as the Subject who initiates and acts decisively in this union. We do well to begin with the union of Christ with the Christian and His self-giving to the Christian, and not *vice versa*. It is here that the union and self-giving of the Christian have their roots.

That Jesus Christ in calling man to be a Christian unites Himself with him means first from His own standpoint that He is unique as the One who in His life and death was humiliated and exalted in the place and for the sake of all, as the One in whom the reconciliation of the world to God and the justification and sanctification of all were accomplished. In all this He has no assistant nor fellow-worker to accompany Him, let alone any *corredemptor* or *corredemptrix*. He is absolutely isolated from all others. Without them, He intervenes for them. But as this One, when it is a matter of the revelation of this work as in-augurated in His resurrection from the dead and con-tinued in the work of His Holy Spirit, when it is a matter of His work in its prophetic dimension, He cannot and will not remain alone, nor can He be solitary in the reconciled world on His way to His future, conclusive and universal revelation. He cannot and will not be the Master without disciples, the Leader without followers, the Head without members, the King without fellows in His people, Himself without His own, Christ without Christians. The fact that the One who is disclosed in His resurrection from the dead and the outpouring of the Holy Spirit is really the omni-potent God who stooped down in unmerited love to man, the Lord who became a servant, has in the time which moves to its end in His final revelation a counterpart in the fact that as the Proclaimer of the act of God accom-plished in Him, in His prophetic office and work, He does not go alone but wills to be what He is and do what He does in company with others whom He calls for the pur-pose, namely, with the despicable folk called Christians. He attests to the world the reconciliation to God effected in Him, the covenant of God with man fulfilled in Him, as He associates with Christians, making common cause and conjoining Himself with them. He does not merely do this ideally or partially, but really and totally. He does not merely comfort, encourage, admonish or protect them remotely or from afar. But as He calls them to Himself in the divine power of His Spirit, He refreshes them by offering and giving Himself to them and making them His own. That He wills and does this is—in analogy to the mystery and miracle of Christmas—the true *ratio* of Christian existence as this is celebrated, adored and proclaimed within the community of Christians in the common administration of the Lord's Supper, instituted to represent the perfect fellowship between Him and them which He has established—an implication which we cannot do more than indicate in the present context.

We now turn to what must be thought and said concerning this union of His with Christians from their standpoint. There is, of course, no one, apostle, saint or the Virgin, who can contribute in the very slightest to what is accomplished for all by the one Jesus Christ in His life and death. In relation to His high-priestly and kingly work even a Paul can only know what has been done for us by God in Him (1 Cor. 2^{12}). But those to whom He reveals and makes known this life and death of His as the act of God for their salvation and His own glory do not confront this act of revelation, this work of atonement in its prophetic dimension, as hearers and spectators who are left to themselves and ordained for pure passivity. What kind of vocation, illumination and awakening would it be, what kind of knowledge, if they were merely left gaping at the One who discloses Himself to them ? No, as surely as He does not will to tread alone His way as the Proclaimer of the kingdom, so surely they for their part must be with Him, companions of the living One who are made alive by Him, witnesses in His discipleship to that which He wills to reveal to the world as having been effected in Him, namely, to the reconciliation accomplished and the covenant fulfilled in Him. This is what He makes them as He calls them to Himself, as He does this really and totally, as He does not leave them to themselves, as He does not remain outside them, as He gives Himself to them, as in the divine power of His Spirit He unites Himself with them. That they may become and be those with whom He unites

Himself by His Word ; that they may be those who are born again from above by His presence and action in their own lives ; that they may be continually nourished by Him—this is, from their standpoint, the *ratio* of Christian existence. Here again we are naturally reminded of the mystery and miracle of Christmas, and must make provisional reference to the Lord's Supper. " I in you " (Jn. 14^{20}, 15^4). " I in them " (Jn. 17$^{23, 26}$). " I in him " (Jn. 6^{56}, 15^5). According to Jn. 15$^{1f.}$ He is the vine which produces, bears and nourishes the branches, or according to the even stronger expression in Jn. 6^{33} He is the " bread of God which cometh down from heaven, and giveth life unto the world." He gives them His flesh and blood, imparting and communicating Himself to them, giving Himself to nourish them, in order that as He lives they also may and will live to all eternity (Jn. 6^{53}). The same teaching is found in Paul. " Know ye not your own selves, how that Jesus Christ is in you ? " (2 Cor. 13^5 ; cf. Rom. 8^{10}, Col. 1^{27}). He is the One who has apprehended the apostle (Phil. 3^{12}), putting His power in him (2 Cor. 12^9), setting His truth in him (2 Cor. 11^{10}), speaking in him (2 Cor. 13^3), and always magnifying and glorifying Himself in his person (Phil. 1^{20}). And in relation to other Christians He is the One who dwells " in your hearts by faith " (Eph. 3^{17}), or who seeks to be formed in them (Gal. 4^{19}). Whether they are Greeks, Jews, Barbarians, Scythians, slaves or freemen, Christ is in them all (Col. 3^{11}). Χριστὸς ἐν ὑμῖν is the great mystery of God among the nations (Col. 1^{27}). In the strongest possible expression (Gal. 2^{20}), Christ lives in the apostle in such a way that he has to say of himself that he no longer lives, i.e., in himself and apart from the fact that Christ lives in him, but that he now lives in faith in Him who gave Himself for him, this being his own most proper life to which, as one who still lives in the flesh, he can do justice only as he believes in Him. In Col. 3^4, however, " Christ our life " is also said in relation to Christians generally, and again in relation to all those who by the Spirit have been given to know what is given them by God there is made the immeasurable claim : " We have the mind of Christ " (ἡμεῖς δὲ νοῦν Χριστοῦ ἔχομεν, 1 Cor. 2$^{12, 16}$), i.e., in virtue of His life in us we have His reason.

It has always involved an unwise and, on a proper consideration, an attenuating exposition of these verses to speak of an extension of the incarnation in relation to the Christian's *unio cum Christo* and then in relation to the Lord's Supper. We are concerned rather with the extended action in His prophetic work of the one Son of God who became flesh once and for all and does not therefore need any further incarnation. We are concerned with the fact that He as the one Word of God takes up His abode in the called, that His life becomes their life as He gives Himself to them. This is the mystery and miracle of His union with them. Similarly, we do well to refrain from describing the Christian in relation to his fellows (Luther, *De libertate*, 1520, W.A., 66, 26), or, as Roman Catholics do, the priest in the mass in relation to other believers, as an *alter Christus*. In this perfect fellowship the one Christ as the only original Son of God, beside whom there can be no other, is always the One who gives, commands and precedes, and the other, the *homo christianus*, whom He makes His brother and therefore a child of God, is always the one who receives, obeys and follows. The former is the Word of God in person ; the latter, like John the Baptist in the Fourth Gospel, is His witness. In this distinction, of course, neither remains alone. Both become a totality. For it is not too great or small a thing for Christ to give Himself to the Christian, to cause His own life to be that of the Christian, to make Himself his with all that this necessarily implies. This is the high reality of His vocation to the extent that this takes place and is to be understood as His union with the Christian.

In the reality and power of the union of Christ with the Christian, however, their fellowship has also the meaning and character of a union of the Christian with Christ. Their fellowship would not be complete if their relationship were actualised only from above downwards and not also from below upwards, if it were not reciprocal. A justifiable concern for the unconditional predominance of the freedom, grace and decision of Jesus Christ which establish the relationship should not mislead us into suppressing or minimising the fact that His action has its correspondence in an action of the Christian. According to the guidance of the New Testament the declaration concerning the communication of Christ with the Christian necessarily includes a complementary declaration concerning the communication of the Christian with Christ.

That Christ links Himself with the Christian settles the fact that the latter, too, does not go alone. To do justice to Christ as his Counterpart he is not directed to believe in Him and to obey and confess Him on his own initiative or resources. He is certainly summoned to believe, obey and confess. And both as a whole and in detail this will always be the venture of a free decision and leap. It will always be a venture in which no man can wait for or rely on others, as though they could represent him or make the leap for him. Even in the community and therefore with other Christians, he can believe, obey and confess only in his own person and on his own responsibility. But does this mean on his own initiative and resources ? No, for the act of the Christian is not to be described as a leap into the dark or a kind of adventure. We have only to consider what kind of a free decision or leap is involved to see that, if there is any action which is well-grounded and therefore assured in respect of its goal, it is the faith, obedience and confession of the Christian. The Christian undertakes these things as through the Spirit he is called to do so by the risen One in whom he believes and whom he obeys and confesses. And in the knowledge given him with his calling, he is not merely required but empowered to do it. In Jesus Christ he knows and apprehends himself as a member of the world reconciled to God in Him, as a man who is justified and sanctified in Him in spite of his sin, as a legitimate partner of the covenant fulfilled in Him. Believing in Jesus Christ and obeying and confessing him, he simply does the natural thing proper to him as the man he is in Christ and therefore in truth. He simply realises his true—the only truly human—possibility. He simply exercises the freedom given him as the man he is in Christ and therefore in truth. The decision or leap of his faith, obedience and confession consists in the fact that he takes himself seriously as the man he is and recognises himself to be in Jesus Christ instead of immediately forgetting his true self (who and what he is in Christ), like the man who looks at himself in a mirror and then goes on his way (Jas. 1[23f.]). It consists in the fact that he

253

begins to act on this basis, i.e., on the basis of Jesus Christ and as the man he is in Him. He believes, obeys and confesses as, now that Christ has united Himself with him, he unites himself with Christ, giving himself to the One who first gave Himself to him, and thus choosing Him as the starting-point and therefore the goal of His thinking, speech, volition and action, quite simply and non-paradoxically because this is what He is, because there is no other starting-point or goal apart from Him, because in truth he is not outside Him but within Him.

Here again, however, we must consider the opposite side and therefore add that as the Christian unites himself with Christ it is also settled that he cannot part from Christ. In his relationship with Him He alone is the One who gives, commands and leads, and the criterion of the genuineness of all the faith, obedience and confession of Christians will always necessarily consist in their allowing Him alone to be what He alone is, neither openly nor secretly trying to subject Him to their own dominion, in the exercise of which their faith would at once become unbelief, their obedience, disobedience and their confession denial. This does not mean, however, that they can refrain from immediately and directly recognising their own cause in His cause, i.e., in the occurrence of His prophetic work in the world. For as they recognise Him, they can and should recognise themselves in Him, what they themselves are in truth. Except by the self-deception of Jas. $1^{23f.}$, how could they break their solidarity with Him? As those they are and know themselves to be in Him, as members of the world reconciled to God in Him, as justified and sanctified sinners, they cannot possibly leave Him in the lurch instead of following Him. In the freedom given them as those they are, they have only one option, namely, to believe in Him, to obey Him and to confess Him, and in so doing, in making this movement, to unite themselves with Him as He in His turning to them, in calling them and making Himself known to them, unites Himself with them. Called, illumined and awakened by His prophetic Word, for this Word they can only be in truth the men they are. What other can they do, then, as those to whom Christ has given Himself, than to give themselves to Him, to exist as His, and therefore continually to seek

254

and find their life in Him, in whom it is their truest life ?

The New Testament gives us every reason to draw very distinctly this line from below upwards. For rather strangely, but quite unmistakeably, it is not merely no less but much more noticeable in the New Testament than the opposite line which is original and must thus be regarded as decisive in our description of the whole relationship. It certainly receives more frequent mention. While the authors of the New Testament presuppose the being of Christ in the Christian, with no fear of injuring the supremacy of the divine initiative they do in fact look more in the opposite direction, namely, to the being of the Christian in Christ. The whole emphasis of the speech concerning the vine in Jn. 15[1f.] is obviously laid on the fact that, as the branches can bear fruit only as they abide in the vine, so the disciples, if they are to be what they are fruitfully, must abide in the One who speaks to them. This is brought home in many different ways, and it is impressively repeated in the First Epistle of John (3[6, 9], 4[16]). For χωρὶς ἐμοῦ, " without me ye can do nothing " (Jn. 15[5]). That they are called to abide in Him presupposes that the free and responsible participation of Christians in their status is envisaged in the description of the fellowship between Christ and them. It presupposes that they are already in Him, and obviously because first and supremely He is in them and has made their being a being in Him. " I in you " (Jn. 14[20]), comes first, but secondly and on this basis it must also be said : " Ye in me." That Christians are in Christ, that their Christian existence is everywhere realised in the fact that it unites with His in which it has its origin, substance and norm, is the insight which in the New Testament dominates especially the thinking and language of Paul, though it also finds expression in the First Epistles of Peter and John. The statement usually has an indicative character. But we have to remember that even indicatively it speaks of the history in which the union of the Christian with Christ takes place, so that we need not be surprised that it may become the imperative so characteristic of the Johannine passages. Christians are now quite briefly described as οἱ ἐν Χριστῷ Ἰησοῦ, or usually even more simply as ἐν Χριστῷ or ἐν κυρίῳ (Rom. 8¹, 2 Cor. 5¹⁷, Eph. 2¹³, 1 Pet. 5¹⁴). And they are described in this way because they are in Him (ἐστέ, 1 Cor. 1³⁰, 9¹, ²; ἐσμέν, 1 Jn. 2⁵). And they are in Him because Christ has adopted them into unity with His being (Rom. 15⁷), which means that in virtue of their baptism they have put Him on like a covering garment (Gal. 3²⁷), and must continually do so (Rom. 13¹⁴). This historical being in Christ is decisively determined, of course, by the fact that first and supremely God was " in Christ " reconciling the world to Himself (2 Cor. 5¹⁹). It is thus determined by their election made and revealed in Christ (Eph. 1⁴, ⁹, 3¹¹), by their redemption accomplished and manifested in Him (Col. 1¹⁴), by the grace of God addressed to them and recognisable in Him (1 Cor. 1¹⁴), by His love (Rom. 8³⁹), by His peace (Phil. 4⁷), by the eternal life of which they are assured in Him (Rom. 6²³). As they are in Christ, they acquire and have a direct share in what God first and supremely is in Him, what was done by God for the world and therefore for them in Him, and what is assigned and given to them by God in Him. But their being as thus determined by God is a concretely active being. In the one reality ἐν Χριστῷ God and man do not confront each other abstractly as such. On the contrary, there is a direct and concrete confrontation of the divine and corresponding human action, the former kindling the latter and the latter kindled by it. Conscious of being an ἄνθρωπος ἐν Χριστῷ (2 Cor. 12²), Paul is very definitely activated as an apostle. He can be absolutely certain of his convictions " in him," as in respect of the distinction of meats in Rom. 14¹⁴. He can have " in him " the joy with which he confidently makes his request of Philemon (v. 8). He can be sure " in him " of speaking the truth both from God and before Him (Rom. 9¹, 2 Cor. 2¹⁷). " In him," too, he can be quietly confident in respect of His communities (2 Thess. 3⁴, Gal. 5¹⁰) and thank God that He always causes him to triumph in Christ and to spread abroad the savour of His knowledge (2 Cor. 2¹⁴). Nor does Paul ascribe here to himself anything that he does not also basically ascribe both indicatively and imperatively to all Christians and to the whole community. " In him " he makes his boast in respect of them (1 Cor. 15³¹). Has not he Paul as an apostle begotten them again

in Christ Jesus through the Gospel (1 Cor. 4^{15}) ? Called
" in Christ," are not all Christians " in him " saints (Col. 1^2)
and believers (Col. 1^4, Eph. 1^{15}), hoping " in him " (1 Cor.
15^{19}) and " in him " called to obedience in their own
particular situation (Eph. 6$^{1f.}$) ? " We all, with open face
beholding as in a glass the glory of the Lord, are changed
into the same image from glory to glory, even as by the
Lord who is the Spirit," without whom it would be impossible (2 Cor. 3$^{18f.}$). Hence Paul can see in one or
another his fellow-labourer (Rom. 16^3) or fellow-servant
(Col. 4^7) " in Christ," and in Epaphras his fellow-prisoner
" in him " (Philem. 23). They are all light " in the Lord "
(Eph. 5^8). They can and should all glory " in the Lord "
(1 Cor. 1^{31}, 2 Cor. 10^{17}, Phil. 1^{26}). They can and should
all rejoice " in the Lord " (Phil. 3^1, 4$^{4,\ 10}$). The apostle
greets them " in him " in his letters (1 Cor. 16^{19}, Phil. 4^{21}).
And " in him " he also admonishes them, here too presupposing that they are " in him," that as Christians they
are within and not without, so that they have only to be
told to continue to walk " in him " (Col. 2^6, 1 Pet. 3^{16}) and
to be reminded of the mind which is self-evident " in Christ
Jesus " (Phil. 2^5) and of that which is " fit in the Lord "
(Col. 3^{18}). To what can those who are in Him be meaningfully admonished, invited and summoned but—in a rather
different expression—to stand as who and what they are
(1 Thess. 3^8, Phil. 4^1) ? In relation to the historical character of this being of theirs, however, it is indeed meaningful
to admonish, invite and summon them to do this. How
could they be what they are in Christ if they did not continually become it ?

This is not by any means a full list of the New Testament
references to the εἶναι ἐν Χριστῷ. To give such a list it
would be necessary not only to mention and co-ordinate
many others, but also to introduce a series which we have
left aside, namely, the passages which, without any basic
alteration of meaning, substitute διὰ Χριστοῦ or ἐν ὀνόματι
Χριστοῦ for ἐν Χριστῷ. But we have certainly adduced
sufficient to show what powerful witness there is in the
New Testament to the union of the Christian with Christ
which is our present concern.

It is perhaps relevant to our purpose to add a brief
linguistic enquiry into what has been said both materially

and in the biblical discussions concerning the two aspects of this union, i.e., that of Christ with the Christian and that of the Christian with Christ. What is meant by the word " in " when we say that Christ is in the Christian and the Christian in Him ? Is this a mode of expression which demands demythologisation because of its evident localising ? We may confidently reply that the word certainly has in all seriousness a local signification. If, in the fellowship between Christ and the Christian and the Christian and Christ, it must be maintained—for this is the limit beyond which there can be nothing more to demythologise—that we have an encounter in time between two personal partners who do not lose but keep their identity and particularity in this encounter, then the " in " must indeed indicate on both sides that the spatial distance between Christ and the Christian disappears, that Christ is spatially present where Christians are, and that Christians are spatially present where Christ is, and not merely alongside but in exactly the same spot. Hence we say that Christ is in Christians and they in Him. Yet while this is true, it has surely become obvious both in our material presentation and in our survey of the biblical evidence that in this context the word " in " transcends even though it also includes its local signification.

The first statement, namely, that Christ is in the Christian, has the further meaning that Christ speaks, acts and rules—and this is the grace of His calling of this man— as the Lord of his thinking, speech and action. He takes possession of his free human heart. He rules and controls in the obedience of his free reason (2 Cor. 10[5]). As a divine person it is very possible for Him to do this in the unrestricted sovereignty proper to Himself and yet in such a way that there can be no question whatever of any competition between His person and that of the Christian, whether in the attempt of the latter to control His person, or conversely in its suppression or extinction by His person. It is very possible for Him to do it in such a way that the human person of the Christian is validated and honoured in full and genuine freedom, in the freedom of the obedient children of God. That Christ is in the Christian means, then, that as the Mediator between God and man He does not exist merely for Himself and to that extent

258

concentrically, but that in His prophetic work, in the calling of His disciples and Christians, with no self-surrender but in supreme expression of Himself, He also exists eccentrically, i.e., in and with the realisation of the existence of these men, as the ruling principle of the history lived by them in their own freedom.

The second statement, namely, that the Christian is in Christ, has not only the local but also the higher meaning that his own thinking, speech and action has its ruling and determinative principle—and herein it is the work of his gratitude corresponding to grace—in the speech, action and rule of Christ. His free human heart and reason and acts are orientated on Him, i.e., on agreement with His being and action. In the power of the Word of God which calls him, and therefore in the power of the Holy Spirit, this orientation is his only possibility, already in process of realisation. Again, there is no rivalry between the human person and the divine. There is thus no danger that the former will be overwhelmed by the latter. There is no danger that it will necessarily be destroyed by it and perish. Rather, the human person, experiencing the power of the divine, and unreservedly subject to it, will necessarily recognise and honour it again and again in its sovereignty, finding itself established as a human person and set in truly human and the freest possible movement in orientation on it. That the Christian is in Christ means *mutatis mutandis* for him, too, that as one who is called by the one Mediator between God and man in the exercise of His prophetic office he cannot exist for himself and to that extent concentrically, but that, without detriment to his humanity, awakened rather to genuine humanity, he also exists eccentrically, in and with the realisation of his own existence, being received and adopted as an integral element in the life and history of Christ.

This, then, is the Christian's *unio cum Christo*. We recall that in this high view and doctrine we are not presenting a climax of Christian experience and development in face of which the anxious question might well be raised whether we have reached the point, or will ever do so, where in respect of our own Christianity we can sincerely say: " Christ in me, and I in Christ." On the contrary, we are presenting the last and most exact formulation of what makes us Christians whatever our development or experience. We have seen that Paul particularly in the New Testament does not think of restricting his insight in this regard to himself and a few other Christians of higher rank, but that as he speaks of himself he also speaks of the generality of Christians, not excluding the very doubtful Christians of Galatia and Corinth and not excluding the doubtful nature of their Christianity. If, as we have attempted in concentric circles, we think through what it means that the goal of vocation, and therefore of Christianity as divine sonship, is always attachment to Christ, co-ordination and fellowship with Him, discipleship, appropriation to Him with the corresponding expropriation, life of and by the Holy Spirit, then we are infallibly led at last to the point which we have now reached and described, namely, that a man becomes and is a Christian as he unites himself with Christ and Christ with him. And we remember that from the purely material standpoint this is the starting-point for everything else which is to be thought and said concerning what makes the Christian a Christian.

[IV, 3, pp. 538–549]

INDEX OF PASSAGES

262

HARPER TORCHBOOKS / The University Library

J. Bronowski & Bruce Mazlish	THE WESTERN INTELLECTUAL TRADITION: *From Leonardo to Hegel*	TB/3001
Edward P. Cheyney	THE DAWN OF A NEW ERA: 1250–1453. *50 illus.*	TB/3002
Carl J. Friedrich	THE AGE OF THE BAROQUE: 1610–1660. *49 illus.*	TB/3004
Myron P. Gilmore	THE WORLD OF HUMANISM: 1453–1517. *64 illus.*	TB/3003
L. H. Gipson	THE COMING OF THE [AMERICAN] REVOLUTION: 1763–1775. *30 illus.*	TB/3007
Wallace Notestein	THE ENGLISH PEOPLE ON THE EVE OF COLONIZATION: 1603–1630. *23 illus.*	TB/3006
Louis B. Wright	THE CULTURAL LIFE OF THE AMERICAN COLONIES: 1607–1763. *30 illus.*	TB/3005

HARPER TORCHBOOKS / The Academy Library
[*Selected titles*]

Jacques Barzun	THE HOUSE OF INTELLECT	TB/1051
Max Beloff	THE AGE OF ABSOLUTISM, 1660–1815	TB/1062
Jeremy Bentham	THE HANDBOOK OF POLITICAL FALLACIES. Intro. by Crane Brinton	TB/1069
Henri Bergson	TIME AND FREE WILL: *The Immediate Data of Consciousness*	TB/1021
H. J. Blackham	SIX EXISTENTIALIST THINKERS: *Kierkegaard, Jaspers, Nietzsche, Marcel, Heidegger, Sartre*	TB/1002
Crane Brinton	ENGLISH POLITICAL THOUGHT IN THE NINETEENTH CENTURY	TB/1071
Helen Cam	ENGLAND BEFORE ELIZABETH	TB/1026
Cochran & Miller	THE AGE OF ENTERPRISE: *A Social History of Industrial America*	TB/1054
G. G. Coulton	MEDIEVAL VILLAGE, MANOR, AND MONASTERY	TB/1022
Wilhelm Dilthey	PATTERN AND MEANING IN HISTORY	TB/1075
W. A. Dunning	RECONSTRUCTION, POLITICAL AND ECONOMIC	TB/1073
F. L. Ganshof	FEUDALISM	TB/1058
W. K. C. Guthrie	THE GREEK PHILOSOPHERS: *From Thales to Aristotle*	TB/1008
Marcus Lee Hansen	THE ATLANTIC MIGRATION: 1607–1860. Intro. by Oscar Handlin	TB/1052
John Higham, *Ed.*	THE RECONSTRUCTION OF AMERICAN HISTORY	TB/1068
J. M. Hussey	THE BYZANTINE WORLD	TB/1057
Dan N. Jacobs, *Ed.*	THE NEW COMMUNIST MANIFESTO	TB/1078
Henry James	THE PRINCESS CASAMASSIMA. A novel. Intro. by Clinton Oliver	TB/1005
William James	PSYCHOLOGY: *The Briefer Course.* Ed. with Intro. by G. Allport	TB/1034
Hans Kohn, *Ed.*	THE MIND OF MODERN RUSSIA: *Historical and Political Thought*	TB/1065
Samuel Noah Kramer	SUMERIAN MYTHOLOGY. Illustrated	TB/1055
Paul Oskar Kristeller	RENAISSANCE THOUGHT: *Classic, Scholastic, Humanist Strains*	TB/1048
Bernard Lewis	THE ARABS IN HISTORY	TB/1029
Ferdinand Lot	THE END OF THE ANCIENT WORLD	TB/1044
Arthur O. Lovejoy	THE GREAT CHAIN OF BEING: *A Study of the History of an Idea*	TB/1009
Niccolo Machiavelli	HISTORY OF FLORENCE AND OF THE AFFAIRS OF ITALY	TB/1027
John Stuart Mill	ON BENTHAM AND COLERIDGE. Intro. by F. R. Leavis	TB/1070
John B. Morrall	POLITICAL THOUGHT IN MEDIEVAL TIMES	TB/1076
Jose Ortega y Gasset	THE MODERN THEME. Introduction by Jose Ferrater Mora	TB/1038
Erwin Panofsky	STUDIES IN ICONOLOGY: *Humanistic Themes in Renaissance Art*	TB/1077
J. H. Parry	THE ESTABLISHMENT OF THE EUROPEAN HEGEMONY: 1415–1715: *Trade and Exploration in the Age of the Renaissance*	TB/1045
Raymond Postgate, *Ed.*	REVOLUTION FROM 1789 TO 1906: *Selected Documents*	TB/1063
George E. Probst, *Ed.*	THE HAPPY REPUBLIC: *A Reader in Tocqueville's America*	TB/1060
Priscilla Robertson	REVOLUTIONS OF 1848: *A Social History*	TB/1025
Ferdinand Schevill	THE MEDICI. Illustrated	TB/1010
C. P. Snow	TIME OF HOPE. A novel	TB/1040
N. N. Sukhanov	THE RUSSIAN REVOLUTION, 1917 *Vol. I*, TB/1066; *Vol. II*, TB/1067	
Twelve Southerners	I'LL TAKE MY STAND	TB/1072
A. F. Tyler	FREEDOM'S FERMENT: *Phases of American Social History*	TB/1074
Dorothy Van Ghent	THE ENGLISH NOVEL: *Form and Function*	TB/1050
J. M. Wallace-Hadrill	THE BARBARIAN WEST: *The Early Middle Ages*, A.D. 400–1000	TB/1061
W. Lloyd Warner	SOCIAL CLASS IN AMERICA: *The Evaluation of Status*	TB/1013
Alfred N. Whitehead	PROCESS AND REALITY: *An Essay in Cosmology*	TB/1033

HARPER TORCHBOOKS / The Bollingen Library

Rachel Bespaloff	ON THE ILIAD. Introduction by Hermann Broch	TB/2006
Elliott Coleman, *Ed.*	LECTURES IN CRITICISM	TB/2003
C. G. Jung	PSYCHOLOGICAL REFLECTIONS. Edited by Jolande Jacobi	TB/2001
C. G. Jung	SYMBOLS OF TRANSFORMATION: *An Analysis of the Prelude to a Case of Schizophrenia.* Illustrated. *Vol. I*, TB/2009; *Vol. II*, TB/2010	
Erich Neumann	AMOR AND PSYCHE: *The Psychic Development of the Feminine*	TB/2012
Erich Neumann	THE ORIGINS AND HISTORY OF CONSCIOUSNESS. *Vol. I*, TB/2007; *Vol. II*, TB/2008	
St.-John Perse	SEAMARKS. Translated by Wallace Fowlie	TB/2002
A. Piankoff	THE SHRINES OF TUT-ANKH-AMON. Ed. by N. Rambova	TB/2011

Jean Seznec   SURVIVAL OF THE PAGAN GODS: *Renaissance Humanism and Art. Illus.*   TB/2004
Heinrich Zimmer   MYTHS AND SYMBOLS IN INDIAN ART AND CIVILIZATION. Illus.   TB/2005

HARPER TORCHBOOKS / The Cloister Library

[Selected titles]

Augustine/Przywara   AN AUGUSTINE SYNTHESIS   TB/35
C. K. Barrett, *Ed.*   THE NEW TESTAMENT BACKGROUND: *Selected Documents*   TB/86
Karl Barth   CHURCH DOGMATICS: A Selection. Edited by G. W. Bromiley   TB/95
Karl Barth   THE WORD OF GOD AND THE WORD OF MAN   TB/13
Nicolas Berdyaev   THE DESTINY OF MAN   TB/61
Martin Buber   ECLIPSE OF GOD: *The Relation Between Religion and Philosophy*   TB/12
Martin Buber   TWO TYPES OF FAITH: *Interpenetration of Judaism and Christianity*   TB/75
R. Bultmann   HISTORY AND ESCHATOLOGY: *The Presence of Eternity*   TB/91
R. Bultmann &   FORM CRITICISM: *Two Essays on New Testament Research.* Translated &
K. Kundsin   edited by Frederick C. Grant   TB/96
Jacob Burckhardt   THE CIVILIZATION OF THE RENAISSANCE IN ITALY. Illustrated Edition. Introduction by B. Nelson and C. Trinkaus. *Vol. I,* TB/40; *Vol. II,* TB/41
Edward Conze   BUDDHISM: *Its Essence and Development*   TB/58
Frederick Copleston   MEDIEVAL PHILOSOPHY   TB/76
F. M. Cornford   FROM RELIGION TO PHILOSOPHY: *The Origins of Western Speculation*   TB/20
Mircea Eliade   COSMOS AND HISTORY: *The Myth of the Eternal Return*   TB/50
G. P. Fedotov   THE RUSSIAN RELIGIOUS MIND: *Kievan Christianity*   TB/70
Ludwig Feuerbach   THE ESSENCE OF CHRISTIANITY. Introduction by Karl Barth   TB/11
Sigmund Freud   ON CREATIVITY AND THE UNCONSCIOUS   TB/45
Adolf Harnack   MISSION AND EXPANSION OF CHRISTIANITY, FIRST THREE CENTURIES   TB/92
Friedrich Hegel   ON CHRISTIANITY: *Early Theological Writings*   TB/79
F. H. Heinemann   EXISTENTIALISM AND THE MODERN PREDICAMENT   TB/28
Johan Huizinga   ERASMUS AND THE AGE OF REFORMATION. Illustrated   TB/19
Immanuel Kant   RELIGION WITHIN THE LIMITS OF REASON ALONE   TB/67
Søren Kierkegaard   THE JOURNALS OF KIERKEGAARD: A Selection. Edited by A. Dru   TB/52
Søren Kierkegaard   THE PRESENT AGE. Trans. by A. Dru. Intro. by W. Kaufmann   TB/94
Søren Kierkegaard   THE POINT OF VIEW FOR MY WORK AS AN AUTHOR   TB/88
Alexandre Koyré   FROM THE CLOSED WORLD TO THE INFINITE UNIVERSE   TB/31
Walter Lowrie   KIERKEGAARD. *Vol. I,* TB/89; *Vol. II,* TB/90
Emile Mâle   THE GOTHIC IMAGE: *Religious Art in 13th Century France.* Illus.   TB/44
Gabriel Marcel   HOMO VIATOR: *Introduction to a Metaphysic of Hope*   TB/97
A. C. McGiffert   PROTESTANT THOUGHT BEFORE KANT. Preface by J. Pelikan   TB/93
T. J. Meek   HEBREW ORIGINS   TB/69
H. Richard Niebuhr   CHRIST AND CULTURE   TB/3
H. Richard Niebuhr   THE KINGDOM OF GOD IN AMERICA   TB/49
F. Schleiermacher   ON RELIGION: *Speeches to Its Cultured Despisers.* Intro. by R. Otto   TB/36
P. Teilhard de Chardin   THE PHENOMENON OF MAN   TB/83
D. W. Thomas, *Ed.*   DOCUMENTS FROM OLD TESTAMENT TIMES   TB/85
Paul Tillich   DYNAMICS OF FAITH   TB/42
Ernst Troeltsch   SOCIAL TEACHING OF CHRISTIAN CHURCHES. *Vol. I,* TB/71; *Vol. II,* TB/72
Evelyn Underhill   WORSHIP   TB/10
Johannes Weiss   EARLIEST CHRISTIANITY. *Vol. I,* TB/53; *Vol. II,* TB/54
Wilhelm Windelband   A HISTORY OF PHILOSOPHY. *Vol. I,* TB/38; *Vol. II,* TB/39

HARPER TORCHBOOKS / The Science Library

[Selected titles]

L. von Bertalanffy   MODERN THEORIES OF DEVELOPMENT: *An Intro. to Theoretical Biology*   TB/554
Harold F. Blum   TIME'S ARROW AND EVOLUTION. Illustrated   TB/555
David Bohm   CAUSALITY AND CHANGE IN MODERN PHYSICS   TB/536
J. Bronowski   SCIENCE AND HUMAN VALUES   TB/505
W. H. Dowdeswell   THE MECHANISM OF EVOLUTION   TB/527
C. V. Durell   READABLE RELATIVITY   TB/530
R. W. Gerard   UNRESTING CELLS. Illustrated   TB/541
Werner Heisenberg   PHYSICS AND PHILOSOPHY: *The Revolution in Modern Science*   TB/549
Max Jammer   CONCEPTS OF FORCE   TB/550
J. M. Keynes   A TREATISE ON PROBABILITY. Foreword by N. R. Hanson   TB/557
D. E. Littlewood   THE SKELETON KEY OF MATHEMATICS   TB/525
H. T. Pledge   SCIENCE SINCE 1500: *A Short History.* Illus.   TB/506
W. V. O. Quine   MATHEMATICAL LOGIC   TB/558
O. W. Richards   THE SOCIAL INSECTS. Illustrated   TB/542
Paul A. Schilpp, *Ed.*   ALBERT EINSTEIN: *Philosopher-Scientist.* *Vol. I,* TB/502; *Vol. II,* TB/503
Hans Thirring   ENERGY FOR MAN: *From Windmills to Nuclear Power*   TB/556
Stephen Toulmin   THE PHILOSOPHY OF SCIENCE: *An Introduction*   TB/513
G. J. Whitrow   THE STRUCTURE AND EVOLUTION OF THE UNIVERSE. Illus.   TB/504
Edmund Whittaker   HISTORY OF AETHER & ELECTRICITY. *Vol. I,* TB/531; *Vol. II,* TB/532

1609:

WINTER OF THE DEAD

A Novel about the Founding of Jamestown

Elizabeth Massie

TOR®

A TOM DOHERTY ASSOCIATES BOOK
NEW YORK

This is a work of fiction. All the characters and events portrayed in this book are either products of the author's imagination or are used fictitiously.

1609: WINTER OF THE DEAD

Copyright © 2000 by Elizabeth Massie

A Tor Book
Published by Tom Doherty Associates, LLC
175 Fifth Avenue
New York, NY 10010

www.tor.com

Tor® is a registered trademark of Tom Doherty Associates, LLC.

ISBN-13: 978-0-765-35604-8
ISBN-10: 0-765-35604-X

First Edition: March 2000
Second Edition: March 2007

Printed in the United States of America

0 9 8 7 6 5 4 3 2 1

To my mother, Patricia Spilman, outstanding artist, mother, and a very wise woman. You encouraged in me a freedom of spirit, a peace of self, tolerance, compassion, and the wings to fly forward to new places. I love you!

❧ Introduction ❧

THERE WAS A story told among the Powhatans in the late sixteenth century that strangers from across the great waters would come and destroy their people. The strange men would have golden hair, be of light skin, and would carry sticks that spit fire. That story came true.

In 1607 three ships arrived on the shores of what is now the state of Virginia, carrying adventurers from across the Atlantic Ocean. These voyagers did indeed have fair skin and hair, and they brought with them tools, swords, and strange heavy objects that shot fire from their muzzles—muskets and pistols.

With great hardship, disappointment, and determination, these men established the first permanent English settlement in the New World. Gentlemen, sailors, and laborers made the difficult voyage for the purpose of finding gold and riches for the Virginia Company of London, an organization of wealthy men who financed the expedition and who expected a good return on their investments. And among the men who made the trip, there were also teenaged boys, young men with as much desire for adventure as those older than they.

"Hostage exchange" was common practice with many explorers in the sixteenth and seventeenth centuries. It was seen as prudent by seasoned adventurers to have boys in their early to mid teens to be used as commodities to trade—like beads, tools, or other trinkets—to the natives of strange, new lands. Sometimes these boys were considered permanent "goodwill gifts"; other times they were traded for a native as a "cultural exchange"; other times a boy was expected to live among the natives, learn the language and customs, then escape and return to the explorers in order to convey all they had learned, thus giving the explorers an advantage. Whether these boys knew why they had been brought on a particular voyage is unclear; they may have believed they had been selected to be choppers of wood, builders of homes and fortress walls, bearers of arms, and haulers of water. For if they had truly known their destiny, would they have agreed to the long sea journey in the first place?

It is recorded that two boys—Thomas Savage in 1608 and Henry Spilman in 1609—were among the exchanges made between the Powhatans and the men of the Jamestown settlement. These two boys lived to adulthood, served as interpreters during the later years in Jamestown, and wrote about their experiences.

But what of the other boys who came to America with John Smith and Christopher Newport? Their experiences were certainly as traumatic and exciting as those of the others who sailed on the *Susan Constant,* the *Godspeed,* and the *Discovery.* Nathaniel Peacock and Richard Mutton were real people, two of the young men on the original journey in 1607. What happened to them? Did they live? Did they die during the cruel summers and winters of the early years, when the settlement was on the verge of collapse, when natives were attacking with a vengeance and disease was rampant and starvation became so intense that some men took to robbing the graves of the dead to find meat?

Here is a story of what these boys might have faced, set against the backdrop of true and often horrific events. Many of these characters were real people. Nathaniel and Richard were small players in a dramatic portion of United States history. Yet to these boys, the part they played was frightening, challenging, and personal.

1

March 11, 1607

   At last, praise God, the Susan Constant *has eased its rolling and I am able to write. For 50 days we have been sailing
from London across these wretched waters, and for these many
days we have been biding our time, some not as well as others.
Unlike some men down here on the 'tween deck, I have a strong
stomach and the pitching of the ship rarely bothers me. But
the other passengers, many gentlemen and wealthy fortune-
seekers, whine like babies when we rock back and forth in the
waves. They complain and then they vomit. It isn't the jarring
sea which makes me sick, but those prissy men and the fact
that I am responsible for cleaning up what they spit out. Yet
I must act like they do not bother me. They do not like me,
but it is best that I act humble and stupid so they will leave
me alone.*

   *Gentlemen. I've never had to spend so much time in so close
quarters. Back in London, I could run from them and put
distance between us, but not here. Here, I must endure them.
Here, each one of us is trying to make a "home" out of a space
of perhaps two feet wide and five feet long. Some of the gentlemen who boarded first laid claim to barrels, maneuvered
them so they were side by side, and put their mattresses across*

the tops so they would not have to sleep on the floor. Others have nailed canvas sheets from the ceiling in order to make themselves little private closets. As a simple laborer, and a boy at that, I was required to find my space last. I sleep here, near the stern, under the clacking tiller which thumps constantly as it works the rudder. The other commoners here on the Susan Constant mind their own business and fraternize primarily with each other. They do not bother me, but they have not befriended me, either.

My name is Nathaniel Peacock. I am fifteen years of age, born on the 15th of February in the year of our Lord 1592. It has been a very long time since I've held a pen to write. Paper and ink are hard to come by for such as myself, a poor orphan boy from the London streets. But I won't be a poor boy for long. Soon I will be a rich man with all the money and goods I want, because we are going to Virginia, a land of beauty and wealth, named for the Virgin Queen Elizabeth who reigned until 1603, the time when our King James ascended the throne. In this land of Virginia I shall be able to act as I want and not as I must.

My written words are awkward and splotched, as much from unfamiliarity with this pen as from the shifting of the ship on the water. But as long as I can get my hands on ink and paper, I intend to keep a journal of my adventures.

We have been traveling since December 20th of last year. It's been a much longer journey than planned. We have faced sleet and rain and thunderous waves. Twice we've gone six-on-four rations as commanded by Captain Newport, allowing six men the food of four so we do not run out before we find an island on which to refresh our supplies. We have seen the near-death of our Reverend Hunt from seasickness and have seen his miraculous recovery. But we are together still, and still are headed west.

There are three ships crossing the ocean—the Susan Constant, the Discovery, and the Godspeed. The London Company, a group of rich men seeking yet more fortune, raised the money for the ships and the crew and the supplies to take this voyage. The Company named Bartholomew Gosnold to be captain of the Godspeed, and they named John Ratcliffe to be captain of the Discovery. Here on the Susan Constant the solemn Captain Christopher Newport is in charge. It did surprise Richard and me that John Smith wasn't named captain of this ship. Smith, as everyone knows, is a brave and daring man indeed.

It was John Smith himself who spotted my companion, Richard Mutton, and me outside the Charging Boar Tavern in London last September, and offered us the chance to sail the sea to Virginia. We had been stealing from the passersby as was our usual morning activity, and at first when Smith called to me, I was certain he had seen me take a coin pouch from an old man. To be caught stealing small things in London is to be beaten. To be caught stealing valuables is to be hanged, and I daresay what I'd taken from the old codger had value. But Smith hadn't witnessed the theft. He merely bowed to us and then asked if we were healthy and free to travel. I hesitated, but when he introduced himself as Smith, I assured him right away that we were indeed of good health and free to go wherever he wanted us to go.

Smith said there was a voyage to go to the New World of Virginia in December. I said yes. I also said I could use hammer and nails and an axe, that I could tend animals, could cook, and could fight with musket or sword. All lies, of course, but to get by in this world, one must act many roles. Richard was not as enthusiastic as I to go. He was afraid the gentlemen on the trip would treat us poorly. Why, Richard reasoned, should we get on a ship to be treated poorly in close quarters when we could be treated just as poorly in London where we had room to run away? But I say you must act whatever part you are given at whatever moment that is, and soon you will get what you want. If we act as humble laborers, then we will survive the voyage to gain the wealth we so deserve in Virginia. We could never get wealthy in London, no matter how *many old men we robbed. But the Spanish have found gold on their voyages west and so shall we. In Virginia, I've heard tell there is gold lying about the ground, just waiting to be picked up and put into one's pocket.*

The blotch on the paper just now is where my hand jerked, throwing off a rat who had nuzzled up to my elbow and proposed to be my friend. I think he's wandered off to bed down with one of the gentlemen.

Poor rat.

I stole this paper, the pen, and the inkwell from the wooden box of Samuel Collier, John Smith's brattish page. The boy is red-haired and freckle-faced and believes he is better than me although he is two years my junior. He has a mattress near Richard's and mine, on the other side of a pea barrel and potato barrel. I know how to play the part of meek laborer in front of the men, but Samuel best watch it if he finds himself alone with me.

In spite of the others' complaints, my companion Richard Mutton and I are bearing the trip well. We do what we're told, running errands, bringing food to the men, cleaning rubbish and wastes, killing rats and mice and tossing them overboard, mending loose boards alongside the sailors. Sometimes we make a game of throwing the rats, to see who can pitch one the farthest. I usually win. Whatever our tasks and however poorly the men on the Susan Constant *treat us, I keep thinking of the reasons Richard and I came along in the first place.*

There are, of course, the reasons the London Company gives for our venture. Those are of bringing profits to the Company and of establishing a settlement in Virginia where English goods can be shipped in exchange for New World commodities.

There are the reasons King James gives, those of spreading Christianity to the heathens of Virginia, finding a route to the East India Sea, and establishing a stronghold in Virginia to halt the further spread of Spain and France's claims between the 34th and 45th degrees of north latitude.

But Richard's and my hearts are set on our own expectations. And dreams of them make everything worthwhile.
Riches. Treasure.
Gold!

2

THERE WAS MOVEMENT across the 'tween deck, a sound of shoes clattering on wood. Nathaniel Peacock glanced up, brushed a strand of matted brown hair from his eyes, and squinted. It was late at night, well after suppertime. In the faint lights of the lanterns scattered around where the gentlemen and other workers lounged, Nathaniel could see red-haired Samuel Collier climbing down the ladder from the main deck. The boy was wearing his hat, the broad-brimmed black one with the jaunty, bouncing feather.

Quickly Nat capped the inkwell and slipped it and the pen beneath his mattress. Then he lay down, keeping his eyes open to slits to watch the approach of the page. In one hand he held the papers of his journal close by his side, hoping they would dry soon so he could stash them safely under his straw-stuffed pallet. In his other hand he held the five pebbles he'd scooped up from the River Thames shore, a last connection to the world he'd left behind. Beside Nathaniel, fourteen-year-old Richard Mutton slept on his own lumpy mattress.

Samuel worked his way carefully through the clusters

of gentlemen and commoners on the floor. As were Nathaniel and Richard, Samuel was always cautious not to disturb the men. Even though tonight most were preoccupied—playing cards, rolling dice, chewing the remainders of their evening meal of hardtack and cold pork, coaxing tunes from flutes, sipping beer from mugs, and fumbling with lanterns in an attempt to make them burn more brightly—one misstep from a boy could send any of them into a rage. An upset gentleman was a dreadful experience. Nathaniel, for doing nothing more than spilling gruel or sloshing waste water, had been punched in the ear and kicked in the gut.

When Samuel found his mattress, he paused and put his hands on his hips and frowned as if something was wrong. Could the boy tell that Nathaniel had been into his wooden storage box?

Samuel drew his nose up and sniffed the air. This close, even in the pale light of the lanterns across the floor, Nathaniel could see his twitchy blue eyes and his bright red hair.

"Something stinks," Samuel said.

Nathaniel said nothing. Samuel was constantly trying to pick a fight, and if Nathaniel was going to match wits with this boy, he'd do it on his own terms and in his own place, not here with witnesses. Instead, he closed his eyes and pretended to doze.

"You hear me, Peacock? I said something stinks, and I think it's you, you London vermin! What was Smith thinking to invite you and Mutton along? Such a waste of space, I say. Illiterates and indigents! Pah! We have been so much better to have brought along a few extra pigs. At least pigs are worth their weight in victuals!" He waited as if he hoped Nathaniel would jump up and get himself in trouble. Even though Samuel was of less status than any of the men, Nathaniel and Richard were less than Samuel, and an outright fight within earshot of the gentlemen would likely bring about more of a punishment for Nat than for Samuel.

Nathaniel said nothing.

"Waste of space." This time Samuel's words were softer, as if he was speaking to himself. Clearly he thought Nathaniel was sleeping.

A moment later, Nat heard the page shuffle around beneath his thin blanket and then go still.

Go to sleep, you spoiled puppy, Nat thought.

Then, when the ink was dry on the page, he hid the paper behind the barrel at his head. He lay flat, crossed his arms beneath his head, and stared up at the low 'tween deck ceiling. The five pebbles were cool in his fist.

The boat hull creaked. The cannons, poised at shuttered portholes, bumped back and forth on their blocks. From the hold below the 'tween deck, Nat could hear the sheep and pigs and chickens in their crates bleating and grunting and squawking to each other. The ship's tiller just above and behind Nat's head thumped steadily as it worked the rudder, taking them farther across the sea toward Virginia. The bell rang from the upper deck, indicating it was time for a change of watch.

Nathaniel watched the light from the men's lanterns cast eerie, dancing shadows about the barrels and hull. Some of the shadows were shapeless and vague; others reminded him of things he'd left behind in London. One moved like the jaws of a mad dog which had bitten through the leg of his trousers the day the ships had left the port at Blackwall. Richard had seen it as a bad omen for the trip, but Nat had seen it as a good omen because the dog had missed the flesh of Nat's leg entirely. One shadow fluttered like a swan on the Thames River, and another hovered like a stray cloud in London's oft gray sky.

Unlike Richard, Nathaniel did not miss the reeking old English city. Nat had been born there, and had been raised by his mother, a barmaid, until he was six and she had died of fever. Cast out by the bar's owner, Nat had lived on the streets and had slept in various stables and barns until, nearly a year later, he was taken in by a street peddler who sold fish from a rattly push-cart. Nat had helped the man catch and hawk his goods, and the man had given Nat food and shelter in the man's shack. He'd also given Nat something most street boys would never have. He'd taught Nat to read and write.

The peddler, a large and cheerful man called Boonie, had been as poor as any beggar, but the man had a love for literature, and had kept a tattered but beloved collection of books in a little chest. From these, Nat had learned to read, and on paper scrounged by Boonie Nat had learned to write. It seemed as if only the rich had paper, ink, and quills, but somehow Boonie would bring these things home and the two of them would write. Nat was certain the man had stolen the paper and ink, but it didn't matter. He had a skill that the gentlemen had, and it would serve him someday. But he had never told anyone, not even Richard. Some secrets were best kept close.

Nat was nine when Boonie had died from a mule kick to the head, and Nat had lived alone ever since. He had formed partnerships with other street boys, taking what food and clothing and bits of coal they could in order to survive. But the partnerships had come and gone. Some of the boys had been caught at their thievery; others had stolen from Nathaniel and run away. Some of the boys had died. Not long after Nat's eleventh birthday, he'd met Richard. The two worked as a team in snatching vegetables from street-side stands or lifting valuables from rich women's baskets, but Nat didn't consider Richard a friend.

Nat rolled over onto his elbows and took the ink and pen back from under his mattress. Laying the pebbles aside, he smoothed the paper as best he could on the tiny floor space by his mattress, squinted in the murky light, and wrote,

It is a good thing not to have friends. They can betray you. They can die. A man alone has the most power. A man alone shares with no one, and is the better for it. A man alone is truly a man.

And at last, with the rhythmic rocking of the ship, Nathaniel let sleep take him away for a little while.

3

March 13, 1607

NAT AND RICHARD stood on the main deck in the bright sun and cool breeze, hurling rats and mice over the rail into the ocean waves. There had been seven buckets full of the vermin, some caught among the barrels and the gentlemen's pallets on the 'tween deck, others on the main deck and in the cook's small brick galley. One particularly large and hairy rat had bedded down with the overweight and haughty man Edward Brookes, and the man had shrieked like a woman until Nat had clubbed the rodent with a poker.

As of yet, Richard and Nat hadn't had to go down through the square hatch in the floor of the 'tween deck into the lightless hold and catch rats down there. So far, only the sailors had swung down on their ropes to feed the animals and to work the pumps. The 'tween deck was smelly indeed, with the sweat and expensive perfumes worn by the gentlemen, but the fumes that drifted up from the hold were far worse. Who knew what kinds of creatures made their home down there among the waters of the bilge? And Nathaniel knew

that Richard was claustrophobic, especially in unfamil-
iar, unlit places. It had taken the boy a few weeks to
lose his discomfort on the 'tween deck.

Catching and dumping rats was preferable to other
chores the two boys were given. It was much more fun
to collect the animals and play at who could toss one
farther than it was to clean spilled urine or to swab
down vomit.

"Look!" Nat said to Richard, nudging him on the
arm as the rat he'd tossed arched and dropped into
the water a good thirty feet from the ship. "Aha! Quite
a distance old ratty flew there! I'm winning."

"My last one was at least that far," grumbled Richard.
"We can't be certain, can we? Who shall go out to measure?"

"Your arms are just too short," said Nat, grinning.

Richard scooped another rat from his bucket and
threw it, but a gust of wind kept it from going very far.
The little dead creature, its toes curled and its glazed
eyes open, dropped only ten feet from the ship.

"Pah!" grumped Richard.

But Richard's less-than-cheerful humor didn't
bother Nathaniel. The day was too pleasant, the sun
too kind, to make him think of anything but what lay
ahead. In not many weeks, they would step off onto the
land of Virginia, where gold and pearls abounded,
where urchin boys could become gentlemen and pompous pages would give them the respect they deserved.

"It seems to me that Samuel Collier would better
serve this trip killing rats and mice than to do whatever
silly errands John Smith has him do," said Richard. He
ran his hand under his nose, wiping away sooty mucus
from a lingering case of sniffles. "I hate the page."

"So do I," said Nat. "But as I've told you, you must
act as if he does not offend you. Stay out of his way.

Act as if he does not exist and we will be the better for it."

"I cannot ignore him. He constantly chides us!"

"But we must act our station so the men will leave us alone as much as possible. When we get to Virginia, we can improve our status. We can even steal silver and pearls and run away to live in a gold-filled Virginia hill if we want! But until then, we must be quiet, dim-witted laborers."

"I hate the gentlemen, too," said Richard. "They see us as no more than stray cats on a London alley."

"Behave as a cat and you will be seen as a cat. Behave like a humble ship's boy and you will be seen thus."

Richard rolled his eyes and gestured with upturned hands. "I cannot act as well as you! You have always been able to make people believe what you want them to. You could play a part at the Globe Theatre, I am certain. But not me, I—"

"Stop chattering!" It was a sailor who had seen the boys pause in their work. "I'll clout you! Back to work!"

"Yes, sir!" said Nat. Richard scowled.

"Only one more rat for us each," said Nathaniel, looking into the buckets. "Here is your chance to best me."

Nat and Richard threw their rats at the same time. Nat's went much farther than Richard's, plopping into the foamy green water and then disappearing.

"Idiot's game," said Richard.

"Ah, but it gives us the chance to stay above deck a bit longer, Richard," said Nat. "If we dumped them all at once, we'd have to go back down at once, and I don't know about you, but I prefer fresh air to stale."

"Hmm," said Richard.

The boys stood for a few more seconds, staring out at the vast water, pretending to toss rats from the now empty buckets. All around them, sailors went about their business, checking riggings, climbing the foremast, the mizzenmast, and the mainmast to constantly check and alter the sails, shouting to each other and to the crews of the *Discovery* and the *Godspeed* not far away. The huge white sails on the three ships billowed, and the red and white St. George's Cross flags snapped briskly in the wind. Over the past few days, there had been rough weather and the cook had been forced to put out the fire in his oven so a stray spark would not set the ship afire. Today, however, Nat could smell sweet, roasting meat from the small galley under the Great Cabin.

Nathaniel and Richard were in the clothes they'd worn since they had left London. Both had moth-ruined wool breeches, ratty silk stockings, weather-hardened leather shoes, and simple white linen blouses. Nathaniel also owned a brown cloak, given him by the charitable wife of a wheelwright who lived in Downing Street near the Thames. The cloak was now part of his mattress, covering the straw-filled bag to keep it less scratchy.

"How are you faring, my men?" came a familiar voice. John Smith stood with his arms crossed by the mainmast. Even though he was dressed as dandy as any lord, with a velvet doublet and cloak, embroidered breeches, silk stockings, and pistol and dagger at his waist, it was clear he had felt the effects of the long journey; his face was drawn and more pale and his cheekbones were prominent. Yet his voice was strong and his head held high. Smith often had a kind word for those below his station, and it was a pleasant distraction for Nat and Richard.

"Fine, sir," said Nat, bowing obediently. "It looks as though we'll have good weather for a time. Praise God."

"Praise God indeed," said Smith. He strode to the

railing and with a smile said, "Watch." He held out an open hand, showed it to Nat and Richard, then closed it and gave it a shake. When he opened it again, there was a shilling where none had been.

Nat's eyes widened. "How did you make that appear?"

"Oh," said Smith. "I have learned a lot in my travels. I have learned how to make things appear and disappear. This can be very useful at times. Very useful indeed."

"I can imagine," said Nat. So, not only was Smith dramatic and loud and confident, he was good at sleight of hand. What an amazing life this man must lead. *I would like to be just like him someday,* Nat thought.

But as Smith moved the shilling from one hand to the other, his face grew somber. He glanced over his shoulder. Captain Newport and Captain Gabriel Archer had come out of the Great Cabin beneath the stern's quarterdeck and stood talking quietly and looking at Smith. Newport was tall with broad shoulders and very little hair. Archer had a narrow face and fidgety eyes.

"The bad weather may have calmed," Smith said softly, "but the environment on this ship is more unpredictable now than ever. It will not be long before we are embroiled in a great turmoil."

Richard frowned. Nat said, "What . . . ?" But then he knew it was best to keep quiet. Best to act like he didn't understand. But he did understand. Many of the gentlemen on the ship didn't like Smith. They were jealous of him and thought he was too arrogant. Often they grumbled about his attitude. Now it seemed as if the other captains might also feel the same way. This couldn't be good for the voyage. With some luck or perhaps some divine interference, the men would keep their distrust to themselves and not cause any trouble before they reached the shores of Virginia. Not only was there the peril of rough seas, unpredictable winds on a long trip such as this, there were also Spanish ships on this very same sea who would welcome the chance to attack and rob an English ship. If the men fought seriously among themselves, they would be less able to deal with other dangers they might meet.

But then Smith smiled and clapped Nat and Richard on the shoulders. "And where is my page, that good-for-nothing? Go send him to me. I have errands which need to be done. If he's sleeping, douse him with water!" With a chuckle, Smith walked away, past Archer and Newport, who paused to watch him and then began talking again.

Down below, men were talking, coughing, and spitting. As always, Nat had to pause on the ladder to regain his vision in the dim light. Then he and Richard placed the buckets behind the base of the ladder and wormed through the men to their pallets. Nearby, on his own rumpled mattress, Samuel sat glaring at the two boys. He held his open wooden box in his lap.

"Samuel," Nat said. "Smith is calling for you."

"Yes," said Richard. "He is furious. I've never seen his face so red or his hands so palsied!"

"You," hissed Samuel, without making a move to get up.

"You?" said Nat. "You what?"

"You urchins," Samuel said.

"I beg your pardon for being an urchin," said Nat. "But such is my fate. Forgive me for my worthlessness."

Samuel's eyes drew up and his lip quivered furiously. "You've stolen from me, you stinking beggars!"

"I don't know what you mean," said Nat. Richard dropped to his mattress, already bored with this game of words.

Samuel shook his head. "I'm missing paper and ink,

and no one but you would have the nature to steal."

"Paper?" said Nat. "Why do you think I'd steal paper? Certainly I can't read nor write, I haven't your education."

"You are sneaky and clever!" Samuel snipped. "Just wait, you won't know when my revenge is coming! You two just wait and see!" He slammed his black hat onto his head and stormed away, the feather bouncing.

"What do you think he will try?" asked Richard. "I have never heard him so angry."

"Who knows and who can care?" said Nat.

"Did you steal his paper and ink?"

"Why would I? I am as ignorant of letters as you. Now come. We have work to do."

The day went on as usual, emptying waste, serving food, washing out the most severely soiled clothing of the gentlemen with seawater, repairing loose planks alongside the sailors.

But that night, after all had turned in for the evening's rest, Richard's yell woke Nat with a start.

Sitting bolt upright and blinking the cloud of sleep away, Nat looked to his right where Richard slept. Richard was not there. He then heard Samuel's voice, near the center of the 'tween deck. "Catch them, urchin! You will need them in Virginia!"

"Give them to me!"

Nat jumped up, hopping over sleeping men, trying not to step on anyone's head.

"Samuel!" shouted Richard.

Men were awakening now, yelling and complaining.

"You boys shut your mouths or I'll shut them for you!"

"What is the commotion?"

"I'll give you a wallop if you do not quiet down!"

Nat found his way to the center of the 'tween deck, his eyes now adjusted enough to see what was going on. Samuel had pried the wooden grating from the hold's hatch, and was dangling Richard's shoes over the hole. Richard was reaching out for them, but clearly afraid that if he made a quick move, Samuel would indeed drop the shoes down into the stinking black pit at the bottom of the ship.

"Samuel, give me the bloody shoes!" Richard said.

"Give me my paper and ink back."

"I don't have your paper. Give me my shoes."

"Be quiet, boys!" shouted Edward Brookes. "You will go over the side of this ship into the ocean if I get my wish!"

Nat said, "Samuel, give Richard his shoes before the men beat us!"

"No!" Samuel giggled and threw the shoes into the hold.

Richard gasped, then grabbed Samuel by the collar. "You worthless beast! I need my shoes!"

"Then go get them. I will not stop you. If you need your shoes, by all means, go into the hold and get them."

Suddenly there was a whoosh and a blow, and Nat was struck to his side, his breath knocked out. He lay stunned, struggling to pull air back into his lungs. Edward Brookes then knocked Samuel over, but Richard jumped out of the way in time.

"You boys get to your places before I kill the whole of you!" Brookes said. "And I am a man of my word!"

Samuel groaned, sat up, and said, "I will go, sir. Do not strike me again."

Brookes grunted once more, then, seeming somewhat satisfied, stumbled back to his mattress.

Samuel said quietly to Richard, "Best be after your shoes, boy. I would not be in Virginia with my feet bare. It could be dangerous and quite cold." Then he giggled and walked away.

"My shoes," Richard said, almost as if in mourning.

"I will help you get them in the morning when it is light," said Nat.

"My shoes are leather, and there are more vermin down there than anywhere else on this ship," said Richard. His voice was shaky. "If I wait until tomorrow, they will be chewed to scraps. I will go down now. I have no choice."

"We do not have a lantern, Richard. If I try to borrow one from a gentleman, he will say I am stealing, you know it. Stealing will have me whipped and then tossed overboard."

"All I need is rope. I think the shoes went straight down, so if I go straight down, too, I should find them without too much trouble."

Nat nodded reluctantly. He went to the ladder and found a length of rope coiled on a nail on its side. He tied one end around the bottom rung of the ladder, then took the length to Richard. All around, men flopped over on their mattresses in various stages of sleep, snoring, burping, farting. Richard grasped the rope, whispered, "God help me, I never wanted to go down into that dreadful place," and lowered himself into the hold.

Nat could imagine what was down there with Richard—water snakes swimming in standing water, enormous rats grown fat and vicious with constant feeding on the men's food supplies and an occasional caged chicken. He shivered and gooseflesh stood up on his arms and neck.

"I've never smelled such foul odors," Richard called up.

"Shh! Get the shoes quickly. I'll pull you back up."

There was silence for a few moments, then the sound of Richard swearing as he rummaged below, feeling for the shoes. All around Nat, the men began snoring once more.

Hurry! Get out of that wretched place!

Nat leaned over a bit farther, straining to hear, hoping Richard would not be bit by something poisonous.

And then there was a shrill giggle immediately behind Nat and something struck him between his shoulder blades and he was tumbling headlong into the rancid darkness of the hold. He landed on his side with an "umph!" His left arm was twisted beneath him, and hot, stabbing pains shot through it.

A voice very near him said, "Nat! Is that you?"

Nat croaked, "Samuel knocked me down into this place!"

"The cursed brat!"

Nat got his feet beneath him and stood dizzily. The flooring was as he feared, slimy and damp and uneven. The smell down here was worse than he could have imagined. It was like sticking his head into a waste bucket full of excrement.

"Are you all right? Did you break anything?"

Nat moved his left arm and gritted his teeth against sparkles of pain that traveled the length of it. "I think not. My arm can move, but it hurts dreadfully. God! I cannot have a broken arm. How would I survive the rest of the journey with a broken arm?"

"You can move it truly?" asked Richard.

"Yes."

"Then it is not broken. Perhaps bruised or sprained."

"Yes," said Nat. Then he heard a hissing sound, and the chickens nearby squawked.

"Snakes, Nathaniel!" cried Richard.

"No, I don't think so."

"Or huge, rabid rats like the dog back in London. We cannot see them before they bite us on the legs!"

"Richard, the hissing sound is only water running in

the bilge. Be calm or you will only make matters worse."

"How can they be worse?"

There was a pause, and Nat said, "At this moment, I do not really know." Then, "Did you find your shoes?"

"I found one of them."

"We have to find the other, then we must get out of here straightaway."

Then Richard said, "How?"

"How? What do you mean?"

"You have a hurt arm. How will you get out of here?"

"I . . . ," Nat began. But Richard was right. Richard could pull himself up the rope, but there was no way Nat could do it with only one good arm. "I do not know."

"Don't fret," Richard said, the fear in his voice barely disguised. "We'll find a way. But first the shoe."

Nat swallowed and his throat was dry.

It took a while to find the shoe. Nat grimaced as he felt around the filthy flooring, around crates and barrels as he held his bad arm close to his body. He tried not to think of things waiting in the darkness to bite his fingertips, but every strange sound and sensation caused him to draw his hands back in terror.

And then Richard said, "I have it!"

Nat stood up. His knees were soaked through with stinking water, and his hands were scratched and full of splinters. His arm throbbed.

"Get the rope now and climb out," said Nat.

"What about you?"

"Go on without me. Maybe my arm will heal enough in a day or two and then you can throw the rope back down to me. If not, I'll just stay down here until we land, and if I am not dead, they can take me out with the chickens and pigs."

There was silence, then Richard broke into laughter.

"You are such an actor, Nat! What drama! Now hear me. When I am out, I'll toss the rope back to you. You tie it about your waist and I will haul you up."

"You're not strong enough."

"This trip is making a man of me. Just wait and see."

There was a deep breath and grunt, and Richard was climbing the rope. Nat could feel the air move as Richard's legs kicked out, working to hoist his body upward. A minute later, the whispered call came from above. "Catch the rope now and tie it tightly!"

Nat's hand felt around until it found the rope. He pulled at it to get enough length to put it around himself.

But it was too short.

He pulled again and met with taut resistance. "Richard, the rope is too short to make a loop!"

A quiet curse from above, then Richard said, "Let me find more rope and we will tie them together."

Nat stood in the stinking darkness, not wanting to move now that he was alone in the hold. Visions of tremendous rats sprang into his mind again, and he wished he had tall leather boots like a captain to protect his ankles.

Then Richard's voice came. "Nat, there is no more rope to be found here on the 'tween deck."

"What do you propose, then? That I stay here and rot?"

"Quit whining. I will find more rope in the day, when it is light and I am allowed up deck. Find a barrel. I will have rope in just a few hours. Be patient."

Nat stretched his hand out and moved forward until he found a barrel. He sat atop it and stared out into nothingness.

"Goodnight, Nat," called Richard.

"It is not very good, but what can I do about it?"

Richard swore softly, then was gone.

Nat drew his legs up and crossed them. *There are no poisonous snakes nor rats with deadly jaws,* he told himself. But he kept his legs crossed and away from the floor just in case. His mind went fuzzy, and even though he fought to stay awake, he fell into a restless sleep.

Rope smacking against his cheek made him startle into consciousness. His eyes flew open.

"What?" he said. "Where am I?" Then he remembered. But it wasn't day. Who had lowered rope into the hold while it was still nighttime? He squinted up into the darkness, but could see nothing but the outline of a head.

"Quick," said a man's voice. "Loop this around yourself and tie it tightly. I will get you up."

Nat reached for the rope. His left arm was still sore and now it felt swollen. Carefully he drew the end around himself and tied it, then slid the loop up beneath his arms and took hold. He stood up on the barrel. It was only a matter of six or so feet to the hatch.

"All right, Nat," said the mysterious man. "Pull."

The rope went rigid and lifted Nat up off the barrel a few inches. But then he slammed back down again.

Nat said, "I lost my grip. I am too heavy!"

"Shhh, do not make a business of this," said the man. "The gentlemen are still asleep and I would like to keep it that way. Let me get you out quickly. Hold tight."

The rope inched up. Nat tried to will himself to weigh less by loosening his body's joints. The rope went up another four inches. Then it wavered, but didn't slip. It was pulled jerkily yet consistently upward, and in just a few moments, Nat was able to throw one foot up through the hatch, then another, and then he was pulled to the safety of the 'tween deck floor.

"How is your arm?" asked the man.

"It will be better soon," answered Nat. He pulled

himself out of the rope and then squinted at the man who had helped him. It was Jehu Robinson, a thin, very quiet man whose pallet was near the ladder.

"Thank you," Nat said uncomfortably.

Jehu looked over at the mattresses, occupied by dozing gentlemen, then back at Nat. "I am ashamed these men would not help you," he said. "We could all hear you. They are not all asleep, but hiding with their eyes closed. I suspect they are afraid to dirty their hands or bring out a callus on those smooth, unblemished palms."

Nat said nothing. He didn't know what role to play with this unusual man.

"God forgive us our selfishness," said Jehu. "Now, let us get back to our places before the gentlemen decide our yammering is so bothersome that we should both be dumped down into that hold!"

❧ 4 ❧

March 20, 1607

OVER THE DAYS that followed, there was nothing to see in the ocean but waves, an occasional fish leaping into the air, the fins of sharks slicing the water, and the other ships, sails stretched full, following behind. *Virginia*, thought Nat. *Where are you?* But the minutes on the upper deck were the best entertainment to be had, and Nat relished them. They took their time dumping urine and rodents into the water so they could savor the fresh air. At least Nat's arm was not broken and only ached on occasion.

One cloudy afternoon, as Nat and Richard stared out at the sparkling waves, tossing rats, an argument brewed behind them.

Nat recognized Gabriel Archer's voice immediately. He didn't think it would be wise to acknowledge the disagreement, so he looked ahead at the water, while tuning his ears in sharply. He held his finger to his lips so Richard would follow suit.

"Sir, I have often told you that Captain Smith is a troublemaker. His haughty attitude with the gentlemen has made him so loathsome I scarce can tolerate it. Must we endure him for such time until we are settled in Virginia?"

"We shall." This was the voice of Captain Newport. "I've not seen reason to do anything other than that, Archer. He is a man of much knowledge of the sea. As prone as he is to try to tell others what to do, we need him."

"Indeed!" said Archer. "I've as much knowledge as Smith and my experience is as valuable or more so. Yet I don't scheme to overthrow us all when we've arrived in Virginia."

"I've not heard that kind of talk from Smith, either," said Newport. "Is your imagination heightened by our time at sea?"

"Not my imagination, sir, but my understanding of the conniving mind and the untrustworthy soul."

"I'll listen to this no more," said Newport. "I've work to do." There were footsteps across the deck to Newport's cabin at the stern of the ship.

Archer took a deep breath and blew it out noisily. He grumbled to himself. Then there was a whisper.

Nat glanced over his shoulder quickly. Kendall was there now, standing next to Archer. Both men's capes billowed like dark sails in the sea wind. The two were talking softly, and Nat couldn't hear what was being said. He looked back at the water and dropped a few more mice into the brine.

Then Archer said loudly, "There is the king himself!"

Curiosity took charge of Nat's feet and turned him around. At the center of the deck stood Kendall, Archer, and now Smith. Smith's chin was tipped upward and his hands were clenched at his sides. Surely, Nat thought, these men wouldn't resort to a brawl. That was something street urchins did, not captains.

Smith glanced at Richard and Nat. With a sharp jerk

of his head, he said, "You two. Below, the both of you."

Nat hesitated, and Smith shouted, "I said go now!"

Richard and Nat carried their buckets to the bow-side hatch. Richard scrambled down the ladder and dropped onto the floor. Nat followed, but halfway down, he stopped and climbed back up and peeked his head through the hatch.

Archer had his hand now on the hilt of his sword. Kendall's hand was on the dagger at his waist. Smith, feet planted apart with the rocking of the ship, still maintained clenched fists, but did not touch either of his weapons.

"Hail to our misguided lord!" said Archer. "The man who would crown himself king if chance presented itself."

"King Smith," said Kendall. "What a distasteful sound that is, and what a distasteful smell comes from his direction!"

"Sirs," said Smith. "I've never said I would be king. Do not lower yourselves by speaking in such a manner."

"Hah!" Archer's laugh was deep and without any humor. "You, sir, are the lowest. No one could lie upon this deck and be as low as you. The rats in the hold look down upon you, and the lice stay clear."

Smith's hand went to his sword. "Recant, sir."

"I will not take back the truth. I am not a liar."

"Recant your words or you will regret the moment they left your lips."

"I am not a liar!"

For a moment there was silence, except for the rush of the water and the call of sailors at the masts. Nat's hands trembled on the top ladder rung. The captains' hair and capes lifted and fell in the current of air, waving to each other in childlike taunts. The men stared hard and cold.

And then Smith drew his sword in a flash, and

jumped toward Archer with the point to the man's throat. Kendall brayed and skipped away. Archer's eyes went wide as moons.

"Recant," hissed Smith. "Or your words will be your death!"

Archer sputtered, clearly frightened. Then he managed, "No, sir. I'm afraid your actions here have only proven me correct."

"Nat!" called Richard from below. "Get down here!"

Nat waved frantically to keep Richard still.

Smith stepped up closer to Archer, keeping the point of the sword at the man's neck. There was a bead of blood where the blade touched. Smith's teeth were bared, his nostrils flaring. "Deny your words, Archer!"

But there was a shouting from the door to the Great Cabin. Newport stood, hat in his hands, his mouth open in fury. Slamming his hat onto his head, he hurried down the ladder and shoved Smith and Archer apart. "What is this? On my good ship I have one captain ready to take the life of another?"

Smith sheathed his sword and said, "I have cause, sir. If you'd only seen the behavior of these two, of Archer and Kendall, you'd know why I acted as I did."

But Archer threw his arms apart in a gesture of surprise. "I have no idea of which he speaks! The man charged me, unprovoked, and made to slit my throat!"

Kendall pushed from the side of the ship and stood by Archer. "It's true, my lord. Smith is rabid in his actions! The man would have murdered Archer had you not come upon us when you did. He must be taken into custody."

"Yes," said Archer. "Confine the man, that we might hang him when we reach the next island!"

But Smith stood straight and looked Newport directly in the eye. "Captain Newport, it was not without provocation that I pulled my sword. These two men have played their petty game of jealousy since we set sail from London."

Newport said, "Give me your weapons, Smith."

"Sir, these men called me names so foul that no man could tolerate such abuse!"

"We are innocent of such absurd charges," said Archer. "Foul names? His mind plays tricks on him. You saw his actions. We have no option but to put the man in chains."

Newport shook his head in resignation. "Smith, give me your weapons. I will have a court of inquiry tomorrow, but for now, you must be secured in your cabin."

Smith stared angrily between Archer and Kendall, but then reluctantly handed his dagger and sword to Newport.

"He should be put into the galley, Captain Newport," said Archer. "What punishment is it that he be allowed to stay in his own cabin, where I myself must sleep?"

"Sleep elsewhere, then, until court is held," said Newport. "But until he is found guilty, he will not go into the galley."

Newport then gestured to the door to Smith's cabin. Kendall and Archer glanced at each other. Then Archer said, "Will you not at least bind the man? He is a danger, sir, you saw it with your very eyes!"

"Not until the court!" said Newport. "Now I will speak no more of this until morning."

Nat watched as Newport put Smith into his cabin. Then the captain called to a sailor and spoke with him quietly. The sailor stood, arms crossed, outside Smith's door. Clearly the cabin was to be guarded until court was held.

Someone tugged on Nat's shoe, and he looked down. It was Edward Brookes. The man was holding a waste bucket. "Make yourself useful, boy," he said.

"There are three more buckets ready to be emptied. Now, be quick!"

That night, when Nat lay down to sleep, his mind wouldn't let go of what he'd seen. He pulled out his paper, flattened the rumples from the surface, and uncapped the ink. He wrote,

If Archer and Kendall knew I saw the truth. If they realized that I saw the provocation Smith was subjected to, they would throw me into the sea like a pan of vomit.

He rolled onto his side and tucked his hand beneath his head and shivered. Then he wrote,

What will happen in the court of inquiry tomorrow? If Smith is found innocent, all will be well, except that Archer and Kendall will continue to make their trouble. But if Smith is found guilty, he will be confined in the hold, down with the vermin and the stench of the bilge. And when we reach land, he will surely be hanged.

When Nat went to sleep at last, he dreamed of a rope about his neck and men laughing at him. He was being hoisted up to mizzenmast to the great blue sky, unable to breathe.

He clutched at his throat and screamed as the rope grew tighter and tighter.

Nat's legs kicked out as his vision shattered; he found himself in the blackness of the 'tween deck, lying on a thin, straw-stuffed mattress.

He sat up. His hands went instantly to his neck, and he was relieved to find the dream noose gone. He wondered if he had called out in his sleep, but no one around seemed disturbed, not even the irritable Samuel Collier.

Nat lay back down and linked his fingers beneath his head. Maybe he hadn't yelled, but he was surprised that the dreadfully loud hammering of his heart hadn't startled any of the gentlemen out of their mysterious, mindless sleeps.

5

March 21, 1607

THE COURT OF inquiry was held out on the upper deck, and only gentlemen were allowed to attend. Nat paced the 'tween deck, rolling his pebbles in his palms, wondering if he should go up the ladder and tell what he had seen. They certainly couldn't hang Smith if they knew the truth of the incident. Surely Newport was a man concerned with truth and fairness.

But in spite of the taunting dream, he knew it was best to say nothing. To play the idiot.

Richard was curious about what was going on up the ladder, but he didn't let on. He was weaving a small mat with some loose straw he'd found, bending over it and pretending to be intensely content to be at this task.

Samuel sat on his pallet, driven to distraction by Nat's pacing.

"Sit down, urchin," he commanded. "With so much back and forth you'll tip the ship over and we'll all drown."

"Tell the lapdog to be silent, Nat," said Richard, looking up from his weaving.

"I will not be silent," said Samuel. "I am free and I may speak as I wish."

Nat took a breath and blew it out through his teeth.

Then there were men's voices and footsteps on the ladder. Nat's hands found each other and made a single, tight fist.

It was a pair of sailors, who squinted about and then gazed at Nat.

"You, boy!" called one sailor. "You are the one!"

"Me?" asked Nat. His heart pounded in anticipation.

"You are called for to speak at the inquiry!" said the sailor.

Dear God! Nat thought. *Someone knows I was watching! Who could it have been? What am I to say? What is to happen?*

"What're ya waiting for, get up here now!"

Nat glanced at Richard and Samuel, who were both watching with the same stunned expression. Then he followed the sailors up the ladder and to the Great Cabin at the stern of the ship.

He'd never been inside this room and had never expected to be. Whatever cleaning or vermin extermination was done for Captain Newport was handled by one of the sailors. It was not a large space compared to the width and breadth of the 'tween deck, but it had a feeling of light and grandeur. There were two oak cots against either side, with a desk covered in rolled charts, instruments, pens, and inkwells, a cabinet for clothing, a shelf for books, and several lanterns hanging on brass hooks. Small square windows revealed the sea to either side, and they allowed in plenty of sunlight, enough for men to see during this daytime hour without lighting the lanterns.

But it was crowded this morning. Men stood in tight clusters, all facing the side of the room where Captain Smith stood in his shackles. Newport was at the desk, hands folded, clearly exasperated yet keeping his emotions in check. Archer was up, pacing as best he could in the cramped quarters. This inquiry had been going on for over an hour now.

Nat was shoved against the wall by the door, behind Kendall and Edward Brookes. Most of the men in the cabin didn't seem to notice he had been brought in, and the few who did gave him disdainful glances.

"Mutiny," Archer was saying. "The man is clearly up to it. It is clear he's planned it from the beginning. Smith has no respect for those in command, such as yourself, Captain Newport. He sees himself as the dashing rogue, hero to the underlings such as the sailors, commoners, and laborers, winning their favor for his own gain."

"Untrue," said Smith simply.

Archer pointed a finger at Smith, close enough to brush the other's nose. Smith did not flinch. "Look at your own history, Smith. Fighting with the Hungarians for adventure, not for the good of England but for your own glory, I daresay! Caught and sold as a slave by the Turks, escaping to Russia and then home again, full of tales which catch the fancy of those who listen. But if they listened more carefully and more deeply, they would see what we see, nothing but a braggart after his own interests."

"Yes!" echoed several other gentlemen.

Archer continued, "I daresay you were never taken slave but conjured the elaborate tale to make yourself into somewhat of a legend! And you see the opportunity to be legend yet again, at the expense of the Virginia Company!"

"I was provoked into the fight with you," said Smith. "I would not raise my sword but for the same reason you would, sir. To protect the honor of my name. If I was unshackled at this moment, I would raise it again for what lies you have said against me just now."

"Indeed!" said Newport at his desk.

"I care for the welfare of this expedition as much as the next," said Smith. "I have said it before and will say it again, it is your jealousy speaking. You wish you had but a fraction of the courage I have!"

"Arrogance!" said Archer.

"Truth," said Smith.

Captain Newport shook his head, then his gaze fell upon Nat. "There is the boy you requested, Smith."

God save me!

"Boy," said Captain Newport, one eyebrow raised beneath his cap. "Smith has made a request that you be brought in to tell what you saw on the deck yesterday."

"Me?" Nat was shocked that he could find his voice. "What I saw, sir?"

Smith looked at Nat straight on, and in an even tone said, "You witnessed the altercation from the onset, boy, did you not?"

"I . . . ," began Nat.

"You were on the ladder, making for the 'tween deck, but you stopped, and I saw you watching there. I am not a successful warrior nor—" he gave Archer a quick, cold glance "—a cunning man who escaped the clutches of Turkish slavery because I do not observe what is about me. And I observed you, boy. On the ladder. Tell these fine gentlemen what you saw."

"Well, sir . . . ," said Nat.

"Of course he will testify on behalf of Smith," said Kendall, giving Nat a shove and knocking him against the door. "This smelly little hold mouse? That is what Smith is hoping for, to win the affections of the common folks so they will do his bidding!"

"So they will lie for him," said Archer.

"Regardless," said Captain Newport. "Boy, have your

say. You have been called to testify as to what you observed yesterday from the ladder."

What do I say? Nat thought frantically. *If I speak on behalf of Smith, I am in danger of the others. If I speak on
behalf of Archer, I am in danger of Smith.*

"Speak!" demanded Newport.

"The sun was in my eyes, sir," said Nat. "So brightly
I could not tell a cloud from a sail. I saw nothing."

"No?" said Newport. "Then tell us what you heard."

"There were several men below me on the 'tween
deck who were in a row, so loud a row that I could
make out nothing but the argument. I heard not a
word spoken between Captain Archer and Captain
Smith." Nat did not look at Smith, but at the floor. It
was a nice floor, even and covered with a piece of
Oriental rug.

"Ah," said Newport. "Then take the boy back where
he belongs. That was a waste of our time!"

A soldier grabbed Nat by the upper arm and steered
him out through the door. Nat was left on his own to
go back down to the 'tween deck.

Richard nearly pounced on Nat, tossing his weaving
aside. "What happened?"

"Nothing," said Nat as he plopped onto his pallet.

"What did you say?"

"I said nothing. I had nothing to say."

"Damn you!"

"So be it."

Nat drew up his knees and waited. It was another
hour before there was word from above. Edward Brookes clambered down the ladder and wiped his hands
in satisfaction.

"Well," he said as he pointed a finger in Samuel's
direction. "You are no longer a page. You are now a
laborer like these other two boys. We'll have you killing
rats and dumping our pails."

Samuel was incredulous. "No longer a page?"

Edward Brookes giggled. He dabbed at his face with a dainty, chubby finger. "Smith has been found guilty of attempting murder and mutiny. He is confined in the galley, and will not be allowed out until we stop for more supplies. There, we will hang him by his neck until he is dead."

"Guilty?" Samuel's word was barely a whisper.

"Yes," said Archer, who was just now coming down the ladder. "Praise God justice has prevailed. The man will hang and we will all be the better for it."

"And I am to clean the waste buckets and kill vermin?"

"Unless you want to hang like your master for disobeying the order of a gentleman," said Edward Brookes. He rubbed at a fold of fat beneath his chin. "You'll do exactly as you are told."

Samuel went silent. The gentlemen, clearly pleased for the most part with the verdict, settled down and picked up their dice and their cards and their flutes. The commoners drew together and whispered in disappointed voices.

"Nat," said Richard. "Smith is going to hang."

"Yes."

"We'll have no one to take our part should things get bad! He was the only one who treated us as men."

"I know."

"There must be something we can do!"

"Absolutely not. We must continue as we have."

"But, Nat, he will hang!"

"I am sorry for Smith. But what I feel matters not at all. I should just as well believe the sun should be purple, and the waters of the ocean filled with cattle to be caught and brought a-deck for our meals."

"You do not care?"

"I can't care. And neither can you."

"If you were unjustly sentenced for an imagined infraction," said Richard, "I would come to your part!"

"If it was life or death, you would not. And I would not for you, either. Now, be quiet. The men are listening to us."

Richard went silent. Nat could feel the confusion and anger steaming off him. But Nat couldn't change the facts. Smith was a survivor. If anyone could escape a hanging, this man could. And if not, then there was nothing Nat could do about it. He and Richard needed to survive, too, and on this cursed ship it would take a blind eye and deaf ear to accomplish that.

6

April 19, 1607

Smith is a survivor! I can learn much from watching him. We sailed along the islands of the West Indies days ago and disembarked on several occasions to replenish supplies of food and water. We stayed three days on one lush tropical isle named Nevis.

Archer told us, "Here we shall wash our clothes and ourselves. We shall eat good foods of this place and recover our strength. Then we shall take care of our prisoner and leave his body like carrion for the scavenging natives!"

"Ah," said Edward Brookes. "Entertainment for us all."

Richard, Samuel, and I were compelled to carry several gentlemen's goods up the ladder, but when we got out on deck, we found soldiers, gentlemen, and captains alike staring in amazement over the railing at the shore.

John Smith was standing on the sandy beach, alone. He was in full uniform, with his helmet in place, breast armor on, and cape swept back, showing his sword, dagger, and powder horn. From his boot top protruded yet another, smaller dagger. In one hand was a musket. Smith was smiling as if to say, "Come and get me, any who dare!"

Archer shook his fist. "How did that man get ashore? How did he gain access to weapons?"

Kendall shouted, "Who helped this murderous villain gain transportation to the shore?"

No one answered. Each man seemed as confused as the other. The pinnace had been lowered into the water already, so clearly someone had rowed the captain ashore.

I couldn't imagine who had done this, but was glad.

Archer complained angrily to Newport as the gentlemen took their turns being rowed to the beach. The pinnaces from the Discovery and Godspeed also carried their passengers to the banks of the island, although once on the land, no one went to take hold of John Smith. Instead, everyone stood back and watched as Smith settled himself on the ground with a few curious, naked natives who had come from the forest, and tried to hold conversation with them.

Richard and I were in the last shuttle. As I climbed down into the pinnace, I heard Archer tell Newport on deck, "The carpenter Edward Pising will bring tools. There is wood here. We will carry out Smith's sentence in spite of his trickery."

The sand on the island was warm. Sailors brought the store of weapons ashore. Even Richard, Samuel, and I were outfitted with helmets and muskets. Once everyone was off the ships and gathered around, we knelt while Reverend Hunt blessed the land and the ships and the voyage.

"Protect us and let us carry Your glory into this land," Hunt prayed.

Then everyone stood and looked again at John Smith.

Archer said, "We will now build a gallows for Smith!"

But Newport said, "Indeed? I have decided I will not go after Smith. See how quickly he has made friends of the savages yonder? He is invaluable. Leave him be."

Archer was incredulous. "Leave him be? We held court and he is condemned to die! Kendall, support what I say."

Captain Kendall came and stood beside Archer, but the eye he kept on Smith showed hesitation.

Reverend Hunt then approached Newport and the other two captains and said quietly, "God may have His hand in this.

Smith has befriended the savages, blessing our presence with peace rather than war."

"I cannot believe my ears!" shouted Archer.

"Do you mean to confront him, then?" asked Newport. "Go ahead, Archer, if you feel you cannot face another day without hanging John Smith!"

Archer glared at Smith, who had stood now and had turned again to face the company of men. The wind tossed his cape; the smile on his face was defiant and confident.

"Face him and his talents with sword and dagger," said Newport. "But you and Kendall will do it alone, for I will have nothing to do with the man's death."

Archer stared at Smith for another moment, then spun on his heel and stalked away. Kendall trotted after.

With Newport's unofficial pardon of Smith's conviction, we all went about exploration. We journeyed inland and found a large, warm spring which was just the proper temperature for long and soothing baths. Smith was back in the fold; he chatted with a number of the men and laughed with others, while Archer, Kendall, and their close friends scowled uselessly.

Days later we sailed west to an equally lovely island of the West Indies called Mona. It was here, on April 7th, that we lost the gentleman Edward Brookes on a lush green hillside. A long hike proved too much. I heard the gentleman George Percy explain to another that Brookes's fat melted inside him and he died. I learned much from the sniveling Brookes. I learned what type of man I will never become, regardless of the wealth I gain in Virginia.

We are on our ships again, with no more stops between here and Virginia. Samuel has grown melancholy and quiet. Even with his master out of chains, he seems as if he's lost some of his nastiness. I think I liked him better when he was obnoxious. At least, he was more interesting.

Soon we will be there. Soon.

Soon I shall walk barefoot in the gold I have come to know so intimately in my dreams. I shall build my home and send *for servants from London to work for me, to tend my animals and raise my garden and stand guard over my treasures. I will be strong like John Smith, and cunning, and quick. I will never be cold again. I will never be poor again. I will never be hungry again.*

The time is so close. The time of suffering is nearly done! Thank God.

7

April 26, 1607

VIRGINIA!" Nat's eyes opened.

"It is there!" came the shout from up deck. "The shores of Virginia, and it is as good and fair a land as we have ever seen!"

Everyone went up to the deck and stared. Nat wormed his way beneath shoulders and elbows to the railing.

Virginia! We have made it!

"Praise God from whom all blessings are bestowed!" said Reverend Hunt.

"Amen!" shouted the men. Above, on the roundtops, sailors cheered and howled in the pale morning light.

Nat turned his face to the breeze and took a long breath of the Virginia coastal air. The three ships sailed more closely to the land and dropped their anchors. The pinnaces were lowered and made ready to carry some of the men ashore. Across the water, there was visible a beautiful land, different from England and Mona but lovely in its own right. Sparkling sand, waving waterside plants, and tall needle-leaved and broad-leaved trees stood back from the beach like watchful citizens.

"Cape Henry," said John Smith as he stood near Nat and nodded at the land. "We shall name that fine point of land Cape Henry in honor of the Prince of Wales."

No one argued or disputed this name, because although Nat could tell by some of the gentlemen's expressions that they wouldn't have cared for any name suggested by Smith, it seemed the right thing to do on behalf of the prince.

The pinnace set off to the shore. Newport sat at the helm, and behind him were Smith, Archer, and Kendall and several sailors and soldiers. The *Godspeed* and *Discovery* also launched their small boats filled with explorers. Nat could see from his vantage place on the ship's deck there were two boys on the *Godspeed*'s pinnace. Nat envied them; they would be among the first to step on Virginia's soil. The small boats reached the shore and the men climbed out and ventured over a sandy knoll where they could no longer be seen.

"I would like to be with them," said Nat to Richard. "I imagine I could be a good soldier here. I told Smith that I was a soldier."

"Just act as a soldier and you shall be one," said Richard.

Nat laughed. "You're learning!"

Suddenly the carpenter Edward Pising grabbed Nat by the arm and said, "We have some repairs from the last storm. You boys come with me." Nat and Richard spent the next hours driving nails into loosened boards all around the upper deck and in the cabins.

When the afternoon shadows grew long, the workers took a break, munching handfuls of hardtack and prunes and drinking their allotted beer. Nat ate quickly, knowing soon they would have better food from the land of Virginia. No longer would he have to worry about saving a stale biscuit.

Then Edward Pising dropped his biscuit, tilted his head, and squinted in the direction of the shore. "Listen," he said.

Richard and Nat listened. There was a faint sound above that of the slapping waves, something like singing, high-pitched and resonant.

"What is that?" Nat wondered aloud.

Then they could hear that it was not singing at all but screams. From over the sandy knoll rushed the Englishmen. They ran in sheer terror, struggling in the sand, muskets held high. Some were yelling, others shouting. They jumped into the pinnaces and frantic sailors splashed knee-deep as they pushed the boats off into the deeper water.

"Lord save us!" said Edward Pising. "Savages!" Breaking from the scrubby vegetation and racing down after the men were several natives. They carried bows and arrows, and as they ran they set the bows straight and aimed at the retreating men.

"Watch out!" screamed Richard.

"Lay low!" cried the carpenter.

The natives drew back on their bows and released. Arrows arced in the air, coming down in a rain over the men of the *Susan Constant*'s pinnace.

Some arrows missed and fell into the water. Several others struck men in shoulders and arms. A sailor, now waist-deep in the water, struggling to climb aboard, was struck in the back and went down. Newport pulled him onto the boat by his shirt collar.

"Row!" cried Nat. Sailors hopped in with the others, and men frantically tugged the oars to steer the boats back to the mother ships. Smith stood straight in the small boat, gesturing wildly with his arms, shouting and directing the others. Archer stood up as well, as if even in this desperate situation, he could not let Smith take command.

On the beach, the natives lined arrows on their bow-strings and aimed again at the pinnaces. They let the arrows fly. Archer spun to face the beach, and his hands flew up in front of his face as he saw the arrows flying at him.

And then he screamed.

An arrow pierced his hands, one in front of the other, pinning them together. Archer fell backward into the boat. Another man grabbed the arrow and tore it free of Archer's hands. Archer screamed again.

"Row!" cried men from the deck of the *Susan Constant*.

Newport was at the stern of the boat then, legs planted apart to keep from tipping over. He raised his musket at the natives, who were yet again reloading their bows. He pulled on the trigger. The blast was loud and smoky, and the natives stopped midload to stare wide-eyed at the weapon pointed in their direction. But they shot arrows again, and again, men in the pinnaces were hit. Cries filled the air. Richard put his hands over his ears.

More men loaded the muskets with powder and ammunition, readied them, then fired across the waves at the attackers. Natives at last turned, and with loud wails and shouts, ran back over the sandy knoll and disappeared.

The boats were quickly rowed the rest of the distance to their ships, and the men, wounded and unhurt, were hauled up to the deck.

Men crowded about and had to be shoved back by the captains and the sailors. The man who had been shot in the back was severely wounded. The arrow still protruded from his body, and there was a second one in his thigh. It took two men and much effort to pull the bloody sticks from him.

"Be strong, Matthew Morton," said the sailor who held the arrow and then broke it in half angrily.

John Smith, sweating and rumpled but not wounded, said, "You took an arrow for us. That shows goodly faith and courage."

Matthew Morton clutched his belly and groaned as the blood ran through his fingers.

This is not acting, Nat thought. *This is truly a brave man. Could I be so brave?*

Morton was carried carefully and respectfully into the galley by two other sailors.

Captain Archer sat on the deck by the center hatch, making a great deal of noise.

"I am mortally wounded!" he shrieked. "My hands are so badly pierced I shall surely die!" Nat could see the holes in the hands, welling with red blood, coursing down his wrists in thick rivulets. His shirtsleeves were soaked.

The surgeon said, "Be still, and we shall do what we can." He motioned for help, and Archer was lifted to his feet and taken to Newport's cabin.

Newport stayed on deck, clearly undeterred by the attack. "We shall wait a short time before we return," he said. "The savages know our power, they will not likely attack again soon. Tomorrow morning we shall go ashore and assemble the shallop. Tomorrow we shall explore. Tomorrow we shall bless Virginia in the name of God and the king."

Gentlemen and commoners alike nodded in agreement. And then Newport said, "And now, as instructed, we shall open the box in which is listed the council for Virginia. We shall know who is to be the leaders in our new land."

Gentlemen and commoners nodded again, but this

time it was clear they nodded for different reasons. Gentlemen hoped they would find the council list to their liking, and that John Smith would not be part. Sailors, soldiers, and laborers hoped that Smith would be on the list.

Newport, Smith, and several other gentlemen went to Newport's cabin. With a pleased tossing of his head and winking in Richard's direction, Samuel Collier followed. Captains from the other ships were hailed and invited to come onto the *Susan Constant* to hear the reading. They came in their pinnaces, which were tethered to the *Susan Constant*'s side. The men came aboard and without a word, went to the Great Cabin.

No one wanted to go below. Everyone wanted to know who was on the list. There was small talk to pass the time. Richard leaned against the ship's railing by Nat and said, "I do not think Smith will make the list. He was charged with attempted murder and found guilty."

"The list was made before we left," Nat said. "I think Smith will be included. And I'll wager my first piece of Virginia gold that I'm right."

The night sky grew dark, and stars made their twinkling appearances overhead. Everyone was restless. How long did it take to open a box and read names? But at last the door to the Great Cabin swung wide and Newport came out. His face was set in a serious mood and it was impossible for Nat to tell from that expression if Smith was in or out. Newport held a piece of rolled paper.

"We have our council," Newport said simply. "These are the men who will share in the leadership of the Virginia colony."

It was as though everyone on deck took a breath at the same time. "Christopher Newport," said Newport, and there were murmurs of agreement. "Edward Maria

Wingfield, Bartholomew Gosnold, John Ratcliffe, John Martin, George Kendall." Then Newport clenched his fist. He glanced back over his shoulder to the Great Cabin where the other men still tarried and then out at the men on the deck. Then Newport said no more, turned and went inside.

"I heard there were to be seven councilors," said Edward Pising. "He read only six."

"I do not understand," said a gentleman. "But I am glad Smith was not on the list!"

Everyone retired below deck.

Richard punched the side of his mattress to soften it a bit and said, "You owe me your first gold."

Nat didn't answer.

It wasn't long before Samuel Collier came below. He looked drawn and tired and upset. Nat didn't want to speak to the boy, but curiosity overcame dislike. "What happened in the Cabin that had Newport looking so troubled?"

Samuel dropped to his mattress and took off his hat. "John Smith was on the list."

"What?" asked Nat.

"He was on the list, but the other councilors say they will not seat him. Wingfield and Kendall were the most adamant in their objections. They convinced the others that Smith would be bad for the colony. They said he had selfish interests. Smith agreed to abide by their decision temporarily. Somehow, he will show them he is fit to council. But not for now." The boy then lay down and went silent.

"I will take your first-found pearl if you would rather keep the gold," Nat said to Richard with a laugh.

Richard grumbled softly and rolled over to sleep. Nat looked at the blackness of the 'tween deck ceiling. Smith was on the council. This would be a good thing for himself. Smith could be counted on. Smith, at least, didn't see Richard and Nat as less than human.

8

May 12, 1607

The past days have been filled with excitement and work. We all went onshore, armed and helmeted, ready for adventure. But I found adventure is, for now, the privilege of others, not common boys. The first act was to give thanks to God for His mercy. Laborers cut down a tree and constructed a large cross. It was erected on the beach of Cape Henry, and the Reverend Hunt gave a long oration on God's anger and power. We knelt in the damp sand and prayed. Seabirds circled overhead, and I thought I could hear a distant chanting of savages and pulsing of drums.

I sense they are anxious we are here. They do not want us taking their mountains of gold. I would not want anyone taking my gold, either, but these are people who are not even Christians, and I've heard gentlemen say that God doesn't reward those who do not worship Him properly.

After our prayer, we stood, and the mood shifted to anticipation. Gentlemen and soldiers gathered together to explore the cape. They left us commoners behind to assemble the shallop. I wanted to explore so very much! I have suffered the journey on the ship as well as any of the others! But I had to keep my thoughts to myself.

I have finished my midday meal, and in moment—

"Boy!" came a sharp voice. It was one of the carpenters in charge of putting the boat together. "Put that dabbling away, you've done with your meal now back to work!"

Nat cursed under his breath and slipped the pen and paper into the front of his shirt. Then he stood and went back to work on the shallop.

The shallop was a boat larger than a pinnace, made of wood brought from London and constructed on the very sands of Cape Henry. It would be used to carry twenty-five men up rivers to investigate. The wood was already measured and cut, so that all the workers had to do was fit it together.

Nat, Richard, and a boy named Nicholas Skot from the *Godspeed* had been put to this task, helping lay out the wood and hold planks in place while Edward Pising ordered them and the other laborers about. Samuel Collier had been allowed to go inland with the explorers, carrying supplies for John Smith.

"Where is the other boy?" Nat asked Nicholas as they stood side by side with a curved length of wood as nails were driven in. "Was there not a boy your size, named James or John? I saw him at the spring on the island of Mona."

Nicholas said, "James Brumfield. He was killed."

Richard's eyes went wide. "Killed? How? When?"

"He went ashore yesterday with the others in the pinnace, and was pierced by an arrow."

"Were you on the pinnace, too?" Richard asked.

Nicholas nodded. "We both were on the expedition ashore. It was fine for a while. And then . . ." He paused. His eyes tightened. "Then there were the shouts, the arrows, and then James was cut through. I tried to hold the blood in his chest, but it poured out so dreadfully fast. I couldn't push the life back in, though God knows I tried."

"Here! Hold the plank still!" shouted Edward Pising. "Be quiet and pay attention. We must have this right!"

The work went well into the late afternoon. Nat held planks as still as possible and watched Edward Pising carefully. This work was hard. The man's hands were scarred and tough as weathered wood. Nat knew he would be responsible for helping build once they settled; then, of course, he would find gold and pay for another boy to come to Virginia and do his work for him.

A sailor smacked Nat soundly on the head, jostling him out of his thoughts. "We're done with this plank. What do you think? We will now let you sit down for tea? Come to this side now and make yourself of some worth!"

The shallop was done by nightfall, and the gentlemen returned from their exploring and sat about the fire, talking and laughing as the stars traveled their course.

The following morning, as Nat restoked the fire with wood he had collected earlier, Newport selected men to take the shallop on an exploration up the wide river to find a site for the permanent colony.

John Smith did not look at all bothered that he had been banned from his seat on the council. In fact, he was as animated and excited as ever. His cape flapped like a seabird's wing, and his face was flushed with intensity. He came over to where Nathaniel and Richard stood eating hardtack beneath a brine-weathered tree and said, "You, Richard Mutton. You look strong enough to make an expedition and small enough to take up just a little space. You seem fit and quick. A few of our older soldiers are still recovering from the savage attack. Although my friend Archer is going with us, his wounded hands will not be much good for a number of days yet. We need another armed man."

Richard looked from Smith to Nat and back to Smith. "Yes, sir," he said.

"But . . ." began Nat. "But, sir, I am stronger and bigger, as you can well see. Do you remember in London? I told you I was a soldier!"

Smith held up a hand. "This time Richard will go with us. You will have another chance."

Richard looked uncertainly at Nat, then followed Smith down the beach to the shallop, where men were placing arms and bundles. Samuel Collier was with them, wearing his feathered hat, holding Smith's personal items. Soon everyone was settled. With a splash of the oars, they pushed off and headed northwest.

Nat stood alone, holding on to a thin branch of the tree, watching as the shallop vanished. *Curses!* he thought.

There was work to do, and Nat threw himself into it. There were oysters and other shellfish to gather from the shallows, wood to gather to keep the fire burning, and with a stream nearby, clothing to wash.

Every so often, Nat would steal a glance of Nicholas Skot. He stopped himself several times from speaking to the boy, reminding himself of his own decision to remain aloof. If he made it here in Virginia, he would make it without sentiment, without pity. It was too bad that Nicholas was mourning his friend. What good would that do him?

The shallop was gone a very long time. One day ran into another, and even though Nat had enough to do to keep busy, he found himself frequently stopping and staring out across the river and wondering how long the shallop would be gone. Had they run into trouble at the hands of the natives? Was Smith still alive? What adventure was Richard discovering? Did he already have a pocketful of gold? Jealously made the backs of Nat's arms hot.

While putting mussels into a pot on the fire, Nat listened to the conversation of Jehu Robinson and another man who were seated nearby on the sand. "It is May eleventh already," said Jehu. "The shallop has been gone many days. I wonder if bad fate has befallen them."

The other man, older with a blistering face and clearly a commoner, said, "Whom did they take but gentlemen and a handful of soldiers? Gentlemen! Men who went only to be seers of sights. They have no skill in arms, save a prissy duel, and they have not the brawn to do battle at arm's length. It could well be that at this moment, John Smith is rowing the lot of them, dead bodies all, back to Cape Henry. And thus the delay."

Jehu said, "You might well be right."

The older man nodded. "They could have taken me. I am strong and could outwit any gentlemen on our expedition. I do so dislike gentlemen, and this trip has not given me reason to change my attitude. Well, sir, except for you."

Jehu smiled.

Nat stirred up the mussels and went back down the beach to dig for more. Perhaps, he thought, he might just turn up some Virginia pearls for his effort. This was the land of riches, after all.

It was another two days before the shallop came into view on the river. Nat was glad to see the boat, but what if the old commoner was right and there were dead men there, rowed by battered captains? But as the shallop neared the shore and a sailor jumped out to pull it in closer, Nat saw that every man was there, and safe. They talked nonstop with each other; they carried strange items of feathers and fur, obviously given them by natives.

Richard's complexion was ruddy now, and as he hopped from the shallop and waded through the water to the beach, Nat thought he even seemed taller.

"Tell me!" Nat said, grabbing his arm. "What have you seen, Richard? What did you find? Gold? You brought me some, surely!"

But Richard held up a finger, nodding toward Captain Newport, who had pulled his hat from his bald head, tucked it beneath his arm, and stood before the fire with his hands spread as if ready to make a proclamation. "We have found many riches here in Virginia," the captain said. "There are natives who welcomed us with friendliness. They laid down their arrows and bows, and there were celebrations and dancing on our behalf. Chiefs or presidents, called *weroances,* of many tribes greeted us with signs of peace, and we were served in a manner most fair."

"And what riches have you found?" asked Edward Pising. "Have you gold hiding in your pockets?"

But Newport shook his head. "Our riches have been the peace with which we have been greeted by the natives of Virginia. And the land which is rich for growing crops, and the fresh waters in streams and ponds all about."

Many of the gentlemen who had not gone on the shallop frowned. Nat gave Richard a questioning glance. Richard nodded solemnly, affirming what Newport had said.

"No gold yet?" said one gentleman. "Surely it is not deep in the ground that we must dig for it?"

"Surely you were not looking carefully," said another. "Fear of natives kept you from watching your steps and certainly you trod on top of the gold without knowing it!"

"We will sail our ships in the morning to find our

settlement site," Newport said. "Get a good sleep to-night."

The men set several new fires, and around these they all gathered and fell into sleep, with only the watch keeping eyes open for natives or wild animals.

Nat, Richard, and Nicholas Skot sat in the cold sand, and once again Nat interrogated Richard.

"Tell me what you saw," he said. "I should have gone and so you owe it to me to tell me what you discovered."

Richard sat with his legs crossed, looking toward the fire several yards away. He seemed older. Even his voice sounded a bit different, deeper maybe, more adult. But his enthusiasm hadn't waned.

"There is a river, I cannot say how long it is," he began, the light from the fire dancing in his eyes. "It may reach the East India Sea, some of the men believe. Thick trees and flowers line the way, with tributaries from deep within the forests. Birds and animals drank along the river, such as I've never seen before. Some animals had no fur on their tails; making them look like rats, yet not rats. Others were so quick, I couldn't see anything but a flash of teeth and claws!"

"And the riches?" said Nicholas. "Newport said you found none, but surely you picked up something!"

"We met many savages, frightful but curious. As Captain Newport said, they gave us meat and drink, some tasty, some foul. They danced and performed for us."

"And what of the savages' gold?" asked Nat. "Did you spy it in a tent? Do they wearing it around their necks?"

"I saw no gold."

"None at all?" asked Nat.

"No," said Richard. "But I don't doubt it is here. We'll find it, don't worry."

"I hope so," said Nicholas.

"We will," said Richard.

"We will," said Nat, stretching out to sleep. "I'm not concerned. We will find it in good time. All in good time."

❧ 9 ❧

May 13–19, 1607

"A T LAST," CAPTAIN Archer said, standing on deck with the bandages still on his hands and a small but rare smile on his face. "Such will be our new home."

The *Susan Constant,* the *Godspeed,* and the *Discovery* had traveled all day, sailing up the broad river, which had been named the James in honor of the king of England, and as the shadows had begun to grow long over the river, the place of settlement was found. It was a wooded peninsula, lush and inviting. There seemed to be no native villages nearby. The water was deep enough close to shore that the sailors threw out ropes and moored the ships to the trees. It was decided to wait until morning to unload to have benefit of sunlight to get a fortress up as quickly as possible.

And morning came very early. Before even a hint of light had filtered down into the 'tween deck, there was noise and movement on the upper deck. Everyone rose quickly and made ready to disembark. First, however, they would all attend the swearing in of the new council.

All the gentlemen who had been named to the council came onto the deck of the *Susan Constant,* and a vote was taken by the members to choose a president. Although Nat was certain Captain Newport would be the one, it was a man Nat didn't know, Edward Maria Wingfield. Nat watched John Smith as the oaths were taken and an oration given. The captain seemed to be in his own world, glancing between the new council members and the shore. His eyes were bright with ideas and his head tilted on occasion as if he were listening carefully to his own thoughts.

The sun was fully up now, and the gentlemen took their personal items across the plank to the place they had named James Towne. Sailors unloaded the barrels and crates, hauling smaller ones out through the cannon hatches on the ships' sides, hoisting the others through the center hatches with ropes. The pigs and chickens and goats were unusually noisy as if they knew they were, at last, home.

Nat balanced himself across the plank from ship to shore. The paper he had stolen from Samuel was rolled up and tucked into his waistband at his hip. He touched it tentatively. He'd have to find a place to hide this. Pulling his fur hat down over his ears, he jumped from the plank to the land. The ground was soft and damp.

Laborers grabbed axes and hatches and immediately began to fell trees to split into planks for a church and a fortress. Soon additional wood would be cut into clapboard cargo to be sent back to England when Newport returned later in the summer. Some sailors returned to the ships to look the vessels over again and, from the sounds of laughter and singing Nat heard from shore, to enjoy some of the remaining beer and whisky in celebration. The tents, smelling of mold and filled with rot-holes, were pitched and patched for use until cottages could be constructed. The work went on for many days.

Richard and Nat were assigned the task of stripping branches from trees felled by the larger men. A disgruntled Samuel Collier had been put to work dragging logs alongside Nicholas Skot. As Nat worked, he watched for the opportunity to speak with John Smith. Nat wanted to go on an expedition like Richard had. It was his turn. He wanted to be scouting instead of slinging an axe. He wanted to learn about the forests and the streams and the dangers in Virginia. He wanted to be able to come back and sketch his own maps for his own use later on. Nat knew it would be a little while before he could actually search for gold— only mindless gentlemen would think gold was the first item necessary for living in this wilderness—but when he had a home and food and a knowledge of the land, he would then go out on his own and find his fortune.

Virginia was a curious place. The trees were stately and wide, and of kinds that Nat had never seen. The animals that peeked from the forest were strange enough to cause one to pause and look. Once such animal was like the stag hunted in England, but it had a softer face and a tail that flashed white when it was startled. Another animal was short and black with a white stripe down its flat back. Nicholas Skot had tried to catch one such animal several days earlier and had been sprayed with an essence so foul he was forced to bathe several times in the water of the James before he was tolerable again. The stink lingered several days. Virginia's weather was pleasant, with temperatures comfortable enough to work without heavy outer layers.

"Do you remember telling Smith you knew how to do this?" Richard asked Nat on an early morning as he chopped branches from a downed tree. His shirt was tied at his waist. Nat's was on a rock. Several hundred feet away, other men were pulling planks into upright positions to fashion the walls of the fort. "We were standing on the street in London. A lifetime ago!"

"I remember," said Nat. "Aren't you glad you listened to me, little man? We will be rich gentlemen soon."

Richard nodded exuberantly. "My arms hurt from this work, but that is all right. I shall hope that Smith finds me worthy to once again go scouting. It was most amazing, Nat! You cannot imagine until you do it yourself. Meeting natives, tasting of their food, watching their pagan ceremonies as they welcomed us. Terrifying but incredible."

Nat swiped at a fly buzzing in his ear, feeling the burn of jealously rise up the back of his neck once more.

"I should want to take another trip up the river," said Richard. "Farther on this time—"

"Richard, say no more about your trip up the river. You've told me time and again, and I've grown more than weary of it."

But Richard did not hear the tone in Nat's voice, or he didn't care. "Farther on, and who knows what we might find? It makes me shiver to think of it, but not from fear but from excitement. If only—"

Nat had let go of his axe before Richard could utter another word, and had slammed his fists into his friend's chest, sending him flying to the ground with a "whoof!"

"Enough!" Nat said, bearing down on Richard with all his weight, causing the smaller boy to cough and wriggle beneath him. "I'm sick unto death of your bragging!"

But Richard's eyes flashed fury, and he grunted, "I do not brag! I tell what I've learned, and I alone! Maybe Smith saw I was the better choice of the two!"

"Not true!" said Nat. Richard bucked hard and rolled

over, throwing Nat off. He tried to jump to his feet, but Nat grabbed his leg and jerked it out from under him, toppling him. Nat hopped to his feet and kicked at Richard, but Richard was up again, throwing wild blows with his fist in the direction of Nat's face. Most missed; several smacked his jaw soundly, bringing on a star-rush of pain.

"You do not even know how to fight!" Nat tried to laugh. "You are truly a child, Richard, and don't even know how to act a man!"

Richard rushed Nat and fell into him. The two took the air for a moment, then struck the ground, knocking the breath from Nat's lungs and a grunt from Richard's lips. The arm Nat had hurt in the hold of the ship was cut through with a new shard of pain.

And suddenly Nat was being kicked soundly in the side, and it wasn't Richard, for Richard was prone beside him, pounding him with his hands and panting.

"Stupid dogs!" came a voice from above, accompanied by more painful kicks to the ribs. "Stop that fighting before I throw you both into the river for the fish to eat!"

Nat rolled away from the boot and stood, his head swimming and his stomach threatening to pitch its contents. Richard received a few more kicks to his hip before he was able to get up. The disciplinarian was Edward Pising, clearly in no mood for boys.

"You're more trouble than you're worth!" the man swore, waving the hatchet he held in his sweaty hand. "If I see this again, I'll knock your heads off, don't think I won't!"

Nat snatched up his axe, trying to ignore the ache in his side and the fresh agony in his arm, and went back to stripping bark. Richard did the same. Neither spoke.

The morning wore on. Men stopped from their jobs

of chopping, digging, and hammering to eat a meal of
clams, berries, and leftover beef and hardtack from the
ships. Gentlemen, who had occupied themselves with
ordering the laborers about and complaining about
everything from the smell of their tents to the lack of
gold lying about on the top of the ground, sat by their
fires and adjusted their collars and dabbed their sweaty
foreheads with their handkerchiefs. The council president, Captain Wingfield, sat with Gabriel Archer, John
Ratcliffe, and several of the gentlemen. Wingfield
seemed to think gentlemen were right in keeping their
hands clean. He seemed as lazy as the worst of them.

I should not want to be a man such as Wingfield, Nat
thought. *He is even worse than the blubbering Edward Brookes. Brookes was not a very bright man, and in that is his
excuse. But Wingfield is clearly shrewd. Yet look at him, dal-
lying around as if the rest of us were servants.*

When no one was watching, Nat took a helmet, musket, and powder horn from the store tent and sneaked
into the woods by the clearing. He knew it was dangerous and that the council would not approve, but he
had to get away for a little while. Until Smith invited
him on an expedition, he could at least check out the
woods near the settlement.

He walked through the pines, as thick and as close
together as old women telling each other secrets. He
held the musket shoulder height. The underbrush was
dense. Thorns grabbed his ankles, biting through the
cotton stockings and into his flesh. Briars wrapped his
sleeves and ripped them. But he kept on walking. He
followed a winding stream a short ways, then climbed
a boulder, slick with moss. He watched carefully, remembering the details of the landscape. When he had
the chance, he would draw a map and keep it with his
journal pages. This way he could return when the
chance arose and find his riches alone.

The shadows in the woods were deep. Sunlight was swallowed up in the throats of the trees. Birds screamed overhead, mocking the young Englishman as he stumbled ahead. A vine wrapped around his bad foot and with a grunt he fell on his face, the musket flying from his grasp. His head struck a log, making a gash in his cheek and throwing stars in his field of vision.

"Ow," Nat moaned, rolling over onto his back and touching his face. Above him was the tangle of branches. Beneath him, the ground was slick and damp with mosses and lichens. Cautiously he rolled to his side.

"I'm doing poorly as an explorer," Nat sputtered, then took a long, deep breath. "Good thing Smith can't see me now. Brawling and tripping! Pitiful! Enough, now. Act as an explorer and you will be an explorer."

He looked straight ahead.

Staring at him from the brush was a pair of eyes.

Screaming, Nat sat bolt upright. His hands went out before him to protect himself. And then something came down firmly on his shoulder.

He screamed again.

A voice said, "What is the matter with you, Nat?"

Nat's head snapped around. Jehu Robinson stood there, one hand on Nat's shoulder, the other on the hilt of his sword.

"I saw eyes!" Nat said, panting. "There, look! Savages staring at me, ready to cut me to pieces!"

Nat and Jehu looked into the brush.

A strange animal, short, squatty, and fat, winked at them with a wet, confused gaze. The animal seemed to be wearing a black mask and its tail was encircled with rings. Its nose twitched, and it lumbered off beneath the low branches of a pine tree and out of sight.

"Savages?" asked Jehu. He stood up and chuckled.

"If that is the savage we expect to find near James Towne, then I would fear very little for our safety!"

Nat put his hand to his forehead. His legs hurt, his arm ached, his bad foot throbbed, and his face burned. And now embarrassment was heaped on top of it all. *I look like a fool!*

"Can you walk, Nat?"

Nat nodded. He wouldn't make things worse by letting on how bad he felt.

"Good, then. Come back with me to the site. John Smith is looking for you and I told him I knew where you were. I saw you go into the woods."

"Smith is looking for me?"

"Yes."

Why? Maybe Samuel's sick and he needs another page for a while. Maybe Smith's tent has torn and needed stitching. Surely it's nothing more than a menial task.

But maybe it is something important.

Nat snatched up the musket and followed Jehu back to the clearing. His heart beat heavily with expectation and he forgot how hurt he was. He glanced once over his shoulder and thought he saw eyes again, watching him intently from behind a tree trunk. But then Nat blinked and the eyes were gone.

Men were finished with the midday meal and were back at work. The steady thumping and cracking of axe and hatchet filled the air. Gentlemen paced about, sipping from their mugs, dabbing their noses, avoiding the suggestions by the council that they try their hand at digging for shellfish along the riverbank or shaving bark from the trees.

But what caught Nat's eye immediately was the shallop. It was back in the water again, and a number of men were inside, dressed in helmets and armor, grasping oars, readying to set off on another exploration.

Several bundles of provisions were in the boat. Smith stood by the shallop, talking to one of the soldiers and pointing up the river. Nat hurried over.

"Ah," said Smith, turning to Nat. "I need you to come on this trip. Bring your cloak and get into the shallop. Keep that helmet and musket and take up armor. We leave in just a moment."

Nat hurried to where he'd left his cloak hanging on a prickly branch of a pine tree. Richard was still slinging his axe, but he stopped when he saw Nat.

"I've been chosen," Nat said.

Richard wiped his face. "Chosen for what?"

"To go on an expedition up the river with John Smith!"

Richard threw down the axe. "You? They asked for you to go instead of me? But I've already proven myself! Where are they going?"

"Does it matter? An adventure. Now I must go. They are nearly ready to leave."

Richard grabbed his axe and slammed it into the wood with so much force that a huge shower of splinters rose into the air like a swarm of locusts.

Nat couldn't help but grin. Richard was such a child sometimes. But down at the shallop, as Nat put his musket inside, Smith said, "Oh, please ask the Mutton boy to come, too. I need him on this trip."

Nat's grin fell. He walked halfway back to Richard, waved at him, and jerked his thumb in the direction of the shallop. Richard understood. With a whoop and cheer, he ran for his gear and joined the others by the river.

The shallop was pushed into the water, everyone took a paddle, and they headed northwest.

🗫 10 🗫

May 19, 1607

THE SHALLOP WAS more comfortable than the pinnace, although it was in no way a luxury ship. There was a bit more room, and with so many men rowing, twelve on each side, none had the full brunt of the task. Nat sat near the back between two men he did not know. He didn't talk to anyone, but followed the others' lead in dipping, pulling, and lifting the oar through the river's bright water.

Richard was near the front of the boat next to Smith, and he was rowing, too, although he could barely keep up.

Why did Smith want him along? Nat wondered. *He surely is no help at all.*

In the humidity off the river, Nat's face, arms, and back were quickly covered in a slick sheen of sweat, and his arms grew tired with the motions. But he would die before he let the men know this. He was acting a sailor.

He felt good. He felt free.

Men near the back of the shallop gossiped about the precious metals they hoped to find on this particular trip, while in the front, Smith directed loudly, boasting that it would not be long before he helped them discover a short passage to the Pacific Ocean and secured himself yet more fame in the eyes of all English sailors and the king himself. "We find ourselves far remote from men and means," said Smith. "Yet it is here that we shall discover the glory of a new route and bring England's power beyond that ever known on earth! All other countries henceforth shall be cowed by the mere mention of England's name and shall keep away for fear of our immutable power."

There was murmured agreement, and Nat found his smile widening in spite of the growing weariness of his arms. Virginia was truly the place of opportunity for all.

They had been gone just over an hour upriver when Smith directed the shallop into a smaller tributary. This they followed until the creek became too shallow and reed-infested to venture farther. They would have to go back and travel farther upriver. Everyone climbed from the shallop and stood hip-deep as the shallop was turned around.

And then an arrow smacked into the shallop, nailing a sailor's forearm to the wood. He shrieked. Men spun about in the stream, trying to shoulder muskets and prepare for a fight, but it was too late. On the bank was a gathering of natives, bows drawn and arrows pointed at the Englishmen.

There was a very long moment of silence and staring. The only sounds were that of the water coursing around the men and the shallop, the birds nearby, and the heavy breathing of the man whose arm was pinned to the wood.

Richard, up to his neck in the murky water, lost his balance, cried out, slipped, and went underwater. Smith grabbed him up and shook him, growling that he should hold still and wait quietly.

Another long minute passed as the men in the water and the natives on the shore studied each other. The natives were nearly naked, wearing only leather or grass loincloths. Their hair was shaved on the right side; the left was very long and coated with some sort of oil. Some of the men had this hair twisted into a knot with birds' wings and pieces of antler woven through. One man's hair even appeared to have a dried human hand laced in it.

Nat felt his bladder go loose with fear; and it was only with a very small sense of relief that he was standing deep in the water.

Suddenly one native jumped into the water as the others stood motionless, the bows and arrows still trained at the Englishmen. The native reached the pinned sailor, wrapped his hands about the arrow, and jerked it free. The sailor made no sound other than a horrific grunting through his teeth, and he drew the bloodied arm up to his chest.

Now that the natives had made a move, Smith seemed confident to do the same. He raised one hand, palm flat, and dipped his head in a small movement of greeting. Nat sensed the gesture was to mean peace, although with the wounding of the sailor, Nat found it hard to believe Smith could offer anything on peaceful terms. But Smith was a survivor, and Nat had no choice but to follow his lead.

Several soldiers and sailors made the same gestures that Smith had. The natives conferred quietly among each other, and then one whirled his hand to welcome the settlers onto the bank of the creek.

Slowly, eying each other cautiously and the natives even more so, the men pulled themselves from the creek and followed the natives into the woods.

Two young natives, about Nat's age, brought up the

rear, slapping their bows in the brush and talking softly.

Nat and Richard were near the back of the group, keeping as close to the other men as possible without running into them.

"They are going to kill us," Richard murmured. "How could Smith have let us go with them this way? Should we have not fought with our muskets?"

"Be quiet," Nat said, although he was certain the terrified pounding of his heart could be heard as surely as the pounding of English boot-steps on the ground.

They came to a clearing, and in it, a tiny village. About fifteen houses sat about in no sense of pattern and with no true lanes. These houses were small with rounded roofs and covered with mats of marsh reeds. In one spot there was a grove of fruit trees, and in another place a variety of crops were growing. A tiny, three-sided hut on stilts was in the center of the garden, and a boy holding a long branch peeked out and stared at the strangers. Small boys in loincloths and small girls with no clothes at all came out from the houses and watched, wide-eyed, as the Englishmen were led through the village. Adults then joined them, men and women, who knelt on the ground and dug at the dirt with their nails and made loud noises.

Let those be sounds of joy and not of vengeance! Nat prayed.

They came then to a cabin much longer than the others, and covered with bark instead of the reed mats. Smith, who had regained a straight, confident stride and smile, went into the longhouse with three of the natives while the rest stayed outside and worked at maintaining their composure. The wounded man had torn a strip of his white sleeve and wrapped the arm up. The citizens of the town gathered near, speaking with the native warriors who had brought the men to the village. There was laughter and dramatic waving of hands in describing the encounter. Nat watched them out of the corner of his eye, trying not to seem concerned or afraid, but trying desperately to figure out what they were conveying to each other.

"Are they going to torture us?" Richard whispered.

"Hush!" said Nat. He tried again to decipher the natives' words and motions. It was worthless. The language and the gestures were agonizingly alien.

After nearly twenty minutes, John Smith came back out of the house, led by the natives who had gone in with him. And then came another native, dressed in a mantle of such feathered, pearled, and shelled finery that Nat knew he was a leader. He held his head high, and his eyes were narrowed in an expression of superiority. All the other villagers showed respect for him by stepping back and not looking him in the eye.

They were taken next to a place near the center of the village where woven mats had been placed. The leader, who Smith explained quietly and briefly was the village *weroance,* lowered himself onto a mat at the head of the circle. Only then did everyone else sit. For the next half hour the Englishmen were entertained with strange dancing and singing. While a man beat on a leather instrument and sang, men and women alike took turns dancing before the *weroance* and the visitors. Feet stamped in rhythm with the drumming. Natives in the circle clapped along. The singing was bizarre and hypnotic.

Then food was served, a wide array of cooked fish, beans, berries, fruits, and a bland gruel. Nat, sitting crossed-legged as everyone else, tried to eat, although his stomach would have none of it. It clamped and clenched, trying to throw the morsels back into his mouth along with stinging bile. With great effort he forced the food down. After that, he only pretended to eat. Although the air was cool, sweat beaded on his arms and neck, and he swiped at it anxiously. Next to him, Richard seemed to have as much trouble partaking of the food as Nat.

At last the dancing and music stopped, and the *weroance* stretched and stood. The shells on his mantle clicked heavily. John Smith waited until the *weroance* nodded, and then he, too, stood. He went over and gestured to the *weroance*. None of it made sense to Nat. The *weroance* tilted his head as if considering, then swept his hand out toward the nearest field of crops.

And then Smith pointed at Richard.

Richard gasped.

Nat's heart froze. The fish he had been holding between his teeth was coughed out involuntarily. He spit it into his hand and then wiped it into the dust.

Why is he pointing at Richard?

"Mutton," Smith called. "Come over here to me."

The Englishmen looked at Richard. Several seemed as confused as he, but others nodded solemnly in understanding.

"Richard Mutton, come here!"

Richard stood shakily and walked over to John Smith. Was Smith going to introduce Richard to the leader as a gesture of friendship? Was Smith so proud of Richard that he wanted to point him out to the leader? Or, perhaps, had the *weroance*, who had begun to study Richard's pale blond hair with his fingers, decided Richard was some kind of strange creature?

Smith put his hand on Richard's shoulder. Richard looked at the ground.

What is going on? Nat wondered.

Smith said, "You will stay here, Richard. You have been traded for goodwill and for baskets of food these savages will give us to take back to James Towne."

Nat's mouth dropped open. He stared at Smith in

utter disbelief. Fear had sucked more color from Richard's face than seasickness ever had.

"Men," Smith said to his soldiers and sailors. "Come with me, and we will be given all we can carry on our shallop. Baskets of all the good things we feasted on this day. It will help keep our settlement alive until our own crops come in good and strong."

Then Richard grabbed at Smith's sleeve. "Wait! What is this you are doing to me? Have you lost your mind, sir?"

Smith laughed. "Some would say I lost it long ago. Now sit, Richard. These natives will not harm you if you are not obstinate. You are but a boy. Do you really think I brought you to Virginia as a laborer? You are much too small. Be silent and the natives will not find you a threat." He strode off to join his men, but Richard ran, too, and stopped just in front of the captain. He grabbed Smith's sleeve.

"You cannot leave me, sir! I cannot survive here in this place!"

Smith clenched his jaw. "Get back before I knock you back!"

"Don't leave me!"

"This is the way of explorers, trading boys for food or goodwill," said Smith. "It has always been so."

"Please!" Richard's voice cracked and spun into sobs. "I do not know what to do. How should I act, sir?"

Nat's stomach twisted.

A soldier said, "Push the boy aside, Captain. These savages will have little to do with such demonstrations as that boy is having." The soldier grabbed Richard by the neck and shoved him backward. Smith led the men away. Nat trailed, afraid to look back over his shoulder. Afraid of what he would see in the eyes of the natives and in the eyes of the boy who had made this long, difficult journey with him from London.

"Nat, don't leave me!" he heard Richard cry.

"I have no choice!" Nat said to himself.

And he didn't turn around. The sound of taunting, laughing village children made the hair on his arms stand up. But he marched on.

❧ 11 ❧

May 24, 1607

We are back at the fort at James Towne. I am again assigned to strip tree bark and to help set the planks in the ground to secure the walls.

But my heart is sick. It is all I can do to keep my mind from the terror I saw in Richard's eyes when we left him behind with those savages. What is happening to him now? What is his fate? And the last words between us were angry. It is too late to take them back, but they haunt me.

Nicholas Skot and Samuel Collier have become skittish. They work at dragging wood from forest to fort but, like Richard, neither is a large boy. I told them what happened to Richard, and they wonder if they will be the next to be traded if there is a need. Back on the ship I would have enjoyed the fear I see in Samuel's eyes, but now it is only a reminder of Richard's fate. Nicholas has told me he will run to the woods before being taken like a sheep to slaughter at the hands of John Smith.

Smith. I know the captain is brave and strong and does what he deems right, but I know now that I do not want to be a man like Smith.

And so when my mind has a moment of rest from thoughts of Richard I wonder—whom should I imitate? Where is a man I can act like? Where is a man I can become?

12

June 9, 1607

Three days ago, as John Smith was out again exploring, we at the James Towne fort were attacked by natives. Such a frightful howl we heard as we stood with our axes and awls, bringing down yet more trees to be split and hauled to the place of construction. We dropped our tools and took up our muskets. Many hadn't time to load the powder and shot before a rain of arrows came down on us. Men dropped like stones, wounded in shoulder and leg and chest. But I was able to fire as the natives came into sight at the edge of the clearing, hitting one native in the throat. He dropped his bow and his knees buckled. His eyes glared at me as he fell dead to the ground. I only remember one other man with such hate and fear in his eyes, and that was a convicted traitor in London as he was taken away on a wagon to be drawn and quartered.

Two hundred warriors there were, according to Edward Wingfield. More than all of us together. Yet the roar of our muskets scared them off and we were left to tend our injured men.

I asked Edward Pising why we would be attacked. As many others, I had thought we had established goodwill. But Pising said he did not know. Perhaps this was another village whom *we had not appeased. Perhaps we had done something offensive which the savages had witnessed while peering at us from the forest.*

"Who can know their minds? Surely not us," he said. "And this shows we can in no way trust them as Smith is bound to think at times."

Now, with some bandaged and others healing in their tents, we work faster than before. We must get our fort constructed.

13

August 19, 1607

"THE CROPS WE'VE raised are deplorable," said Jehu as he and Nat jammed their shovels into the soil within the palisade walls of James Towne fort. The man's black hair was stringy and his eyes pinched with worry. He had also lost a great deal of weight since May, as had all the other settlers. "What seed we brought from England was half moldy when we put it into the ground. We'll be lucky if we see any fall vegetables or wheat at all."

"How do you know so much?" Nat asked. "You are a shareholder who has come to Virginia to find gold. Gentlemen don't know about crops and digging."

Jehu tossed a shovelful of soil out onto the nearby pile. He and Nat were digging a new well. The first one had not provided enough water for the settlement. This second one would hopefully give enough fresh water for the men and animals and crops alike. The water in the James River was brackish, laced with salt and grit. Some men, in moments of desperate thirst, had drunk of the river and found themselves seriously ill or dead.

"I was not always a gentleman," said Jehu. "My fortune came from good planning and a little bit of luck. My parents were farmers from Scotland, but I learned merchanting when I went to live with my uncle in London at fourteen. I have been successful and lucky. Yes, I want gold. But I want to survive to enjoy the riches, and that will take the efforts of us all."

Nat nodded, and slammed his shovel into the growing hole of the well.

The Virginia summer sun above was barely tolerable. No longer were breezes fresh and the air agreeable as they had been in May. Days and nights alike were hot and oppressive. Insects sucked blood of the men, leaving many unwell. Some had died from the bites of these insects; other had perished from eating spoiled food left from the voyage and drinking the river water. A total of twenty-seven men were dead. Even Bartholomew Gosnold, the captain of the *Godspeed*, was so ill with an intestinal disorder many doubted he would recover.

Food was growing scarce; the men had eaten adequately the first weeks, dining on the remaining victuals brought from England. Now deer and squirrels were killed by those who could hunt, and the river gave up fish, turtles, and crabs to those who could gather them, but there was not enough to feed everyone. The garden outside the James Towne fortress was tended regularly, commoners and laborers hoeing, watering, and keeping away as many scavenging animals and burrowing insects as possible. But the crops that had come up were meager. Beans were tiny and few; peas were the same. Cabbages and squash were riddled with an unknown blight. The wheat crop was scrawny. Come autumn, life would be harder still, with little food in store.

If the gentlemen would learn to hunt and garden like com-

moners, Nat had written in his journal two nights prior, *then there might be enough food. But they are worthless. They complain and eat, no better than leeches. There is even talk that our council president Edward Maria Wingfield has been pilfering food from the storehouse to feed himself and his friends. I believe it may be true, as he seems less thin than the rest of us. Lazy, selfish man! But how long can the storehouse feed him before there is nothing left? He will have a hard lesson once his own belly screams at him. Indeed, all these gentlemen have hard lessons to learn if they are to survive more than this summer!*

It is best for me to watch out for myself, for if I depend on others, I shall surely starve.

Jehu and Nat worked another few hours on the well, then took a break. Nat put his helmet on his head and picked up his shirt and musket. He went out through the fort's gate, along one of the grassy pathways, past the fenced gardens and down to the river's edge. He sat on a favorite stone and slipped his shirt on. The fabric made him sweat more, but at least it kept most of the biting flies off his skin. Gazing out across the wide stretch of water, Nat thought about many things. As always, Richard came to mind first.

I wonder if he is alive. Perhaps he is truly safe. I'll never know. There was nothing I could do. If I'd come to Richard's aid, what might have happened to me? As I had to be silent when at John Smith's court of inquiry, I had to be silent at Richard's trading.

Natives, whom Smith called Powhatans after the name of the chief Powhatan of all the native villages in the near and far reaches of this land, had attacked off and on through the summer, but no attack was as severe as the one in June. This had encouraged the men to hasten the completion of the fort. The soldiers set cannons atop bulwarks at the corners of the fort. The Powhatans were, it seemed, a warring group of people with minds impossible for Nat to understand. They appeared friendly at times, then bloodthirsty at others.

Smith had at last gained his seat on the council because of his ability to deal with the unpredictable Powhatans. If it weren't for him, Nat was certain that the whole settlement would be dead or enslaved by now. But Nat no longer trusted Smith on a personal level.

Nat had fared better than most men since May. He covered himself with river mud at times to keep mosquitoes and biting flies away, he slept lightly to listen for impending attacks, and he always hid away in his sack a portion of biscuit or dried meat from each meal so that when cold weather came, he would have something to keep going. As of now, he had many handfuls of salt beef and pork, some dried apples, and a number of rock-hard biscuits. Most of it was wormy, but Nat had pulled the worms out. It was not the first time he'd hoarded food. In London he could go days without finding a fresh supply, and keeping a bit aside was a wise boy's actions. If the other members of James Towne were smart, they would be doing the same.

Some of the buildings in James Towne were already complete, including the church, the storehouse, and cottages for the council members and some gentlemen. The structures were tedious to build, made of woven willow and hazel branches and plastered with thick mud and covered with thatched roofs.

But many men still slept in the rotting tents. Nat shared a tent with Samuel Collier, a young tailor named William Love, and an older laborer named John Laydon. Neither Love nor Laydon was a big talker, and the animosity between Nat and Samuel remained strong. This was good; Nat didn't have to endure late-night banter from any of them.

"There is a gold-seeking party leaving in the morning. Are you going?"

Nat looked around. Jehu was there, standing behind the stone on which Nat sat, slipping his own shirt on over his broad shoulders and scanning the river with squinting eyes.

"Gold? Now?" said Nat. "Those men are fools. Will gold feed them or protect them from attack? I think not. Gold is in my future, not my present."

"Wise," said Jehu. He sat on the rock beside Nat, picked up a stray; flat pebble, and flung it toward the water. It skipped four times and disappeared. "Can you do more than four?"

Nat took a flat stone and hurled it. It skipped three times before it went under.

"I've been thinking. There are many plants here in Virginia," said Jehu. "Different from those in England, but some of which are edible, I'm certain. If only we had a way of finding out which we can eat and which are poisonous. We could then gather the good plants and dry them to add to our store for the coming winter."

"We could ask the Powhatans," Nat said sourly.

"We could," said Jehu. "But the more we can discover ourselves, the better. We don't want to seem helpless to the natives, although I think they already see us as such. I have heard your belly growl, Nathaniel. Don't tell me you aren't hungry and that you don't want to ease that pain."

"I hear my belly, but I don't feel it. I've been hungry much of my life. London was a harsh mother. Hunger is so familiar I scarcely notice."

"Ah, but you will. Give it time."

Nat threw another stone into the water. It skipped twice and sank. "Are you proposing we choose a committee to taste plants? Those that kill the men we will not eat and those the men survive we will harvest?"

"A committee, no," said Jehu. "But volunteers might take small tastes."

"There will never be such volunteers," Nat said.

"I will volunteer. A small taste of a dangerous plant will likely only make one sick. Will you join me? If we discover new foods, what a great thing that will be. We can be of service to all the men here."

"No," said Nat.

Jehu nodded slowly. "I understand," he said. He patted Nat on the shoulder and went back to the fort.

"He will only get himself killed," Nat said to himself. "If not an arrow or bad water or an insect bite, he will intentionally poison himself. Idiot."

Nat went back to the fort when Reverend Hunt rang the bell for the daily worship in the church, and Jehu didn't mention his plan again.

❧ 14 ❧

September 4, 1607

I've a little time to write. This ink and paper is from the bratty page's sack of goods. I sit in my smelly tent, but neither Samuel Collier nor John Laydon nor William Love, the three who share this tent with me, is here at the moment.

More than fifty of our men are dead now, with Captain Gosnold one of the number. Some men have been killed by the illnesses and starvation, others by arrows, and still another recently executed for treason against the crown. He dared to jump up during our worship service and shout that the king was a tyrant who cared nothing about us here in James Towne. Soldiers took him and dragged him out of the church and on the spot, without inquiry or comment, shot him under the order of the council. Poor fool! This action seemed to me more savage than savages, for surely the man was mad with fear and hunger.

The Susan Constant and Godspeed, which left with Captain Newport in June, will be gone until early winter, most likely. No new supplies can be counted on until then.

Many men seem to think we have been abandoned, like the colony that was begun on Roanoke Island south of here years ago. They were left alone and when someone at last came from

England to see the progress and bring more settlers, they discovered that the entire colony was gone. Everyone had disappeared. Taken away or killed by natives is the guess. Is that what will happen to us?

If Richard is alive, is he perhaps better off with natives than with incompetent Englishmen? I miss having someone to complain to about Samuel and Archer and the whining gentlemen.

This afternoon, while I was clearing thistled brush from the edge of the forest, I again spied a pair of eyes glaring at me from behind a boulder. Another animal, I thought, but this time a large one. I held still in case it was a bear, making no sound. No one working near me had any idea that there was danger so close, within several feet.

I continued to stare at the eyes. Then they shifted and widened, and I knew the eyes to be human and not animal. I felt a shout rattle my throat, but it did not come out. A Powhatan, so close he could have slit my throat as I bent to chop the brush. I prayed God that I would not be murdered where I stood.

"You pause there! Peacock, get back to work!" Captain Archer shouted to me. The man, who would never so much as lift an axe, had come out with those of us who would, and he was standing, throwing his hands all over and shaking his head madly, like a crazed fishwife.

I didn't know what else to do, with the Powhatan watching me. And so I did what I most often do, I began to act. When Archer looked elsewhere, I imitated him silently, throwing my own arms around, tossing my head back and forth and wagging my tongue.

The Powhatan began to laugh. I saw the bushes shake and I heard a high chuckle. Such a strange, soft sound! I had no idea a native could laugh. He parted the brush with his hands and smiled at me. It was a boy, a bit younger than myself, wearing bear grease and a leather cloth, his black hair unadorned and slicked back. He pointed at me as if he liked the joke, then let go of the brush and vanished.

I remind myself daily that I will become what I'd imagined back in London. An adventurer, a wealthy, independent man. I know how to plant crops now, and I have learned to cut and strip wood. It is a start. Gold may have to wait until next year. But I will have it.

Jehu continues his lone search for edible plants. I have told him I cannot feel hunger. That was a lie, but I will never show my discomfort. Jehu has discovered some berries which are quite good and dry quite well. He has found a tuber which is tough but meaty. As of now, he has only been mildly sick with a wild bean he tasted. God watches over fools, it seems. Maybe God will watch over James Towne.

15

September 7, 1607

"DO THAT AGAIN, young Peacock," said John Laydon as he sat down on a tree stump with a tin plate of wheat gruel in his lap. The food was tasteless and watery, made of remaining grain from the bottom of the barrels brought on the ships in May and some tiny beans from the James Towne garden. Soon there would be no food at all except what the men produced themselves. Yet many gentlemen still refused to work. John Smith insisted that the council force everyone to work, but Wingfield, Archer, and Kendall would have nothing of it. They didn't want to make enemies of the gentlemen. At the moment, everyone, including the gentlemen, was seated within and without the fortress, eating the slimy gruel.

Nat was seated on the ground. His shirt was off and he could see his ribs straining at the skin of his chest. "Do what again?"

John Laydon leaned over and with a tired smirk said, "The imitation of Archer. I saw you the other day when we were cutting trees. You performed a hilarious rendition of the captain. I told several friends and they want to see it."

Nat noticed that a couple of other men had turned and were grinning at him. Was Laydon serious?

Laydon said, "Archer is not nearby. Please. We need something to laugh at."

The other men nodded.

Nat checked to make sure that no one else was looking his way, stood and went through the motions. He shook his head, snarled, jabbed his finger at Laydon, and jammed his hand on his hip, as he'd seen Archer do many times. John Laydon and the other men clutched their bony sides and howled with laughter.

"Good show!" said Laydon.

Nat sat and licked the remaining gruel from the plate.

In the days that followed, word spread around James Towne that Nat was a comedian. He was stopped as he drew water from the well, while knee-deep in the river digging for mussels, and even as he tried to sneak away to walk in the woods.

"Psst," said one soldier standing on the bulwark. "Peacock, show me an imitation of our council president, the dreaded Edward Maria Wingfield."

Nat wrinkled his nose and made his lip twitch. Then he stomped his foot and leaned back, pretending to down a mug of the beer Wingfield enjoyed so much, then staggered as if intoxicated. The soldier chuckled heartily.

"Hey, there, boy," said the gentleman Benjamin Beast as Nat passed Beast's cottage late one evening on the way to his own tent. "Come in, I've something for you to do." Nat went inside the cottage, which was dark and stank of diarrhea and vomit. There, another gentleman named George Walker was sick, rolled up in a blanket and shivering.

"My friend is ill. I want you to cheer him," said Beast. "We understand you have a talent for satire. Please perform as Captain Smith, that crooked, impudent old arse!"

So Nat pretended to be Smith the way the gentlemen saw the man. He tossed back an invisible cape, tugged at a neck ruff, and crossed his eyes as if on the verge of insanity. Then he went into a mock battle with invisible Turks, cutting off heads and bowing. Beast and George Walker chortled and nodded, then gave Nat his leave. Beast pressed a bruised half apple into Nat's hand as a thank-you.

Back in his tent, Nat lay down on his straw mattress near the dozing, whistle-nosed Samuel Collier, and took out pen and page. He wrote, *If entertaining keeps me in good graces with the men of James Towne, so be it. I will not always have to perform at their beck and call. But for now, if they want a drunken councilor, I'll give them one. If they want a lazy sailor, they can have him. If they ask for a constipated gentleman, thus I shall be.*

❧ 16 ❧

September 12, 1607

WHAT IS WRONG with your face, boy? It is covered with maggots! Let me get them off before they eat your eyes!"

Nat dropped his hoe and straightened from his work in the wheat garden, beads of sweat rolling down his face. Before him, standing unsteadily with a sword in trembling hands, was Jehu Robinson. Two other gardeners stopped their work and stared.

"He's gone mad," one man hissed.

"Nathaniel Peacock," said Jehu. His words were slurred. "You've got worms all over your head. Hold still while I chop them away!"

Jehu wrapped his fingers around the handle of the sword, and with a grunt, swung it up and over. It arced by Nat's ear and Nat jumped out of the way, swearing.

"Jehu! What have you eaten? You are delirious!"

"Nat, wait!" said Jehu. "The worms are in your nostrils now. You will smother to death!" He lifted his sword and lashed out at Nat again. Nat again darted out of the way.

"Jehu, drop the sword!"

The two men in the garden ran out of the gate and up toward the fort, calling for help. "We've a madman!"

Jehu continued to wield the sword, Nat continued to dodge him. The man's awkward movements made it easy to keep away from the blow of the deadly blade. "Please, Jehu," said Nat. "What have you eaten that has you so crazed?"

Jehu paused for a moment, then pulled several leaves from his pocket. They were ordinary-looking, with thorny stems. "These taste peculiar," Jehu said. His eyes went shut, and then opened again, filmy and senseless. He dropped the leaves.

"Put down the sword," Nat said. "Please."

"But the worms . . . !"

"There are no worms, man, listen to me!"

There was whooping and shouting now at the fort. Nat looked up and saw three soldiers rushing down to the wheat garden, muskets at the ready.

"Drop your weapon, Jehu!" said Nat.

Jehu spun around on his toe and saw the soldiers racing at him. He shivered violently and raised the sword. "Devils!" he screamed. "You've devils in your midst!"

"Jehu," said Nat. "There are no devils. Lower the sword."

"Don't you see them?" shrieked Jehu. "God help me, they are sharp-toothed devils, come to slay me!"

"No!" said Nat.

Jehu charged forward, out of the garden and up the ridge toward the men, brandishing his sword. There was a moment of silence as the men paused to aim the muskets and then there was an explosion as three muskets fired. One musket ball struck Jehu in his right shoulder, shattering it instantly and making him drop the sword. The other hit his right knee, and he collapsed with a wail on to the ground. The third lodged in the man's gut, and his shirt flowered with a bright red blossom of blood.

The men with the muskets came over cautiously and poked at Jehu with their shoes.

"He's dead," said one.

"Brain fever of some sort," said a third man. "He's best off dead than a danger to himself and the rest of us."

But he might have recovered, Nat thought. *If they had only disarmed him and put him in a cottage, he might have come through this in just a little while!*

"You, boy," said one man to Nat. "Help take this man into the fort. We'll give him a proper burial."

Nat wanted to cry out at these men, to scold them for their haste, for now dead was a man who had no other thought over the past months than how he could help the settlement survive. But Nat could not cry out. He would not bring their wrath down on himself.

Nat took Jehu's arms and a soldier took his legs. They proceeded into the fortress, where he was laid in the chapel and Reverend Hunt bid all to attend a funeral service. The men gathered solemnly, helmets in hands, listening as the minister spoke of Jehu's generosity and wisdom.

Nat stood near the back beside the open doorway, between Nicholas Skot and Samuel Collier. Nicholas was clearly upset, and wiped his eyes with his hands as the reverend spoke. Samuel, for all his ingrained haughtiness, seemed distracted and dazed, staring down at his shoe tips and rolling his lips in and out between his teeth. It was hard to breathe inside the church, even though the building was not as crowded as it had been months ago with so many men dead. Nat's chest ached in what was more than just heat exhaustion. Something harsh and stinging pressed behind his eyes. He thought not only of Jehu, but of Richard—poor Richard, vanished among the Powhatans and never heard from again—and of his dead mother and of the dead boy James Brumfield, killed on the shore of Cape Henry, and of the dead boys he had once thieved with back in England.

If you cry, they will never again see you the way you want them to. You dare not cry, not now, not ever!

Nat clenched one fist in the other, and bit the inside of his cheek until it bled. But the tears did not come.

Jehu was buried within the fort. Then everyone went back to their normal routines, the gentlemen preparing for the next gold search, the councilors making sure laborers wasted no time on the construction of more cottages within the fortress, the soldiers manning the cannons which faced the forest, and the others wearily raking the river bottom with wood rakes for clams and crabs and chasing animals from the gardens and grumbling that they wished they had the hunting skills of the cursed natives.

After Jehu's burial, Nat paced the fortress. He walked back and forth from the church, past the tents and cottages and storehouse to the gate and back again. From within some of the cottages he could hear the moans of those who were ill with fever and starvation. His nerves clawed the inside of his skin.

"Jehu, you moron," he said to himself. "I told you not to try plants you didn't know!"

He picked up several stones and hurled them through the fence of the sheep's pen. It struck a ewe and her lamb, who squeaked and took several sideways, stumbling steps.

Then Nat stopped in front of Captain Smith's cottage. Smith was not there. Nat glanced around, then went inside.

The captain's home was neat. His wood and canvas cot had a wool blanket neatly folded at the end. On a wooden stool were writing utensils and a comb and knife. Several small crates were beneath the cot. Clothes, an extra shirt and vest and pairs of stockings, hung on nails driven into the wood framing.

Nat stooped down and pulled the crates from beneath the cot. He opened the first. In it were books and scrolls. Nat shut it and opened a second. Here were even more clothes, smelling of mildew, and an extra pair of shoes. Nat slammed it, too.

The third crate, smallest of them all, had a lock. Nat stood and kicked the lock solidly with the bottom of his shoe. The lock didn't break, but the lid of the crate cracked and Nat tossed the lock aside. He opened the box.

"Ah," he said in a whisper.

Here were trinkets, the ones Smith used when coaxing the Powhatans into peace or food. There were small looking glasses and bits of smoothed metal and patches of silk fabric stitched into pouches with drawstrings. At the bottom, blue glass beads. They were smooth and cool. These seemed to be the most popular trade item. Back in July, three entire deer were given to James Towne in exchange for a single bead, which the *weroance* who had approved the gift immediately strung with deer sinew and put around his neck as a symbol of his status.

He scooped up six of the beads and shoved them into his pocket. They clacked softly against the pebbles from the bank of the Thames.

A spear of excitement jabbed Nat's gut as he collected a helmet and left the fort. It was like being in London again, snatching a fish from the monger's barrow. He was a good thief. It was a talent he'd not practiced in quite some time. Now he would bury the beads where no one would find them and accuse him of theft, which would surely bring a noose to his neck. In time he might be able to use these beads to trade for food for himself.

The forest was more dense than it had been in the spring, with summer growth holding tight, the leaves of the tall trees linked together overhead in a solid canopy and the vines growing lush below. Nat carefully avoided one particular vine with tri-leaves which the men had discovered gave a dreadfully itchy rash where it touched.

This part of the woods was familiar. Nat had walked here enough to know the rise and fall of the land. He had even sketched a simple map from his memory, and the map was safely stored in his sack with his journal pages. He felt nearly as home here among the trees as he did back at the fort, although he knew to always walk softly and listen well. He'd not seen any sign of gold, but that didn't mean it wasn't there. It was probably just below the soil, and soon he would take time to dig.

Then he found a good spot. It was close to the river, although the water was hard to see because of the undergrowth. The ground was mushy and covered with pine needles. Nat clawed soil up with his fingernails and tossed it aside. He reached into his pocket for the beads. He would put them here, cover them with soil and leaves, and mark the place with stones.

Suddenly something slammed into Nat's back and sent him flying through the air. He struck the ground on his shoulder with a grunt. Instantly Nat rolled onto his back and jumped to his feet. He would fight, he would survive!

Standing there with a look of triumph on his face was the Powhatan boy he'd seen from the garden. The boy had his hands out before him, one empty and one holding a writhing, copper-colored snake. Nat stared, his knees shaking.

The boy pointed at Nat, then the snake. He made a wriggling motion with his free hand, indicating that the snake had been traveling along the ground. Then he made a jabbing motion as if showing the snake had wanted to bite Nat on the ankle.

Nat slowly nodded at the boy. *Thank you.* The boy nodded back. *You are welcome.* The boy laughed. Nervously Nat laughed, too.

The boy whirled the struggling snake in the air and slapped it hard against a tree trunk. The snake went limp. The boy smiled and pointed at the snake and then to his mouth. Did the boy mean that the snake could be eaten? The boy held the snake out to Nat. Nat took it. He stared at it. Then he remembered how much the Powhatan boy had enjoyed the imitation of Gabriel Archer. Nat dropped the dead snake on the ground and then hunched over and pretended to sneak up on it. Then he quickly snatched it up and struggled with it as if it were still alive.

"Ah!" shouted the Powhatan, thrilled with the act. He began to slap at the dead snake, too. Both Nat and the boy laughed. Nat threw the snake against a tree, wiped his brow dramatically, and put the snake into his pocket. The head hung out limply.

"Ahhhh!" the boy repeated, smiling. The boy stared at Nat expectantly. Nat stared at the boy.

Laughing Boy, Nat thought. *It is what I will call him. But what does he want? He saved me from that serpent, surely. I suppose I should thank him for saving my life, but how do I do that?*

Nat thought of the rocks in his pocket. Maybe a smooth stone from London would be a good gift. Nat pulled out a quartz and gestured for the boy to take it.

The boy took the rock, turned it over, shook his head, and threw the rock to the ground.

Reluctantly Nat drew a glass bead from his pocket. The boy's eyes widened at this, and he took it with a whistle of admiration. He smiled at Nat, opened the leather pouch he wore tied to his waist, and dropped the bead inside. And then, as swiftly as before, he jumped off the path and was gone.

"He knows how to survive," Nat thought, pulling the snake half out of his pocket and then cramming it back again. "I bet I could learn a lot if I spent time with him. And I bet he would help me search for gold. I wonder if we'll meet again."

And the thought was funny, Nat realized as he finished burying the rest of the glass beads. For the first time he could remember, he was thinking that someone to help him might be all right. If only on occasion.

17

November 8, 1607

My excursions into the forests now often find me with a companion. Every ten days or so, as I work in the pitiful, dying gardens, harvesting the last of the crops and killing the late-season insects, I see familiar eyes by the boulder at the edge of the woods. It makes me glad, for I know I will have an adventure and will have some time away from the sickness and arguments of James Towne!

Laughing Boy has taught me how to hunt the way the Powhatans do. He showed me that two hunters can more easily kill a deer by chasing the animal into an inlet of the river, where it struggles in the soft river bottom and cannot get out. This makes it an easy target for musket or arrow. The first time, however, it was I who fell into the river bottom and struggled there, while Laughing Boy howled at me with joy and had a great moment at my expense. But we tried again and again, and it was not long before I was feeling agile and prepared.

Three times now I have come back to the fort with a deer, but not before Laughing Boy and I have made fires with tinder and sharpened stones and cooked and ate a portion of the animal. The men at James Towne were impressed that I, sim-

ple comedian that I am, was able to single-handedly hunt a deer. Of course, they demanded that I share. And so I handed the animal over, with a story that a bear had chased me with the carcass, and ripped part off.

"All three times a bear chased you?" Samuel Collier asked me with a sneer as John Laydon took the deer through the fortress gate. "Who could believe such a story from a boy who not months ago was begging for scraps from the doorsteps of the fishwives of London?"

"Yes," I told the little hot-bird in a whisper. "All three times. The bear thought the carcass was you."

Laughing Boy has also taught me to climb trees and patiently watch for small animals instead of scaring them away with the sound of my footsteps. I've had a hard time handling bow and arrow, but we amuse each other, making fun of my clumsy attempts which often send an arrow flying straight up in the air or smacking down into the ground. But five times now, I've brought back to James Towne several of the ring-tailed creatures, but often as not, I hide one down the front of my shirt to cook and eat on my own at night.

I know I can survive Virginia! I shall outlive them all!

Several times I've tried to show Laughing Boy how to write. He likes to draw the animals he hunts and pictures of what I can only guess are his family. A father, three sisters, and a mother. A weroance.

No man at James Towne could possibly understand my trust of Laughing Boy. But no matter. I have to do what I have to do, and the rest of the settlement can bloody well take care of themselves.

Just yesterday morning I sat down in the woods with Laughing Boy and tried to tell him about gold.

"It's like stone," I said, holding up a gray pebble from beneath a tree. "Like this, but it is beautiful and bright. Yellow, like the sun." I pointed to the sky, where through bare branches the sun could be seen. "It is what will make me a gentleman, and you, too, if you want."

Laughing Boy crossed his legs and his arms and shook his head. Clearly it made no sense to him.

Then I pointed to the pouch at Laughing Boy's waist. He opened it. I pulled out the blue bead. "Like this," I said. "It is valuable, and everyone wants it. Gold. Men kill and die for it."

Laughing Boy chuckled, jumped to his feet, and ran off after a squirrel.

I realized then that gold-hunting would be something I would have to do alone. Damn it all. It would have been easier with two, especially a Powhatan!

❧ 18 ❧

December 25, 1607–January 1, 1608

"WE CAN'T SURVIVE with Wingfield as president," said the bushy-haired gentleman Robert Fenton to the bald gentleman Thomas Sands as the men of James Towne exited the settlement's church on Christmas afternoon. Those who were well enough to attend the service did so, but there were a number who had had to celebrate the morn of Christ's birth from the darkness of their cabins, for their fevers had stolen their vitality. The ground was frozen from an early-morning sleet, the sky was gray, and the air was as cold and cruel as the blade of a sword. Reverend Hunt had spoken for hours on the glorious birth of Jesus and the saintliness of His mother and the love of God, and for hours the men had recited verses and had sung hymns, and Nat's back was tired.

"Hush," said Thomas Sands. "Let us talk outside earshot of those who would disagree." The two gentlemen walked slowly toward the West Bulwark of the fortress. Nat, a scarf torn from the remnants of a wool blanket tied around his ears, followed the men. He acted as though he had business in the pigs' pen, which was only several yards from the bulwark. When he reached the woven fence, he climbed over and proceeded to rearrange the buckets. He was reminded of the times he and Richard had pretended to still have rats to toss into the ocean so they could stay above board longer. There were only two pigs remaining from those brought in May. In the fall the pigs had been allowed to run in the forests to find their own food, but this remaining pair had been brought back to the fort. Many of the laborers suspected that Edward Maria Wingfield was planning a Yuletide feast for himself and some of his closest supporters like Archer and Kendall.

Robert Fenton crossed his arms, leaned against the fortress wall, and spoke in a lowered voice. "John Smith left to explore the Chickahominy River earlier this month, and while he has been gone, Wingfield and his friends have blatantly taken advantage of the rest of us."

Thomas Sands scratched himself beneath the collar of his cloak and then pulled at the curls of his mustache. "Even though he sees the state we are in, even though he sees the very starvation of those he is supposed to govern, he does not expect gentlemen to work. But I work, and you do, as well. We both know now that for even the daintiest man to do nothing is a doom-say for us all. I would rather be a living man than a dead gentleman."

The bushy-haired man agreed. "Wingfield is a fool."

Nat placed the buckets back on the ground and then pretended to reweave a loose branch in the pen fence.

"We should send out a party to find Smith and bring him back," said Sands. "Smith has a clear head when it comes to the needs of our fort. He knows all should work. He knows gentlemen must dirty their hands if they are to live."

Fenton frowned, listening.

Sands continued. "We should bring Smith home to James Towne and settle this once and for all. Let us, as a whole body of Englishmen, gentleman, soldier, surgeon, laborer, all, decide who should govern James Towne. If each man gets a say, I can tell you for certain Wingfield would lose and Smith would be given the presidency of the council."

"Your ideas are radical," said Fenton. "And I understand your anxiousness. But it would be best to wait until Smith returns on his own. This will give us time to talk privately to others and gain their support, so when Smith does indeed show up, we are ready to make our stand. You have heard there is safety in numbers, sir."

"No," said Sands. "If we wait, it will give Wingfield the time to let us all die slow deaths from starvation."

Robert Fenton picked up a stick lying at his feet and hurled it angrily through the air. "Do you hear us, sir? We can't even agree on a simple plan, and yet we are on the same side. How hard will it be to get more than two men to agree to any plan regarding the disposal of Wingfield?"

Suddenly there was a loud squeal, and Nat felt a sharp set of teeth cut through his trousers and into the flesh of his buttocks. "God save me!" he shouted. He jumped out of the fenced enclosure, holding his bleeding wound. One of the pigs eyed him, the animal's lips seeming to be set in a grin.

Thomas Sands rushed at Nat. Nat stumbled back, ready to explain what had happened so the man wouldn't strike him. But Sands only turned Nat around and stared at the ripped breeches and the blood.

"See there," said Sands. "Even our bloody pigs are making a bloody nuisance of themselves, starved as they are in this dreadful land, biting bloody boys in the arse and making bloody messes!"

Robert Fenton looked at the wound, Thomas Sands looked at the wound, and Nat, from over his shoulder, tried to look at the wound. Then all three of them burst out laughing.

"You have adopted the language of the commoner," chuckled Fenton.

"I have indeed!"

"A bloody mess it all is!" said the bushy-haired gentleman. "Bloody fort, bloody savages, bloody diseases!"

"Bloody cold, bloody bad water, bloody Virginia!" said Sands.

"Bloody, damnable Wingfield!" said Nat.

The two men stopped laughing. Thomas Sands spun Nat back around to face him. "Why did you mention our president to us?" he demanded.

"Oh," said Nat, his mind scrambling for an act. "Oh, sir, I beg pardon. Please don't beat me. I meant no disrespect to our good president. I know you men admire him, and I do, too. I'm only speaking because one of these pigs belongs to President Wingfield and I believe the man has taught the pig to bite."

The two men stared at Nat a moment longer, then the soldier let go of Nat's collar. "Well, then, should we just say 'Wingfield's damnable pig'?"

"Of course, sir."

"Fine. Fine." But the men continued to stare at Nat. Then Fenton said, "You are the boy who playacts."

"Yes, sir."

"Who would you entertain us with?"

Nat paused. He wasn't sure who best to act as for these men. If he acted as Smith, like most gentlemen wanted, then they might be offended because they truly liked Smith. But if he acted as someone the commoners hated, such as Wingfield or Archer, then they would know he'd overheard their discussion. "Sir," he said. "My buttocks hurt. Could I do it another time?"

Fenton nodded. "Of course. Go and clean yourself up."

Nat bowed. "Thank you, sir." He hobbled to the well and drew up a small bucketful of icy water. This he dabbed on his wound with a corner of the wool scarf, then inspected the flesh as best he could. It wasn't deep, but it was painful. There was nothing he could do but to wait until it healed. He wrapped the scarf back around his ears and walked out of the fort and down to the river to try to find some shellfish for Christmas dinner.

He tossed rocks into the water to break up the ice at river's edge, but after an hour of poking in the deep mud with a stick, he had caught nothing, and went to bed hungry.

Two days after Christmas, both gentlemen Robert Fenton and Thomas Sands were put into the James Towne jail for, as Wingfield declared, "no less than thirty days." Someone had told the council president that the two gentlemen had spoken against him. Although there were no identified eyewitnesses to the traitorous talk, and all that was spoken against Fenton and Sands was hearsay from an unnamed source, Wingfield declared that an example had to be set.

Nat's tent was not far from the jail, and he had to pass it on his way home at night. He didn't look at the jail because he didn't want to see the faces of the men, pressed to the slats of their tiny windows, gaunt, furious. He knew they believed he had told on them. He knew they believed he was responsible for their confinement.

Neither man spoke to Nat as he went by. But on New Year's Eve, as Nat retired for the evening, he thought he heard Thomas Sands say, "What did you tell for, boy? We were on your side."

And Nat, ever the thespian, acted as if he didn't hear.

And on New Year's Day, John Smith returned to the cheers of many and the silent discontentment of Wingfield and his council.

19

January 4, 1608

At last! I have a cottage! Although I must share it with
Samuel Collier, William Love, and John Laydon. It is smaller
than the other cottages, and not much warmer than the rotting
tent, but it is sturdy and the winds will not blow it down. We
caked the walls thick with mud and have woven door and
window mats with dried grasses from outside the fort. There
is one room, with two cots and two mattresses, a single table,
and John Laydon's trunk.

Although I would not have chosen Samuel Collier to share
a home with me, it makes writing convenient. He has a supply
of pens and ink and paper for the times he takes notes for
John Smith. I steal a little every week or so. He is a sluggish,
careless boy. I don't think he has noticed.

I kept the skins of the deer I killed; they help keep the excru-
ciating cold off me. William Love cried out so dreadfully with
shivers three nights ago I covered him with one of the skins to
quiet him. He still has it.

More men of James Towne have died from weakness, foul
water, and little food. Burials are quick now and with little
dignity, performed at night so the natives, who the soldiers
swear are watching us constantly, won't know how few of us

there are. Our scarce crops from summer are rationed to each man, even the lazy gentlemen who never lifted a finger to help acquire this food. We each are given a bit of wheat and beans daily. It is not enough. But I have seen some of the councilors, even our president Edward Maria Wingfield, go into the storehouse and steal away much more than what is rightfully theirs. If they knew I knew of their dishonesty, they would probably banish me.

The food I saved in my sack from the many months here in Virginia went more quickly than I'd hoped. Some had spoiled beyond hope, and the rest was gone as of November. If it weren't for Laughing Boy, I might be dead now, starved like the others. I do not see the Powhatan as often as I did in the autumn; with his pantomime and stick sketches I know he must spend these winter months hunting with his village. But regularly I find a bundle of corn, nuts, and dried meat left for me where I buried the beads. I gorge myself before I return to James Towne.

Now that the gardens are dead for the winter, most of us do not go beyond the fortress. The soldiers still take turns watching for attacks, but sometimes their weakness causes them to doze, leaving us in danger. There has been much rain and sleet and some snow. My feet are sometimes so numb I can barely stand, but I know if I don't move around, it will only be worse. Very few men look to me for humor now, for which I am thankful. It is too cold to joke.

Thomas Sands and Robert Fenton have been released from their imprisonment, with less than thirty days served. I avoid them as best as possible. I do not like the looks in their eyes. It is not hatred, but a near-pity. I do not need anyone's pity. I only need to survive.

As I write with these stiff fingers, I hear weak shouts from outside my cottage. I hear, "Susan Constant." Susan Constant! The ship has arrived! There will be supplies, food, clothing, weapons. I stop for now.

❧ 20 ❧

January 7–30, 1608

NAT DREAMED OF London, of a stable where he and Richard and another London boy Matthew used to hide when it was cold and rainy. He could smell the scent of clean horses and could feel the warmth of the dusty, brittle straw. Richard and Matthew were nearby, sitting around a small fire, cooking fish scraps and a plump pigeon. Nicholas Skot was there, too, and sitting behind him was Samuel Collier, and one of the new boys, thirteen-year-old Thomas Savage. Boys all waiting for a meal. Nat could feel his mouth water, anticipating the tasty flesh.

But then a spark jumped from the fire and landed in the straw near Nat. "Watch out!" said Richard. Nat tried to get up and away, but his legs were frozen. The straw burst into flames, leaping up and licking the side of Nat's face. Matthew shouted, "Nat, get away now!"

Nat's arms flailed out trying to push the fire back, but still he couldn't stand. The hair on his head began to sizzle. The skin on his face began to melt.

"Get out!"

Get out!

Nat's eyes flew open to the black of night and the shouts of John Laydon in the open doorway. "Nathaniel, Samuel, William, get out! There's fire in the fort!"

In a second he was off his mattress and into his shoes. There was a smell of ash in the cottage, pungent and strong. It stung his eyes. Nat stumbled outside into the frigid night. Samuel and William fell out behind him.

The fort was in an uproar. On the south corner of the fort, Nat could see bright towers of orange-red flames. Cottages were on fire, their reed-covered roofs engulfed, their windows belching smoke. Men raced to the wells, tossing down buckets on ropes and hauling them up again, then running to hurl the water on the structures. There were shouts of panic, there were wails of despair. Many of the voices belonged to the new settlers who had arrived just three days earlier with the supplies and had bedded down in crowded cottages until new homes could be built.

"God help us, why have we come here?"

"We should never have sailed to Virginia!"

"We are doomed!"

"Lord, pity!" said Samuel. "We'll lose everything."

The winter wind was intense, blowing across the tops of the burning cottages and throwing flame tongues onto the buildings next to them.

John Smith, his face blacked with soot, came over to Nat and Samuel and gave each one a sharp smack to the head. "What are you doing there? Go to the river with anything to carry water. I won't have you standing about like simpletons! Hurry!"

Nat darted back into his cottage and grabbed his sack. It might leak, but perhaps it would hold water long enough to get some back to the fort. Samuel followed him, taking up his own smaller sack. They made their way through the chaos within the fort and down the frozen, slippery bank to the river.

The water's edge was covered with a layer of ice. Nat drove his foot through the ice, lost his balance, and stepped into the shallows.

The cold was like a knife to his legs. But he grabbed a handful of grass and pulled himself out. Then he dragged the sack through the water and lugged it back up the slope. Samuel complained the whole way. "A sack can't carry water, mine is leaking. So is yours. This is absurd!"

"Be quiet, boy," said Nat.

There was half a sack of water by the time Nat reached the first burning cottage. A tall man grabbed the sack from him and dumped the water through a smoking window. Then Nat went back to the river.

He lost track of the number of times he ran up and down the slope with his sack. His frozen legs tried to lock up under him, but he pushed them onward. He was aware that Samuel was sometimes beside him, sometimes not, but mostly he was aware of the smells of smoke and the smells of fear. Men shouted, their words no longer intelligible but animal shrieks of terror and anguish.

"We're all going to die!"

"God curse you, London Company, for sending us to our deaths here in this terrible place!"

There was a hazy red glow in the east by the time the fires were at last extinguished. The sun was coming up over the river, its light burning the sky like a cold, taunting fire. Now the damage was visible. Many cottages were destroyed, their grass-and-reed roofs and mud-and-stick walls nothing but smoldering ruins.

The men gathered in the remains of the church, those who had come in 1607 and those who had arrived on the *Susan Constant* just days prior, all looking much the same in their angst and worry, dropping down on charred benches and looking at the ground as if the earth had the answers they sought. The roof was half gone, and just three of the four walls still stood. It was as though God and the devil themselves had battled here, each one trying to claim this house of worship. Nat hated to think it, but it looked as though the devil had given the Lord quite a challenge.

"Where is God?" one man near Nat wondered aloud. "Why has He brought us here for this? We are not as pious as Job, so why must we be tested as severely?"

The Reverend Hunt preached for many hours. He raised his hands to heaven and sought God's help in enduring the difficulties of Virginia. He led the men in the singing of songs and reciting of Psalms, but most of the voices were now scratchy and faint with the ravages of smoke. Reverend Hunt thanked God for the lives and buildings that were spared in the fire. The minister's face and hands were black with ash, and his robe was scorched, yet his words were earnest and sincere.

"Our blessed Redeemer, give us courage to continue our mission here in the New World!"

Most of the men answered, "Amen." Some said nothing.

Over the weeks that followed, the James Towne men worked to rebuild, but this time in wind cold enough to cut flesh. Chopping trees to replace the cottages and plastering frozen mud for walls made joints and muscles ache. At times Nat felt his hands would break off the ends of his arms like brittle icicles. The settlers had so little strength it took three times as long to build a cottage as it had in the summer. Everyone's faces— John Laydon, Samuel Collier, John Smith, Nicholas Skot, and all the others—seemed to have shrunken into skulls. Cheekbones protruded, eyes were hollow and dark, lips were dry, cracked, and often bloody.

I suppose I look as they do, Nat wrote one night as he sat on his mattress after John Laydon had extinguished the lantern and the glow of the moon through the window was the only light available. *It is a good thing I am not wealthy enough to own a looking glass. What a fright I would have.*

Laydon was in his silent prayers now, his eyes closed, his body trembling. Samuel lay on his own mattress, facing away from Nat. Nat hadn't heard Samuel utter more than a few words since the fire. He went to Smith's cottage when called, but other than that, was distant and withdrawn. Maybe he was sick, although Nat had not heard the rasping cough that the dying men had. Maybe he had just given up hope for a good life in Virginia. Maybe he just wanted to go home to England.

Nat looked back at his paper, and couldn't think of anything else to write. He covered the page with one of his remaining deerskins. Then he drew his knees up to his chest and forced himself to sleep.

He awoke when it was still dark, although he could feel the coming morning in the air. His stomach growled, still believing it could demand a meal. Beneath his sack was the sharpened stick Laughing Boy had given him to fish. If he went down to the river now, no one would question him. Even though fish were hard to find in the winter, perhaps he could stir up something in the frosty water.

Quietly he pulled on his stiff shoes and cloak, then went out of the cottage and through the center of the fort toward the gate. Men could be heard through the windows of their cottages, snoring, coughing, and moaning. *What are their dreams?* Nat wondered. The watch in the bulwarks were clearly sleeping; no one stirred as he moved the large wooden post from the latch of the gate and slipped outside.

The stars in the sky were beginning to grow fuzzy as the sun in the east found a fingerhold on the horizon. Pale gray sunlight crawled across the river and the distant trees. Nat knew it would bring no warmth, however. He reached his boulder and stood with the spear raised, staring into the water, watching for a splash.

There was rustling in the trees along the clearing. Nat spun around. Walking softly, sneaking toward the fort, was an entire band of natives.

Nat's mouth opened, but nothing came out. The spear fell from his hands. He took a deep breath and screamed, "Muskets! Quickly, muster now, for the savages are coming!"

His legs loosened and he dashed up the frozen path to the fort's gate. He knew arrows would be flying in just a moment; he knew he would be the first one dead when the natives drew their bows.

But Nat stumbled once, and as he righted himself he looked over his shoulder. The natives were still walking to the fort, but none had bows or other weapons readily at hand. Instead, their arms and shoulders were laden with turkeys, whole deer and some half carcasses, and baskets of dried vegetables, nuts, and corn.

Nat stopped and stared.

At the front of the line skipped a young girl, a bit younger than himself, wearing a deerskin dress decorated in shells and feathers. Her black hair was bound in leather thongs at the back of her neck. Around her neck was a single blue glass bead. She was smiling.

The remaining Powhatans were men, bearing the food. Their faces were solemn but not threatening. They seemed determined to do the job they had come to do. Deliver food.

Unless it's a trick, Nat thought. *Like the Trojan horse, perhaps they are hiding hatchets and clubs in those baskets, ready to kill us if we let them into the fort!*

And then Nat saw someone near the rear of the procession, someone he knew. It was Laughing Boy. He carried a skin bundle filled with ears of dry corn. The boy nodded at Nat, barely, though, as if he didn't want the others to know that he and Nat were acquaintances. *Good,* thought Nat. *If the men of James Towne knew I spent time with a native, they would punish me severely.*

It was only then that the watch came awake in the murky morning light, and began to scream, "Muskets! Muster quickly, we are under attack! All men, muster!"

The cannons on the bulwarks squeaked as they were positioned. Inside the walls, men could be heard shouting, "Attack! We are under attack! Hurry!"

But Nat cried, "They have brought food for us! Wait!"

A soldier at the cannon cried, "Shut up, boy!"

But Nat insisted. "Look, please! They've got food!"

The soldier straightened from the cannon and held up a hand. "Wait, the boy is right! Hold your muskets, men. We have a friendly visit!"

The fort gate swung open and John Smith came out, dressed already in his best uniform. Even his hat was placed carefully on his head and it seemed as if his beard had been combed. Nat had never known anyone who could look so dignified and so in command at such short notice. Surely the man had been sound asleep only a minute earlier.

"Pocahontas!" said Smith, sweeping his arms wide and welcoming the girl. "Welcome to James Towne, and to all those with you. Come in!"

He stood back, his cape flapping, and the natives entered the fort. Nat let them pass, glancing only once at Laughing Boy. As he did, Laughing Boy pointed to the hollow of his throat and tipped his head toward the front of the procession. Nat knew immediately what he was saying. Laughing Boy had given Pocahontas the blue bead. But why?

Everyone was up now, except the men too ill to leave their lodgings. John Smith gathered everyone around and waved his arms. "As I have told the council, because of my travels into the wilderness of Virginia and my visits to many Powhatan villages, we would someday have a time of peace between the natives and ourselves. That time has come. And the daughter of the great Chief Powhatan, Pocahontas, has initiated this feast before us. We are grateful to her for her generosity and pray our people will from this day forward share the land in tranquility."

Pocahontas beamed as John Smith bowed to her. She spun her arms around as if in dance, then said something to the natives behind her. They placed the foods on the ground. Even the most distrustful of the settlers at last laid down their muskets and collected the baskets and the meats. Nat took a small deer, threw it over his shoulder, and followed the other Englishmen to the storehouse. The animals would be skinned and then smoked dry to be eaten over the rest of the winter. The other foods, already prepared, would be rationed out by the councilors until spring:

John Smith conversed with the princess, using those words he knew of her language and a series of gestures. Clearly he wanted Pocahontas to thank her father for sending the food. Nat let his gaze wander over to Laughing Boy, who stood with his arms crossed. Carefully, so not to attract anyone else's attention, Laughing Boy pointed toward the storehouse and then to his forehead. He then touched his neck, nodded at Pocahontas, and shook his head. At last he patted his stomach and pointed at Nat.

Nat understood. It wasn't Pocahontas who had decided to bring food to the settlers. It was Laughing Boy's idea. He knew the settlers were starving. But Laughing Boy had no status to make such a grand proposal. And so he had given Pocahontas the blue glass bead, a rare and wonderful gift, so she would make the arrangements. But for some reason, Laughing Boy didn't really mind that the girl got the thanks, not him.

After Pocahontas and the natives had gone and the sun was up fully, fires were struck to heat up a fine meal of corn and venison. Men sat about, rubbing their hands against the warmth and loudly chewing the meat from the animal bones.

"This is a blessing from God," said Reverend Hunt to John Smith. "The Lord has seen fit to stir the hearts of the savages in order for us to live again."

"Thank God and thank me," said Smith, his mouth full of corn. "The Lord has given me the talent to ease the minds of the savages. I doubt any other settler would have had this effect on their dark hearts. And Pocahontas was so pleased with the appreciation we showed, she will come again."

President Edward Maria Wingfield sat near enough to Nat to be overheard saying, "Smith thanks God for the glory of being Smith. Those savages are never to be trusted." He cracked open the leg bone of a deer and began to suck the marrow from within. "I could see the treachery in their eyes even as they were handing us this food."

Gabriel Archer said, "True. Smith is so bloated with his own sense of worth he would pop if he ran into a thorn." Archer patted the dagger on his belt. "He best watch out for my thorn."

Wingfield nodded seriously and John Ratcliffe put his hand to his mouth to stifle a chuckle. Nat stared at the portion of deer leg in his hands. He pretended not to hear the councilors' discussion.

21

February 16, 1608

The new boy Thomas Savage is gone from us, traded to Powhatan as a hostage just a month after his arrival at James Towne. Smith and Newport ushered Thomas and his chest of clothing from us, and far up the river. They returned with a savage to live with us and learn our language. I did not know Thomas well, but that he was a tall boy for thirteen, and silent and respectful to gentlemen. So I do not think I shall miss him, but a cold chill ran down me when, again, I saw how easily a boy is gotten rid of. The savage who came to James Towne with Smith is a little older than I, but not much. His name is Namontack. He spends his time with the carpenters and with Reverend Hunt, learning how we build, how we speak, and how we pray. Newport plans to take him back to England. I will have nothing to do with him, not knowing how to trust him or if I should even want to.

Perhaps Thomas will find Richard and Richard will not be so alone in the wilderness. Perhaps, if Richard is still living.

Perhaps.

The New World is full of perhaps.

22

April 30, 1608

Pocahontas comes to our fort several times a week, bringing food and taking messages from John Smith to her father, the great Powhatan. The girl is haughty, bold, but I have a respect for her that I did not have earlier. She does indeed face danger when she comes to our fort. How can she know we won't act abruptly as her people sometimes do? Englishmen can be savage, though most would not admit it.

We are growing stronger with the victuals and the warmer weather. Our moods are a bit improved, though the damage from the fire is not totally repaired yet, and there are still many graves around the settlement.

Sometimes Laughing Boy comes with the delivery of food, sometimes not. I've often wondered how I could ask him about Richard, if he's seen him, if he is still alive. But our communication is still so limited, I doubt I will ever be able to convey my concerns. And I don't really know if I want to know the truth. What if Richard has been tortured to death, burned or gored?

We have begun planting our gardens once more. It is not long until we celebrate our first anniversary in James Towne. Celebrate. Not quite the word I should use. But this year could be better. *The natives have given us some seeds to help us with our farming.*

Amazingly, Thomas Savage was not slaughtered by the Powhatans, but has learned enough of their language to act as liaison at some of the trading expeditions Smith has taken over the past two months. I suppose, then, that he is faring well. Or as well as a child can in the face of everything strange and wild. God knows, I do not envy him. How the world, how circumstance, can turn in but a moment.

The Susan Constant *sailed twenty days ago, back to England, talking some wood to the Company and collecting some more supplies for us. We've got no gold yet. I doubt wood will please the Company much.*

We've got men making glass now, fancy, delicate green vessels for candles and beer. The sand along the riverside is melted down to create these wares.

But no gold.

Not a bit of gold.

23

September 28–October 12, 1608

IT WAS WITH mixed feelings that the men of James Towne had greeted the arrival of more settlers on September 20. There were supplies of food and tools and crates of pigs and goats, for which everyone was thrilled. But like the 120 who had come to James Towne in April of this year, the new men who arrived in September were no more knowledgeable of the way of the wilds than were the first settlers to arrive on the *Susan Constant*, the *Godspeed*, and the *Discovery* over a year ago. The Virginia Company had been angry that no gold had been sent from the New World to England, and they were determined to make sure gold was forthcoming. Instead of carpenters and farmers, which James Towne needed greatly, the Company sent gold refiners and more glassmakers. The new council president, John Ratcliffe, seemed at a loss as to how to manage so many people. He shouted orders, whipped those laborers he felt were disrespectful or had them tossed into the fort's tiny, thatched jail, and stomped around with his head held high as if he were in control, but he was not. John Smith was. Men moved more quickly for Smith than Ratcliffe, a fact not lost on the council president.

More trees were cleared from the surrounding forest and houses were built outside the fort. The ground was scraped to make additional fall gardens in which to raise pumpkins and winter wheat, though most of the newcomers had no idea of how to work a crop. Nat thought James Towne was beginning to sound and smell like London.

But there was something new and curious which had come on the ship from England this time. There were two women. One was a married lady named Lucy Forrest, a tall and quiet woman who spoke only with permission of her husband, Thomas. The other was a young girl named Ann Burras. She was Mistress Forrest's servant girl, and there was nothing quiet about her at all. In her mistress's presence, she was obedient and humble. But when she was off about her duties around the fort, drawing water and washing clothes and emptying chamber pots, she chattered to herself nonstop, complaining about the filthy conditions of James Towne and the constant stares of the men who lived there.

On one sunny afternoon as Nat was patching the walls of the church, he felt a dig in his ribs. He dropped the bucket of mud and it fell to its side with a clatter.

"Oh, I am sorry!" It was Ann, her hands on her hips, her nose wrinkled. A lock of hair had fallen from beneath the hood of her cape. "I meant to tease, not frighten."

"I'm not frightened," said Nat. "But you must learn that here in Virginia there are many things which can startle a man. Often it is a savage with a knife to slit the Englishman's throat or a club of bone to smash in his brains. You are lucky I didn't take you for a savage or I would have thrown you to the ground and stomped your neck."

Ann's blue eyes grew wide and her lips twitched. "Sir, you speak so cruelly to me!"

"No, I speak honestly."

Ann's eyebrows drew together in suspicion. But then she smiled. "You are a strong, honest man, I can see that." Then she tossed her head and strolled off.

Nat made a point of speaking to her every day after that. He watched her as she worked with Mistress Forrest washing clothes and preparing meals over the fire outside their house. He helped her carry water and gave her his last deer hide. In spite of her nasal voice, she was not an ugly girl at all.

"Winters in Virginia are harsh," he told Ann one evening at the riverside. "Many men starved last year."

"How dreadful."

"It is true," said Nat. "You need only see the graves to know what we endured."

Ann scowled and looked away across the river.

"But," Nat continued, "I'm a good hunter. I can always get more. In fact, I am a true survivor here. I have a secret supply of treasure in the forest."

Ann looked back at Nat, her eyes widening. She glanced around to make sure no one was gazing in her direction, and gave Nat a quick kiss on the cheek.

That evening, as Nat sat on his mattress removing his shoes, John Laydon said, "Miss Burras is pretty, isn't she?"

Nat shrugged. "I haven't noticed," he said. Had John seen the kiss? Probably not. Most of the men thought Ann pretty. But it made Nat feel self-conscious, regardless.

"Play a role for me," said John. "You are our town's

actor, young Peacock. How would Ann act if a man were to ask her to marry him?"

"Do you want a farce or a drama?" asked Nat.

"I'll leave that up to you."

Samuel said, "So you think you can act as a woman?"

William Love, bending over a torn linen shirt, said, "Let's see comedy!"

Nat pursed his lips and ran his fingers through his tangled hair. His eyebrows peaked as he said, "Oh, sir, you ask me for my hand? I am so flattered, but, sir, you are an old man, old enough to be my father! So I must decline, but I thank you warmly for your offer."

Samuel rolled his eyes. William Love laughed. But John Laydon didn't seem amused.

Over the next few days, Ann made a point of waving to Nat and speaking to him. She stopped her complaining when she was near him, and she seemed to make of point of smoothing her skirts and tucking her hair carefully when she saw him coming in her direction.

After worship service in the church on a pleasant afternoon, Ann pulled Nat aside and said, "Show me the treasure you have in the forest."

Nat felt his cheeks go red. He hadn't meant to tell anyone about the place where Laughing Boy, now that autumn had set in, had begun once more to leave food and symbols of peace between the two of them every ten days. Some days Laughing Boy would be there with the gift and he and Nat would go exploring or hunting. Other times the Powhatan only left the gift. But what if Ann saw Laughing Boy in the forest and was terrified? What if she thought food was not truly treasure? Could Nat trust her?

But she smiled and took his arm, and Nat knew it would be all right.

Ann had to wait until early the next morning, when her mistress thought she was washing clothes in the river. She and Nat crept through the tall stalks of unharvested corn and entered the forest.

Immediately Ann seemed uncomfortable. "It's too hard to walk. My shoes are not for such rough ground."

"Watch your step," said Nat. "You'll get used to it."

Ann said, "Humph," and held the hem of her skirt to keep it off the briars. She kept close to Nat, grabbing his shoulder when her balance teetered and grumbling. "Why would you have treasure so far out here? What good is it if you can't grab it up when you want to look at it?"

Nat said nothing.

"Is it gold? Silver? Pearls, perhaps!" said Ann.

Nat felt his teeth grind together. Pearls? This was a mistake. She had never been hungry, even if she was a mere servant girl.

"Nathaniel, where is the treasure? What is it?"

Nat stopped and said, "There is the treasure, Ann." On the ground, wrapped in large sycamore leaves, was a gift of several small squash, three ears of corn, and some beautiful red-gold feathers. "I have lived in Virginia for more than a year. I've learned that there are other treasures besides gold. Food is more precious. Someday I'll find gold, but for now, I give thanks for food. And there, beneath that pile of stones, are five blue glass beads. Worthless to either of us in England, but like money here, I have them hidden in case I find need to give one to the natives. They find them exquisite."

Ann tilted her head and chuckled for a second. Nat thought she would think about it for a moment and then realize what he was saying was true. But her face drew in and she frowned. "Surely you are teasing me," she said. "Now, where is the real treasure?"

Nat put an ear of corn in Ann's hand. "Here. Look at it. It is gold-colored, is it not? And it is smooth like gold. I am given gifts of food regularly, and I hide them in my sack in my cottage until the worst of times. In my sack now are many ears of corn. This way I do not have to depend on the other men of James Towne."

"I thought you were a rich man."

"In a way I am."

"Where does this food come from?"

"A Powhatan boy."

"Powhatan? You mean a savage?"

"Yes," said Nat. "But he is truly not savage."

Ann gave the corn back but said nothing.

Three days later, John Laydon caught Nat by the arm as he was tossing grain to the pigs. "I have a deal for you, comedian. You give me the sack of victuals you have been hiding in our cottage and the glass beads you have buried in the woods, and I won't tell John Smith that you stole from him and have been illegally keeping food to yourself. That will be your death, boy, and you know I tell the truth."

Nat gave John the sack, and the man put it in his trunk. He took John into the forest and dug up the beads. Four weeks later, John and Ann Burras were married in the church with the blessing of Mistress Forrest and Reverend Hunt and under the jealous eye of a couple hundred lonely men.

❧ 24 ❧

December 30, 1608

John Smith has done it again! Samuel Collier was taken on an expedition to the native village of Waraskoyack, and did not return with the men. I heard from Edward Pising that John Smith left Samuel with Powhatan, "assuring the king perpetual love," in order to keep the peace and for Samuel to learn the language. Someday, Pising says, Samuel may come back to us with this knowledge, and, as with Thomas Savage, we will all benefit. I did not know Thomas Savage, but I knew Richard. I knew Samuel. And for all the page's irritable spirits, I would not have wished this upon him.

Nicholas Skot has told me he is afraid he will be next to be taken away, and asked me what he should do. I told him I do not know. Just as we are unable to tell when we offend the Powhatans and bring attack upon ourselves or when we please them and bring about assistance, I am unable to know the heart and mind of John Smith when it comes to matters such as the trading of boys.

I do not hate Smith as the councilors do, but I do not revere him the way the commoners do. His turn has come to be president of the James Towne council and he is a harsher ruler than the others, which is to our benefit. He makes everyone work. *Those not hunting or collecting food are set to building and repairing our homes and the fort walls or splitting logs and putting them on ships to sail for England in a few days.*

But regardless, I cannot stomach the man as I once did.

Smith visits the natives and trades for food when the storehouse supplies grow slim. I think he enjoys the adventure a bit too much, leaving most of us behind to labor. I wonder if he misses the beads I took. I wonder if, on his trips, he has seen Richard. I have asked him, but he ignored me, as if such a matter is past and should remain past. Pocahontas, the young Powhatan girl, still comes on occasion with baskets of food. We are not starving as we did the last winter, and though I avoid Smith, I do give him credit for his steadfast control. He even makes everyone, from carpenter to sailor to tailor to gentleman, drill with muskets daily so we might be better ready if we are attacked again. Captains Archer and Wingfield obey, but they secretly rebel by continuing to steal from the storehouse when no one is around. I doubt I am the only one who has seen them sneaking out with food under their cloaks, but no one yet seems up to challenging them. They must remember the man who was executed for treason our first summer. Accusing our leaders would be nearly as bad as speaking against the king.

William Love seems pleased to have chores other than hunting and fishing. With many new men now, he is busy with tailoring, mending clothes and stitching new trousers from the small stock of fabric which arrived from London. He is not much with a musket. He can't even hit a tree stump. But he does have talent with a needle.

John Laydon and his wife have a cottage to themselves now. I am certain Ann is enjoying the little extra food which was my very reluctant wedding gift. I believe I even saw the blue beads around her neck, hiding just beneath her collar. John and Ann watch me like hawks, seeing if I try to go again into the woods alone. I've not been back since October. A handful of extra food is not worth the hangman's noose. I hope John is happy with Mistress Laydon. He can have her. I wish him luck with such a spiteful girl.

My shoes have holes in them. They won't last another year.

25

June 3–27, 1609

NAT HAD THOUGHT that, once off the *Susan Constant*, his duty of rat-catcher was over. But it wasn't.

The first of the garden's yields came in early June, and the storehouses were filled with potatoes, peas, and radishes. Other crops had been planted now, the corn, squash, beans, and cabbages, which, if all went well, would be ready to harvest in August. It was hot, but there were still occasional cool mornings and evenings, making it seem as though spring had forgotten its time was done. Sometimes, in the early days of June, the men would find themselves feeling more merry than usual, and a gentleman would pull out the flute he'd carried over on the ship and play a happy, dancing tune.

Nat even found his own feet tapping to the music as he sat at the edge of the gatherings. Yes, he knew there was gold still to be found. Perhaps it didn't sit on the top of the soil as he'd thought, perhaps it wasn't glittering in the fields or sparkling in the streams, but it was there, certainly. Underground, maybe. In a cave, at the bottom of a pond or lake. But it was there. And Nat knew that once James Towne had grown strong and no longer had to fight daily for a piece of bread, then there would be time for him to go exploring once more. This time he'd take a shovel.

But then, on a morning in the middle of the month, as the men gathered at the door to the storehouse for their rations of vegetables and last year's corn, there was a shout of dismay.

"Rats!"

"Damn the vermin! They've helped themselves to our store!"

"How dreadful!" said Ann Laydon.

Nat stood on tiptoe to peer over the shoulder of the tall man in front of him. He could see inside the shadowy store, and indeed the place was alive with the creatures. How could they have gotten in and multiplied so quickly in just a week? There had been a few times when the storehouse had borne vermin, but only in small numbers and found before much damage could be done. But this time it seemed as if a sea of rats were swimming in the stock, crawling over and under barrels and crates and in and out of cracks they had gnawed into the wood.

"Back up," demanded John Smith. The men backed up. Smith motioned for Nicholas Skot, who came up reluctantly. His hair hadn't seen a comb in many weeks, and looked like a greasy tangle of seaweed.

"Boy," said Smith. "You and Peacock are assigned to rid this place of the rats. I want every one gone by dusk."

And so Nat and Nicholas were on rat duty. With clubs in hand, they crept through the crates and barrels of food, smacking rats and tossing them out the door. Nicholas said, "Why do we not just shoot the damnable things?" but Nat reminded him what would happen if a matchlock musket caused a spark in the storehouse. A rat infestation would seem like nothing compared to a roaring blaze.

The rats had done serious damage. They had chewed holes into the crates and barrels and had been living inside, eating their fills and leaving rat droppings everywhere. Much of the food was ruined, because it was impossible to separate urine-soaked corn from the dry, the feces-coated peas from the clean.

"I hate rats!" said Nicholas as several ran across his feet and he batted them into heaven.

"And they hate us," said Nat.

By dark, there were still rats in the storehouse, and so Nat and Nicholas were up early the next morning to continue the job. They whacked the creatures as they ran, crushing them beneath the clubs. Nicholas, rolling a barrel over to check for more, was suddenly pounced on by a large, gray creature that ran up his leg to his face.

"God!" he screamed.

The rat bit his cheek before Nat could slap the rat away and crush him beneath his boot.

"I'll have rabies!" cried Nicholas, dropping his club and holding his face in both hands. "God help me!"

"God help you," said Nat. Nicholas was right. There was no telling if he would die from the bite or if it would just take the course of a swelling.

At last the place was rat-free, and the bodies of full-grown rats and clusters of dead baby rats were taken into the woods and pitched. Nat, with a sense of sour humor, nearly asked Nicholas if he wanted to have a rat-tossing contest, but decided against it. But as the last rat crashed into the undergrowth, he said, "It is possible that those creatures will one day look tasty. That the time will come when we wish we had rats for a meal, and hadn't been so hasty as to throw them away."

Nicholas wiped away a tear and returned to the fort.

Nat didn't go back into the fortress immediately, but down to the river, where some of the sailors had launched the shallop. Smith, as usual, stood by supervising, his hands and his hips and his head tilted proudly. He spied Nat and called him over.

"Peacock!" he said. "You boasted at many skills when first we met. I've got men going to Point Comfort to fish. We must have something to fill our bellies. Are you a fisherman as well as farmer, soldier, cook, and carpenter?"

"Yes, sir," Nat said cautiously.

"Then climb aboard and take an oar. I expect you to return with nothing less than brimming buckets."

Nat's stomach clenched. "Is this truly a fishing trip, sir, not an expedition of exploration?"

Smith didn't seem to notice the hesitation in Nat's voice. "Yes, to the Point, or haven't you noticed we need food? Get aboard!"

Nat climbed into the shallop and was given a place near the back. He'd not left James Towne by boat in a long time. It might have been a pleasant change if he was not aware that this might be more than a fishing expedition. It might be another trip of human trade.

But the shallop did indeed row for the Point down the river at the mouth of the bay. Gulls followed the shallop, seeming to think that these men had something they might want. After a half hour of circling, they went off to another adventure. Nat's arms, much stronger and tougher after two years in Virginia, had no trouble working his oar through the water of the James.

The men landed on the sandy beach, hopping out into the small waves of the waist-high water and pulling

the shallop half ashore. A sailor named Jonas and other
named John drew out the huge net and spread it on
the beach, inspecting it for tangles and tears. The other
men took their shoes off and put them in the tall
grasses, laid their muskets beside their shoes, and then
joined in the stitching of the tears. As Nat and John
nimbly knotted the thin ropes back into place, Jonas
said, "Ye think the shallop would take us back to England safely?"

The men chuckled. "Aye," said John. "Let's board
now and we'll be home to our families in, what, three
or four years, ye think?"

"Let's be off then!" said Jonas.

And then John hit the beach on his belly, and motioned the others to do so as well. Into the sand he
sputtered, "Lord help us, its savages!"

There were curses and swearing, and the men
looked helplessly at the muskets they had left by their
shoes.

Nat could see them now. There were two canoes,
each with four or five natives, paddling south past the
Point. Who were they? Where did they come from?
Were they the Indians from Cape Henry? Were they
from farther north, or perhaps up the James River itself? There was too much distance to see their cos-
tumes clearly.

"Does it matter?" Nat muttered to himself. "If they
see us, we are dead."

"Ye've got a pistol, John," whispered Jonas.

"Oh," said John into the sand. "And you think I'll
take the lot of them with one pistol? I'll kill one or two,
and by then they will have come to shore with arrows
and hatchets at the ready."

"I mean in case they see us, fool," said Jonas.

"Hush!"

The Englishmen lay as still as they could. It was

worthless, Nat knew, because the shallop was huge and couldn't be missed, sitting there on the beach like a dead whale. It was just a matter of a few more seconds.

And then, as the faces in the canoes turned to stare at the shallop, Nat thought he recognized one of those faces. It was tanned, but seemed to not be of a native, but of a white man. An Englishman. An English boy.

Impossible.

"They've spied us, Jonas!" said John. "What are we to do?"

"Lie still and wait. We've got no other options!"

Impossible, Nat thought. *I'm only imagining things. I want Richard to be alive and so have allowed the sun on the water to play tricks on my mind.*

Either divine or some other mystical providence must have smiled, because the natives continued to steer their canoes, watching, yet doing nothing else, until they could no longer be seen.

"They were afraid," said Jonas, jumping up and brushing off his trousers. "They know of the strength of the Englishmen!"

"They felt sorry for us," said John, grasping the re-paired net and walking it to the edge of the water. "They decided we weren't worth the bother."

There was chuckling again, but this time is wasn't as hearty.

And as the men took the net into the briny waters to reap, hopefully, a harvest better than what they'd gleaned from the earth outside the fort at James Towne, all Nat could think about was Richard. Had that been he? Or had it been an illusion?

He threw himself into the fishing to try to forget. To not know.

But the fish the crew took back to James Towne three days later was much less than desired.

26

July 4, 1609

God help me, did I see Richard on the bay or was I dreaming? I can't know anymore. Sometimes my mind is muddled with fatigue and hunger, and it makes me want to rip something apart to get away from it! I can't bear feeling out of control! I can't bear feeling my mind is playing tricks on me!

Sometimes when no one is looking, I slap my own face to bring my mind back around to myself. I see the same numbness on the faces of others, too, and it angers me to succumb as they are!

This is our third summer here in Virginia, and we have gone into it with less strength, less vigor, less health and hope than any summer prior, and I fear unless a miracle occurs, we face a winter which could well be our last. As a body needs reserves of fat to live, a soul needs reserves of faith. There is little faith in James Towne. Old and new settlers alike talk among themselves, longing to go back to England, longing to abandon the cottages and fort and let the woods grow back to reclaim it.

Rats are in the storehouse again, but neither Nicholas— who did not die of rabies from the rat bite but whose face grew like a bloated tomato and then subsided to leave it somewhat lopsided and loose—I, nor any other boy here has been put to chasing them and killing them. As most of us are considered in fair health, we are needed to keep watch and tend gardens and make repairs on cottages which mold and rot before our very eyes. And so, what little grain is scraped from the storehouse barrels and from off the floor is cooked up as it is, with the rat droppings boiled in with the food.

Men are ill, writhing in agony in their sweat-soaked beds. Two died yesterday. This morning another died.

John Smith demands everyone but those who are on the brink of death be up and wielding muskets and axes and fishing nets. He threatens constantly, mustering everyone together each morning by the door of the church to lecture us and wave his hands at us as his cape billows behind him like the great hand of God. I have witnessed Smith draw up the sick and wheezing Edward Pising from his bed and push the man, stumbling, out of the fort and into the garden beyond to hoe a patch of peas.

A miracle is what we need!

Who told us there was gold here? Piss on him! If there was some to be had, I wonder how it would taste on the tongue. I wonder how it would feel in the belly.

27

August 11–12, 1609

SAMUEL COLLIER RETURNED to James Towne in July at the request of John Smith, not flayed or half dead but seeming healthy and tattooed with some marks peculiar to the Powhatans. His red hair was cut short and the blemishes on his face had disappeared. He had gained a fair knowledge of the language of the natives but had lost his curt personality, and a cautious silence had taken its place. Nat was not displeased to see his old hut-mate, but Samuel seemed to have less interest in complaining about day-to-day events, which took much of the fun out of having the page around. Samuel moved back into Nat's hut, but spent most of his time by Smith's side, sharing what he had learned. Nat picked up some words which he hoped to try out secretly with Laughing Boy if the chance came, *wingapo*—"welcome," *chespin*—"land," *rawcosowghs*—"days," *toppqough*—"nights," *netoppew*—"friends," but refused to directly ask that Samuel tutor him. One night, when he could no longer hold his question, he called to Samuel from his cot, "Did you see Richard Mutton among the natives? He has been gone a long time, but I wonder if he is still alive."

"No," said Samuel matter-of-factly. "I did not see him. There are at least thirty-two tribes under the Powhatan. Forget Richard. His fate is known only to God."

Gabriel Archer left Virginia in midsummer, back to England to obtain more settlers and supplies, but the ever-arrogant Edward Maria Wingfield was still in the settlement, and Nat often saw him huddling together with the young gentleman George Percy down by the river as if they were plotting. Smith had not been hanged back in the West Indies as planned. Would these men try again to take revenge against the captain? Would they strangle Smith in the night? Would they stab Smith behind the storehouse?

Heat, flies, bad food, and jealousy were a perilous combination.

Pocahontas, who had visited the fort throughout the spring of the year, had not been back in a while. Nat wondered if the Powhatans were angry once more with the Englishmen. It was difficult to know when they would be friendly and when they would not, although John Smith had usually been able to make temporary peace with his ability to converse and reason. The Powhatans had different views on the use of land. According to Smith and now Samuel, they believed that the land could not be owned by anyone, that one might as well try to buy the sky and the sun. And so fear or anger would break out and there would be an attack. To most of the settlers, it seemed as if the natives acted on whim alone, but Nat knew English behavior must seem like whim to the natives. It was a relationship that seemed to have no clear answers. And the Englishmen, once again, were forced to rely on their own food supplies.

Nat had become an experienced gardener. He knew how deep to dig for planting beans and peas. He knew how to tend the new stalks of corn so they wouldn't shrivel. He knew which insects would eat the plants and which would eat other insects. The men who had survived from the first year as well as the newer settlers watched him and listened to his advice.

"I beg your pardon, sir! Don't pour that on the corn," he shouted as one little bearded silversmith tipped over a bucket of water he'd drawn from the James River. "It's got salt in it. It will stunt the growth. It is best if you use well water."

The silversmith snarled, "Preposterous. We can't spare well water for plants. We need it for drinking."

"We need corn, sir. Please fill your bucket with well water."

The man drew up his face as if he wanted to argue, but William Love, loosening the soil around the melon garden next to the corn, interrupted, shouting over the rail fence. "Nathaniel knows what he's talking about. Do as he says."

Grumbling, the silversmith left the corn garden and took his bucket past the new cottages and through the gate of the fort.

"Hello, Nat!" It was Ann Laydon, a basket on her arm half full of berries she had found in the brush at the edge of the clearing. The skin of her face and hands had grown red with the weather, and her belly was round beneath her skirts. She had a baby due in a few months. "Find any treasures under that corn?"

If no one had been within hearing distance, Nat would have scolded her severely. But he just sighed and looked back at his work. There was a little pleasure in knowing that it irritated Ann greatly to be ignored.

"Your skin has become as dark as a savage in this sun," said Ann. "Does that mean you want to be like them?"

Nat rubbed a mosquito bite on his chest and

chopped the soil around a corn plant with his spade, softening it and working out stones.

"Do you hear me, gardener?"

Nat pushed the loosened soil back around the plant.

Ann stomped her foot. "You are impolite indeed! Do you hear me?"

Nat walked to the next plant and began to chop.

"You'll certainly never be a rich man nor a gentleman with your foul manners!" said Ann. She blew a noisy puff of air through her lips and wandered away.

It was all Nat could do to keep from laughing out loud. However, he could hear a chuckle from William Love nearby.

And then William's chuckle stopped abruptly and the man said, "They have arrived!"

Another gardener in the corn replied, "God help us, they best have food. A lot of food."

Nat dropped his own spade and put his hand to his forehead, shading out the glare of the sun. There, nearing the settlement on the sluggish James River, were five ships. More men, and perhaps women and children as well. This place was going to be overrun. As the gardener had said, they best have food. And a lot of it.

There were shouts from the cottages around the fort and from within. Those who were well enough to be up and off their cots were rallying around to greet the new arrivals. The inhabitants of James Towne clustered side by side by the water, staring at the newcomers.

"Which ships are these, now?"

"I see men waving from the deck. They best be in good health, I tell you. We don't need any more folks who are ailing or dying."

"Pray God the Company has at last sent us men who can work. Farmers, carpenters, surgeons, and cooks."

"You think the Company knows how we fare in Virginia? If they sent us a farmer, I will give you my whole food ration for two days!"

Only the first ship, the largest one with a broken mast, was able to anchor close to the pier. The others dropped anchor behind it, and simultaneously, long-boats were lowered. Bedraggled passengers climbed down the sides and into them with haste, like rats escaping a sinking vessel.

"Not surprising they are so eager to get off them stinking things," said William, standing near Nat. "I remember arriving. Land was the most blessed thing to me when the trip was done."

"Hmm," said Nat.

"Only thing," William continued, "they've no idea what they're getting into here. They shall be anxious to climb back up and squeeze down that 'tween deck once they see what we have waiting for them here. Is not the lush pastures and sparkling streams we were promised, to be certain!"

Several other men chuckled sourly. Nat crossed his arms across his bare chest.

John Smith, who had been standing near the rear of the gathering, strode forward onto the pier to be the first to speak. He'd taken time to straighten his hat and the ruff of his collar. The man never ceased to look dignified when the need arose.

Several pairs of hands in the first longboat rose in greeting as the little boat touched the pier. "Hello, there!" called a man in the front. "God be praised, we have found you! God be praised, we have found James Towne!"

"God be praised if there's ale aboard," said the recovering Edward Pising. "I'll drop to me knees in this mud and shout 'glory, hallelujah!' if we've good stout drink in them ships!"

Passengers in the longboat climbed onto the pier

and bowed wearily, gratefully, to John Smith.

"Think there be girls with the men, Nathaniel Peacock?" came a shrill voice. "That should please you, I would think." Ann was right next to him, standing at his shoulder. She wore a smirk on her face, and her hair was free around her shoulders, not pinned up properly.

"You only know what pleases yourself, Mistress Laydon," said Nat quietly. "Now go to your husband. And make a decent style with that hair of yours. It seems as if you fancy the ways of the Powhatan women, with it hanging down like that."

Ann's face drew up and her eyes flashed. She whipped about and stormed over to John Laydon, who put his hand on her shoulder but otherwise didn't seem to notice she was there. He continued to speak with the other men and nod in the direction of the ships on the river.

The other longboats docked at the pier and the passengers continued to unload. There were many men, and yes, a few women and several young children. With a surge of fear and anger, Nat noticed the sickness of more than half; they staggered, they coughed dark spittle onto the soil of James Towne. Some needed the aid of others to walk. Others were carried.

"What we needed was meat and bread," cried Edward Pising. "Not half-dead, worthless people."

Nat watched as the hoard walked, hobbled, and stumbled toward the gate of the palisade through the cluster of settlers. It was pitiful indeed, as Jehu Robinson would have said. Men clung to sick wives; children cried in their mothers' arms. One young woman in a soiled blue gown and shabby velvet cape wept silently as she walked to the fort.

As a man passed, Nat asked, "Why does that woman weep? She does not appear ill as do many others."

"Young Mistress Ford lost her husband on the journey over. He died of the sweating sickness and we dumped his body overboard. She is but eighteen years, had been married but a week before the ships left England, and is now a widow!" The man stroked his chin and cleared his throat. It was a rattly sound; this man was suffering with a lung problem himself. "But she is a stout one, she is. I've not seen her cry aloud nor tear her hair as some of the women have. Instead, she has shown nothing but kindness to others who suffered on the trip, giving them aid and comfort. What a disaster we have endured. Our flagship *Sea Venture* was blown off course and we fear they are lost."

"Dreadful," said Nat.

"Indeed," said the man. He then extended his hand. "My name is Peter Scott. And this is my wife, Martha." He motioned to the small-framed woman behind him, who nodded wearily at Nat. "God be praised, the three of us survived the ordeal on the sea."

Three? Nat wondered. But then he noticed that Mistress Scott was pregnant. How would baby Scott and baby Laydon endure James Towne?

Nat gazed again at the stoic woman in the dirty blue gown as she followed the shabby assembly into the fortress. Then he went back to his spade in the cornfield. There was nothing to do but wait for the order to build more cottages and bury those who would die before the next morning.

William Love also returned to his work in the patch next to Nat's. "Gabriel Archer and John Ratcliffe are back," he said. "I'm certain John Smith would have rather they'd been two of the dead, tossed to the sharks in the depths of the sea."

Nat didn't answer. He chopped for a while, as fast as he could to make the muscles of his arms sting so he wouldn't have to think. Shadows crawled across the ground and Nat chopped and smoothed and raked.

As he neared the corn plants close to the trees, something in the corner of his eye moved. Nat looked up. There, peering from behind the needled branches of a pine, was Laughing Boy. Nat's mouth dropped open. He had not seen the Powhatan in nearly a year, and the change was amazing. Laughing Boy was muscular and very tall, no longer the thin child with whom Nat had explored. His hair was no longer plain, but adorned with shells and feathers. Perhaps he had grown into a warrior. Laughing Boy smiled and gestured for Nat come into the woods.

Nat shook his head. There were too many men around to chance leaving. But he pointed to the sun and then lowered his flattened palm. *I will meet you when the sun sets.*

Laughing Boy understood. He nodded, and then departed.

"It will be good to see him again," Nat said to himself. "There is so much going on now with the new settlers, no one will miss me if I sneak away after dark."

It was more difficult to leave at sunset than Nat had thought it would be. Smith had ordered all able-bodied men who were not posted as watch to either bury the dead, nurse the sick, or get to work planting posts for new houses. Even as it grew dark, he had men set many fires ablaze so they could see and continue digging holes and raising the skeletons of the huts. Soon moonlight added its glow and the work went on without pause.

Nat had never gone alone into the forest at night without a lantern. But if he were to take a light, he would be spotted, and so, with only the aid of the moon's glow, he left James Towne and carefully made his way to the place he and Laughing Boy used to meet. Crickets and tree frogs mocked him. Their tiny, dry

voices seemed to ask, "Why are you here? It's dangerous. Go back. Go back."

He picked up a thick stick and held it before him
like a club.

Laughing Boy was not in the usual meeting place.
Nat held the stick and sat on the ground after poking
with the stick to make sure he didn't sit on a snake.
He waited. And waited.

After what seemed like an hour, Nat brushed himself
off and prepared to return to James Towne. Maybe
Laughing Boy hadn't understood after all. Maybe he'd
decided he really didn't want to be friends with Nat.
He felt his way along between the trees with the stick,
straining to see in the waning moonlight.

The crickets picked up their chorus. "Go back, go
back, go back, go back."

And then another sound caught Nat's ear, and he
stopped short. It was the whistle of a bird. But it
seemed out of place in the night. Nat had only heard
that whistle during the day. His fingers tightened
around the stick. He could hear his heart pounding in
his ears.

"I'm just imagining the sound," Nat told himself after a moment of silence. "I've gotten jittery and my
mind is playing tricks. I am acting like a child." He
strode forward again, this time humming a simple tune
in his mind.

Then the bird's whistle came again, this time from
very close to his left.

And then there was one to his right, and one directly
behind him. There was a rustle of leaves.

Oh, God, I'm not imagining, Nat thought. *I'm being followed by—*

Hands grabbed him then, throwing him to the
ground, driving air from his lungs with a harsh grunt.
His eyes slammed shut with the agony.

"Help!" he managed. A hand jerked his helmet off. A knee punched into his chest, throwing bright sparks of pain through his whole body. His head was yanked back by the hair. A hank of it ripped out at the roots. There were wails around him, screams ghastly and loud and triumphant. Nat's arms were stretched out to the sides and pinned firmly to the ground.

He opened his eyes.

There, holding him like a helpless insect, were four Powhatan warriors. They were painted white and black, and their eyes twinkled in the dark. One had a club of stick and stone, and it was poised over Nat's head.

They are going to smash my skull!

They all laughed at Nat. The sound was as cold as the blade of a dagger.

Nat screamed, knowing at the moment that he did it was a mistake because he was showing cowardice and that was enough to make him worthy of death.

The warriors laughed again, a sound that pierced the air like a devil's cry. The one with the club raised it high, ready to bring it down.

God help me no I'm going to die!

And there was a flash of movement, and the club was knocked away. Nat gasped. He couldn't see anything but two forms wrestling against the backdrop of black trees. His arms were released as the other warriors joined in the struggle. And then someone dropped over Nat's body, protecting him.

One warrior shouted, and the one crouched over Nat snarled something back.

The warriors argued fiercely, but the one over Nat didn't move. For many long minutes, there were heated words in native tongue, between the standing warriors and the one who sheltered Nat. At last the four standing Powhatans could be heard leaving, walking off into the darkness and muttering to themselves.

The form pulled away from Nat. Nat rubbed his eyes with his fists and with effort, drew his legs under himself and sat. It was then he could see clearly, even though the moon offered little assistance. Laughing Boy had saved him. He had risked his own reputation, his own life, for Nat.

Laughing Boy shook his head and made a soft, regretful sound and offered his hand to help Nat to his feet. Nat found his voice. "Thank you," he whispered.

Laughing Boy, who Nat was certain knew no English, nodded and patted Nat on the shoulder. *You're welcome*, the gesture said. He understood the words of appreciation.

Laughing Boy helped Nat to the edge of the woods but would go no farther. Nat waved good-bye and limped back to the fort. When he got to his cottage, William had awakened and the lantern was lit.

"What happened to you?" William asked. "You've got gashes all over, and your eye is swelling shut."

Nat hesitated. He should say nothing, but he was so awed with what he had just experienced, he couldn't keep quiet. "I was rescued in the woods," he said. "I had gone for a midnight hunt and was attacked by four strong Powhatan warriors. They meant to bash in my brains, but another threw himself over me and would not let it happen."

William's eyes grew huge. "Indeed?" he said. "A savage saved your life?"

"Yes," said Nat. He lay down on his mattress and pulled his deerskin over his shivering legs.

The following day, word of the rescue had spread. Even John Smith came to Nat's cottage to speak to him about it.

"You were alone in the woods?" asked Smith, his arms crossed and his eyes narrow. "Who gave you permission?"

Nat answered, keeping his gaze downcast. "Forgive me, but with all the new arrivals and their dire conditions, I thought I might hunt a bit and bring in extra meat."

Smith said nothing, but stroked his chin. He stared out of the cottage window, then looked back at Nat. "I was rescued in such a manner, too. Pocahontas laid her head on mine to keep her father from killing me."

"That is amazing," said Nat.

"You don't believe me?"

"Oh, sir, of course! I only mean that God was surely watching you!"

"Of course He was," said Smith. "God likes me and has a special eye for me. How else could something like that happen?" He left the cottage.

He can't tolerate that I have such an amazing story! Nat wrote hastily on a page. *And now he makes my story his, and makes it more exciting that it is a princess and her father the Powhatan. Pompous! Self-important! And I hope the man never has chance to read my words.*

But neither Nat's tale nor Smith's mattered much. There was work to do among the sick and dying of James Towne. Remembering the rescue made Nat feel grateful, and amid all the sadness, it gave him a sense of wonder.

He wrote, *My friend saved my life. And he is no savage. His name is Laughing Man.*

28

September 2, 1609

John Smith was in the shallop with some of the soldiers when a powder keg exploded. It cut the man to pieces, burning him and tearing him at the same time. He is in his cottage, and although I've not peeked inside, they say it is all he can do to keep from screaming from the pain. He bites leather to keep his agony silent. There is talk he might die. Some say he should return to England if he is to live. What will happen here if he leaves? There is no one who can rule James Towne as well as Smith.

I think about Ratcliffe, Wingfield, and Percy. Did they plan this? Did they bribe one of the soldiers to light the keg in order to kill Smith? I will never know for certain.

Nicholas, Samuel, and I have been put on burial duty as well as gardening duty. There was a stocky and able boy who came with the August ship, one named Henry Spilman, but he was taken as a hostage to the natives just before Smith's accident, and so there are only three boys strong enough now for the digging of graves and removal of bodies. Over the past weeks, many of the new arrivals who were ill have died. I hate to touch the cold skin of the dead. I have to make myself think that they are indeed dead, no more than the carcasses of the deer and bear I have eaten. Mistress Ford must think me foul indeed, walking about with the stench of the dead on my hands. I wish that was not so, but I fear it is.

One of the dead early this morning was a little girl named Martha Angus. Her mother is also sick, but would not let go of the child when we went inside her cottage with our lanterns to remove the body. She just sat on the cot, crying, holding the child in a filthy blanket, kissing the crusted forehead and vomit-streaked lips. At last her husband took the child away and, as weak as he was, came with us to the newest place for bodies on the northwestern edge of the colony near the forest wall. The father made us promise that animals would not dig his poor child from the ground. I promised him, knowing it was a lie. At night it is all we can do to watch for natives, much less a determined fox.

There is little we can do. As I sit and write in the light of my lantern on this late night, I hear voices calling for Samuel and me. Another has died and we must take the body out.

Smith must recover. James Towne is failing.

❧ 29 ❧

October 3–30, 1609

JOHN SMITH WAS dying indeed. The dreadful wounds from the powder explosion had healed badly, and not even the surgeon knew how to put him right. Nat had at last found the courage to look in on the wounded leader, peering through the rear window of the cottage and heart sinking at the sight.

Smith was nearly a corpse, his face pale and scarred, his chest heaving with effort. The great cape hung, burned nearly to a rag, on the wall beside a cross. Reverend Hunt sat beside him, reading Scriptures aloud.

"He leadeth me in the paths of righteousness for his name's sake . . ."

Nat pulled away from the window and forced himself down to the fall garden to pull bugs from the pumpkins.

It was with much anxiety and sadness that the council president was put aboard a ship to go home. Prayers were offered up in the church that Smith return to England safely and that he recover quickly.

The citizens of James Towne watched the sail of

Smith's ship disappear down the river past the trees. Nat and Nicholas stood side by side, staring after the boat. Nat felt as though the sun was setting, not to rise again.

Look out for yourself, Nat, he thought. *Do you see what is happening? The colony is going to fall, likely to never rise again. Remember your own rule. Take care of yourself or you shall go down with it!*

John Ratcliffe, who stood closest to the edge of the river, turned to the gathering and said, "Do not fear, gentlemen and ladies. Godspeed to John Smith, but he is in God's hands now. I have plans which our fine Captain Smith would never have approved but which I have no doubt will lift us from this mire and bring prosperity, wealth, and comfort to us all."

There were murmurs, some of interest, some of doubt.

"Fear not, I am back in charge." With that, the man brushed through the crowd and strode back up the embankment and into the fort.

Nicholas shook his head, picked a piece of grass from the riverbank, and stuck it in his mouth to chew. "We're in trouble now if we weren't already," he said.

"We are for certain," said Nat.

In the weeks that followed, Ratcliffe did nothing to lift the colony from the mire. He spent his time with his gentlemen friends, mingling only with the other settlers at church services. With no supervision now, stealing among the citizenship became commonplace at night when guards were groggy and not very alert. The hogs and chickens, which Smith had ordered left unbutchered until spring, were snatched, one by one, and killed and eaten by those with enough energy to do so. It was a subtle but relentless feeding frenzy under the cloak of night.

And hunger was a great equalizer.

Nat stood in the doorway to his cottage long after Samuel and William had fallen into restless sleep. It was warm for an October night, and the breeze coursing through the fortress carried mixed scents of dead leaves, mud, and sickness. The stars overhead spattered the black sky like sparkling sand. From the cottages within the fort walls and those without came the sounds of coughing, groaning, crying, snoring. An owl cried from the forest.

Few men have been caught or put on trial for stealing from the animal pens and the storehouse, Nat thought. *At this moment, there are but five men inside the jail accused of taking grain, and these men were obviously clumsy! Why shouldn't I give it a try? I am perhaps the best-trained thief among us, and my stomach grumbles while there is food to be taken!*

"Yes," he whispered. "But when you have stolen in the past, it never robbed another of a chance to live."

But if I don't take it, someone else will, he thought. *Would I rather the food be taken by Wingfield or Ratcliffe, or perhaps the watch guard, or some other gentleman? It shall be taken regardless. It might as well be me.*

Nat snatched a small knife he had by his cot into the side of his shoe, stepped outside, and walked quietly around the cottage, past the empty pigpen to the chicken house, then held tightly against the wall and listened for any sign he'd been noticed. The helmeted guards on the bulwarks were not talking to one another, so Nat guessed they were too tired to chat or, God forbid, possibly dozing. The night watch had passed Nat's cottage just a minute earlier with musket, pistol, and lantern in hand, but he would not be around again for another few minutes. Nat knew that if there was a chicken left to be had, he would have it.

The door was latched, but there was a small window with reed-woven shutters tied closed. Nat cut the rope and pushed one side of the shutter open. The window was small, but Nat was thin now, and bony. He worked one arm through the window, then his head and shoulder, hearing with relief the soft chortle of a hen somewhere in the darkness. His second arm went through and with a bit of kicking, he fell headlong into the rotting straw of the chicken house.

Scrambling up, he put his head to the window to listen and look for the night watch. Again, nothing to see but darkened cottages and sheds, the massive, shadowed wall of the fort, and the silhouette of the guards on the bulwark.

There were several chickens in the house, ones John Smith had ordered left alone until spring with the other animals. Smith was right to make such an order. Taking these animals and the grain from the storehouse in the fall was just asking for dire circumstances come late winter and early spring.

But stomachs hurt now. And, as Nat had decided back at his cottage, if these birds didn't go to him, they would surely go to another thief.

He sat quietly until one of the five remaining chickens came pecking within arms' reach. Then he dove on it, snapping its neck with one swift and easy move. The other chickens, sensing danger, scrambled off. He cut off the head, threw it into the dark, and let some of the blood drain into his mouth. It was hot, salty, and thick, but not foul as he would have thought two years ago. The rest of the blood, he let drain into the straw. Then he began the job of stripping feathers. It was difficult, but he ripped as many off as he could, tossing them to the floor.

Stuffing the headless, nearly featherless bird into his shirt, Nat climbed back out through the window, tied the shutter back as best he could, looked carefully for the watch, then sneaked back to his own cottage, where

Samuel was thrashing in sleep and William was speaking in his dreams. Nat hid the chicken beneath his cot. When he was really feeling hungry, he would cook the bird and eat it. It was his now. Nobody could lay claim to it.

As he lay down for just a couple of hours sleep, pulling the mildewed blanket up to his chin, the cottage door slammed open. It was the night watch, waving his lantern.

"Peacock!" the man said sternly.

Christ have mercy! thought Nat. *I'm caught!*

"Sir?"

"And Collier! Up, the two of you. We've a dead man, Alexander Peavey, in a cottage outside. His brother alerted me. We need the body taken out."

"Oh, sir," said Nat. "Of course. Samuel, up, boy! We've work to do."

Nat put on his shoes, pretended to wipe sleep from his eyes, and went to the door. Behind him, Samuel fumbled for his own shoes.

The night watch raised the lantern and stared at Nat, frowning. "What is that? You've got blood on your face, boy!"

Nat touched his face. How careless he'd been! "I bit my tongue while sleeping, sir," he said humbly. "Dreaming the tongue was a slab of beef."

"And the blood on your shirt?"

Where I carried the chicken, Nat thought, and quickly said, "I bit my tongue quite hard, sir. It is paining me dreadfully, you can imagine."

"I can imagine indeed," said the night watch, looking at Nat, at his shirt, and at Nat's cot.

Then Samuel was there beside Nat, shivering in spite of the seasonable temperatures, saying, "Why do they have to die at night? Can't they wait a bloody few hours?"

The cottage was on the south side, outside the fortress, and it took a good two hours for the two of them to take the body out and bury it quietly near the forest. When Nat and Samuel returned to their own cottage, the sun was beginning to show to the east past the trees and down the river.

And the chicken Nat had stolen had been stolen.

30

November 1609

Most of the provisions were gone by the middle of autumn, and the citizens of James Towne began to wail to the councilmen to save them from starvation and destruction. This fall, the number of settlers was larger in spite of the deaths, and the fear of hunger seemed triplefold with the masses.

In early November John Ratcliffe declared loudly hat he would rescue the colony. He would take the shallop upriver and meet with the savages whom Smith had befriended and bring back plenty of grain and meat. Those who had the strength had gone down to the pier to send them off, and with as much pomp as he could muster, Ratcliffe herded forty-eight men into the shallop and they paddled west. Nat watched until the boat could no longer be seen beyond the bend.

"Will they have luck?"

Nat turned to see Mistress Ford behind him. She wore the same blue gown she had the day she had arrived in James Towne, but it was cleaner now. She smiled softly, a sadness at the corners of her mouth.

"Possibly," said Nat. He didn't want to lie to this woman. She seemed strong enough to take the truth. "But it can be very dangerous. The Powhatans have ideas different from ours. They do not believe we should be here, but at times they tolerate us. It is a mystery, and we are at its mercy."

The woman nodded. Then she said, "Do you have a moment? I need help."

Nat had meant to spend time skinning the few groundhogs that several men had brought to the fort the day before. The meat had been consumed already, but the skins, when cured properly, could be stitched together to make a blanket for the upcoming winter. But he said, "All right."

Mistress Ford led Nat to a cottage near a small sheep shed on the eastern side of the fortress. "This is my home," she said. "My name is Audrey Ford. I live here with Sally Martin and the couple Peter and Martha Scott."

I know, thought Nat. There wasn't a settler he didn't know by name now, or a cottage whose residents he couldn't name. But Mistress Ford, clearly a lady in spite of this land of despair, was still a lady, still gracious and polite.

He returned the official greeting. "I am Nathaniel Peacock. A pleasure." He bowed. It had been a long time since he'd bowed to anyone.

"Sally is dying," said Mistress Ford. "Of dysentery."

Nat stopped at the open doorway. Audrey went inside, then bid Nat come, too. He stepped into the shadows.

Sally was a specter beneath a fouled blanket. Her face had caved in on itself and most of her hair had fallen out. Her eyes were closed.

"I promised her she would see the sun once more before she died," said Audrey quietly. "I tried to lift her and take her out, but she is so limp I can't get hold of her to lift her. Will you help me, sir? It is her last wish. God will bless you, and so will Sally."

My job is the dead, not the near dead, Nat thought. *I have other things to do, damn it all.*

In a woven basket in the corner of the cottage were several dead, furry animals. Not groundhogs or squirrels, but rats, their tiny eyes glazed over, their skulls crushed. These people were already catching rats for food. Nat realized that it might not be long before rats would be considered good fare to all of the James Towne citizens.

Nat took a deep breath of the thick, putrid air. Then he went to Sally, slid his arms beneath her, and lifted her from the bed. She weighed nearly nothing. Her nightdress was wet with urine.

Audrey and Nat went outside, walking through wrinkle-nosed settlers and frightened children. They went to the riverside, Audrey holding Sally's bony hand. Nat stood on his favorite rock and turned Sally so the sunlight reflected from the river onto her face. The woman shivered, muttered something unintelligible, and sighed. Then, with a violent spasm, she died.

Audrey put her free hand to her face, burying her eyes for a moment. "Jesus had pity on her soul," she said. "Sally was a fine woman."

Audrey helped Nat dig Sally's grave near the graves of the many who had died since August. Audrey said a brief prayer, and thanked Nat for his assistance.

"Let me know if there is any other way I can help," Nat heard himself say. "I share a cottage with Samuel Collier and William Love, inside the fort by the pigpen. You can find me if you need me."

Giving a gracious but tired curtsy, Audrey walked back up to the cluster of cottages.

It wasn't long before Audrey sought Nat's help again.

The day after Sally died, Audrey found Nat and asked if he would show Peter Scott how to best dress a rat. Nat was patient with the fumbling young Peter, and the two of them had a laugh at the earnest attempt which left the rat in three pieces. In appreciation for Nat's time, Martha mended Nat's torn stockings. Then Nat helped Peter patch the roof on the cottage. In thanks, Audrey gave Nat her dead husband's shoes. She had saved them from the ship. Nat put them on and they fit well. He put his old, holey shoes in the corner of his cottage in case he might need them at another time.

In the midst of the confusion, frustration, and anguish of the colony, Nat had found a place of peace—in the home of the Scotts and Audrey Ford. The exchange of help was easy and Nat looked forward to each new request.

"You are a smart man," Audrey said one evening as they sat side by side on the stone by the river. She wore a yellow gown and her face, thin and drawn and pale, had been scrubbed clean. Her dark brown eyes stared off at the other side of the water. "You know how to build a home, to raise crops, to hunt and to fish. If we survive here in James Towne, you could easily become a councilor with your knowledge."

"Oh, I doubt that," said Nat. "I am not rich. I once thought I'd find gold and become a gentleman, but I don't know if that will ever happen. And only rich men are considered worthy of leadership."

"That is a silly idea," said Audrey. "My husband was not rich, but he was one of the wisest men I ever knew." She hesitated. "And so are you." Then Audrey reached into the deep pocket of her gown and brought out a small leather-bound book. "I want to give you this. It is a book of poems. Do you read?"

"Yes," said Nat. He took the book and before he realized what he was doing, he gave Audrey a hug. He thought she might slap him, but she only smiled more. "I write, too," said Nat. "I've got pages in my cottage. I've written my thoughts whenever I've had the chance to do so."

"May I read them someday?"

Nat nodded.

The next morning, Nat gave Audrey the loose pages to read. And the following evening, she gave them back. They had been sewn together into a true journal, with blank pages at the back. "Peter Scott gave me paper to give you more room to write," she said. "Keep on writing. Your words are precious. They are the words of a gentleman, Nat."

Nat blushed and stammered a thank-you. He slept with the journal under his arm that night. His dreams were pleasant.

On the morning of November 17, the shallop returned from the west. Nat, Peter Scott, and William Love, along with several other men, hurried down to the pier to unload the baskets of food that John Ratcliffe had promised to bring to the fort.

But there were no baskets of food. There were only sixteen men in the boat, and John Ratcliffe was not among them. Those in the boat nearly fell out, scrambling with their fingers and babbling madly.

"What happened?" asked William. "Where is the wheat and corn and venison? Where are Ratcliffe and the others?"

One soldier dropped facedown onto the grass and began to sob. "Dead," he said. "All dead. The Powhatans pretended to be civil, then when we disembarked, they captured up and took us to their village. And Ratcliffe, God pity him! Never have I seen such a terrible fate imposed on a man!"

Nat could taste bile in his mouth. "What?" he managed. "What did they do to him?"

None of the soldiers spoke for a long time. Then one said, "He was stripped naked and tied to a tree. The savages laughed and howled at him, and I knew it was going to be heinous. The women of the village came out then, and armed with sharpened mussel shells, scraped his flesh from his body and threw it into the fire for him to witness! They flayed his legs, then his stomach, stripping the meat away as if he were a deer tied to a stake. And Ratcliffe lived through this, screaming as if his soul were burning in the very pits of hell. When he died at last, he was nothing but bloody bones and twitching nerves."

"Christ have mercy!" cried Peter Scott.

"Christ did not have mercy on Ratcliffe," said one soldier.

"But we ran off," said another soldier. "And even through the rain of arrows, we few escaped. But we bring nothing back except our own miserable selves."

"God help us now," said William. "Smith is gone, the Powhatans are again seeking to destroy us, our leaders do not know how to lead, and we have little food as the last of it was consumed weeks ago. Our storehouses are bare, our cottages crumbling, and many of us sick. God help us."

"God help us," said the soldiers.

God please help us! thought Nat.

❧ 31 ❧

December 25, 1609

Christmas day. In London, Richard and I would celebrate by stealing a pig and cooking it on a fire by the Thames River. I dreamed of better days. I thought they would be here.

I don't even know how to dream of better days now.

There is madness in James Towne. Madness born of illness and death and starvation and dread. The only thing that keeps me from losing my mind are my three friends. Peter and Martha. And Audrey. She is kind, wise, and pretty. I suppose now I can't let her read my journal or she will see these thoughts and think me forward.

Audrey says I am a gentleman. What a strange thought. I am ragged and poor and dirty. Yet she sees a gentleman. I don't even know what it is to be a gentleman, or a man at that. Laughing Man stood up for me when he was in danger. He did what he believed right.

Perhaps that is what changes a boy into a man. Not years, not airs, not wealth. But bravery to say or do what is right.

What is right?

I wish I knew.

For I have witnessed a horror, one too difficult to imagine, but it was not my imagination, for my own two eyes told me it was real.

Many of the settlers stay inside their cottages now; few are able-bodied enough to go out in the biting cold to retrieve water for their household or cook the gruel we make from roots and bark and grubs. The soldiers who are well enough to keep watch at the bulwark do so, though their numbers have dwindled. About thirty men and women are strong enough to hunt for food, picking through the forest and dragging the rivers, but they come up with little. Several men have run off to live with the Powhatans in hopes they would survive better with the natives. Sometimes those of us at James Towne eat once a day. Sometimes we do not eat on a given day.

But I did not want to believe what I saw three nights ago.

Marcus Daniels, boy of fourteen, died just before sunset, and his parents helped Samuel and me remove the body to the burial site. The ground is dreadfully hard this time of year, but the four of us were able to make a grave not quite two feet deep. It was the best we could do, given the cold and given our strength. I went into the woods then, looking for an injured bird, an opossum, something slow-moving to kill to eat. There were a few shriveled berries on a crabapple tree, and their bitter taste was fine to my tongue. There were sluggish grubs, sleeping beneath the bark in a tree, and I tugged them free, crushed them with my teeth, and swallowed them down. But my hunger still clawed at my gut, insistent, determined.

It was on my return that I was aware of commotion in the burial ground. I paused at the edge of the woods, staring in the moonlight, and saw someone huddled over the fresh grave of young Marcus Daniels. His father, I suspected, or his mother, come to grieve in private while the rest of the settlement lay still in the cold embrace of a winter's night.

But then I heard the soft cough, and recognized it, and did not understand why he would be at the grave.

It was Nicholas Skot.

I walked closer, quietly, because I sensed he thought he was alone and to startle him might cause him to cry out and make the guard suspect we were natives on the attack, and shoot at us. But as I approached, moving along the brush and keeping to the trees, I knew I did not want to see what was before me.

But it was too late.

Nicholas had unearthed the body of Marcus Daniels, and had severed both hands and put them into a bucket. He was at work with his knife, cutting the forearm off at the elbow. He panted with effort. His breath was visible on the frosty air. I knew his intentions, and I gasped.

He heard me, and glanced up, his eyes as wide with fear as the eyes of a deer Laughing Boy and I once chased into the shallows of the river to slay. And then, in a whisper barely heard over the hushed whisper of the December breeze, he said, "It is nearly Christmas, Nat. Don't you understand? Christ was born for us, and He said, 'This is my body.'"

"Nicholas, you'll die for this," I said. "If anyone hears of it, they will execute you!"

"You won't tell," he said. I could hear the giddy insanity lacing his words. "My body, take and eat. I have to eat, Nat. I have to eat!"

With that, he scooped up his bucket and ran off into the darkness through the silent cottages and sheds.

I returned to my cottage, and said nothing.

What is right?

I cannot know.

There have been rumors the past two days that graves are being robbed and the dead eaten by our starving colonists. Our leaders say it is an abomination, but they cannot find out who is supposed to have committed this sin.

I will not say, for I do not know what is right.

I have always been proud that illness and hunger have never seen me worth their while. But I fear that is not the case now. I know now how it feels. If I had the strength, I'd journey deep into the woods and find Laughing Man. I would ask him for help. But I can't. It is all I can do to write this. And I am tired now. I must stop. I am so very, very tired.

32

January 8, 1610

N AT, WAKE UP, please!"

Nat's eyes opened, then closed. He was so tired. He wanted to sleep another hour. Another year.

"Nat, wake up. I am sorry to come into your cottage without permission, but we need you. Martha is in very bad condition."

Nat opened his eyes again. Audrey stood over his mattress. He could not make out her face in the darkness, but her voice was laced with genuine fear. "Nat, I think Martha is dying. Please come!"

Nat sat up. His head reeled and he had to wait until it subsided. Then he forced his feet into his shoes and stood up. William and Samuel were still sleeping.

"Come," said Audrey. She threw Nat's cloak around his shoulders, grabbed his hand, and the two of them went outside into the bitter winter night. As they moved toward Audrey's cottage, the young woman said, "Peter has lost his wits with grief. If Martha dies, he will lose not only a wife but a child as well! He is talking out of his mind, Nat. He even tried to strike me away when I went to comfort him. I tried to put a hand on Martha's forehead and he shoved me back. What should we do?"

Nat tried to speak, but it was as if his lips were frozen together.

"At least hold Peter so I can tend Martha," said Audrey. "If I can nurse her beyond this bout of illness, I will, but I cannot if Peter will not even let me near her. Will you hold Peter?"

Nat managed to nod.

They stopped outside the door to Audrey's cottage. A strong gust of wind lifted her cloak and skirts, revealing white, stick-thin ankles in mud-coated shoes. "Peter, it is Audrey. I have Nathaniel with me. We are coming in to help."

There was a low growl, but nothing more. Audrey cast a desperate look at Nat, and opened the cottage door. They went inside. It was not much warmer inside than out.

A single lamp, sitting on the top of the Scotts' small trunk, burned with a dim, sputtering light. Nat's eyes had to adjust before he could even find Peter and Martha. And then he was able to make them out. Peter was crouched in the corner on the dirt floor, wearing only his long white linen shirt, holding Martha tightly in his arms.

"Peter, Nat is here. Martha needs our help. Please let me see her. Talk to Nat while I check on Martha to see what I can do for her."

Peter lifted his head. His eyes were as wild and dangerous as those of the mad dog Nat had killed in London. "Go away!" he snarled.

Martha and Nat took several steps closer. Peter tried to back farther into the corner. Martha groaned weakly, but her eyes did not open and she did not move.

"Peter, you are our friend," said Audrey. "Martha is our friend. We want to help."

Peter's teeth were bared. His lips twitched.

"Peter," said Nat. "Give Martha to Audrey. Come to the other side of the cottage with me. Let us talk."

There was a long moment of silence. Audrey said to Nat, "I gave him some acorn gruel, but he slapped it away. It was as though he no longer can even recognize food."

Nat nodded.

"Peter, listen to us," said Audrey.

Peter looked from Audrey to Nat to Martha in his arms. "Martha," he said. "My Martha."

"Peter," said Audrey.

Suddenly Peter jumped to his feet, wailing and tearing at the air. Martha rolled off his lap into a heap. Peter lunged at Audrey, grabbing her throat in his fingers. Audrey gasped and fell backward, dragging Peter with her. Nat's blurry mind cleared then; he threw himself at Peter. His arms wrapped about the man's waist and with all the energy Nat had, he wrenched Peter away from Audrey. Peter screamed and struggled. His ragged fingernails gouged into Nat's wrists and he bit Nat on the hand.

"Audrey, get out of the cottage. Go find more help. I can't do this alone!" cried Nat.

Audrey darted out of the cottage. Nat continued to hold tightly to Peter even though the man slashed viciously with his nails and chomped with his teeth. At last Nat got one leg beneath those of Peter Scott and knocked the man's body out from underneath him. Peter hit the floor with a cry and Nat held him down.

Nat leaned in close to Peter's face. "Listen to me, man! You are hungry, we all are! But you cannot let it consume you. You must be strong for yourself, for Martha and the baby. Help is coming. We will do all we can to see that Martha makes it through."

Peter's struggles grew weaker and weaker. *Pray God he is not dying, too,* Nat thought. But the man continued to breathe, irregular, shallow breaths. Then Peter looked at Nat. He said, "Nat? Please get off me. You are too heavy."

"You will not fight with me?"

"No," said Peter. "I will not."

Nat got up from the floor and gave Peter a hand to help him up, too.

"Martha," said Peter. "I must go to her."

"Yes," said Nat, "And we will do what we can to bring her back to health."

They went to the corner and Peter knelt by his wife. He lifted her head. And then he threw back his head and roared. "She's dead!"

Nat touched Martha's wrist. He put his finger beneath her nostrils and there was no air moving. Indeed, the woman had died.

"Peter," Nat began. "I am so very sorry, so—"

But Peter's mind snapped again in an instant. He drove his fist against Nat's chest, slamming Nat backward into the trunk. The lantern wobbled but did not fall. Peter ripped at his face and his clothes and babbled dreadful, insane nonsense.

Nat left the cottage. He found Audrey pounding on a nearby cottage door, and he took her hand to stop it.

"No one will help," said Audrey. "I've tried three homes and everyone says we are all sick and dying and they won't leave their own to help Peter and Martha."

"It doesn't matter now," said Nat. "Martha is dead. Peter is indeed distraught beyond reason, but I think it is best to leave him alone with her until he comes to his senses."

"Where shall I sleep, then?" asked Audrey.

Nat took Audrey to one of the empty barns and made her a pallet out of straw. Then he brought his one remaining deerskin to her, covered her, and bid her good night.

Back in his cottage, he recorded the events of the night. *Poor Peter Scott,* he wrote at the end of the entry. *Such a loss, both wife and baby. Perhaps he will find better luck in the passage of time. Perhaps things will turn for the better for all of us. How can it get any worse?*

❧ 33 ❧

January 6–10, 1610

MARTHA SCOTT'S BODY was found in Peter Scott's trunk, chopped into pieces and covered with salt. Her belly had been ripped open and the baby was missing.

Peter Scott was immediately put into the James Towne jail, a small building with no furniture, lanterns, nor fireplace. He was left there for several days, with only a handful of grain tossed in for his meals. The trial would come to pass quickly, as soon as the council could decide what to do about so horrendous a crime.

"He killed her," Nat heard one gentleman say as he collected firewood from the fort's community supply. "Killed her and ripped the child from her and tossed the baby into the river. Then he cut his wife up and salted her for food. He thought no one would look in that ghastly trunk!"

"Killed his own wife," said another man. "I am starving, but I would never murder! Satan has come to James Towne and lives in the person of Peter Scott."

Nat found his voice and said, "Peter did not kill her, she died."

But the gentleman scoffed. "You are his friend, you'd say anything. Now, hold your tongue before I accuse you of assisting in the murder, boy!"

George Percy took Peter Scott from the jail after several days and marched the young man to a tall tree just outside the palisade. As everyone gathered to watch, Peter was drawn up by his thumbs and hung there, his jaws clenched together, his eyes wincing with incredible pain.

"Getting what he deserves," said one man in the crowd.

"God save his soul," said one woman.

"Nat, I was not there when Martha died," Audrey said, tears of frustration and pity coursing down her face. "You were there. Tell them what you saw."

But Nat shook his head. He might be accused of killing Martha, too. *Peter, I'm sorry! There is nothing I can do!*

Percy proceeded to question the tortured man hanging from the tree. "Peter Scott, did you murder your wife, Martha, and cut her into pieces?"

Peter did not move. Nat could see tears on the man's cheeks, but there was no sound.

"Did you cut her into pieces and throw your infant into the river?"

Peter did not answer. Cloth bags were tied to Peter's ankles and filled with stones to weigh Peter and make the pain even more terrible. The questioning went on for fifteen minutes. Nat stared at the ground. He could no longer endure the expression on Peter's face nor the agony in Audrey's eyes.

And then there was a cry of triumph from George Percy, and Peter Scott was cut down from the tree. "He admitted his offense," Percy told the crowd. "He nodded at the last question. His nod confirmed our accusations. This man is a murderer and shall die!"

Nat looked up at last. Audrey said, "Peter did not nod. His head spasmed and Percy, looking for anything to end this ordeal, said he saw a nod! What shall we do? Peter was mad with hunger, and so his tormented mind reasoned that Martha would be food after she died. But he did not kill her! We must stop the execution of Peter Scott!"

Nat turned away from Audrey. There was nothing he could say.

Peter Scott was returned to the jail and a pyre was built in the center of the barren cornfield. All men who were able piled brush and sticks and branches together and planted a post in the center. Nat feigned illness to keep from participating. He lay on his mattress and tossed with anxiety and rage. At Peter for losing his mind and butchering his dead wife's body. At Martha for dying. At Audrey for being kind and drawing him into association with the Scotts. At George Percy for believing torture could secure truth. And at himself for having no courage to say what needed to be said.

The next morning, in the bitter cold, all those who were not sick in bed turned out for the punishment of Peter Scott. George Percy brought the torch, and made an impassioned speech, gesturing with the torch at both the condemned and at the witnesses. His words were punctuated with puffs of mist. He stomped his feet to keep warm, but on and on he rambled about God and the devil and Peter Scott's obscene acts.

Peter, his feet without shoes, and wearing only a torn shirt and moth-eaten trousers, had been lashed to the center post. He stared up at the sky. Every few moments he would shudder with the cold.

"We are Englishmen," said Percy to the settlers. "We are civilized, and will not tolerate less. Hanging is not good enough, not strong enough, for such a deed as Peter Scott performed. He must suffer and we will see that he does."

There were murmurs from the group, some in agreement, some laced with sadness for what Peter was about to endure.

"Peter, have you anything to say before you are sent out of this life?"

Peter said nothing. But then his head turned, and he looked directly at Nat.

Nat felt the stare as surely as a knife to his heart. He put his hand inside his cloak and drew out that which he had brought to the execution, that which he didn't really believe he'd have the courage to show.

"George Percy, sir!" shouted Nat. Audrey turned and stared at Nat with wonder. The mumbling in the crowd quieted. "Percy! Listen to me now, if never before. I must tell you something, and you must hear me out. I know for a fact that Peter Scott did not kill his wife."

"Don't listen to him, Percy!" shouted a gentleman. "He is Scott's friend."

"Let him speak," said Percy.

Nat held up his journal. It was curled and soiled, but inside was a record of the night of Martha's death, the details of what had happened. Nat said, "Most of you here know me. And those of you who do know I don't have friends. I have avoided friends ever since I came to James Towne. I have preferred to be alone, to take care of myself. But what I say is truth, God as my witness."

"Continue," said Percy.

"I went to the home of Martha and Peter the night she died. Audrey Ford called me and I came, hoping to calm the man as Audrey nursed the poor woman. I was with Peter and Martha when she took her last breath. I wrote of it in my journal, and I offer it now as testimony to the facts."

Percy held up his hand. "Mistress Ford, is Peacock giving us an honest statement?"

Audrey said, "I did indeed call him. Peter was crazed with heartache for the dire condition of his wife. I was not there when she died, but I can say Nathaniel Peacock would tell the truth."

There was mumbling in the crowd. Then Nat continued, "Please, sir, read my journal aloud and let Peter be charged with only the cutting of his wife. Surely that is not an offense requiring death."

George Percy squinted at Nat, then Peter, then the journal. "Bring that record to me, boy," he said.

The crowd parted as Nat worked his way to Percy. Some looked at him as he passed as though they hoped the journal might stop the burning. Others scowled as if they were afraid it would.

"Here, sir," said Nat. He gave the booklet to Percy. Percy handed the torch to the torch man. Nat took a deep breath. He couldn't imagine what trouble he'd be in for rescuing Peter, but right now it didn't matter. He had no choice.

I have no choice. Richard, this is for you, too.

Percy flipped through the pages, then tossed the journal onto the pyre. "Make-believe," he declared to the settlers. "Anything to try and rescue this demon!"

"Accuse Peacock of conspiring to murder Martha Scott!" came a cry.

Percy paused, then shook his head and said, "There is no indication that Peter acted in any way but alone. Peacock is just trying to stall what must happen. Now we shall have justice. Peter Scott will face our fire here in this life and hellfire in the next."

Percy nodded to the torch man, who lowered the flame to the kindling and waited until it began to smolder and smoke. The journal caught the first licks of flame and went up like dry leaves.

Nat watched, dumbfounded, horrified. Audrey came over, took his arm, and buried her face in his sleeve. She couldn't watch as the fire grew stronger and stronger, working its way to the center pole where Peter Scott stood, his eyes closed.

Women in the gathering broke into sobs. Men mumbled uncomfortably. Nat said nothing. He stared into Peter's face, and thought, *Peter, I pray it goes quickly for you.*

The fire reached Peter's legs and caught the fabric of his trousers instantly. The blaze raced up his chest to his face. There were several seconds of silent twitching and shaking. The smell of roasting flesh was sharp and pungent. And then, with an unbearably long scream of supreme anguish, Peter Scott gave his consciousness and life to God.

Only a few remained to watch the man reduced to cinders. Nat led Audrey back to her cottage. She sat without a word on her cot, and Nat sat next to her, holding her gently. He could feel her quiet weeping as his chest grew warm and wet.

"You did a good thing," came a voice from the door. Nat looked over to see William Love. "Someone had to speak up for Peter. I can't believe he killed his wife, either. Thank you for trying."

Nat nodded and William withdrew. Minutes later, Edward Pising looked into the cottage. "Master Peacock? You were brave to speak out at such a moment. I didn't know Peter Scott well, but I know in my soul that he could not have killed his wife. He was a fine man. He should not have died. But you gave his death some dignity."

"Thank you," said Nat.

A handful of other men and women stopped by to

tell Nat of their appreciation for his courage. Nat thanked them all in turn.

Night came. Audrey fell asleep, curled up on her cot, and Nat gazed at her for a moment, and then covered her gently with the deerskin. He touched her hair and bid her a sleep without dreams.

He went back to his cottage and found that Samuel Collier had put three sheets of paper on his mattress as well as a pen and small well of berry ink.

34

January 16, 1610

The winter rages on. We've seen snow and sleet and more of us dead. The frozen ground is hard to dig for graves, and our arms can barely wield a shovel. We had nearly five hundred when John Smith was sent back to England. Now there are barely one hundred. Should we have come? I do not know. Will we become like the colony of Roanoke Island and vanish without a trace? I do not know that either. We are in the hands of time and fate.

But I think I have become a man. I have found friendship is a good thing, and that it is better to work together than apart. Lessons which may serve me well if I live. I hope I will.

Audrey is meeting me in a few minutes. We are going to collect acorns. There might still be a few in the forest which can be cooked, and perhaps if I have the strength, I can climb a tree like Laughing Boy taught me and watch for a lumbering groundhog.

Together. It is a good word. Whether for another week or a lifetime. God get us all through this.

Together.

ELIZABETH MASSIE'S YOUNG FOUNDERS

SERIES

View America through the eyes of its young founders

(1609) Winter of the Dead

Two homeless London orphans excitedly accept passage to the New World, a place rumored to be overflowing with wealth. After arriving, the boys are faced with the reality of starvation and disease, and they must rely on their wits to survive.

0-765-35604-X • Paperback

(1776) Son of Liberty

Sixteen-year-old Caleb is a free black living in a slave state. When British Governor Lord Dunmore promises freedom to slaves who join his army against the Americans, Caleb is torn between his race and the Revolution he believes in.

0-765-35273-7 • Paperback

(1863) A House Divided

Twins Susanne and Stephen join opposite sides of the Civil War, communicating despite being separated by war, death, and disease. Little do they know, the Union and Confederate forces will converge on their hometown of Gettysburg in a deciding battle.

0-765-35272-9 • Paperback

(1870) Not With Our Blood

After his father dies, seventeen-year-old Patrick must work long hours in a factory to support his family. When Patrick's friend reveals that he steals from the wealthy mill owners to make extra money, Patrick must choose to join his gang or continue to struggle.

0-765-35605-8 • Paperback

www.tor.com **TOR**